J
Graphic
Y

W9-BWR-862

FRANKLIN BRANCH LIBRARY
13651 E. MCNICHOLS RD.
DETROIT, MI 48205
(313) 852-4797

OCT   2006

Arcana Vol. 4
Created by So-Young Lee

Translation - Youngju Ryu
English Adaptation - Barbara Randall Kesel
Copy Editor - Hope Donovan
Retouch and Lettering - Gloria Wu
Production Artist - Jennifer Carbajal
Cover Design - James Lee

Editor - Bryce P. Coleman
Digital Imaging Manager - Chris Buford
Production Manager - Jennifer Miller
Managing Editor - Lindsey Johnston
VP of Production - Ron Klamert
Publisher and E.I.C. - Mike Kiley
President and C.O.O. - John Parker
C.E.O. and Chief Creative Officer - Stuart Levy

A 🐾 **TOKYOPOP**® Manga

TOKYOPOP Inc.
5900 Wilshire Blvd. Suite 2000
Los Angeles, CA 90036

E-mail: info@TOKYOPOP.com
Come visit us online at www.TOKYOPOP.com

© 2004 SO-YOUNG LEE, DAIWON C.I. Inc. All rights reserved. No portion of this book may be
All Rights Reserved. reproduced or transmitted in any form or by any means
First published in Korea in 2004 by DAIWON, C.I. Inc. without written permission from the copyright holders.
English translation rights in North America, UK, NZ and This manga is a work of fiction. Any resemblance to
Australia arranged by DAIWON C.I. Inc. actual events or locales or persons, living or dead, is
English text copyright © 2006 TOKYOPOP Inc. entirely coincidental.

ISBN: 1-59816-200-4
First TOKYOPOP printing: April 2006
10 9 8 7 6 5 4 3 2 1
Printed in the USA

VOLUME 4
SO-YOUNG LEE

HAMBURG // LONDON // LOS ANGELES // TOKYO

THE JOURNEY THUS FAR...

CHARGED WITH THE MISSION OF LOCATING A GUARDIAN DRAGON THAT WILL PROTECT HER KINGDOM, INEZ AND YULAN LEAVE THE WORLD OF MAN AND ENTER UNCHARTED TERRITORY. ALONG THE WAY, THEY ENCOUNTER THE GENTLE CREATURE, MONG, THE MYSTERIOUS KYRETTE, AND AN ELF NAMED ARIEL. THE GROUP SOON BECOMES EMBROILED IN AN ELVIN FAMILY FEUD, BARELY ESCAPING WITH THEIR LIVES! LATER, ANOTHER THREAT ARRIVES IN THE FORM OF THE DREAM WRAITH NAMED LILITH, AND HER TARGET APPEARS TO BE YULAN...

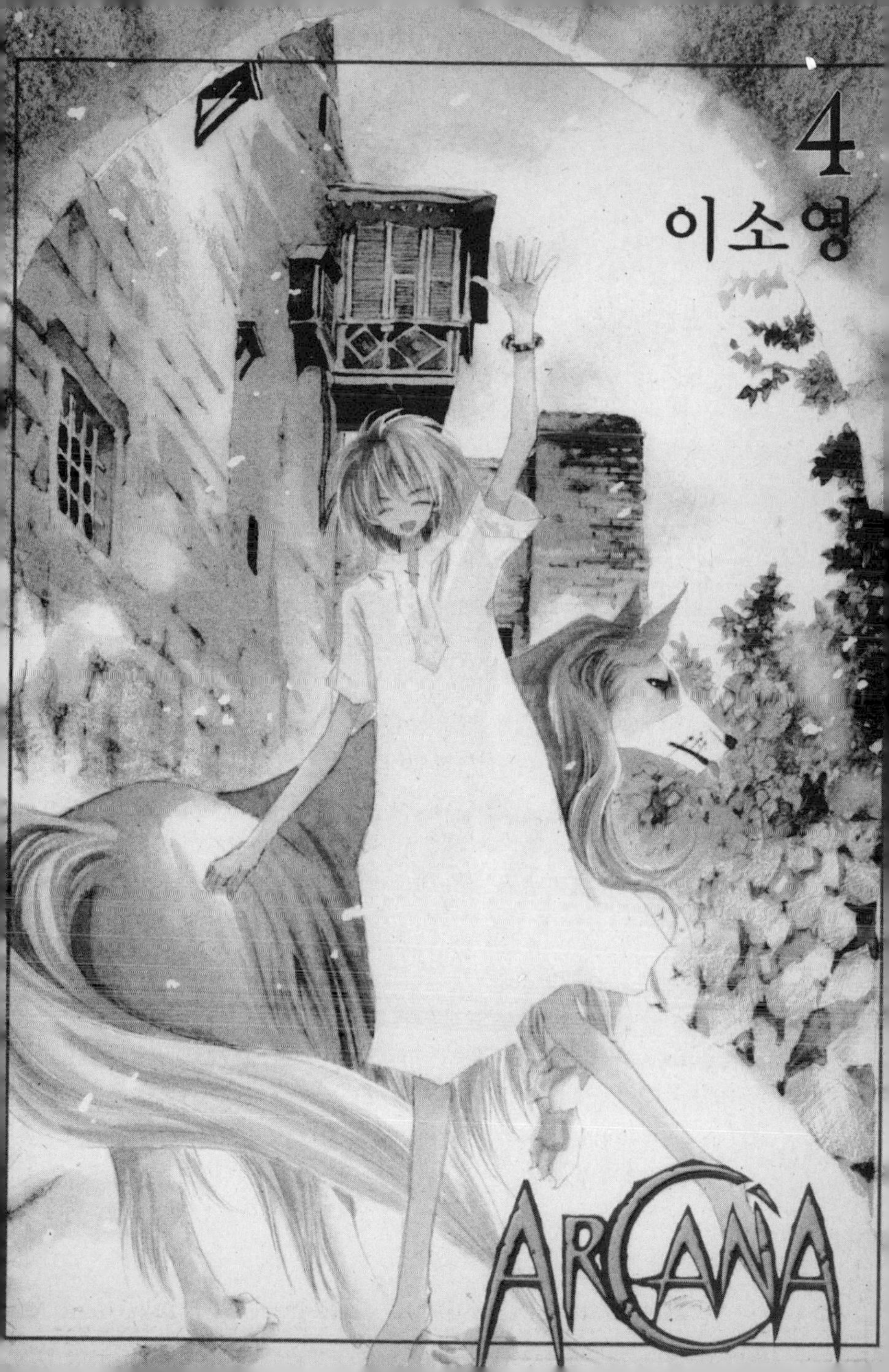
4
이소영
ARCANA

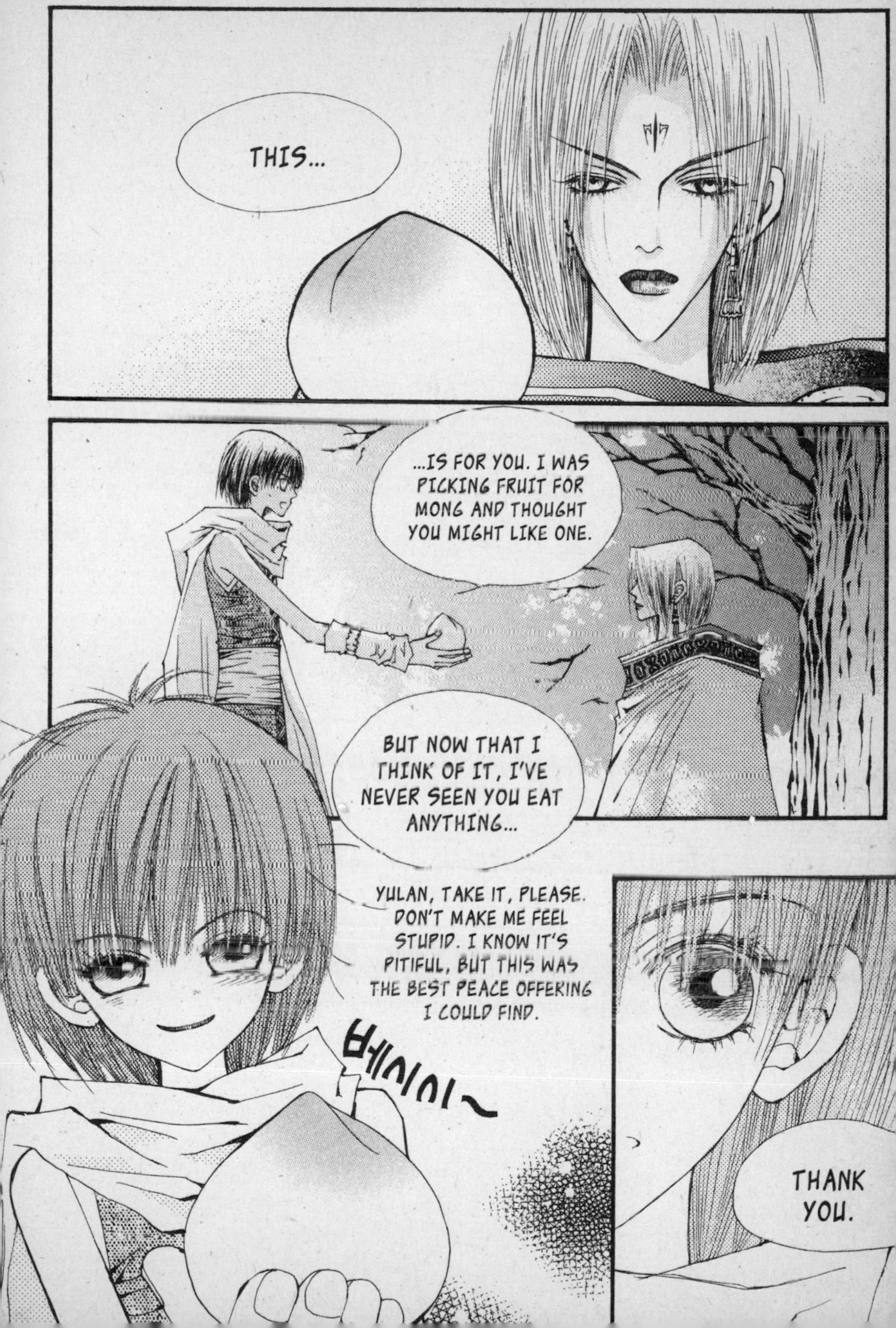
THIS...
...IS FOR YOU. I WAS PICKING FRUIT FOR MONG AND THOUGHT YOU MIGHT LIKE ONE.
BUT NOW THAT I THINK OF IT, I'VE NEVER SEEN YOU EAT ANYTHING...
YULAN, TAKE IT, PLEASE. DON'T MAKE ME FEEL STUPID. I KNOW IT'S PITIFUL, BUT THIS WAS THE BEST PEACE OFFERING I COULD FIND.
THANK YOU.

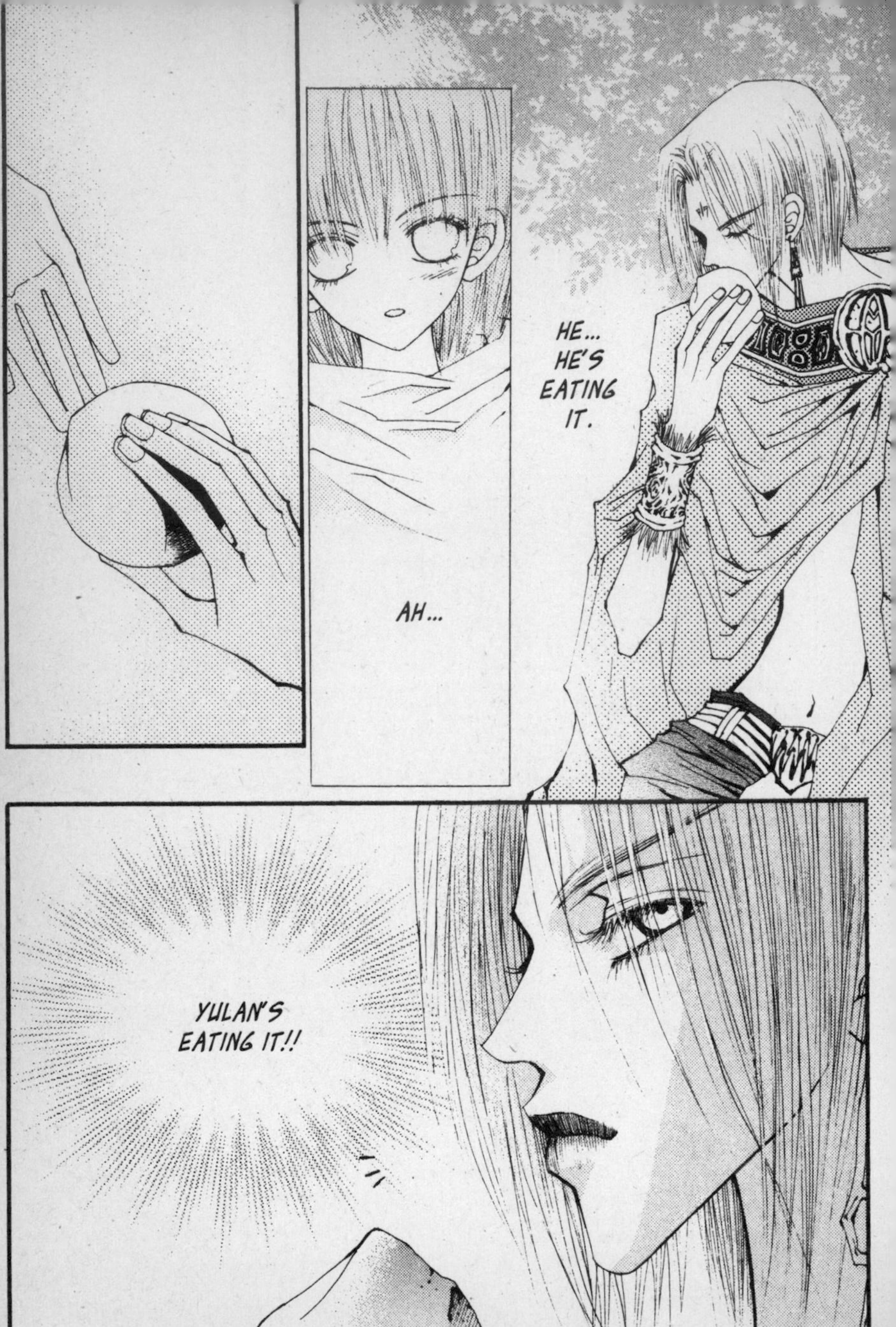
HE... HE'S EATING IT.
AH...
YULAN'S EATING IT!!

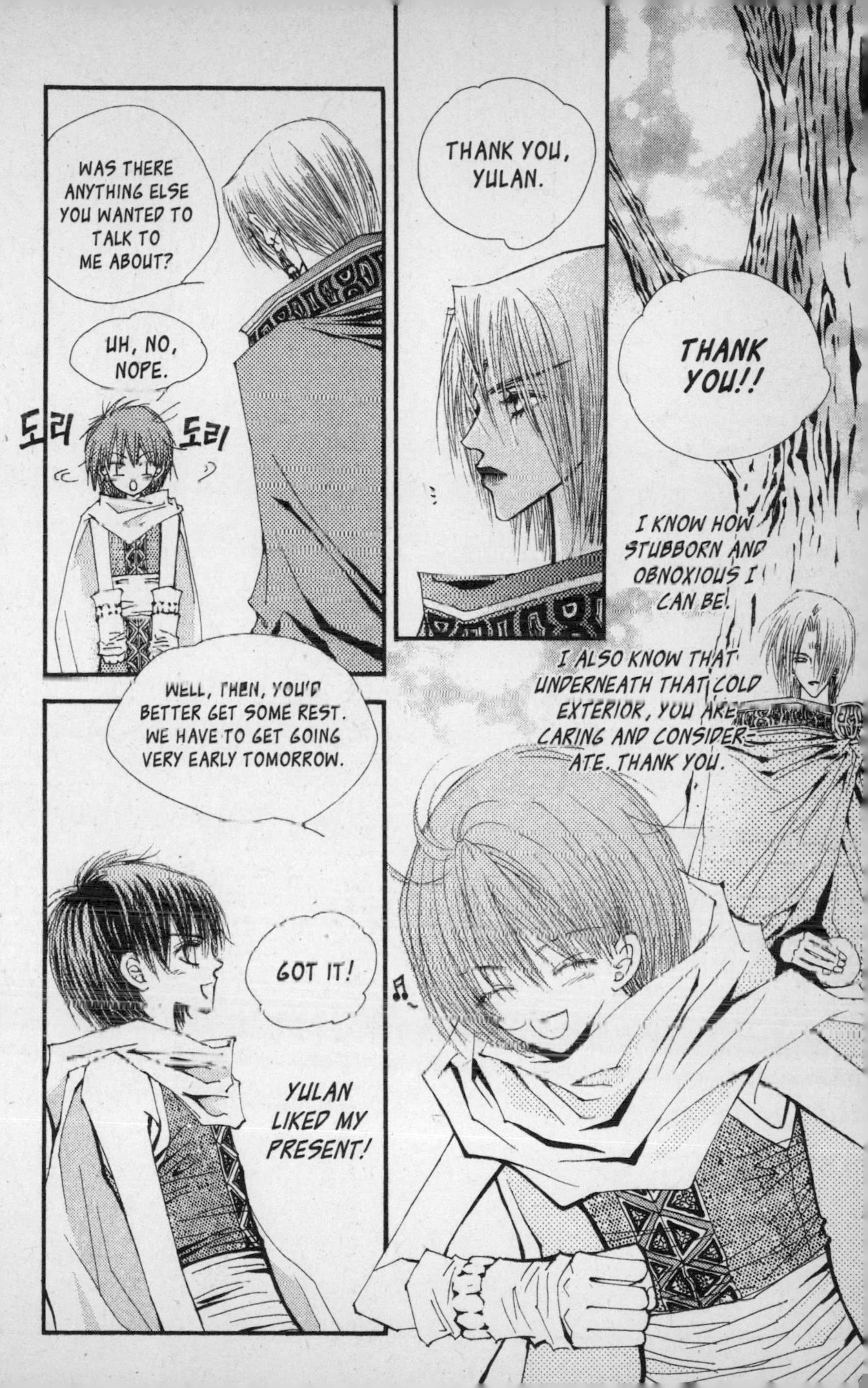

WAS THERE ANYTHING ELSE YOU WANTED TO TALK TO ME ABOUT?
UH, NO, NOPE.
도리 도리
THANK YOU, YULAN.
WELL, THEN, YOU'D BETTER GET SOME REST. WE HAVE TO GET GOING VERY EARLY TOMORROW.
GOT IT!
YULAN LIKED MY PRESENT!
THANK YOU!!
I KNOW HOW STUBBORN AND OBNOXIOUS I CAN BE.
I ALSO KNOW THAT UNDERNEATH THAT COLD EXTERIOR, YOU ARE CARING AND CONSIDERATE. THANK YOU.

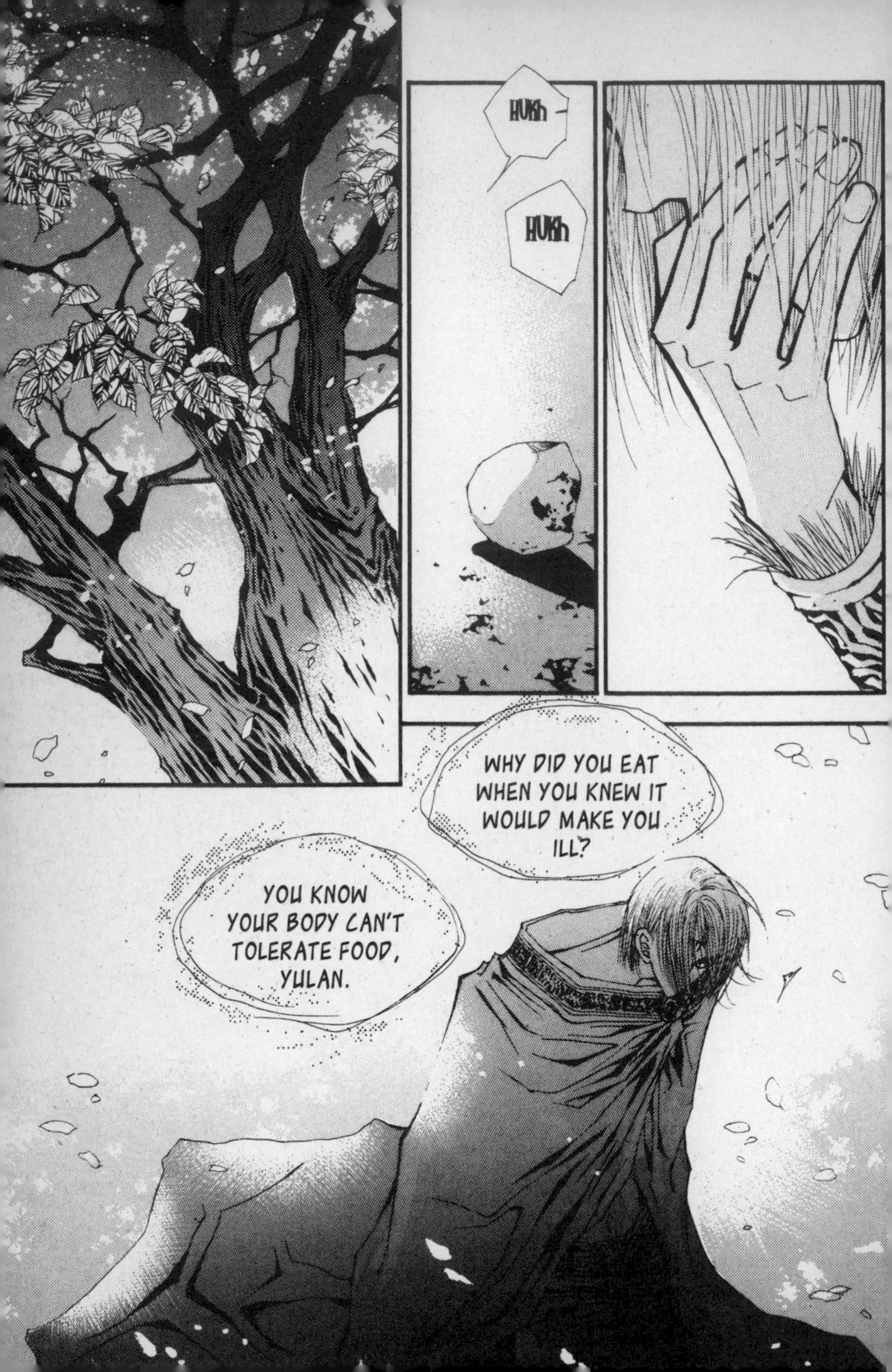
HUKh
HUKh
WHY DID YOU EAT WHEN YOU KNEW IT WOULD MAKE YOU ILL?
YOU KNOW YOUR BODY CAN'T TOLERATE FOOD, YULAN.

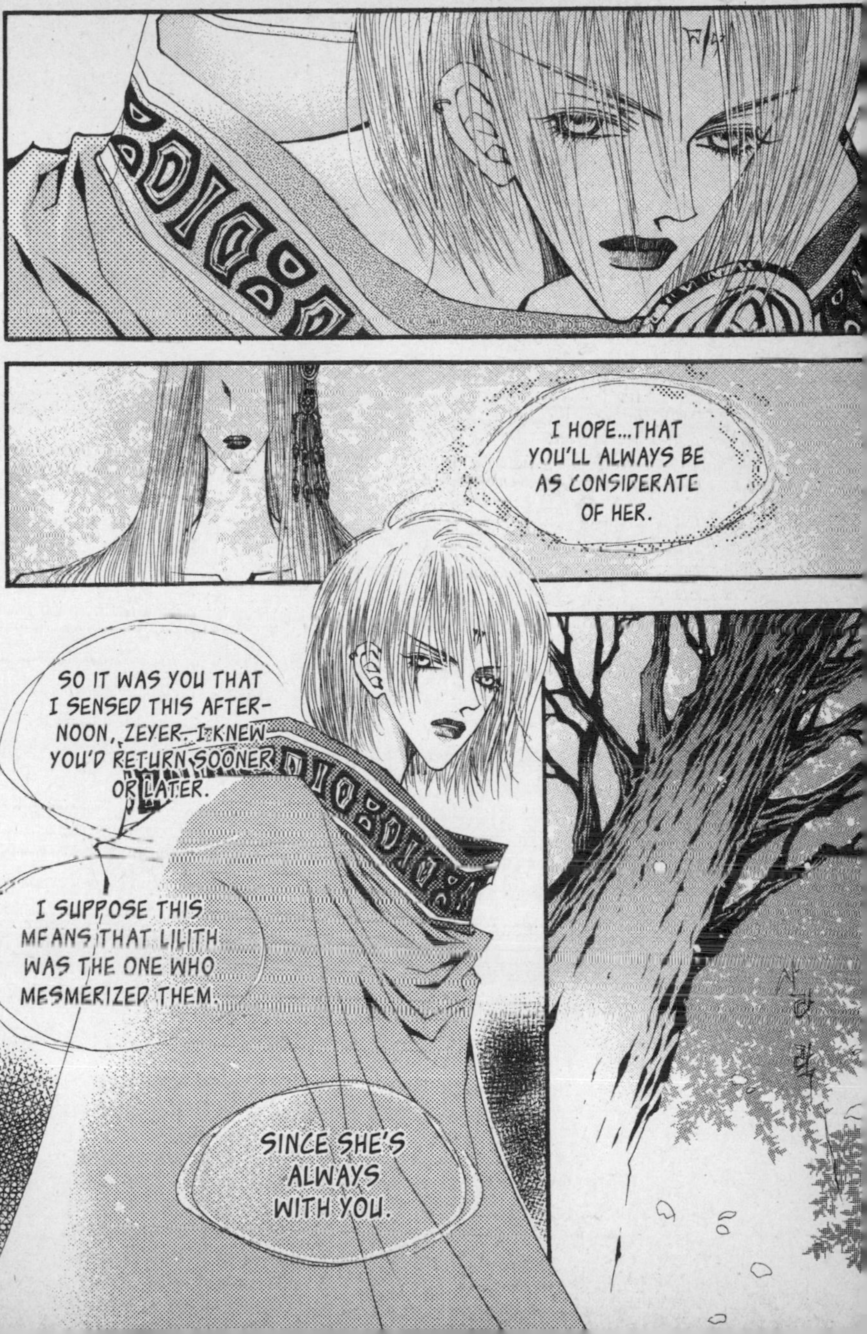
I HOPE...THAT YOU'LL ALWAYS BE AS CONSIDERATE OF HER.
SO IT WAS YOU THAT I SENSED THIS AFTER-NOON, ZEYER. I KNEW YOU'D RETURN SOONER OR LATER.
I SUPPOSE THIS MEANS THAT LILITH WAS THE ONE WHO MESMERIZED THEM.
SINCE SHE'S ALWAYS WITH YOU.

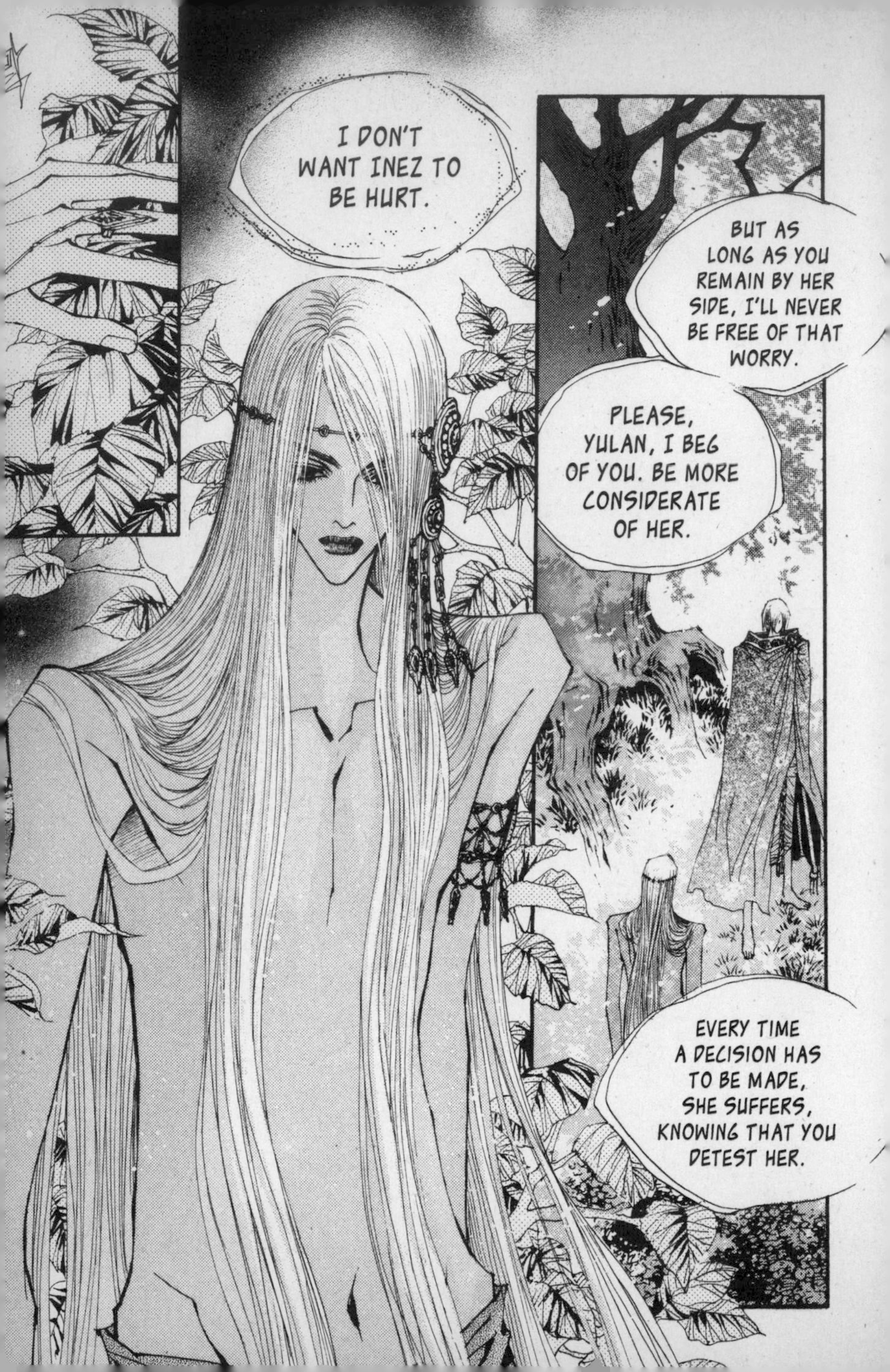
I DON'T WANT INEZ TO BE HURT.
BUT AS LONG AS YOU REMAIN BY HER SIDE, I'LL NEVER BE FREE OF THAT WORRY.
PLEASE, YULAN, I BEG OF YOU. BE MORE CONSIDERATE OF HER.
EVERY TIME A DECISION HAS TO BE MADE, SHE SUFFERS, KNOWING THAT YOU DETEST HER.

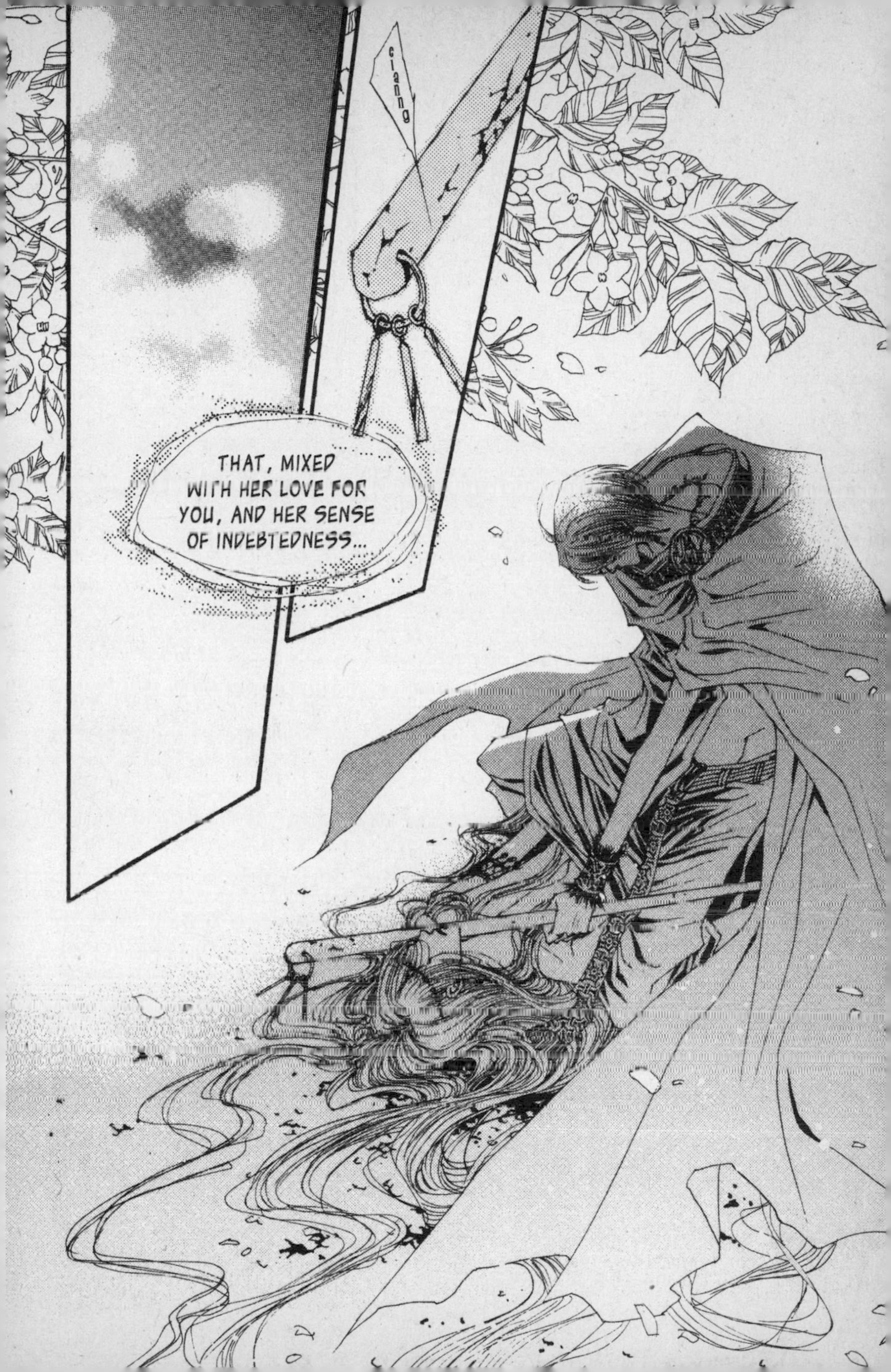
clanng
THAT, MIXED WITH HER LOVE FOR YOU, AND HER SENSE OF INDEBTEDNESS...

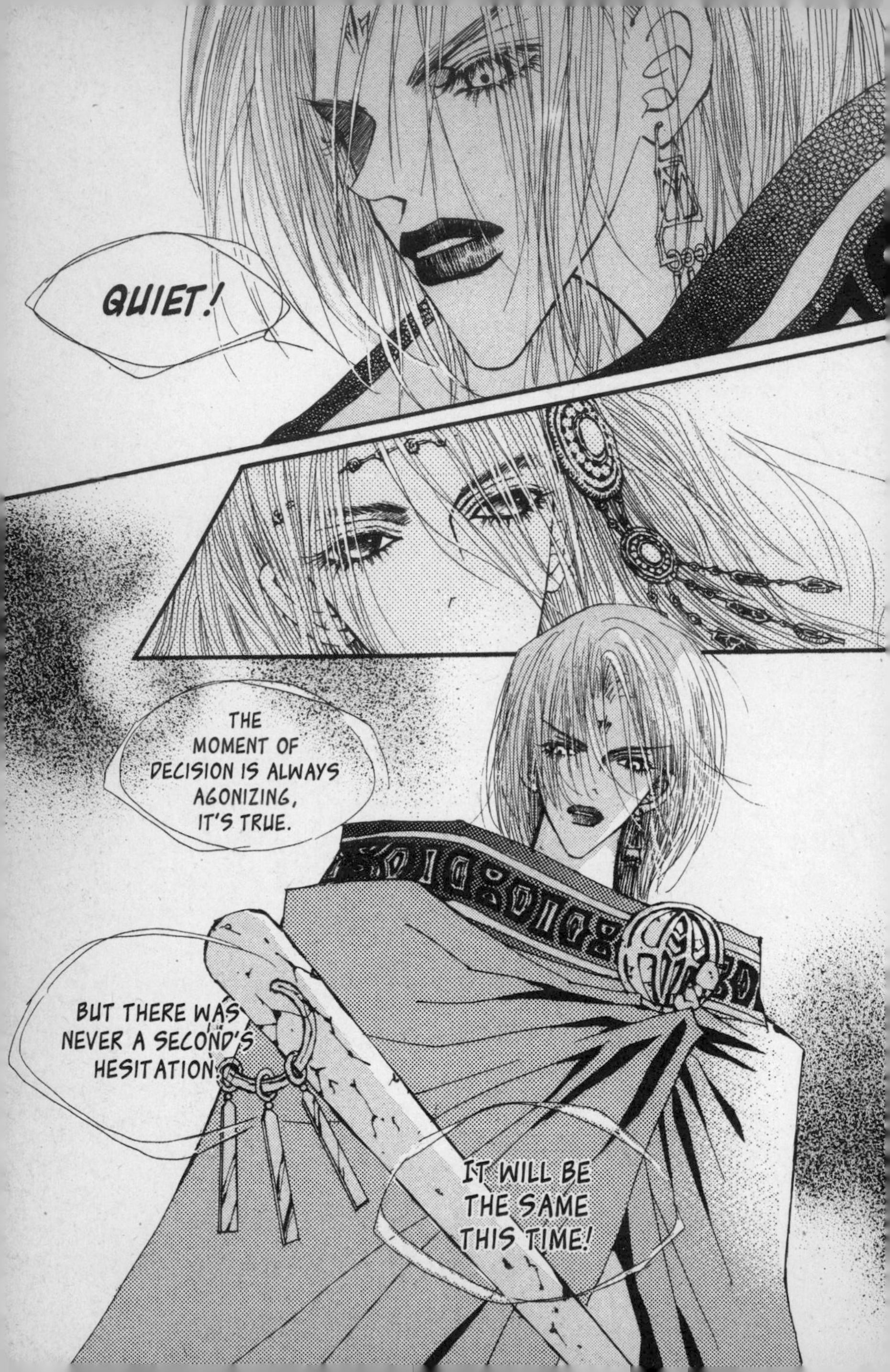
QUIET!
THE MOMENT OF DECISION IS ALWAYS AGONIZING, IT'S TRUE.
BUT THERE WAS NEVER A SECOND'S HESITATION.
IT WILL BE THE SAME THIS TIME!

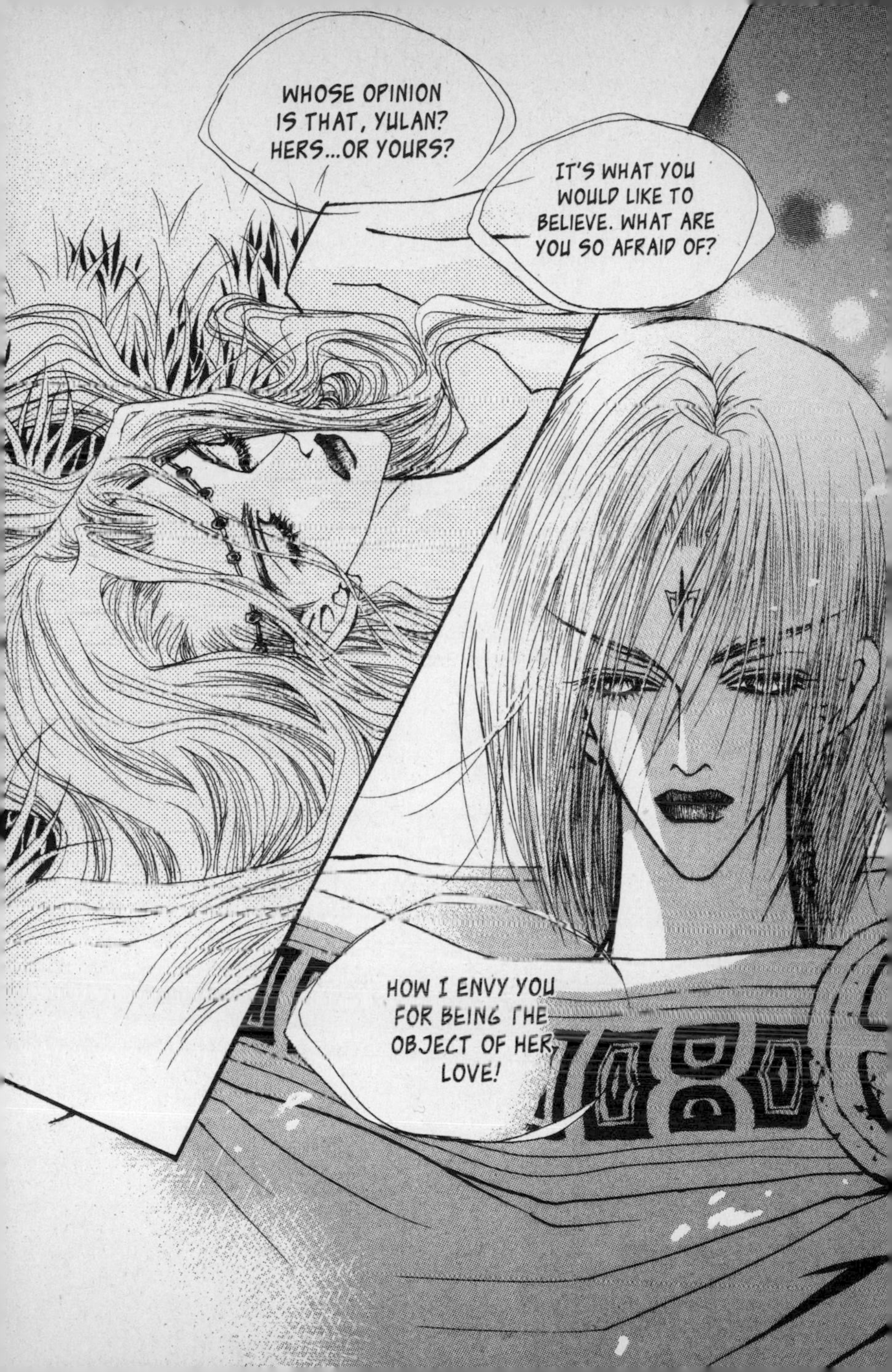
WHOSE OPINION IS THAT, YULAN? HERS...OR YOURS?
IT'S WHAT YOU WOULD LIKE TO BELIEVE. WHAT ARE YOU SO AFRAID OF?
HOW I ENVY YOU FOR BEING THE OBJECT OF HER LOVE!

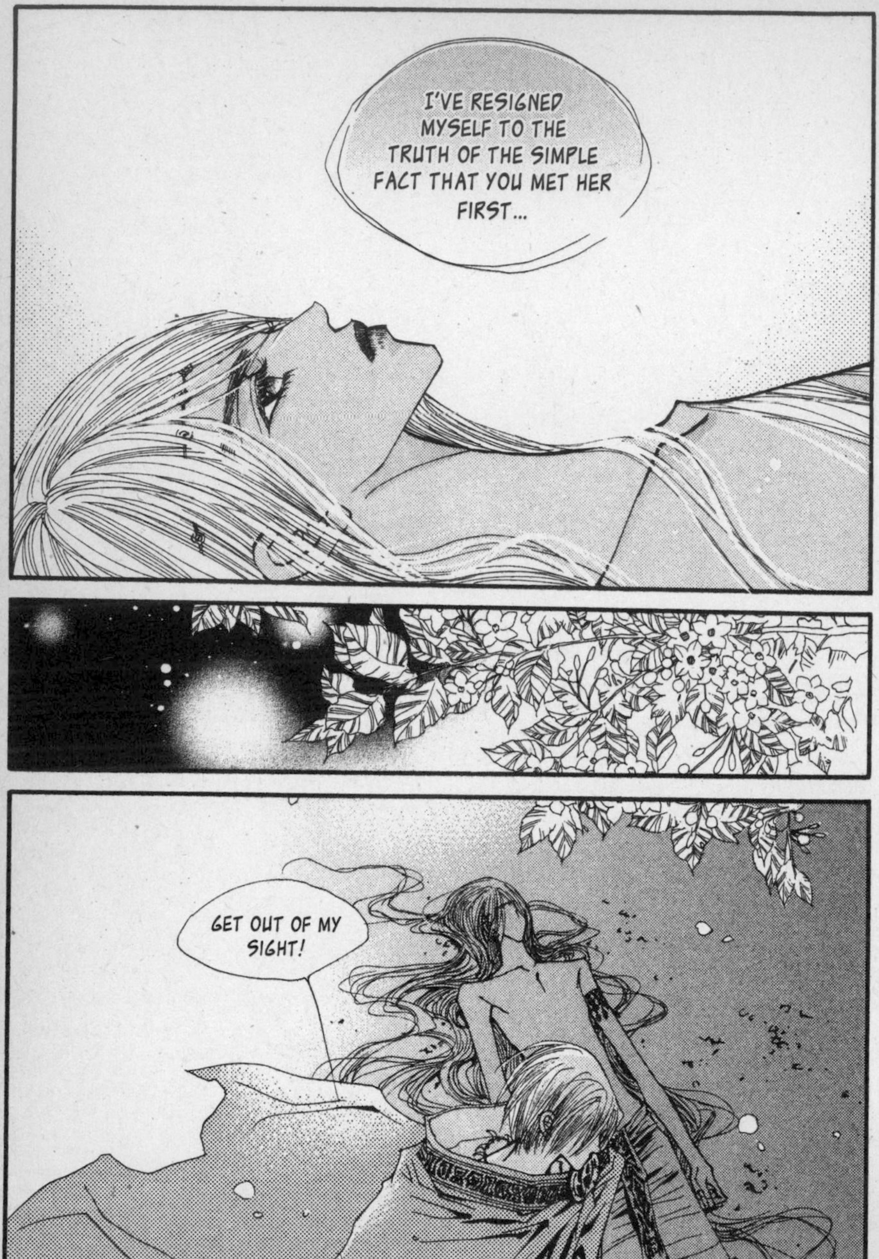
I'VE RESIGNED MYSELF TO THE TRUTH OF THE SIMPLE FACT THAT YOU MET HER FIRST...
GET OUT OF MY SIGHT!

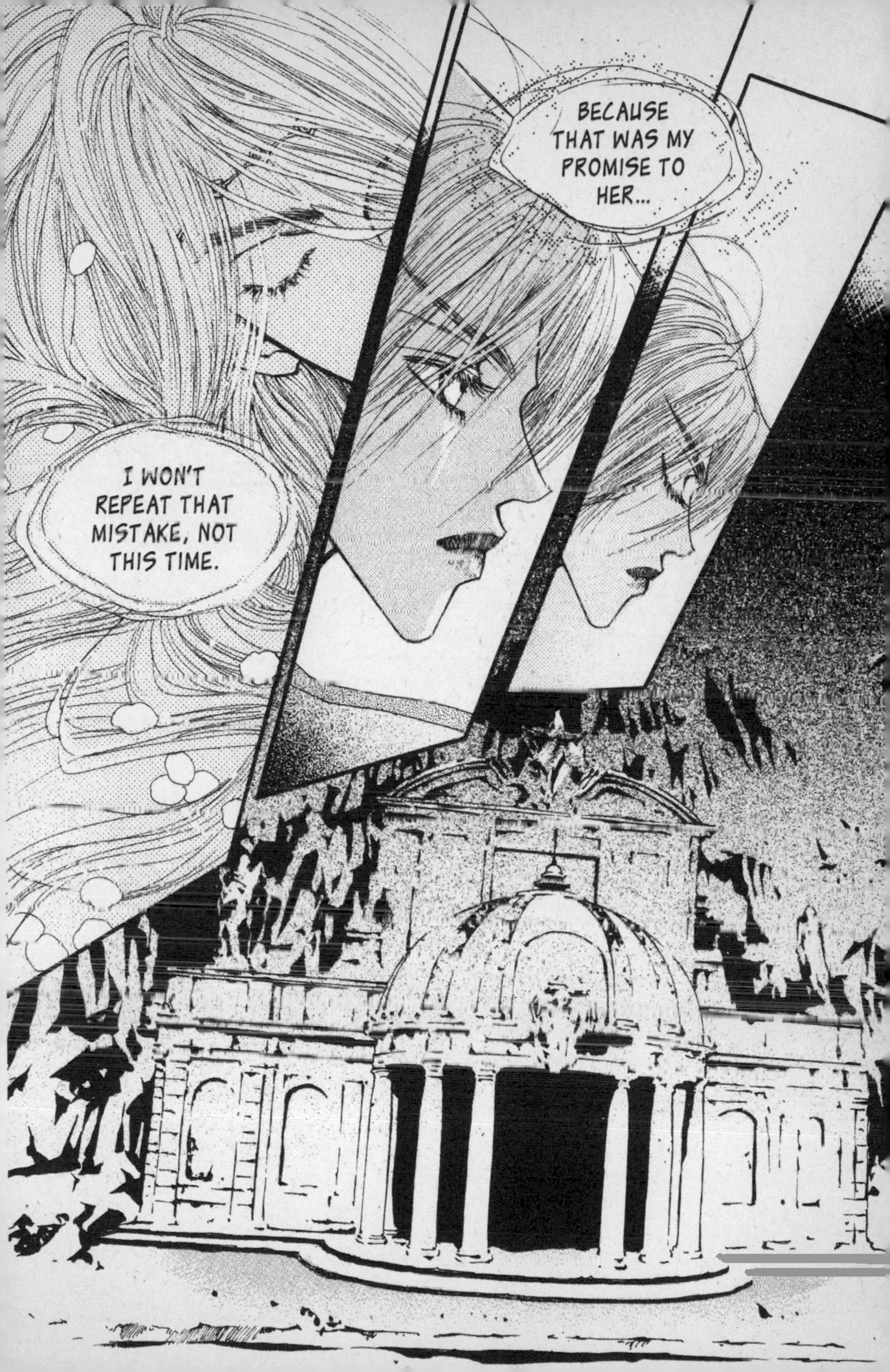
I WON'T REPEAT THAT MISTAKE, NOT THIS TIME.
BECAUSE THAT WAS MY PROMISE TO HER...

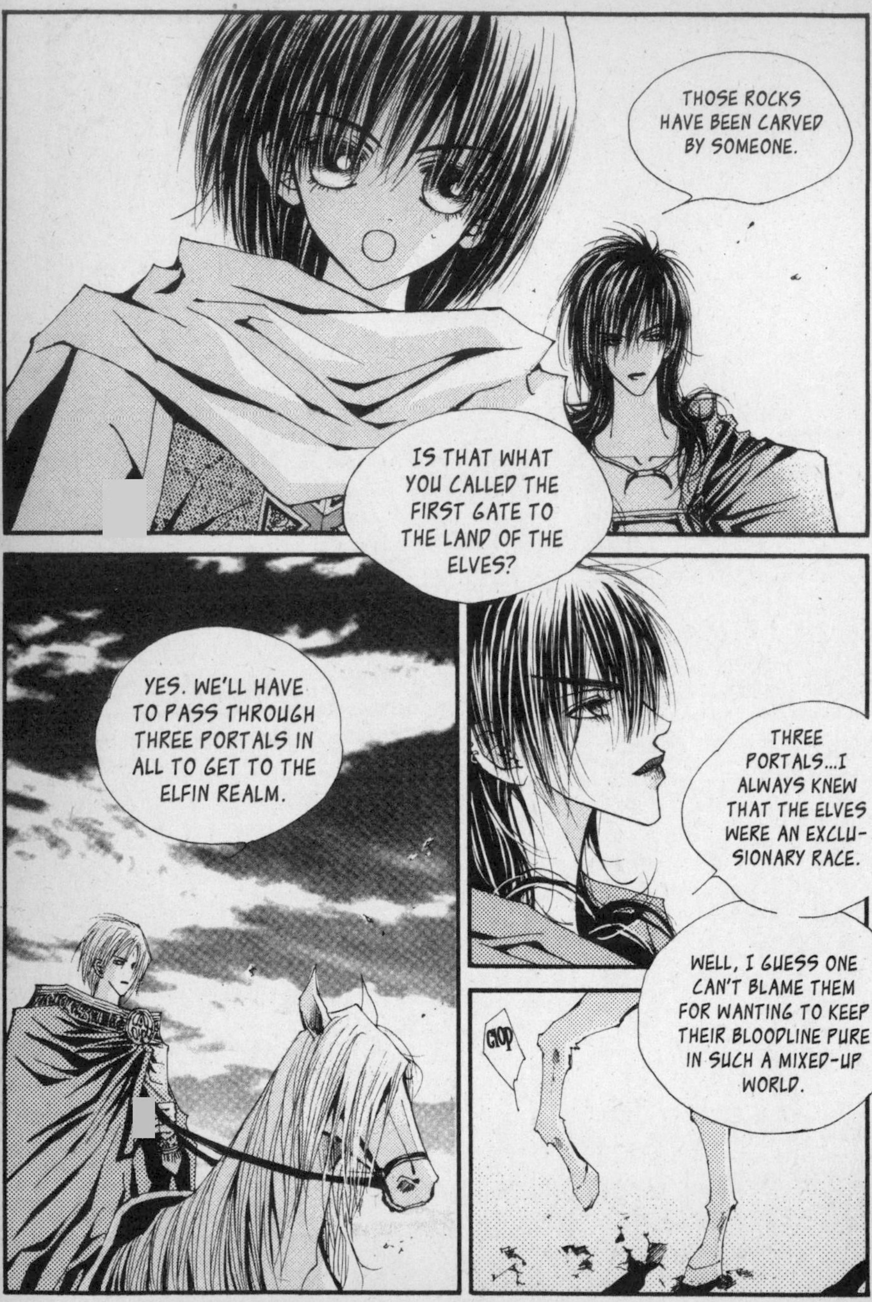
THOSE ROCKS HAVE BEEN CARVED BY SOMEONE.
IS THAT WHAT YOU CALLED THE FIRST GATE TO THE LAND OF THE ELVES?
YES. WE'LL HAVE TO PASS THROUGH THREE PORTALS IN ALL TO GET TO THE ELFIN REALM.
THREE PORTALS...I ALWAYS KNEW THAT THE ELVES WERE AN EXCLU-SIONARY RACE.
WELL, I GUESS ONE CAN'T BLAME THEM FOR WANTING TO KEEP THEIR BLOODLINE PURE IN SUCH A MIXED-UP WORLD.
CLOP

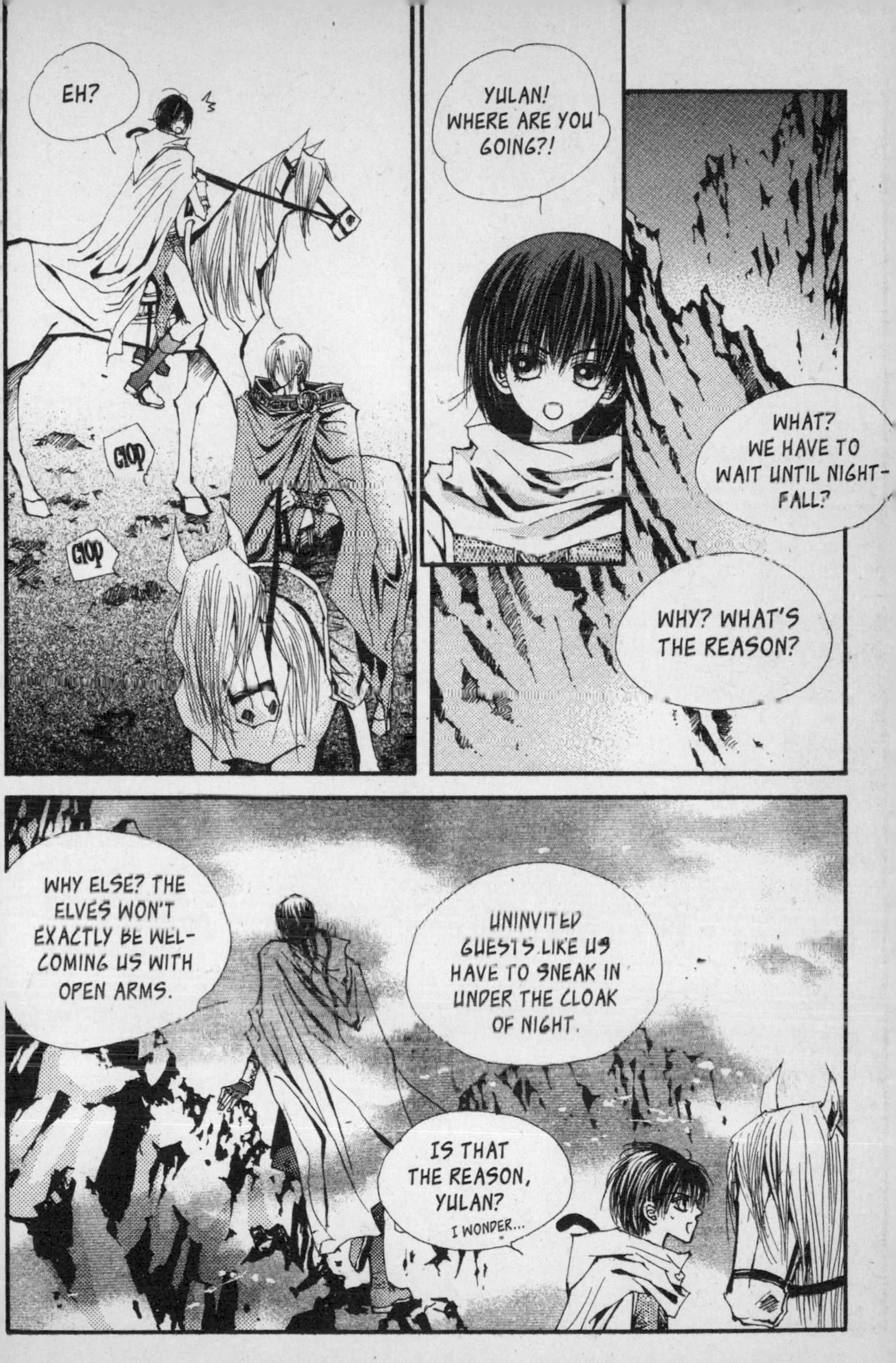
EH?
CLOP
CLOP
YULAN! WHERE ARE YOU GOING?!
WHAT? WE HAVE TO WAIT UNTIL NIGHT-FALL?
WHY? WHAT'S THE REASON?
WHY ELSE? THE ELVES WON'T EXACTLY BE WEL-COMING US WITH OPEN ARMS.
UNINVITED GUESTS LIKE US HAVE TO SNEAK IN UNDER THE CLOAK OF NIGHT.
IS THAT THE REASON, YULAN?
I WONDER...

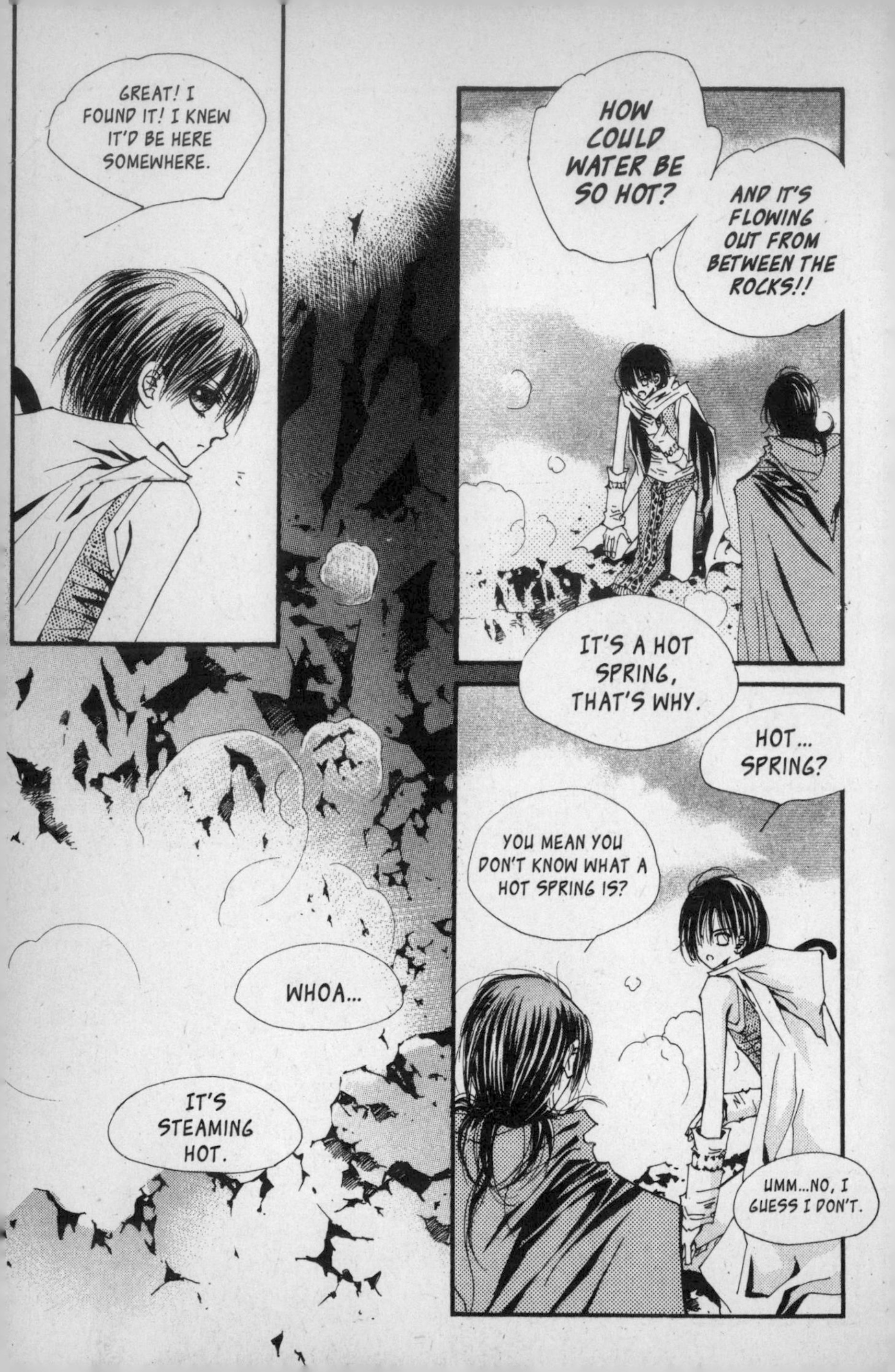
GREAT! I FOUND IT! I KNEW IT'D BE HERE SOMEWHERE.
WHOA...
IT'S STEAMING HOT.
HOW COULD WATER BE SO HOT?
AND IT'S FLOWING OUT FROM BETWEEN THE ROCKS!!
IT'S A HOT SPRING, THAT'S WHY.
HOT... SPRING?
YOU MEAN YOU DON'T KNOW WHAT A HOT SPRING IS?
UMM...NO, I GUESS I DON'T.

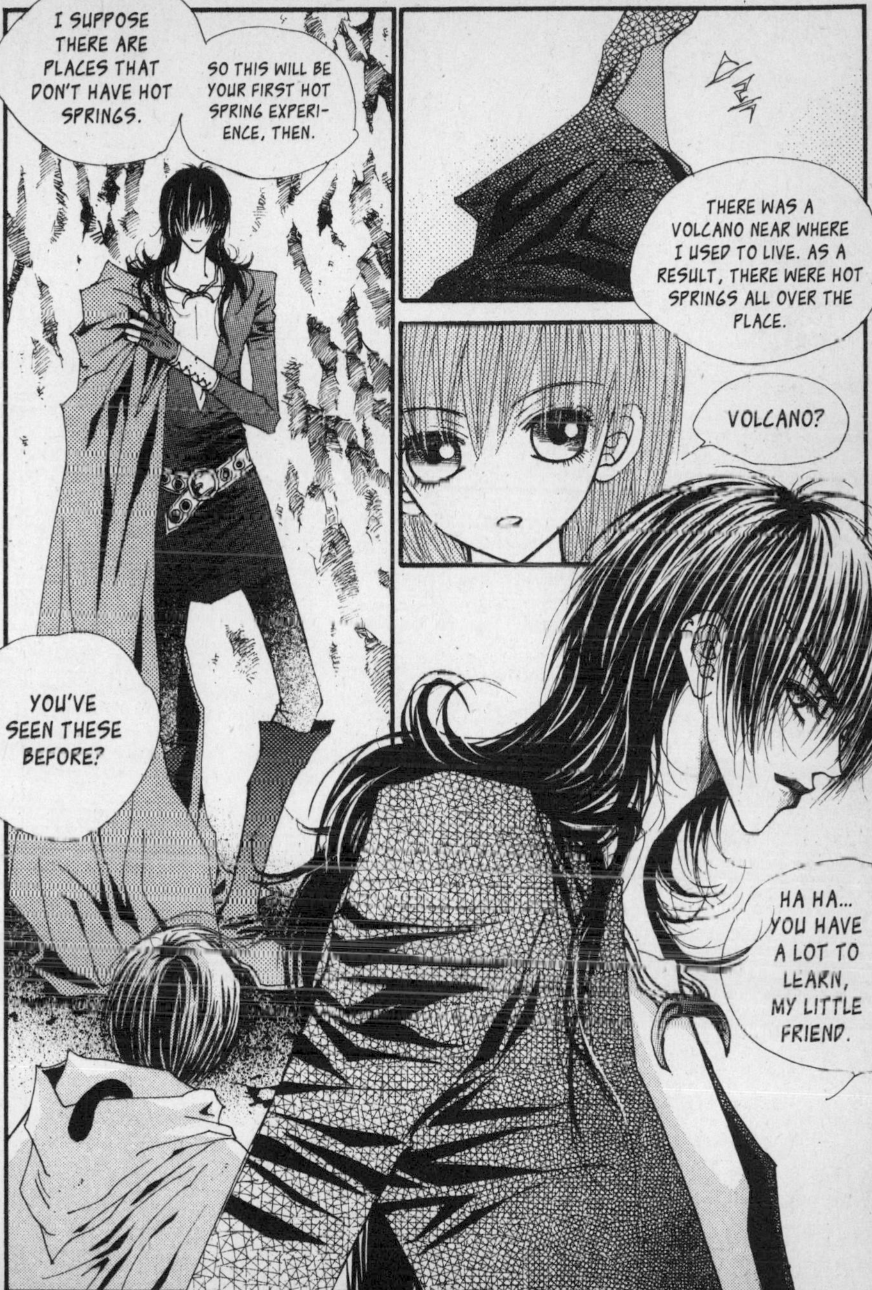
I SUPPOSE THERE ARE PLACES THAT DON'T HAVE HOT SPRINGS.
SO THIS WILL BE YOUR FIRST HOT SPRING EXPERIENCE, THEN.
THERE WAS A VOLCANO NEAR WHERE I USED TO LIVE. AS A RESULT, THERE WERE HOT SPRINGS ALL OVER THE PLACE.
VOLCANO?
YOU'VE SEEN THESE BEFORE?
HA HA... YOU HAVE A LOT TO LEARN, MY LITTLE FRIEND.

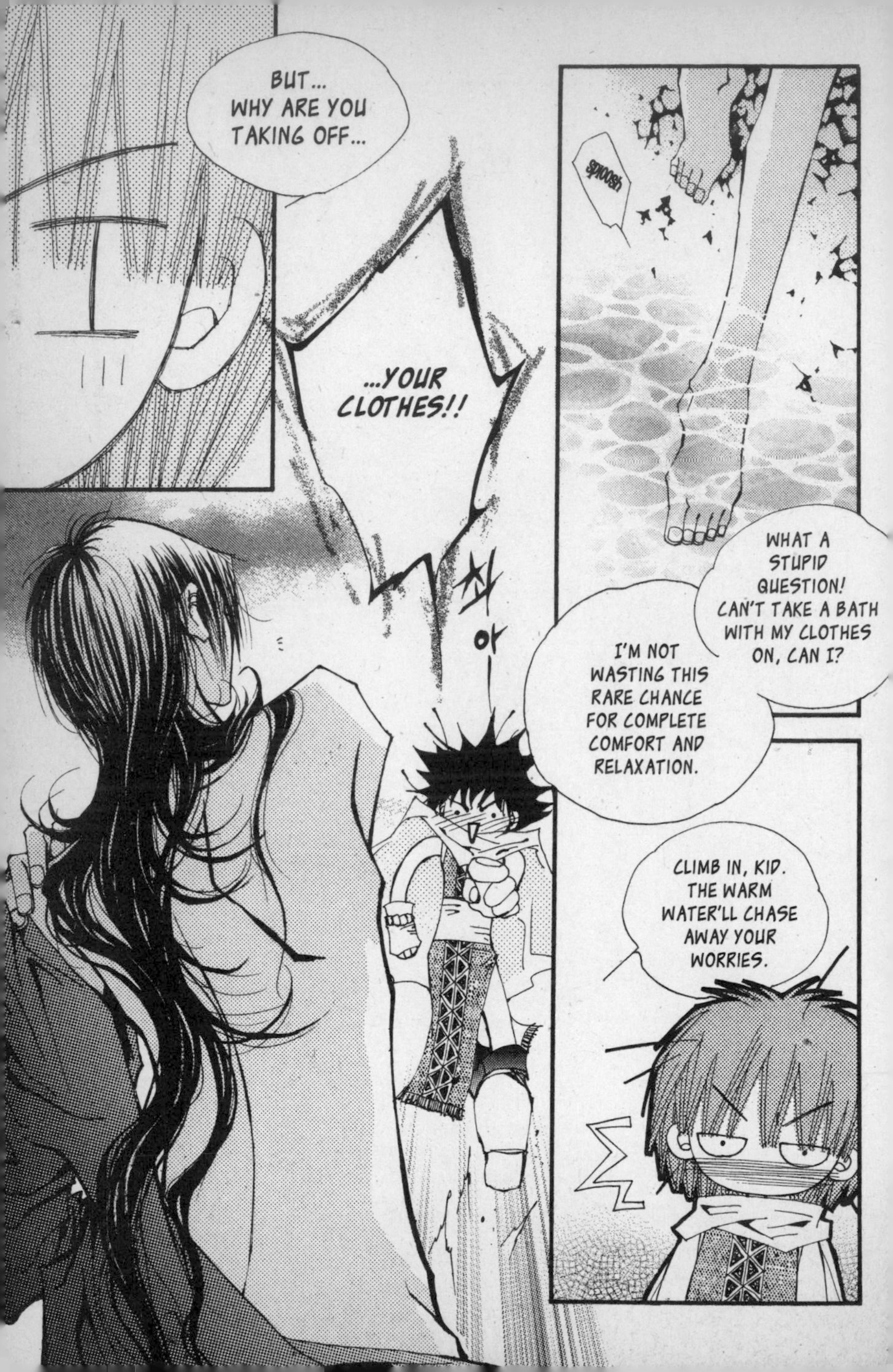
BUT... WHY ARE YOU TAKING OFF...
...YOUR CLOTHES!!
촤아
WHAT A STUPID QUESTION! CAN'T TAKE A BATH WITH MY CLOTHES ON, CAN I?
I'M NOT WASTING THIS RARE CHANCE FOR COMPLETE COMFORT AND RELAXATION.
CLIMB IN, KID. THE WARM WATER'LL CHASE AWAY YOUR WORRIES.

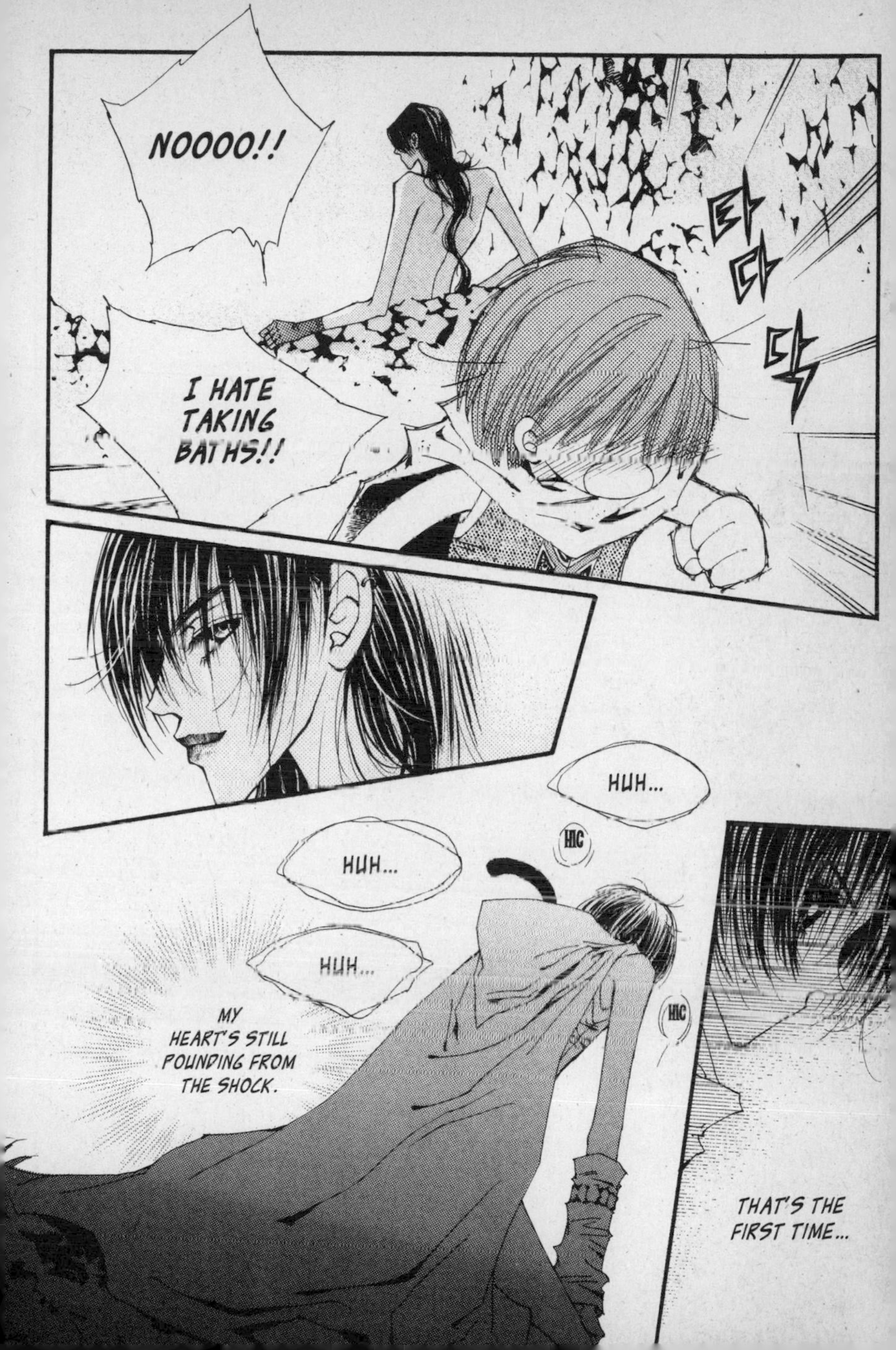
NOOOO!!
I HATE TAKING BATHS!!
HUH...
HIC
HUH...
HUH...
HIC
MY HEART'S STILL POUNDING FROM THE SHOCK.
THAT'S THE FIRST TIME...

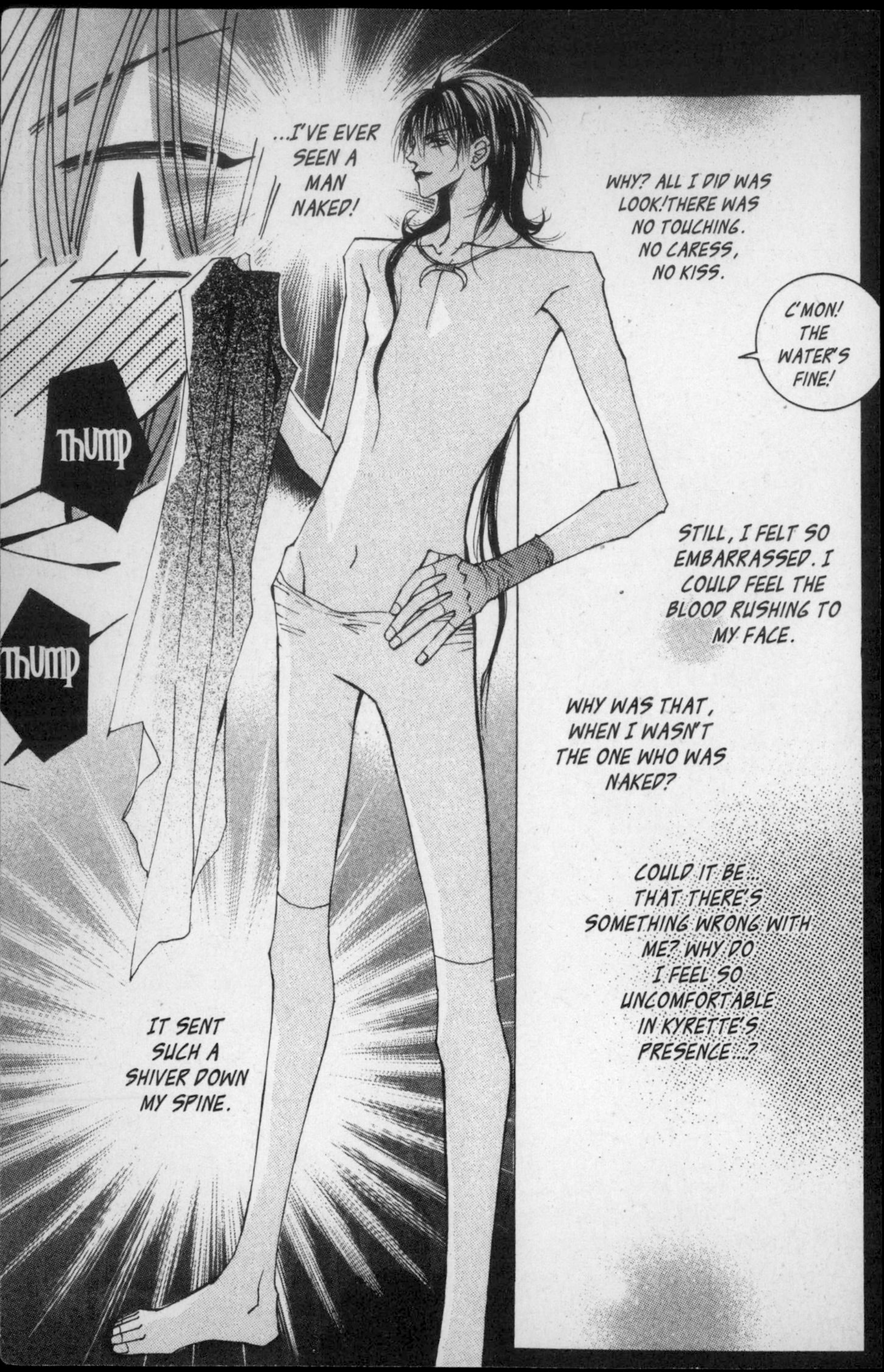
...I'VE EVER SEEN A MAN NAKED!
THUMP
THUMP
IT SENT SUCH A SHIVER DOWN MY SPINE.
WHY? ALL I DID WAS LOOK! THERE WAS NO TOUCHING. NO CARESS, NO KISS.
C'MON! THE WATER'S FINE!
STILL, I FELT SO EMBARRASSED. I COULD FEEL THE BLOOD RUSHING TO MY FACE.
WHY WAS THAT, WHEN I WASN'T THE ONE WHO WAS NAKED?
COULD IT BE... THAT THERE'S SOMETHING WRONG WITH ME? WHY DO I FEEL SO UNCOMFORTABLE IN KYRETTE'S PRESENCE...?

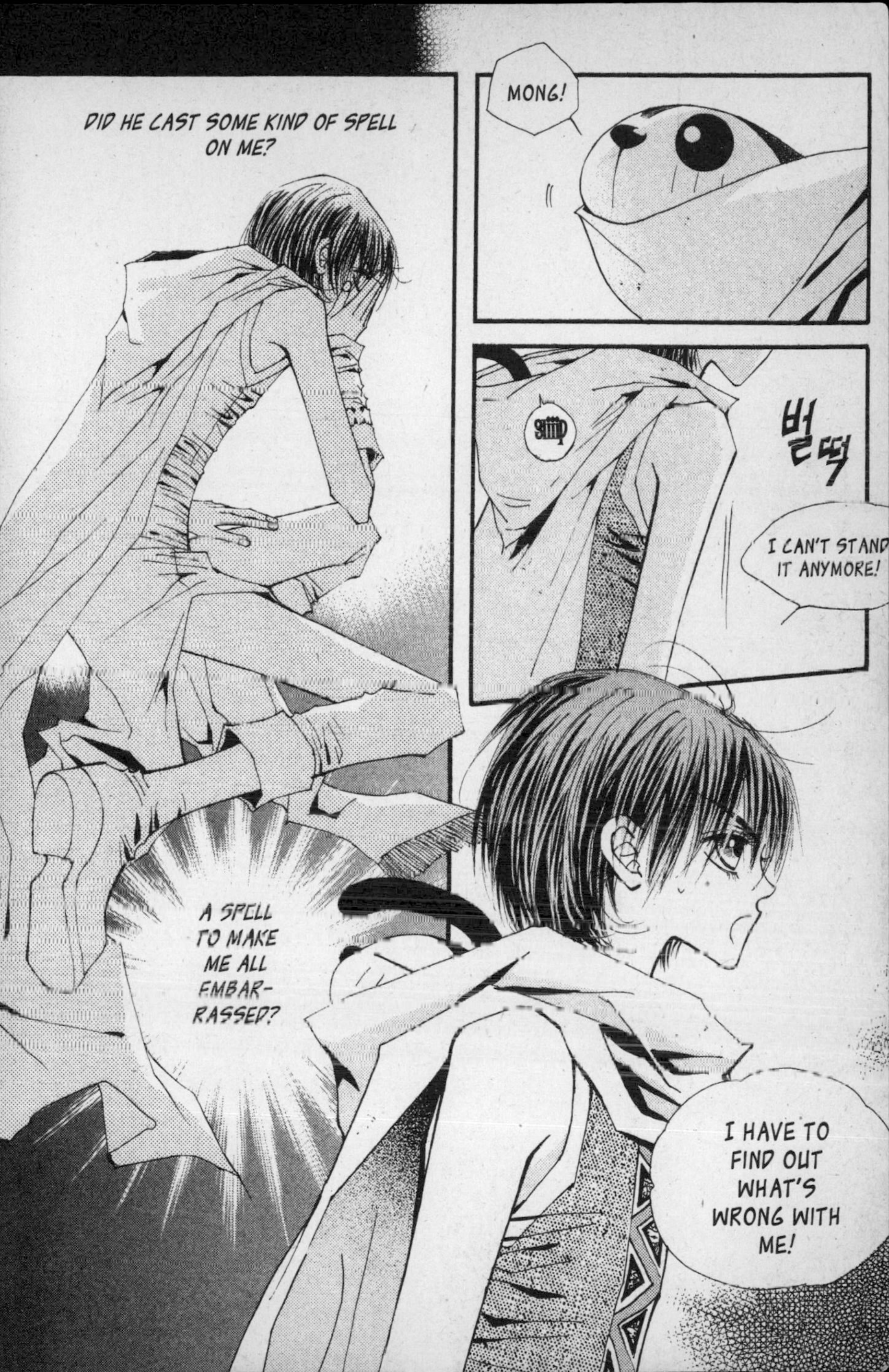
DID HE CAST SOME KIND OF SPELL ON ME?
A SPELL TO MAKE ME ALL EMBAR-RASSED?
MONG!
벌떡
I CAN'T STAND IT ANYMORE!
I HAVE TO FIND OUT WHAT'S WRONG WITH ME!

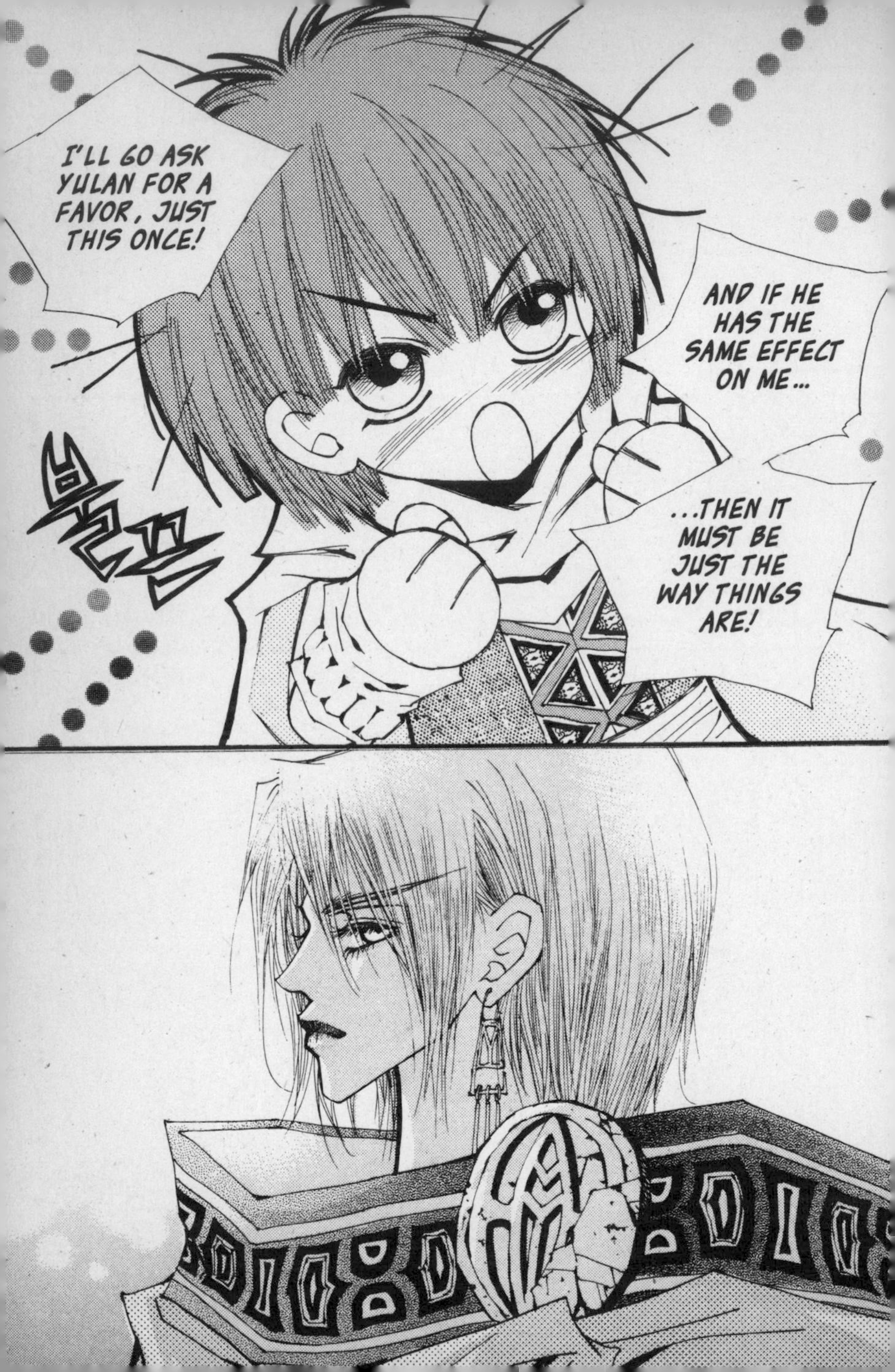
I'LL GO ASK YULAN FOR A FAVOR, JUST THIS ONCE!
AND IF HE HAS THE SAME EFFECT ON ME...
...THEN IT MUST BE JUST THE WAY THINGS ARE!

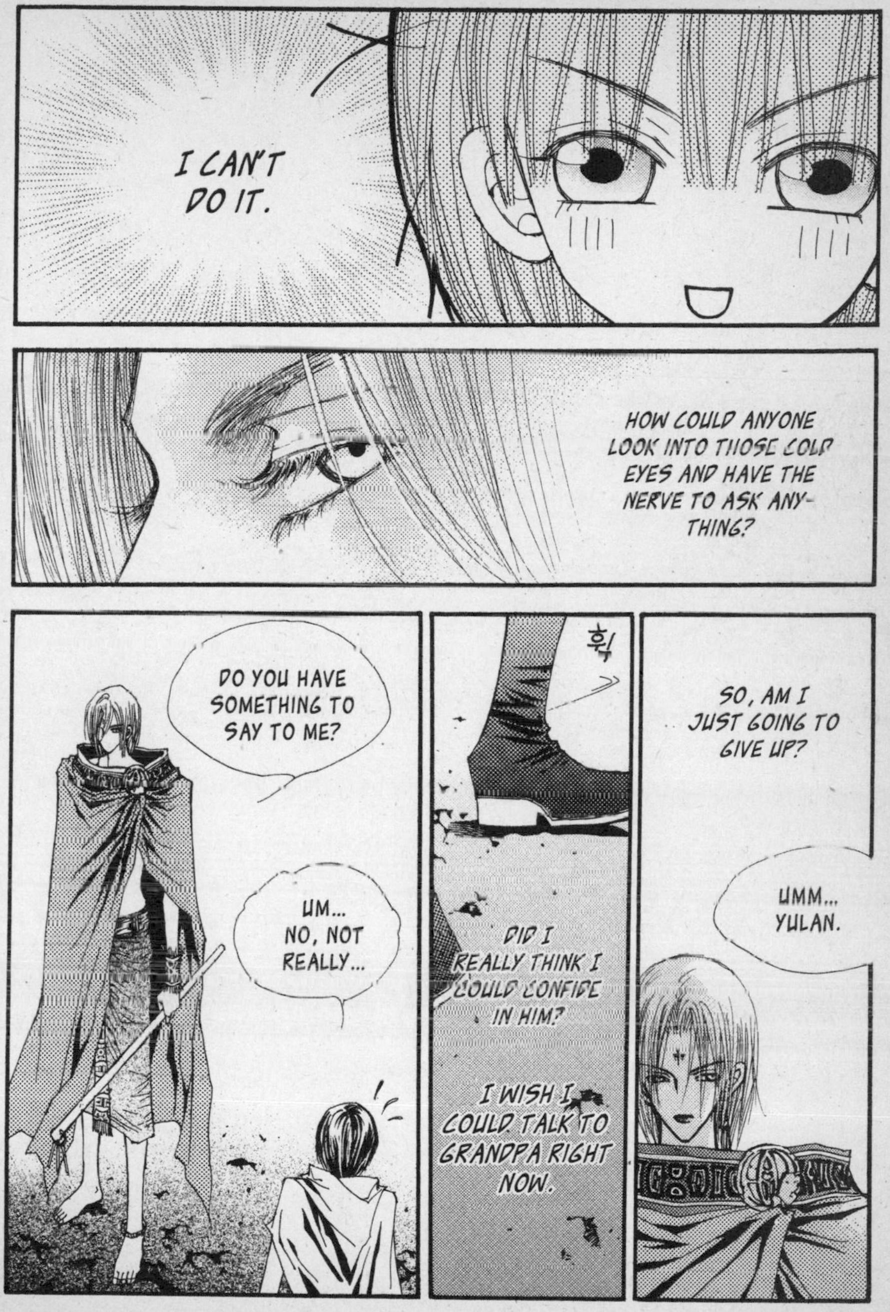
I CAN'T DO IT.
HOW COULD ANYONE LOOK INTO THOSE COLD EYES AND HAVE THE NERVE TO ASK ANY-THING?
DO YOU HAVE SOMETHING TO SAY TO ME?
UM... NO, NOT REALLY...
훅
DID I REALLY THINK I COULD CONFIDE IN HIM?
I WISH I COULD TALK TO GRANDPA RIGHT NOW.
SO, AM I JUST GOING TO GIVE UP?
UMM... YULAN.

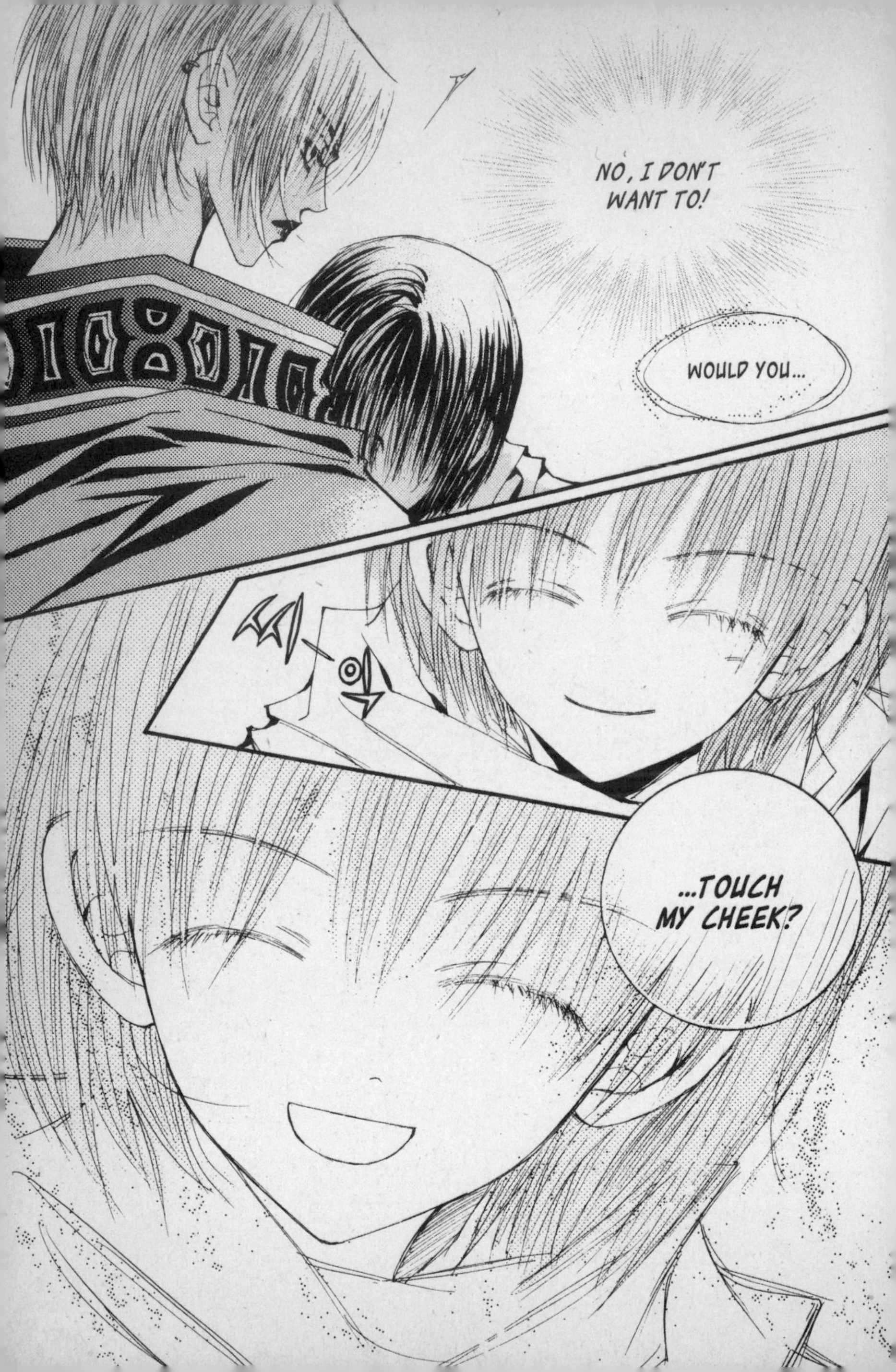
NO, I DON'T WANT TO!
WOULD YOU...
...TOUCH MY CHEEK?

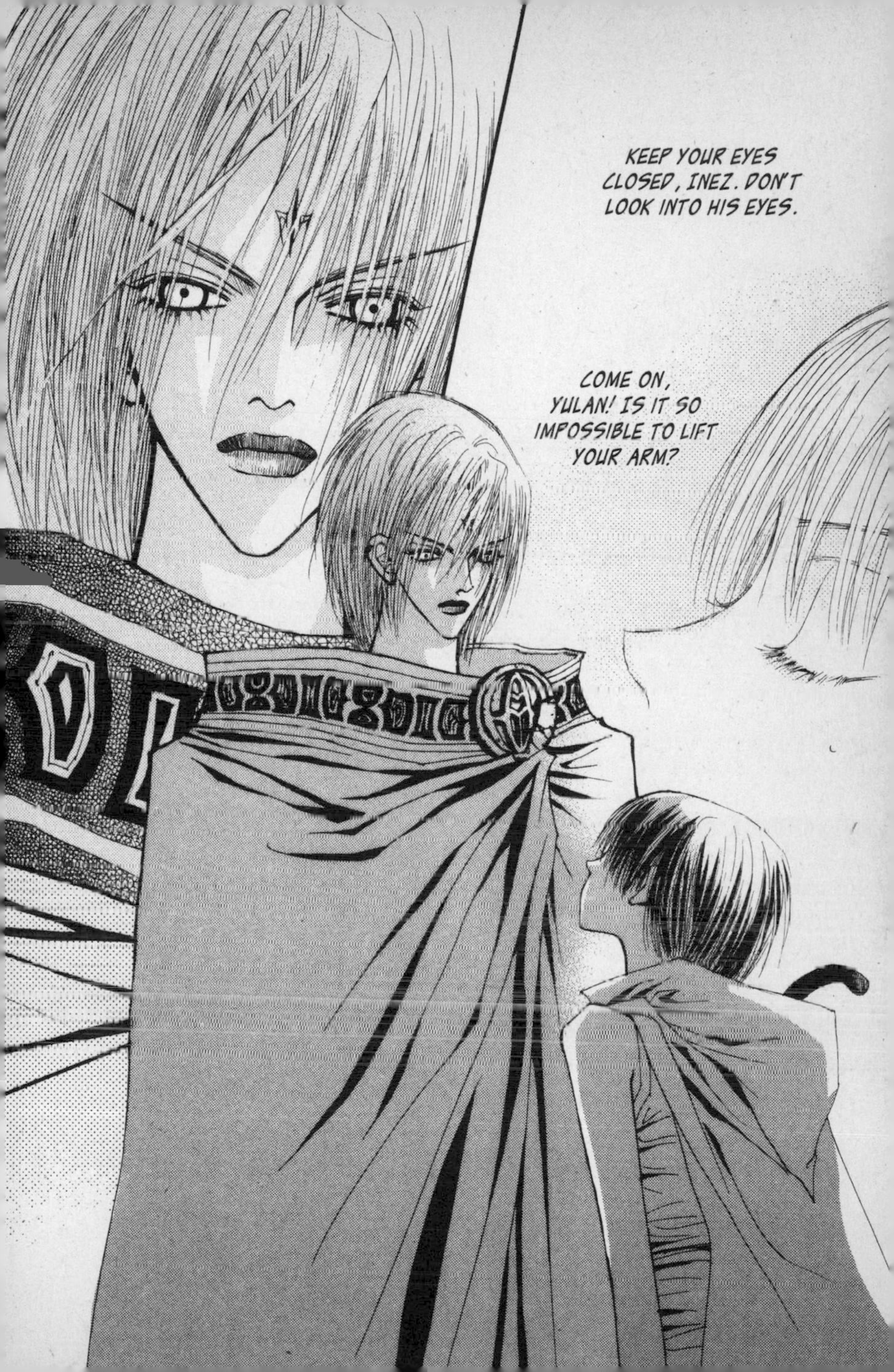
KEEP YOUR EYES CLOSED, INEZ. DON'T LOOK INTO HIS EYES.
COME ON, YULAN! IS IT SO IMPOSSIBLE TO LIFT YOUR ARM?

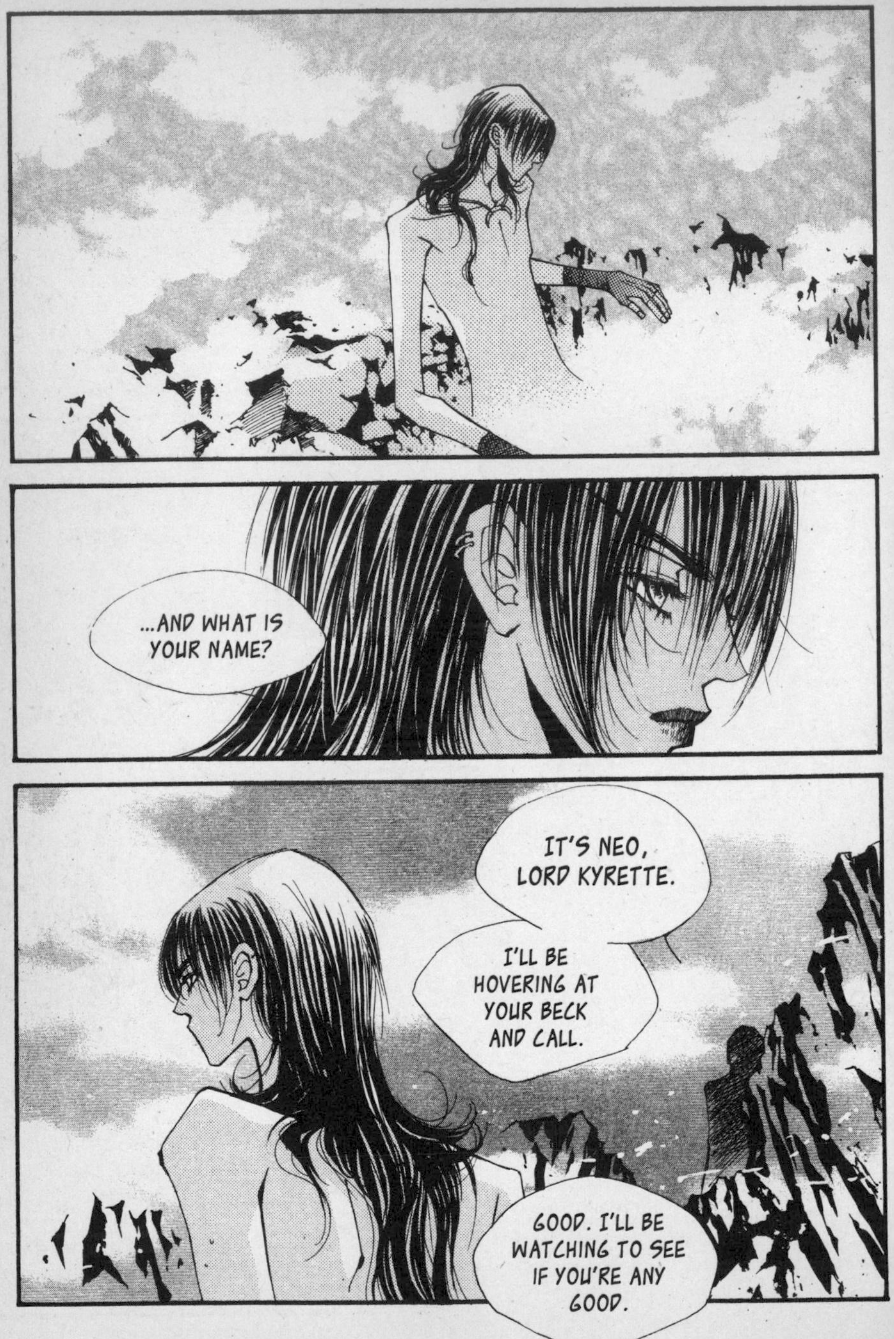
...AND WHAT IS YOUR NAME?
IT'S NEO, LORD KYRETTE.
I'LL BE HOVERING AT YOUR BECK AND CALL.
GOOD. I'LL BE WATCHING TO SEE IF YOU'RE ANY GOOD.

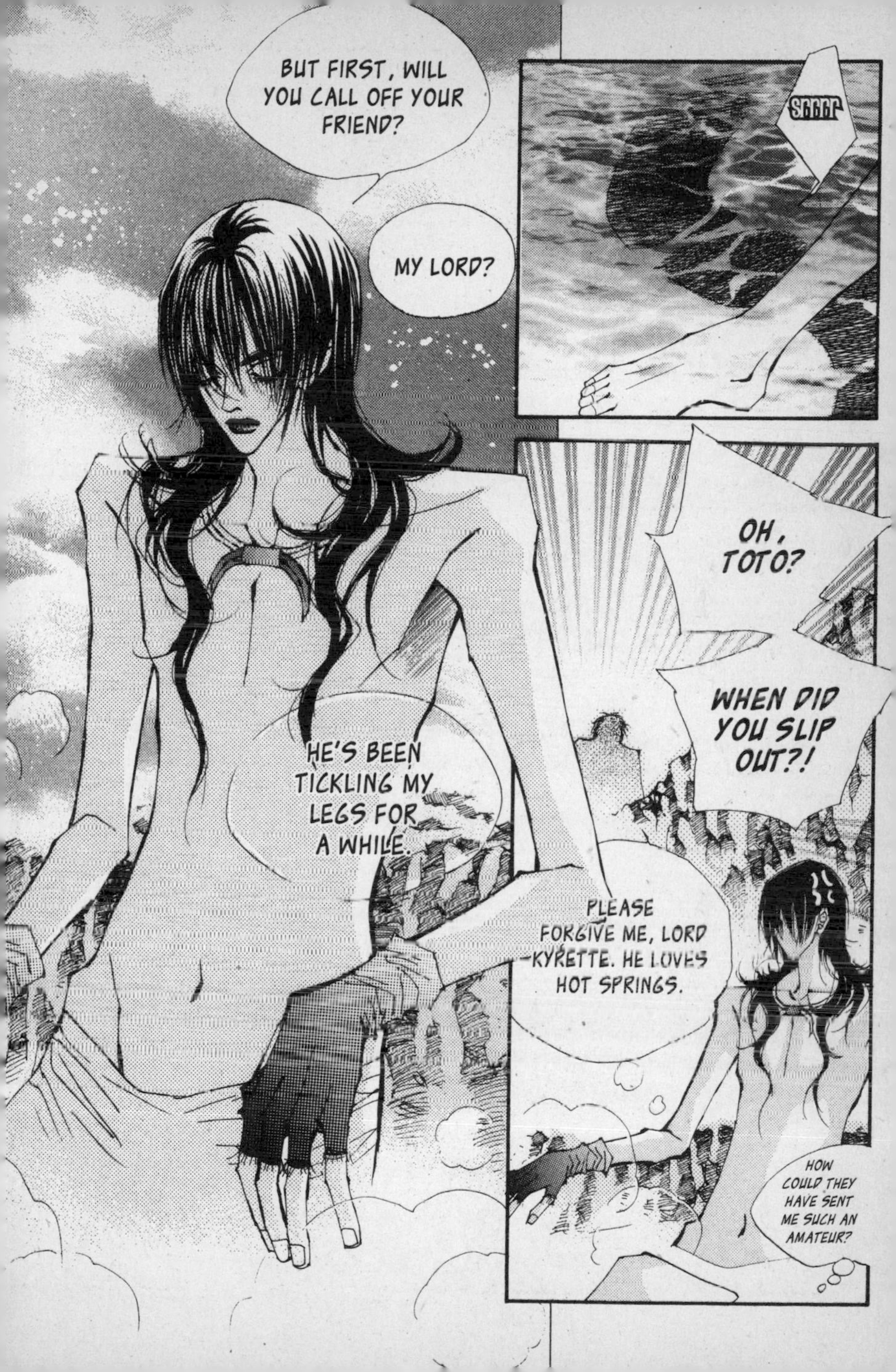
BUT FIRST, WILL YOU CALL OFF YOUR FRIEND?
MY LORD?
HE'S BEEN TICKLING MY LEGS FOR A WHILE.
SGGGR
OH, TOTO?
WHEN DID YOU SLIP OUT?!
PLEASE FORGIVE ME, LORD KYRETTE. HE LOVES HOT SPRINGS.
HOW COULD THEY HAVE SENT ME SUCH AN AMATEUR?

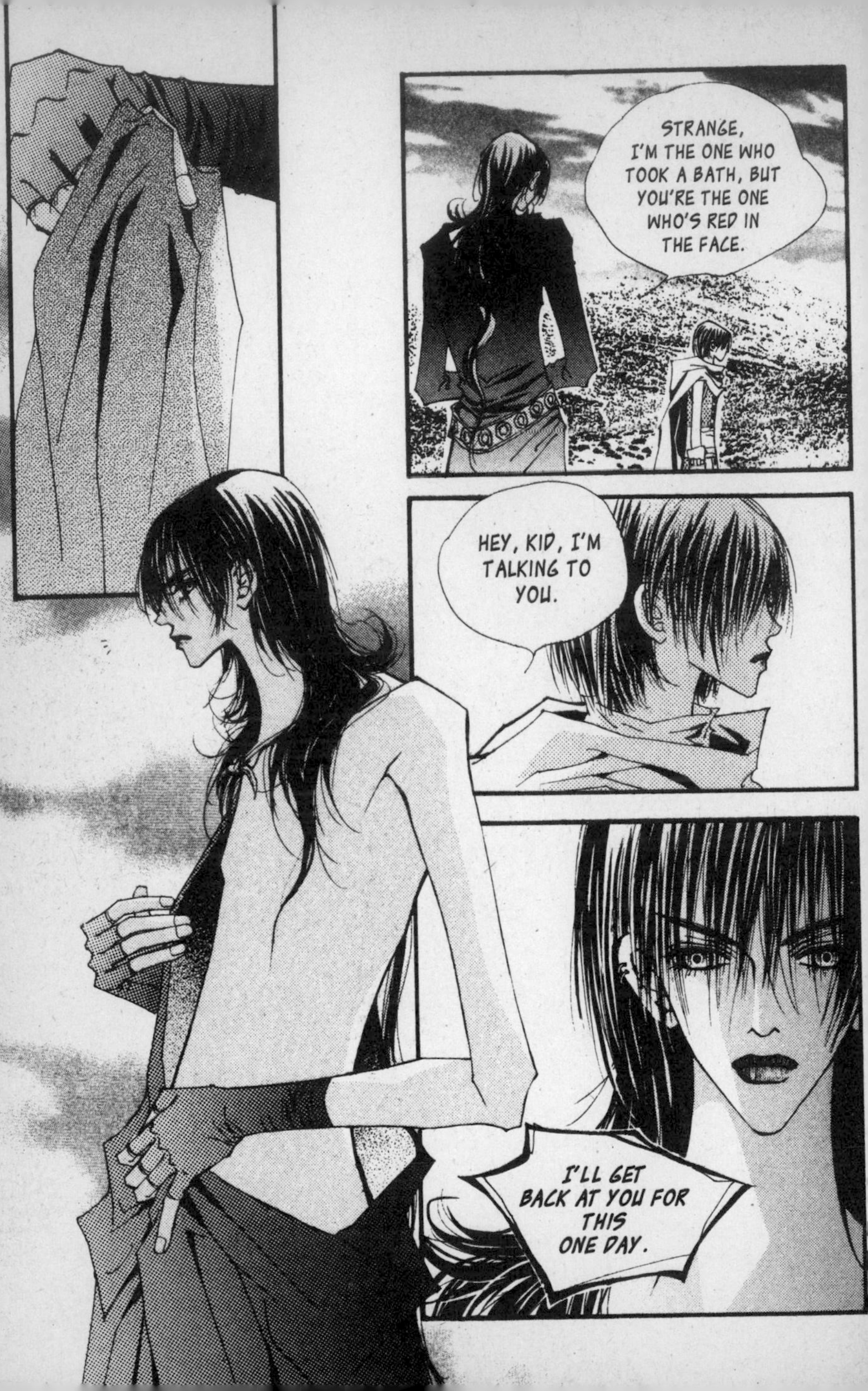
STRANGE, I'M THE ONE WHO TOOK A BATH, BUT YOU'RE THE ONE WHO'S RED IN THE FACE.
HEY, KID, I'M TALKING TO YOU.
I'LL GET BACK AT YOU FOR THIS ONE DAY.

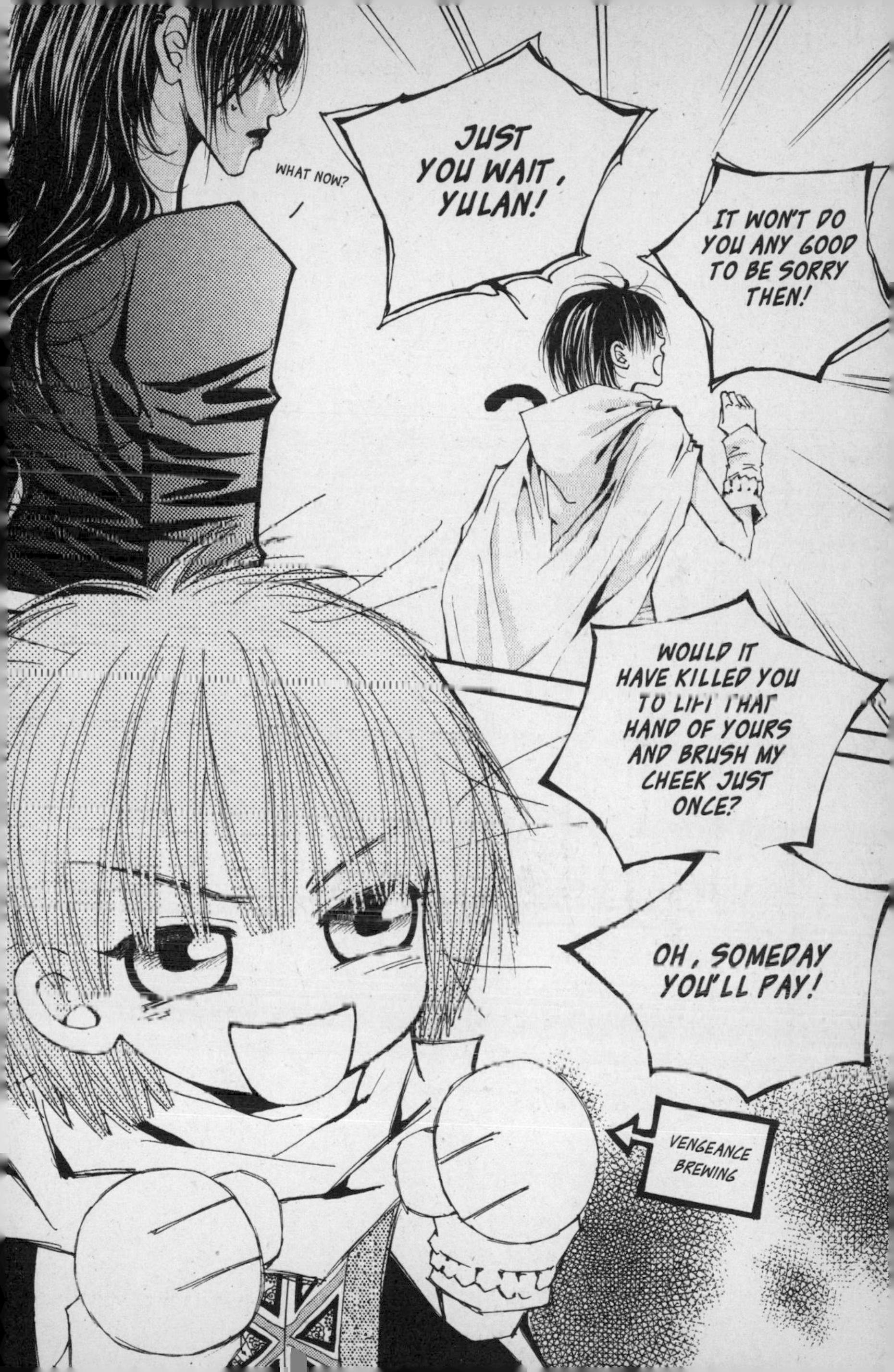
JUST YOU WAIT, YULAN!
IT WON'T DO YOU ANY GOOD TO BE SORRY THEN!
WHAT NOW?
WOULD IT HAVE KILLED YOU TO LIFT THAT HAND OF YOURS AND BRUSH MY CHEEK JUST ONCE?
OH, SOMEDAY YOU'LL PAY!
VENGEANCE BREWING

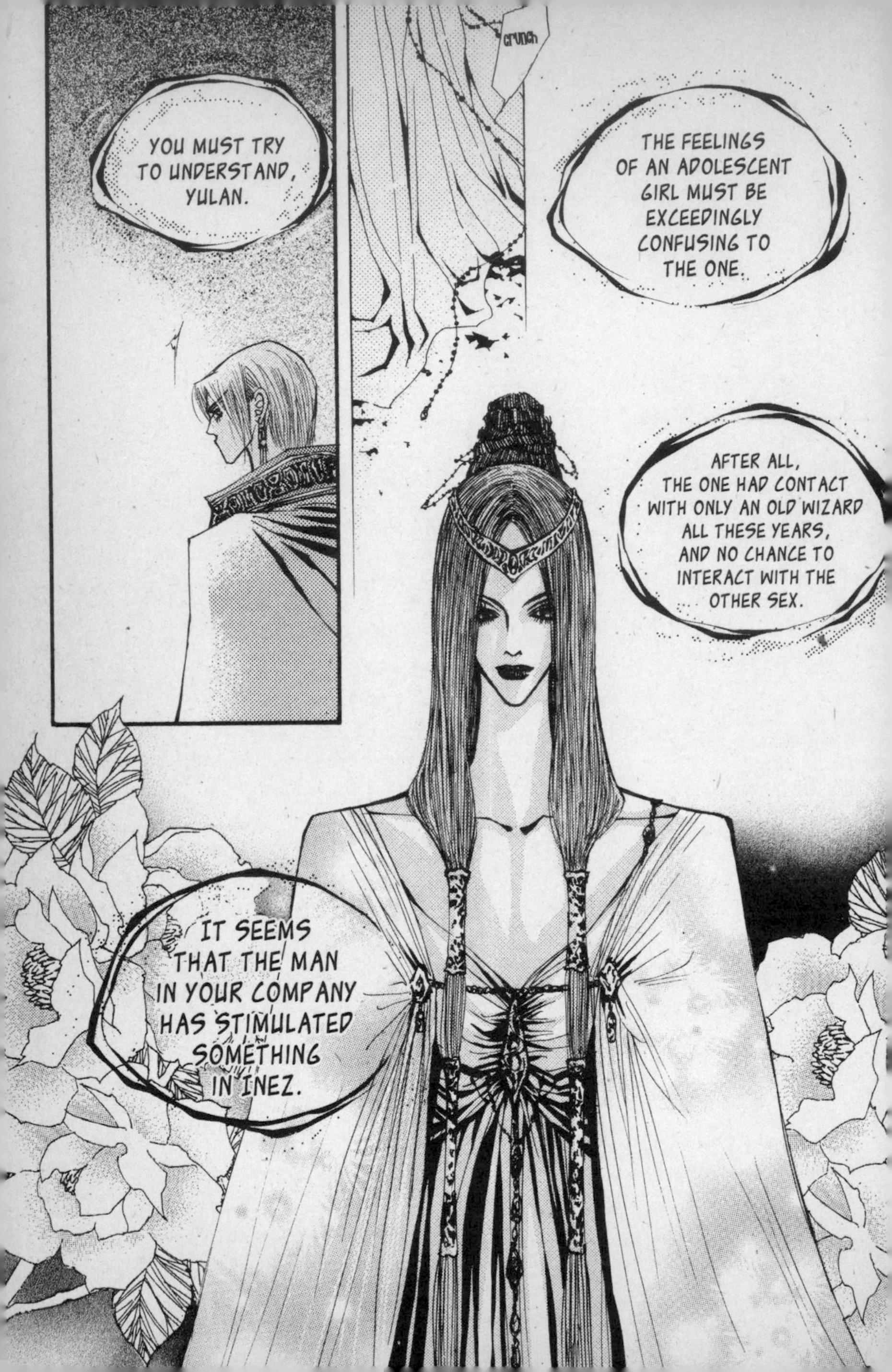
crunch
THE FEELINGS OF AN ADOLESCENT GIRL MUST BE EXCEEDINGLY CONFUSING TO THE ONE.
AFTER ALL, THE ONE HAD CONTACT WITH ONLY AN OLD WIZARD ALL THESE YEARS, AND NO CHANCE TO INTERACT WITH THE OTHER SEX.
IT SEEMS THAT THE MAN IN YOUR COMPANY HAS STIMULATED SOMETHING IN INEZ.
YOU MUST TRY TO UNDERSTAND, YULAN.

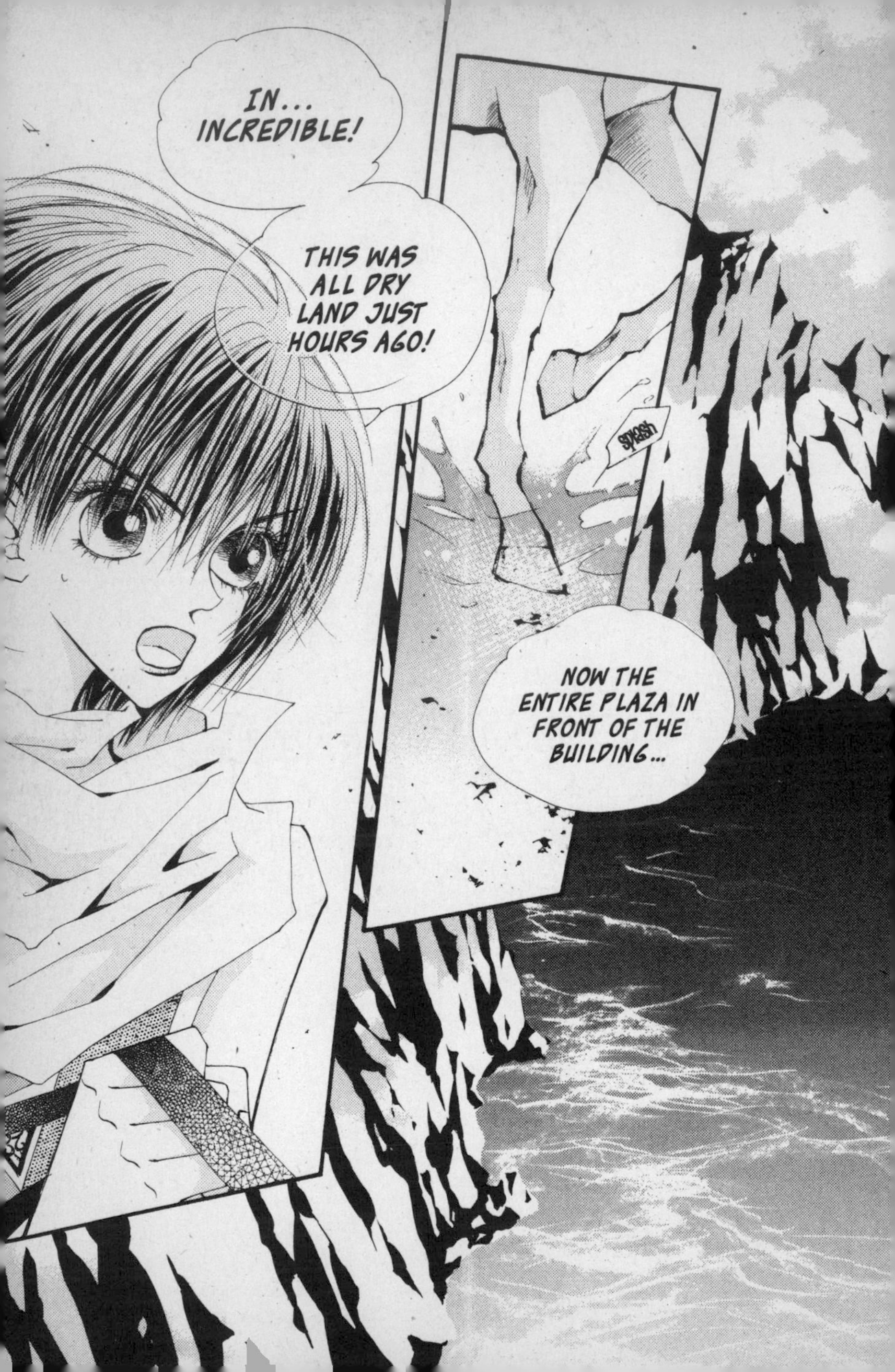
IN... INCREDIBLE!
THIS WAS ALL DRY LAND JUST HOURS AGO!
splash
NOW THE ENTIRE PLAZA IN FRONT OF THE BUILDING...

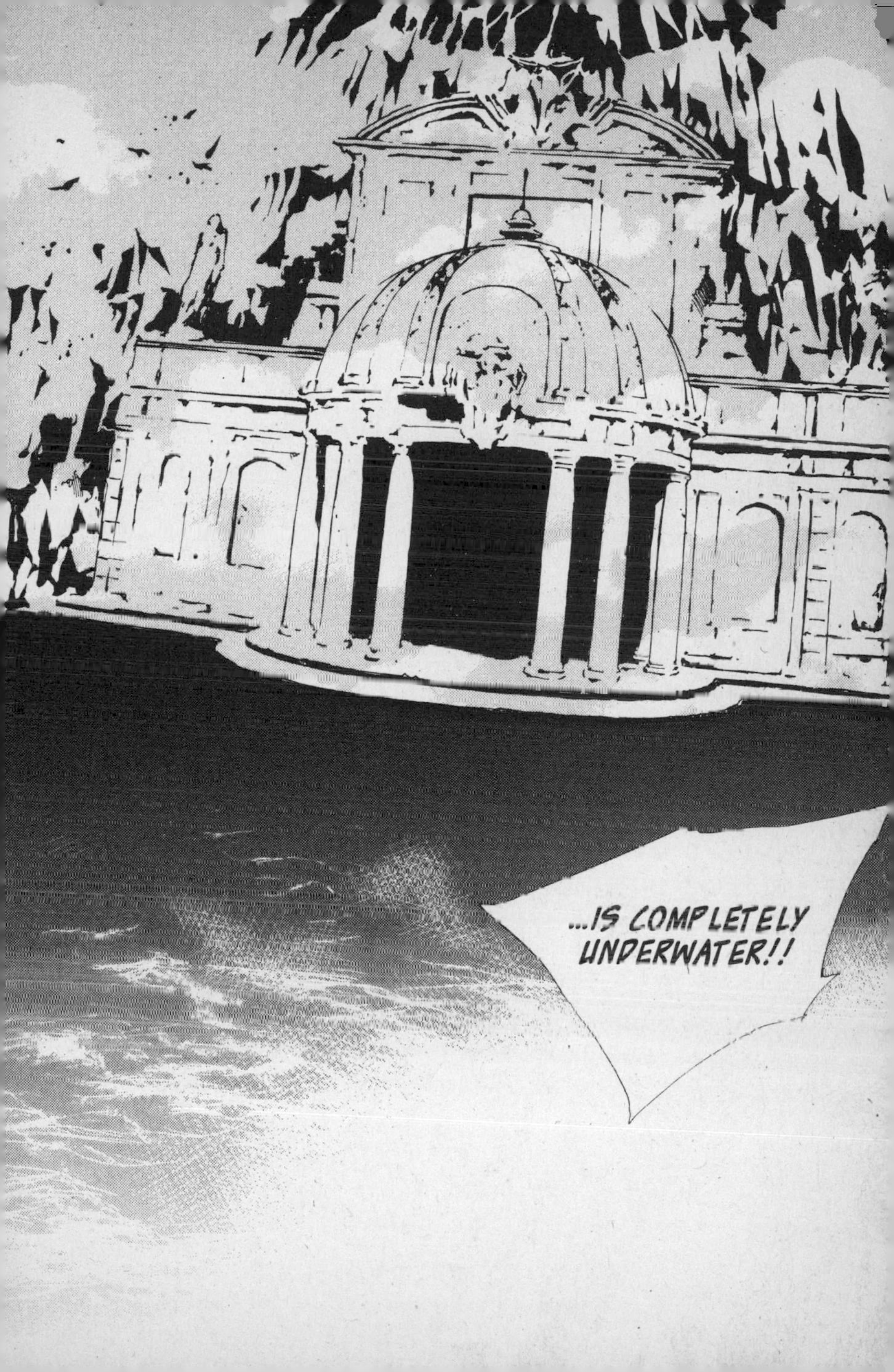
...IS COMPLETELY UNDERWATER!!

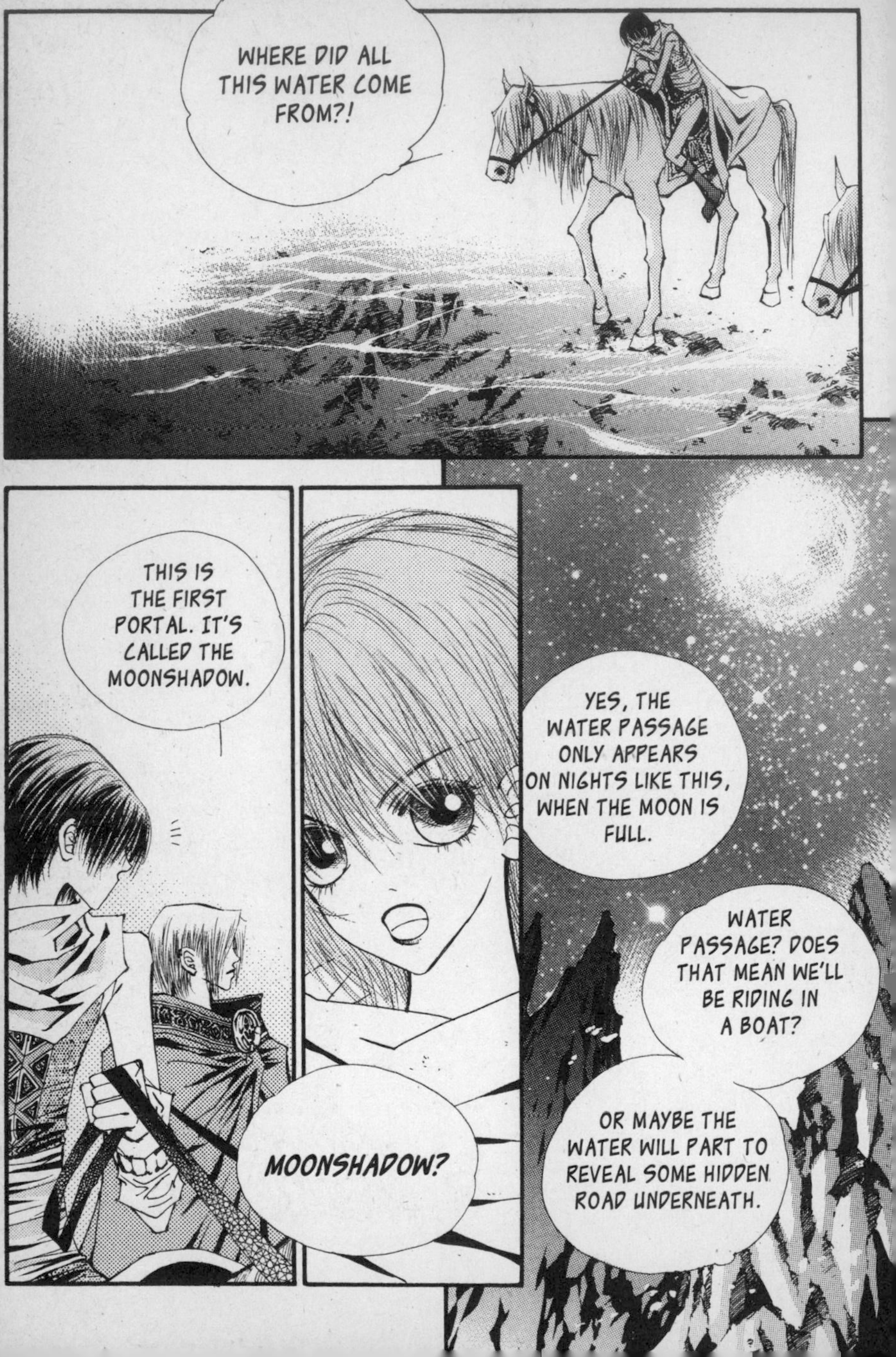
WHERE DID ALL THIS WATER COME FROM?!
THIS IS THE FIRST PORTAL. IT'S CALLED THE MOONSHADOW.
MOONSHADOW?
YES, THE WATER PASSAGE ONLY APPEARS ON NIGHTS LIKE THIS, WHEN THE MOON IS FULL.
WATER PASSAGE? DOES THAT MEAN WE'LL BE RIDING IN A BOAT?
OR MAYBE THE WATER WILL PART TO REVEAL SOME HIDDEN ROAD UNDERNEATH.

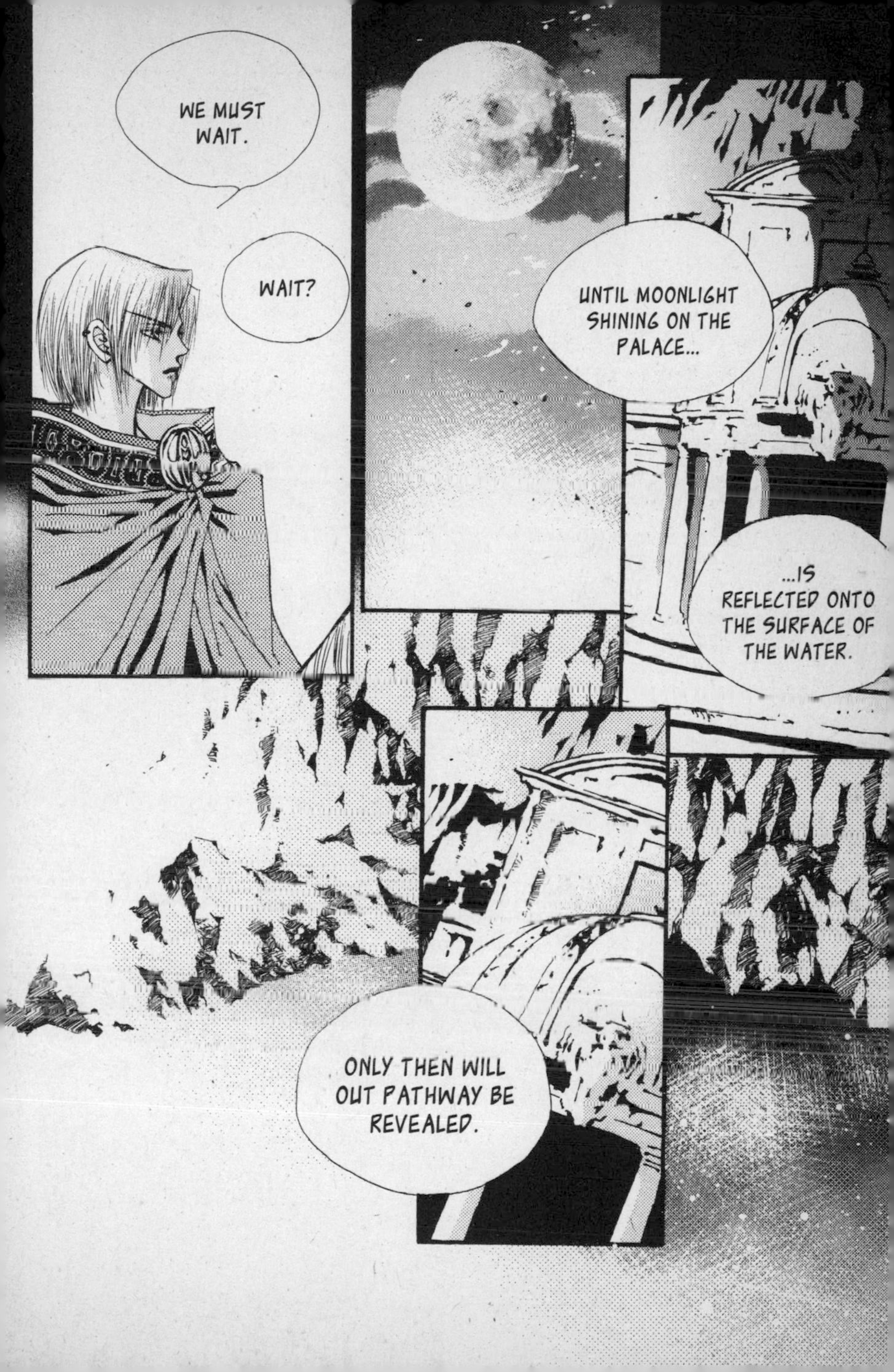
WE MUST WAIT.
WAIT?
UNTIL MOONLIGHT SHINING ON THE PALACE...
...IS REFLECTED ONTO THE SURFACE OF THE WATER.
ONLY THEN WILL OUT PATHWAY BE REVEALED.

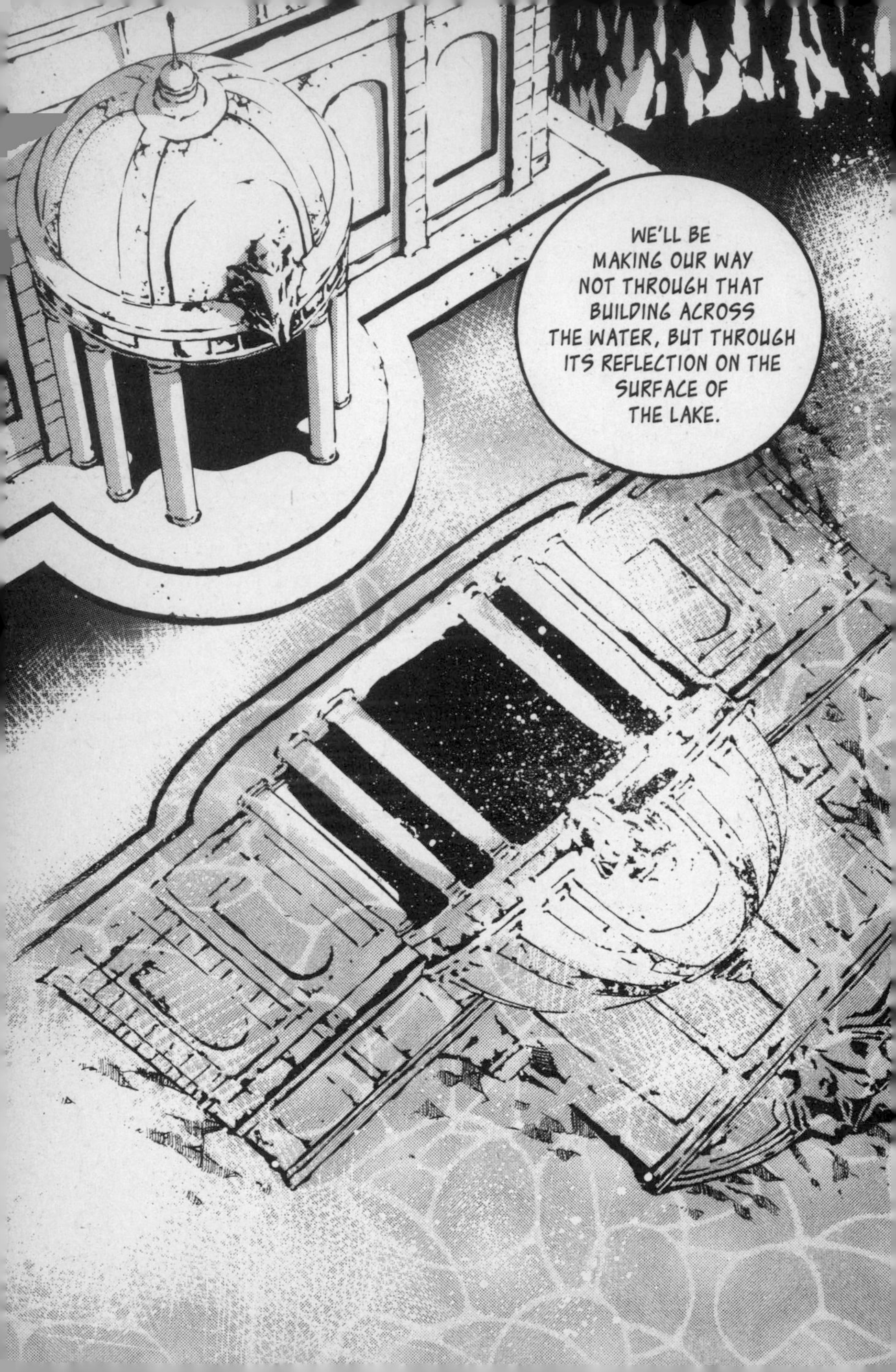
WE'LL BE MAKING OUR WAY NOT THROUGH THAT BUILDING ACROSS THE WATER, BUT THROUGH ITS REFLECTION ON THE SURFACE OF THE LAKE.

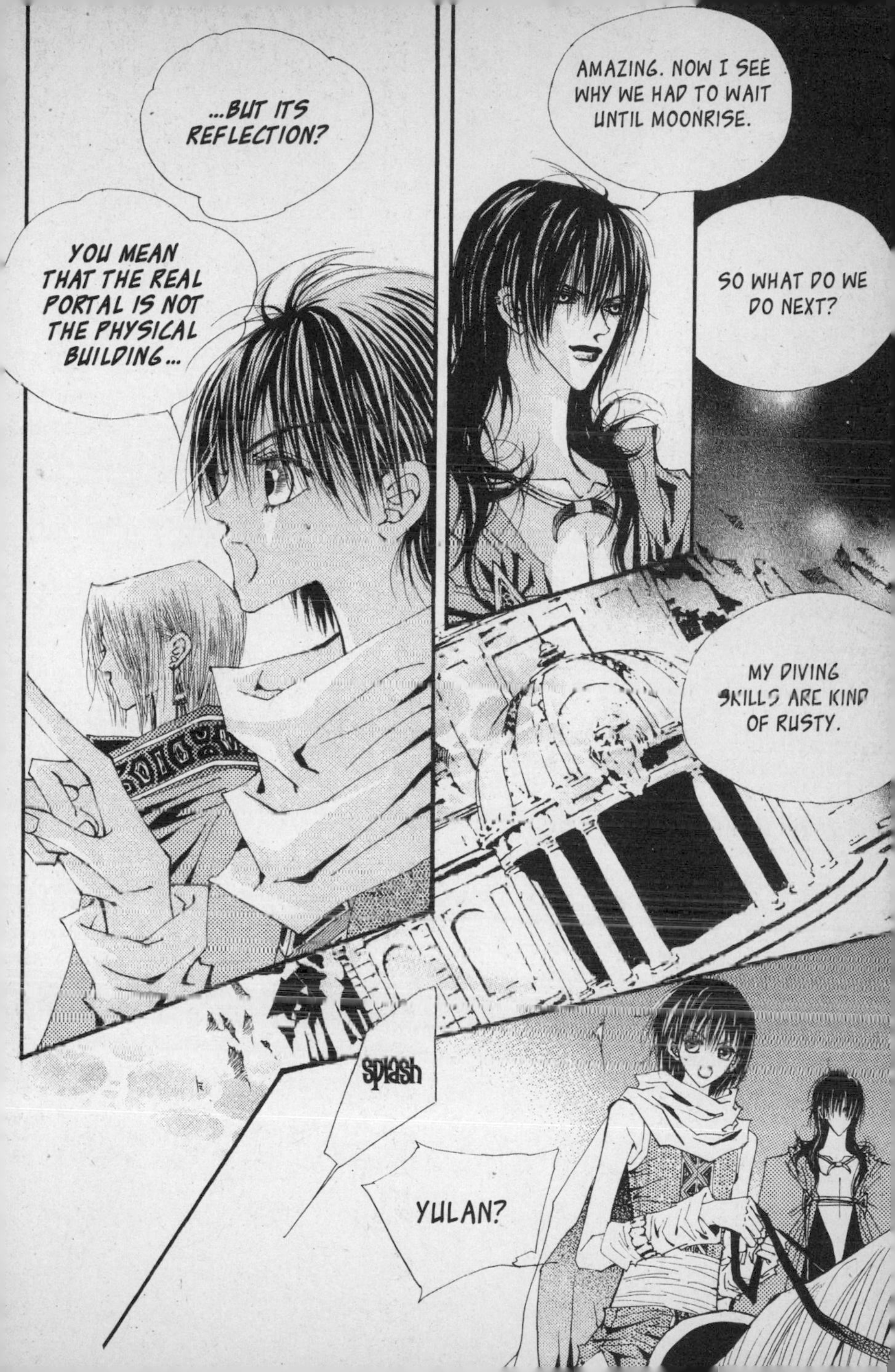
YOU MEAN THAT THE REAL PORTAL IS NOT THE PHYSICAL BUILDING...
...BUT ITS REFLECTION?
AMAZING. NOW I SEE WHY WE HAD TO WAIT UNTIL MOONRISE.
SO WHAT DO WE DO NEXT?
MY DIVING SKILLS ARE KIND OF RUSTY.
SPLASH
YULAN?

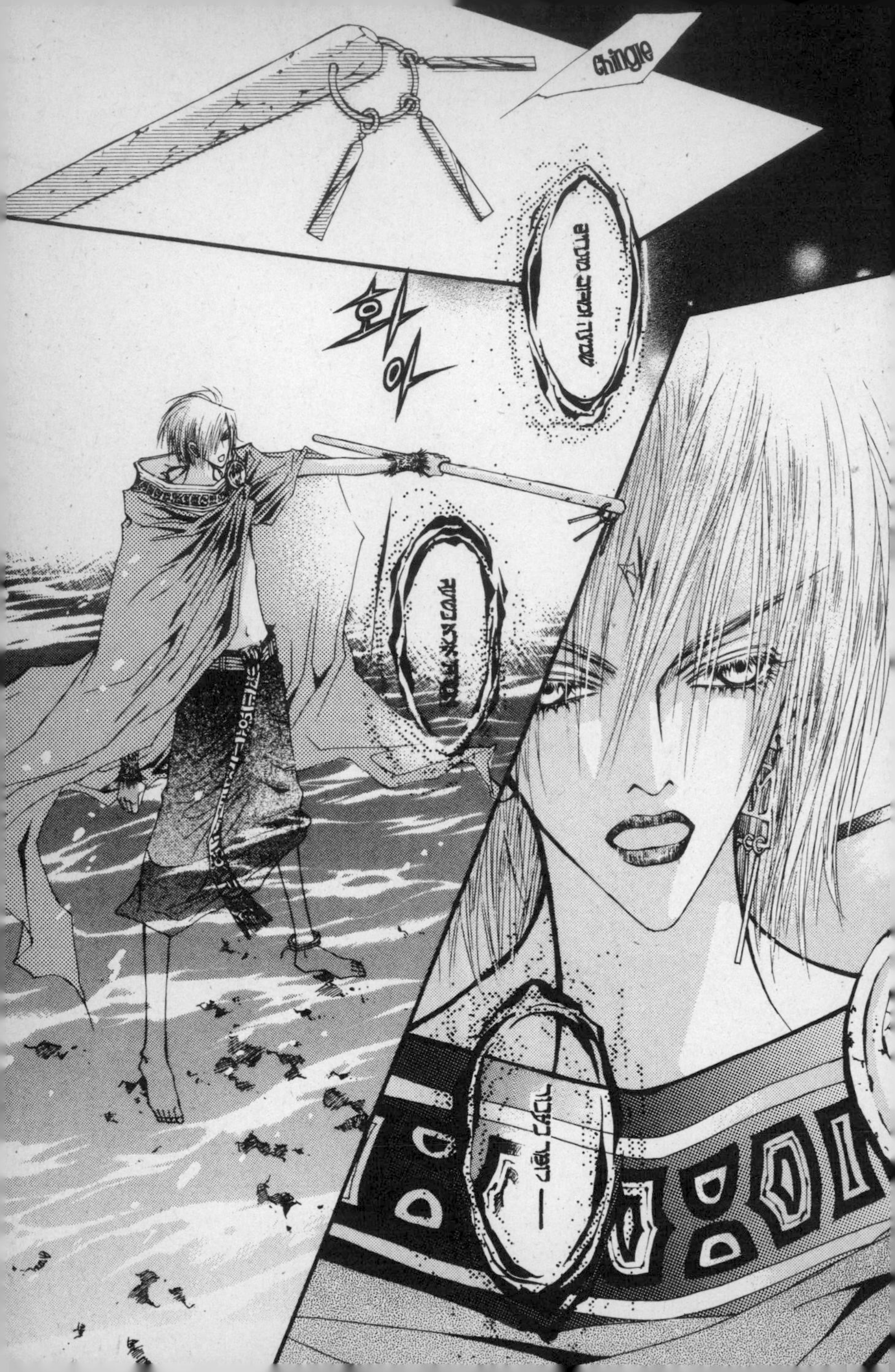
Chingle

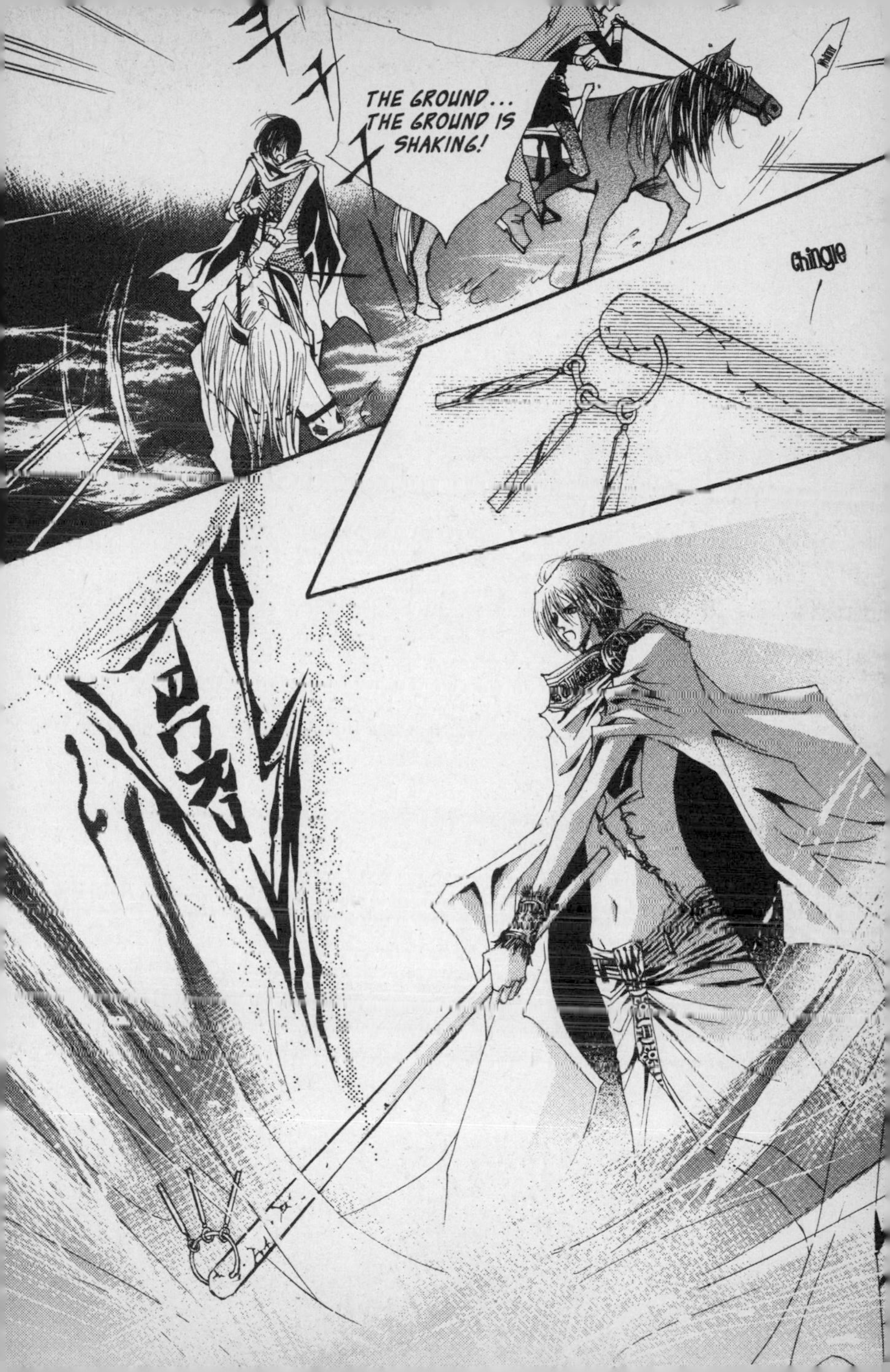
THE GROUND... THE GROUND IS SHAKING!
Chingle

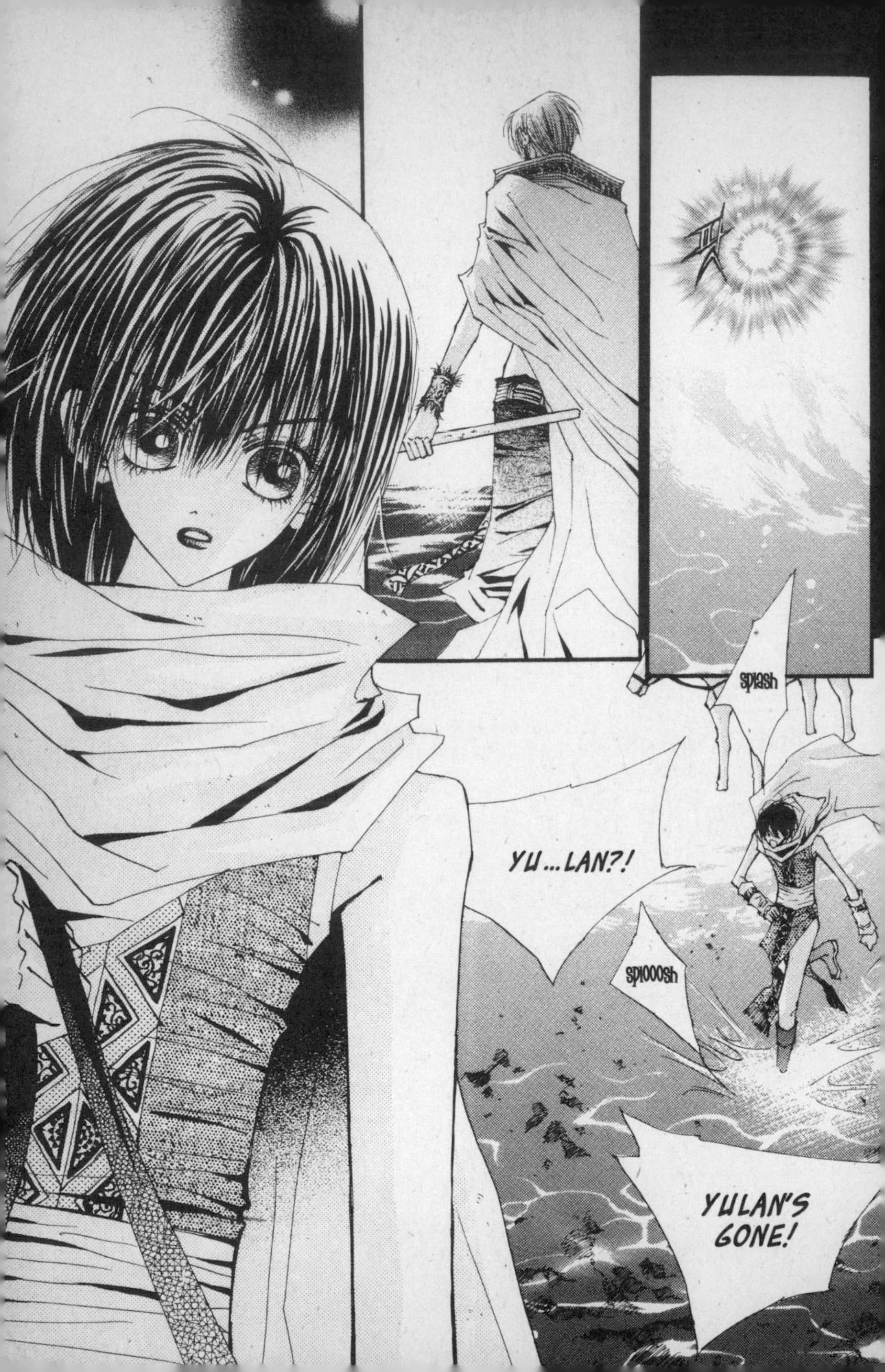
splash
YU...LAN?!
splooosh
YULAN'S GONE!

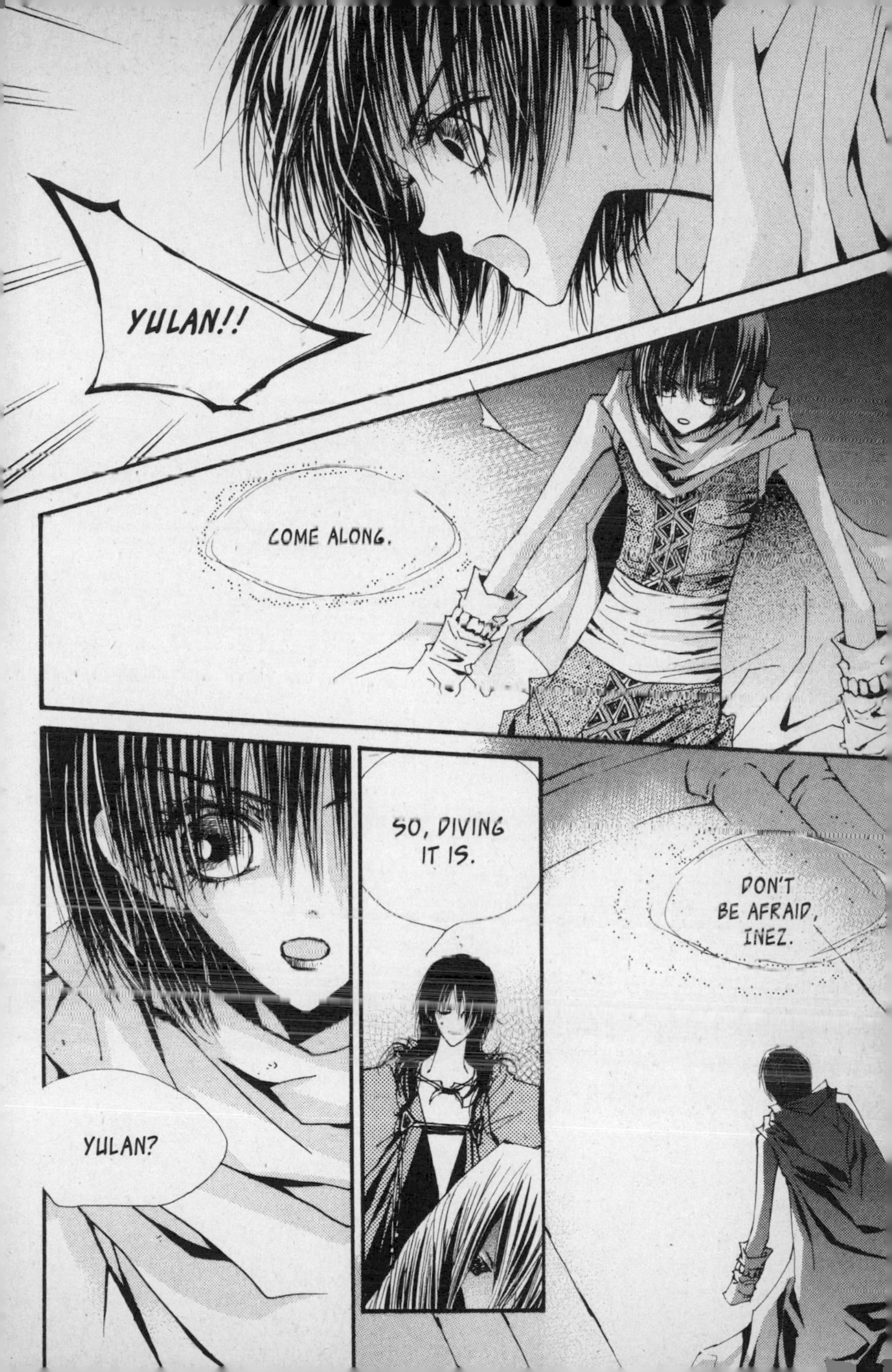
YULAN!!
COME ALONG.
DON'T BE AFRAID, INEZ.
SO, DIVING IT IS.
YULAN?

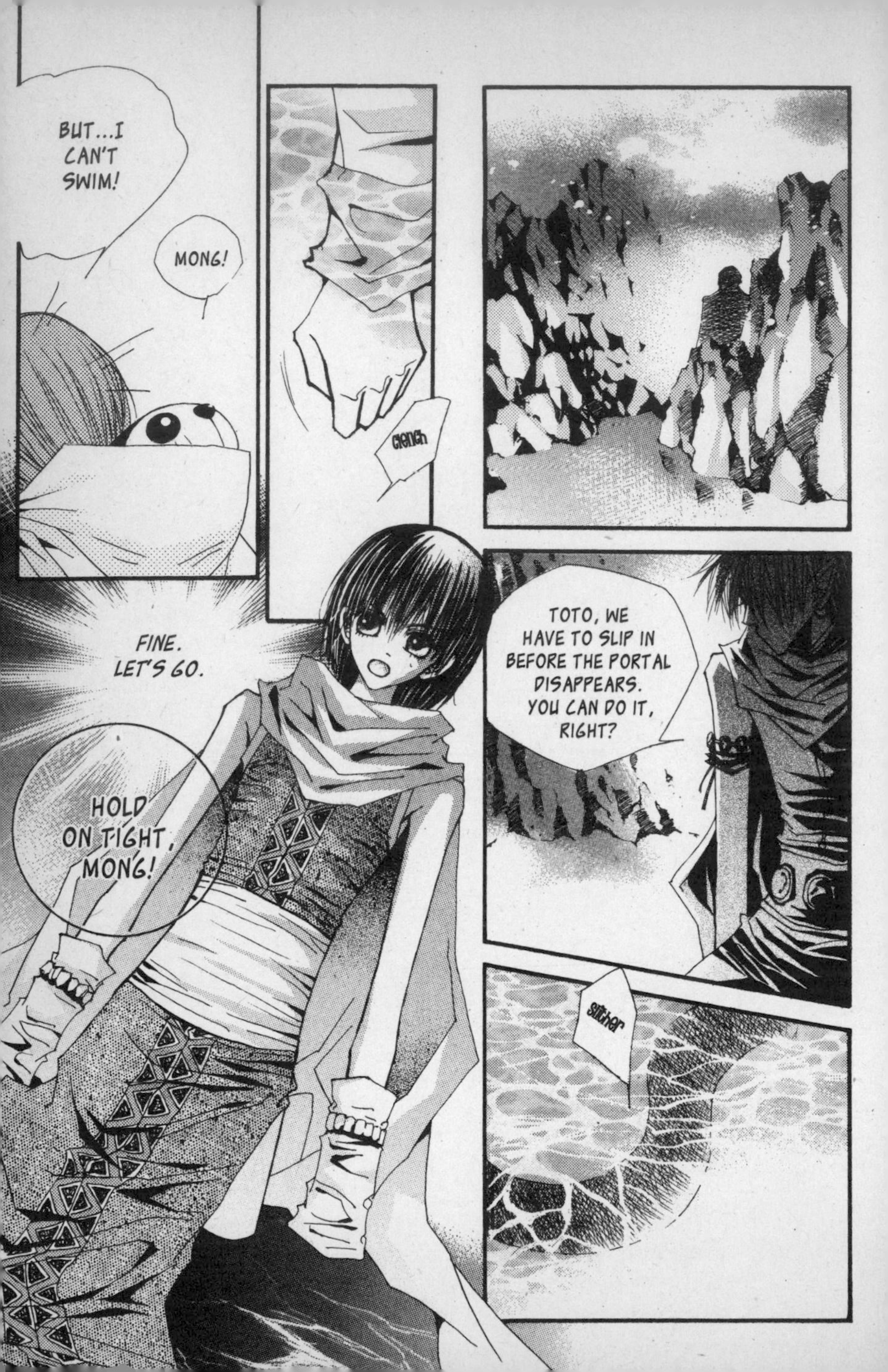
clench
BUT...I CAN'T SWIM!
MONG!
TOTO, WE HAVE TO SLIP IN BEFORE THE PORTAL DISAPPEARS. YOU CAN DO IT, RIGHT?
slither
FINE. LET'S GO.
HOLD ON TIGHT, MONG!

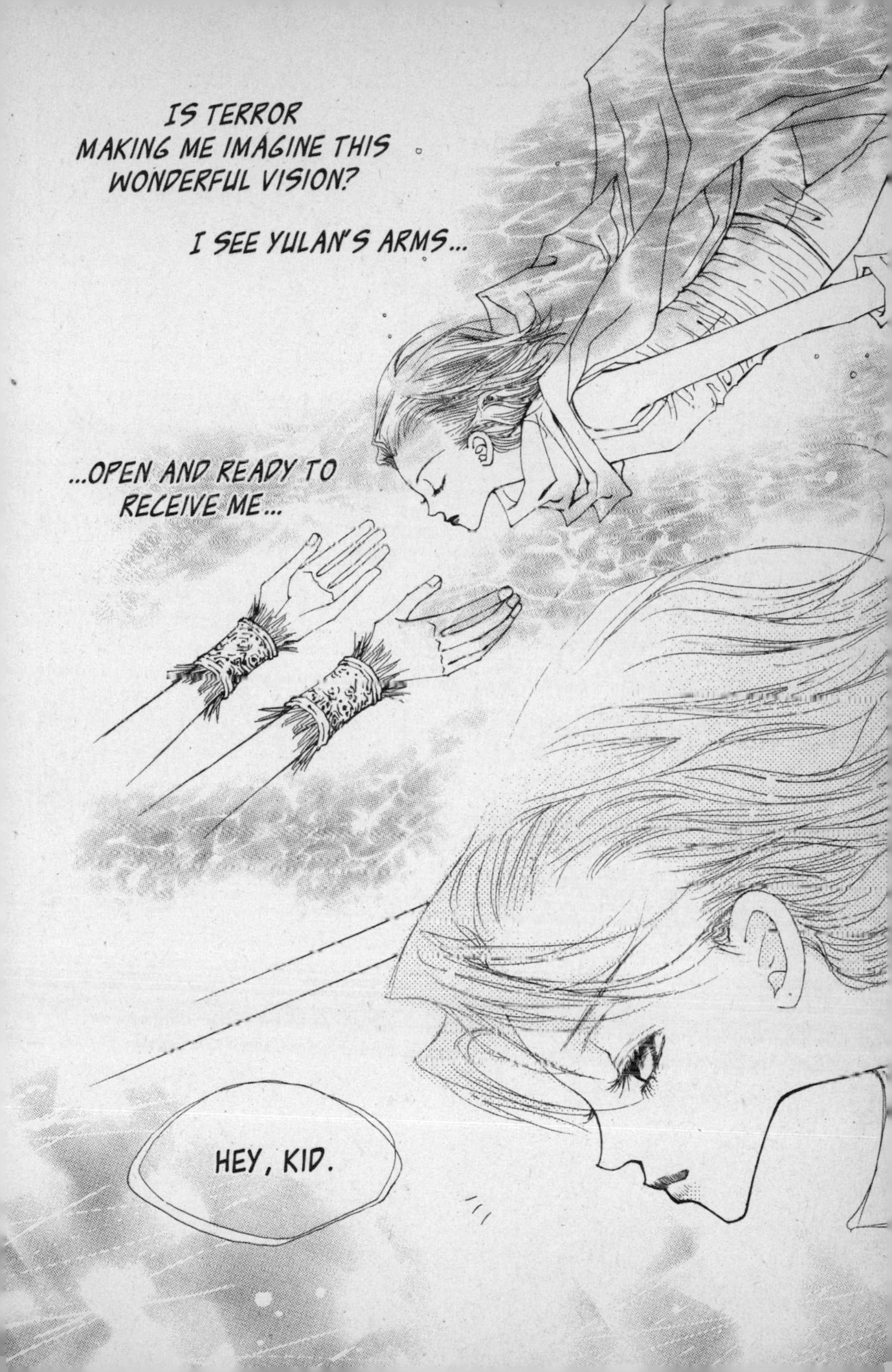
IS TERROR MAKING ME IMAGINE THIS WONDERFUL VISION?
I SEE YULAN'S ARMS...
...OPEN AND READY TO RECEIVE ME...
HEY, KID.

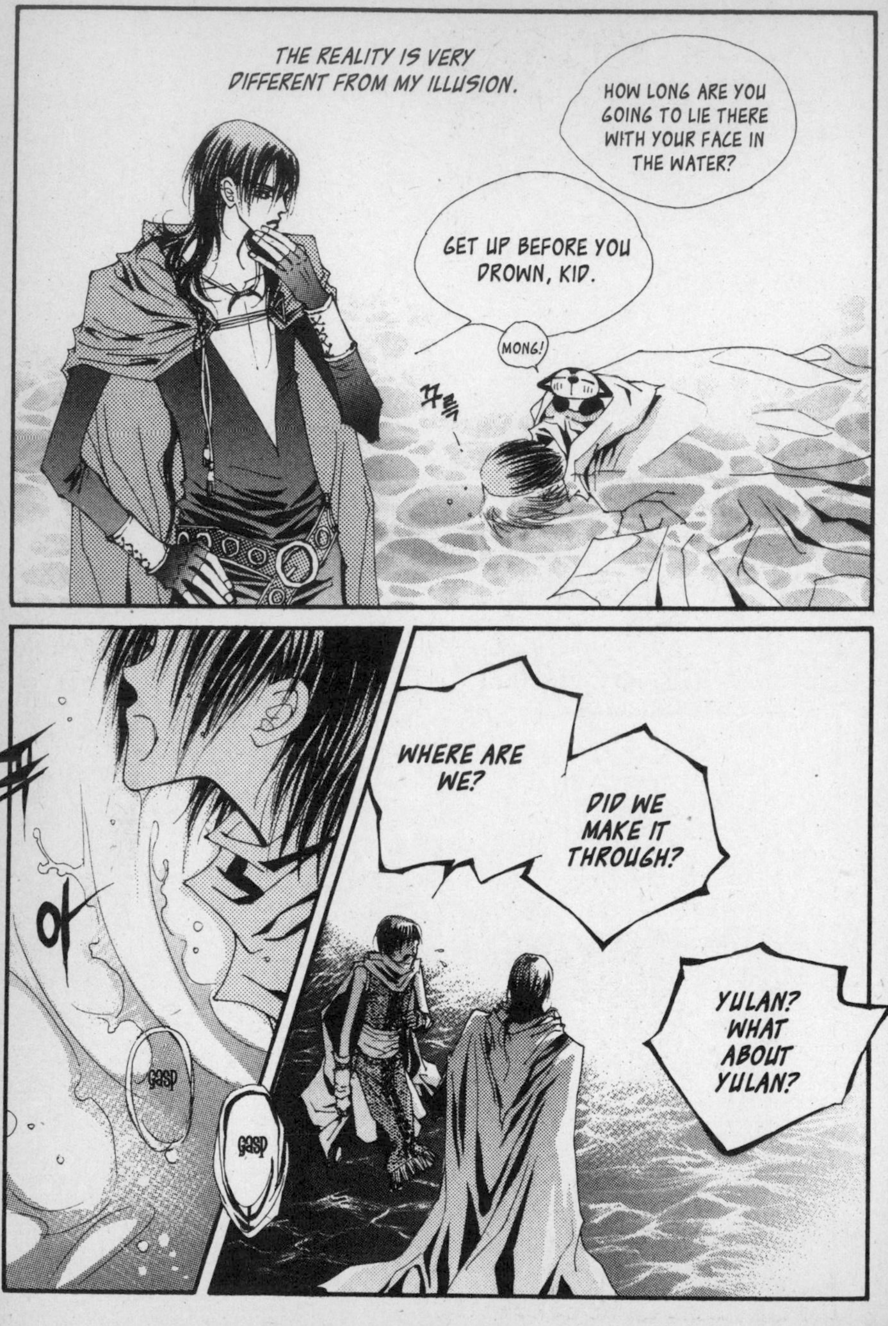
THE REALITY IS VERY DIFFERENT FROM MY ILLUSION.
HOW LONG ARE YOU GOING TO LIE THERE WITH YOUR FACE IN THE WATER?
GET UP BEFORE YOU DROWN, KID.
MONG!
GASP
GASP
WHERE ARE WE?
DID WE MAKE IT THROUGH?
YULAN? WHAT ABOUT YULAN?

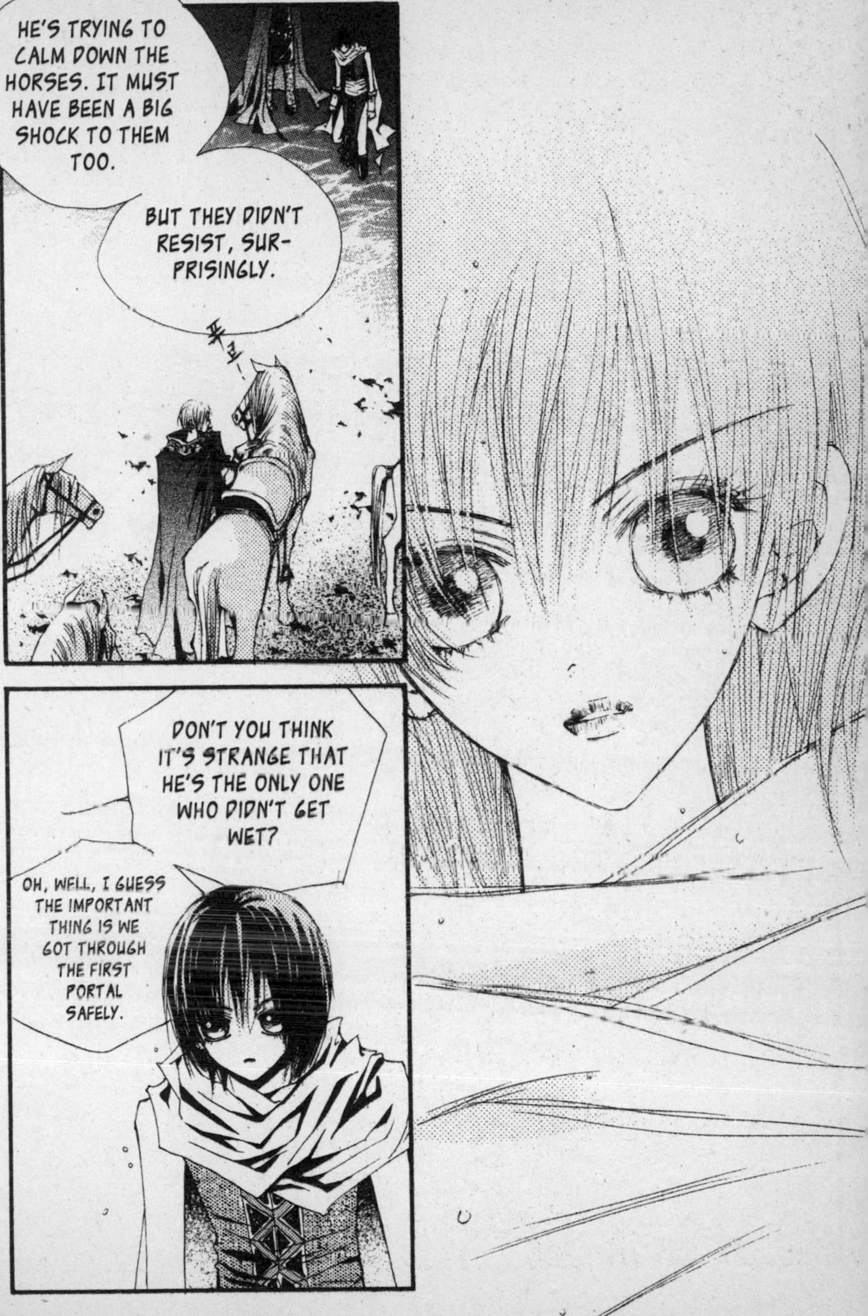
HE'S TRYING TO CALM DOWN THE HORSES. IT MUST HAVE BEEN A BIG SHOCK TO THEM TOO.
BUT THEY DIDN'T RESIST, SUR-PRISINGLY.
DON'T YOU THINK IT'S STRANGE THAT HE'S THE ONLY ONE WHO DIDN'T GET WET?
OH, WELL, I GUESS THE IMPORTANT THING IS WE GOT THROUGH THE FIRST PORTAL SAFELY.

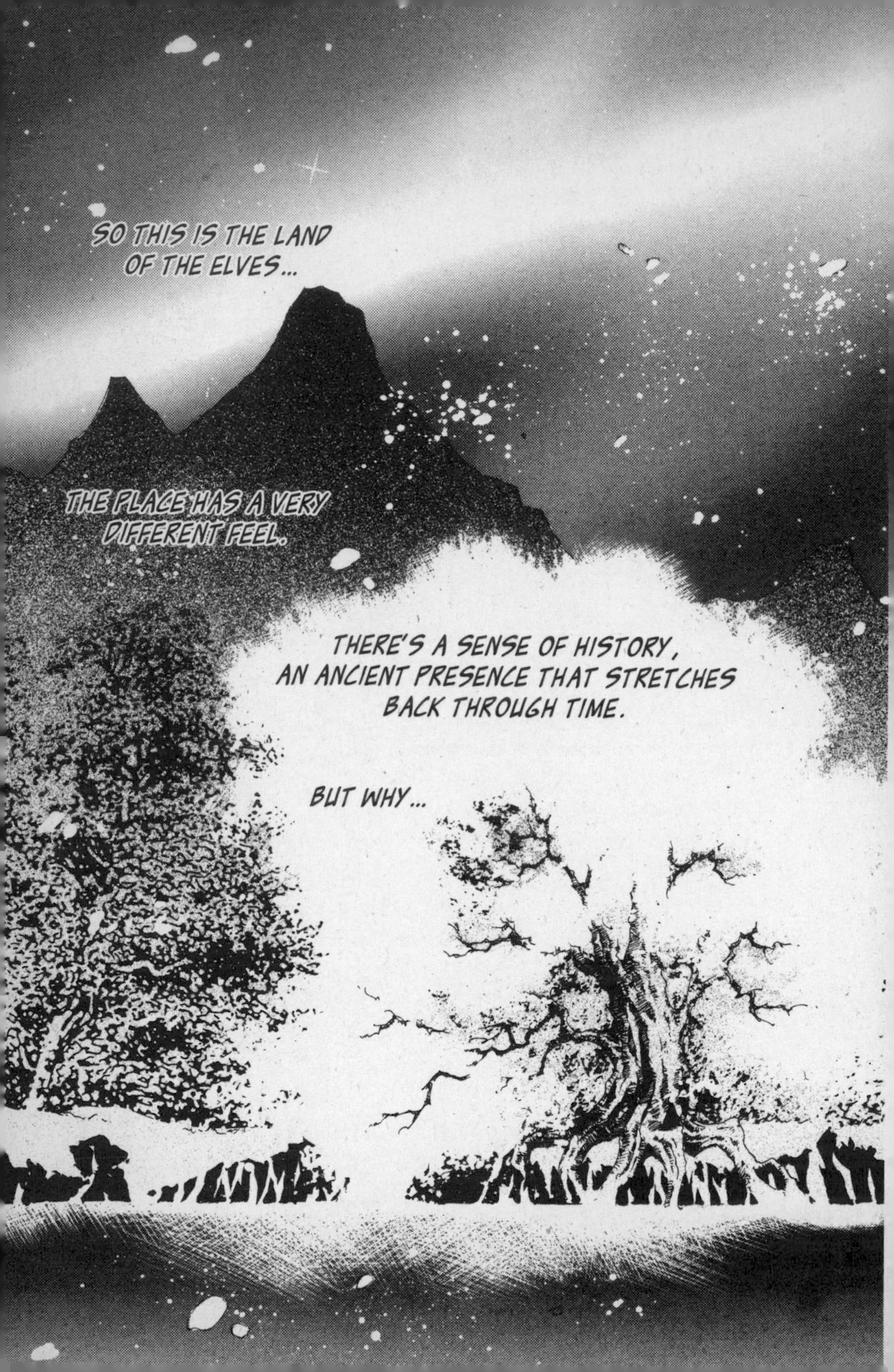
SO THIS IS THE LAND OF THE ELVES...
THE PLACE HAS A VERY DIFFERENT FEEL.
THERE'S A SENSE OF HISTORY, AN ANCIENT PRESENCE THAT STRETCHES BACK THROUGH TIME.
BUT WHY...

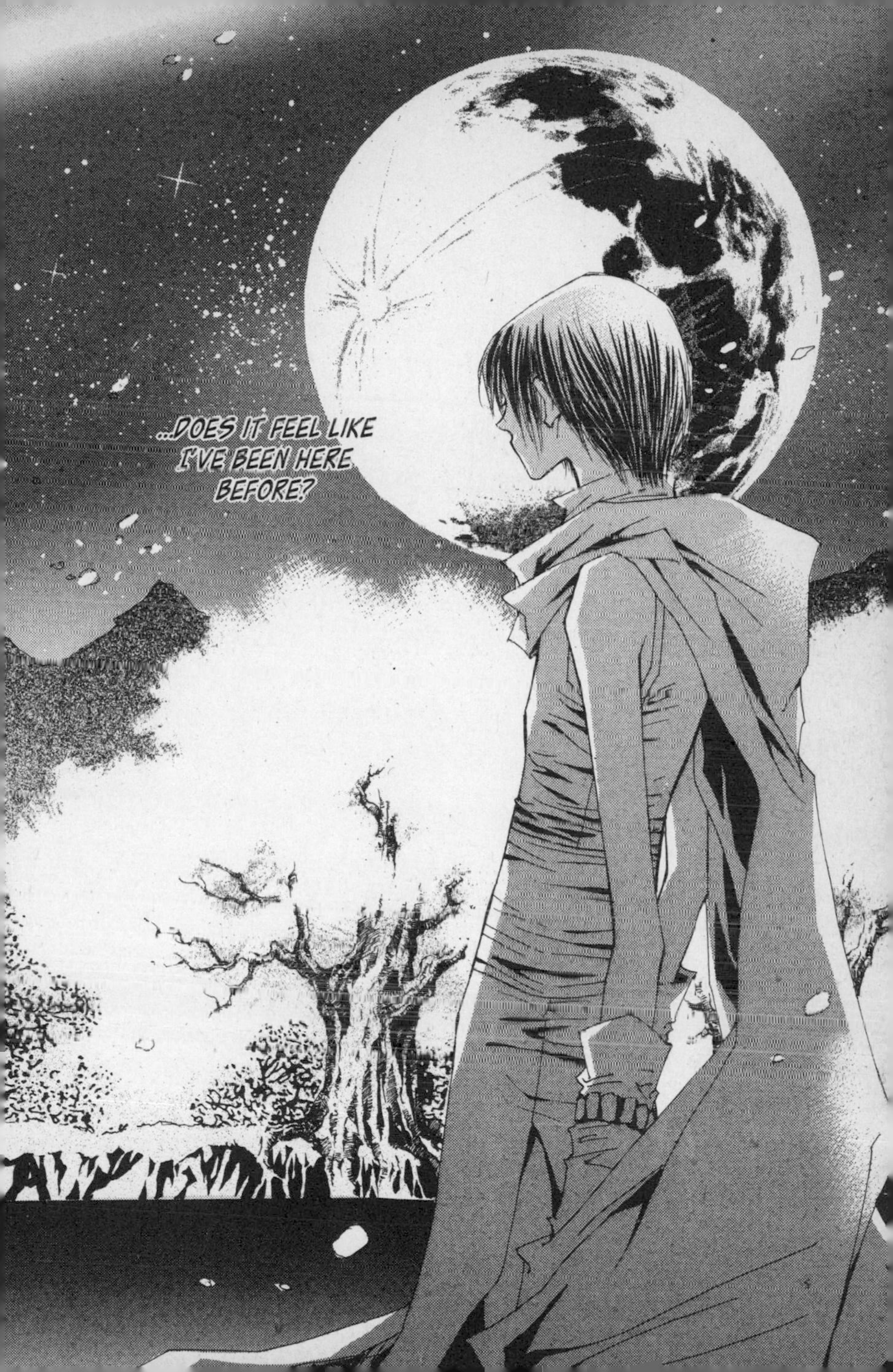
...DOES IT FEEL LIKE I'VE BEEN HERE BEFORE?

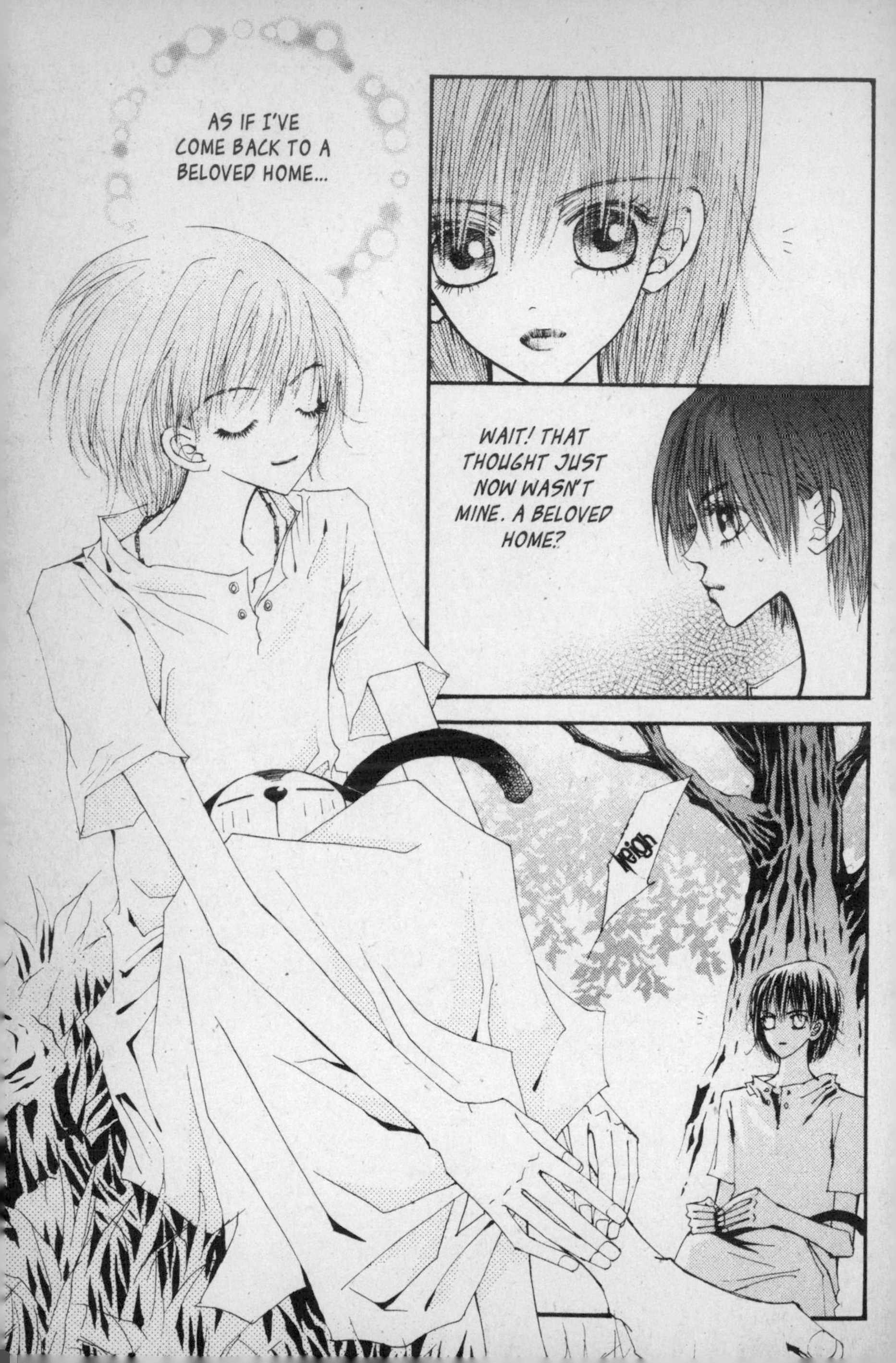

AS IF I'VE COME BACK TO A BELOVED HOME...
WAIT! THAT THOUGHT JUST NOW WASN'T MINE. A BELOVED HOME?
leigh

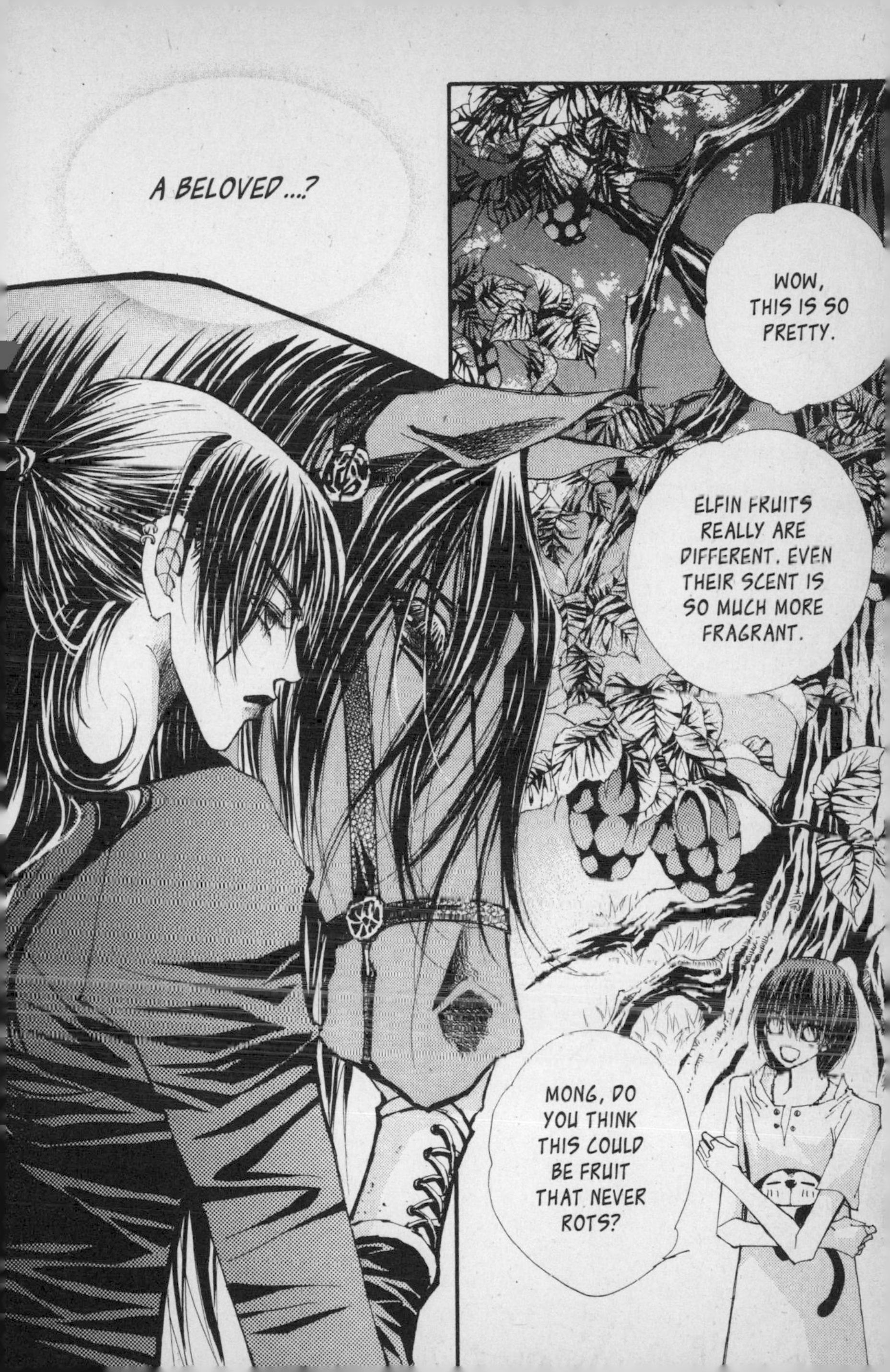
WOW, THIS IS SO PRETTY.
ELFIN FRUITS REALLY ARE DIFFERENT. EVEN THEIR SCENT IS SO MUCH MORE FRAGRANT.
A BELOVED...?
MONG, DO YOU THINK THIS COULD BE FRUIT THAT NEVER ROTS?

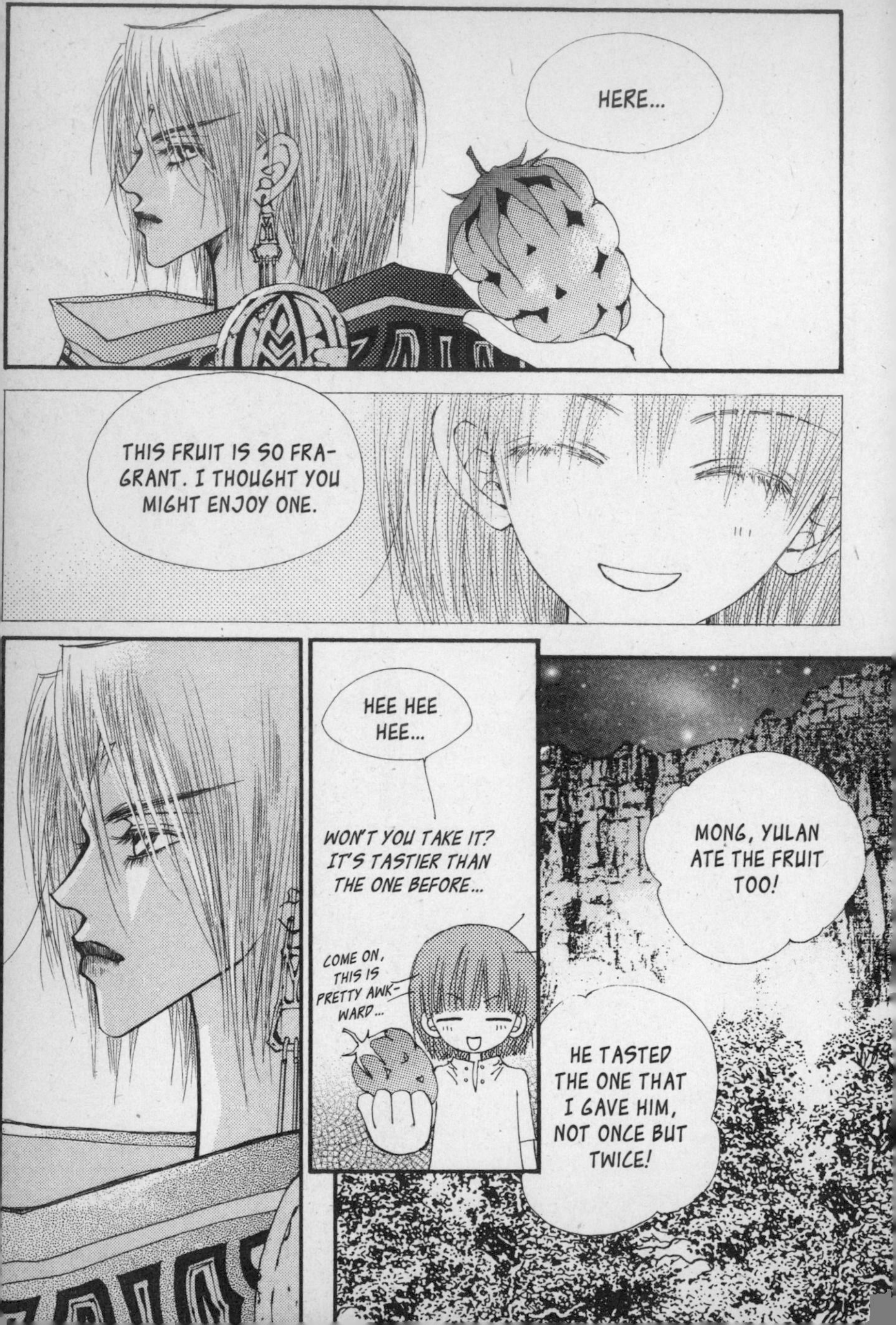
HERE...
THIS FRUIT IS SO FRA-GRANT. I THOUGHT YOU MIGHT ENJOY ONE.
MONG, YULAN ATE THE FRUIT TOO!
HE TASTED THE ONE THAT I GAVE HIM, NOT ONCE BUT TWICE!
HEE HEE HEE...
WON'T YOU TAKE IT? IT'S TASTIER THAN THE ONE BEFORE...
COME ON, THIS IS PRETTY AWK-WARD...

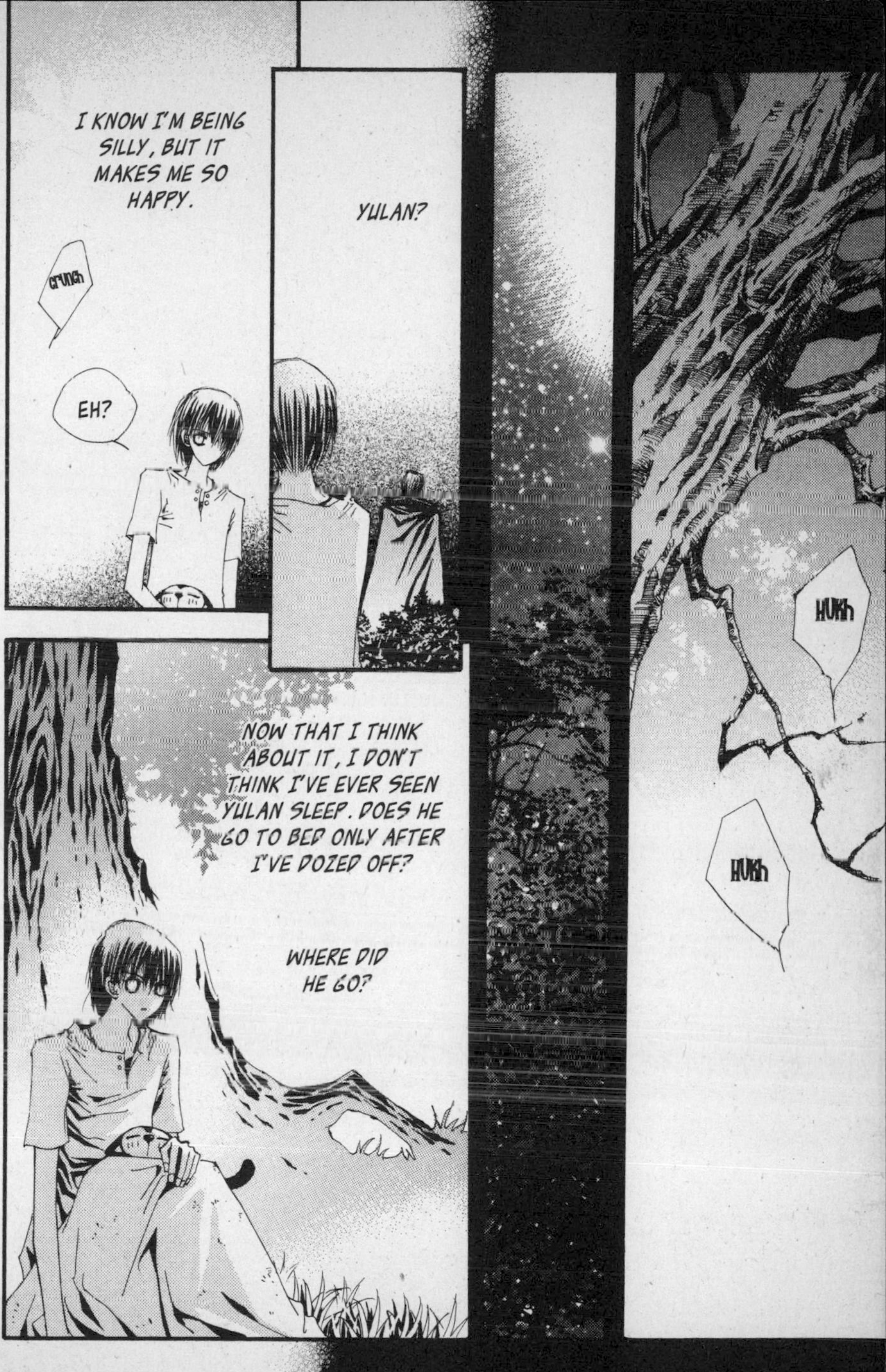

I KNOW I'M BEING SILLY, BUT IT MAKES ME SO HAPPY.
crunch
EH?
YULAN?
NOW THAT I THINK ABOUT IT, I DON'T THINK I'VE EVER SEEN YULAN SLEEP. DOES HE GO TO BED ONLY AFTER I'VE DOZED OFF?
WHERE DID HE GO?
HUKh
HUKh

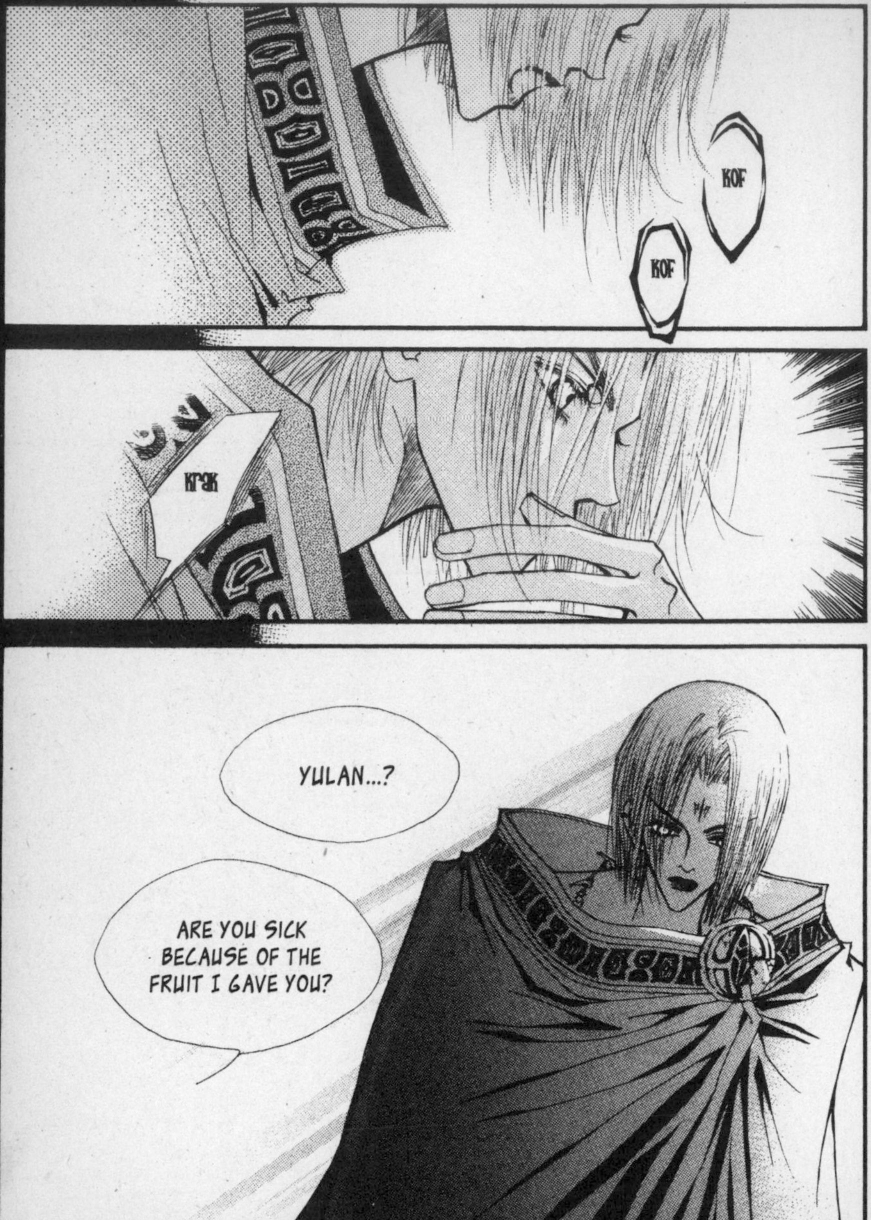
KOF
KOF
KRAK
YULAN...?
ARE YOU SICK BECAUSE OF THE FRUIT I GAVE YOU?

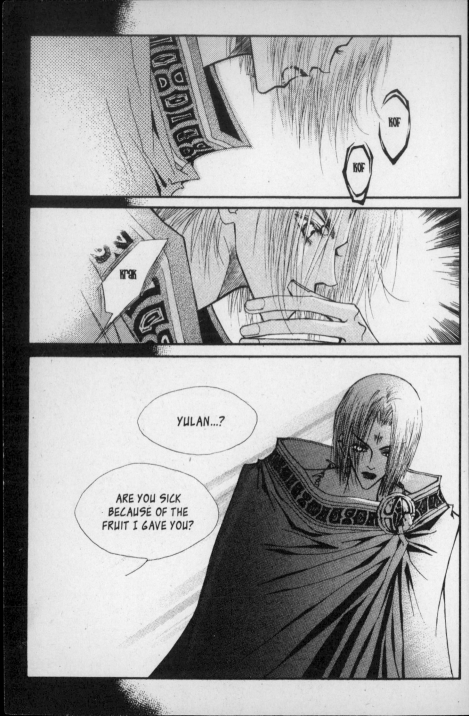

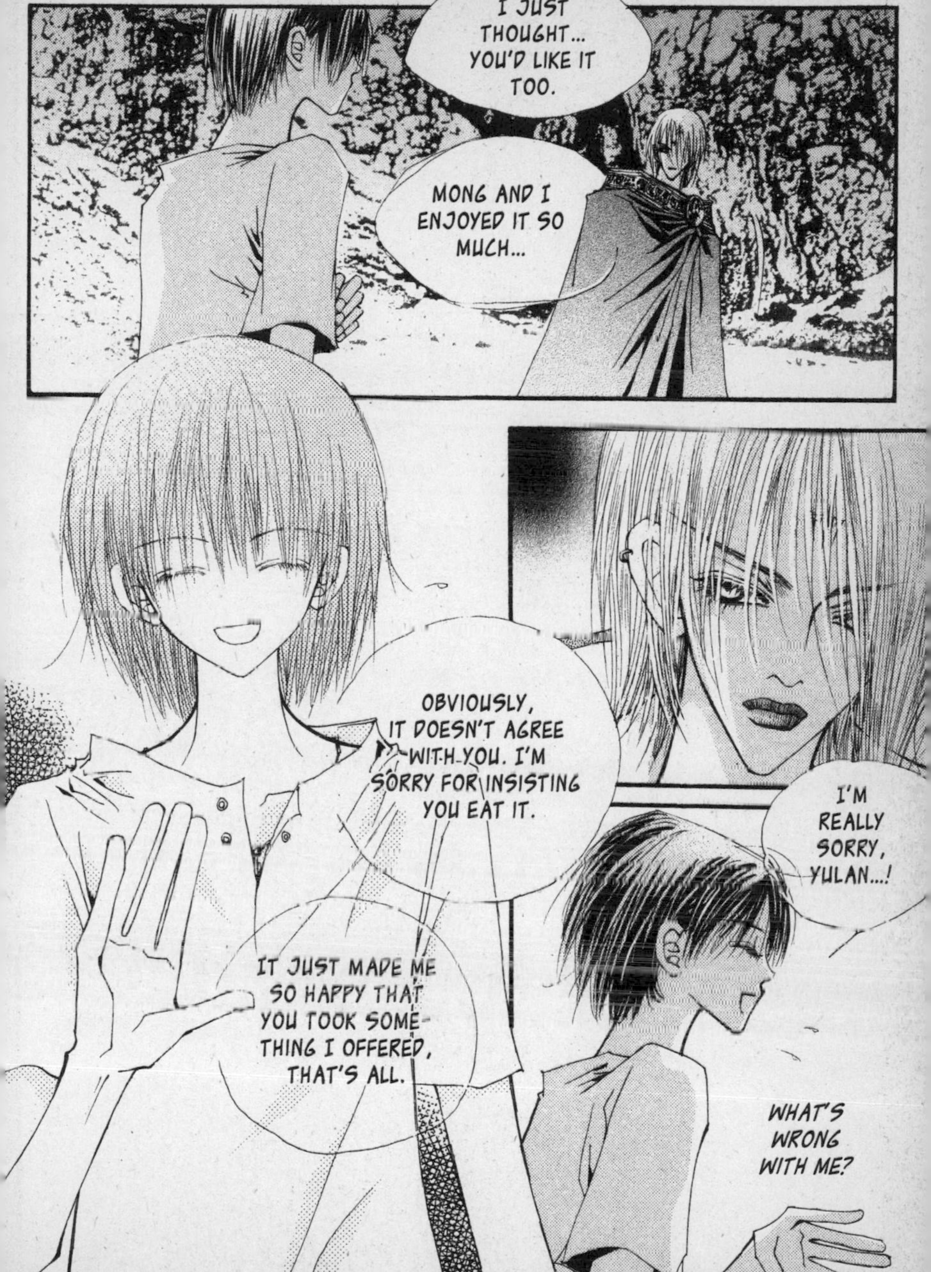
I JUST THOUGHT... YOU'D LIKE IT TOO.
MONG AND I ENJOYED IT SO MUCH...
OBVIOUSLY, IT DOESN'T AGREE WITH YOU. I'M SORRY FOR INSISTING YOU EAT IT.
IT JUST MADE ME SO HAPPY THAT YOU TOOK SOME-THING I OFFERED, THAT'S ALL.
I'M REALLY SORRY, YULAN...!
WHAT'S WRONG WITH ME?

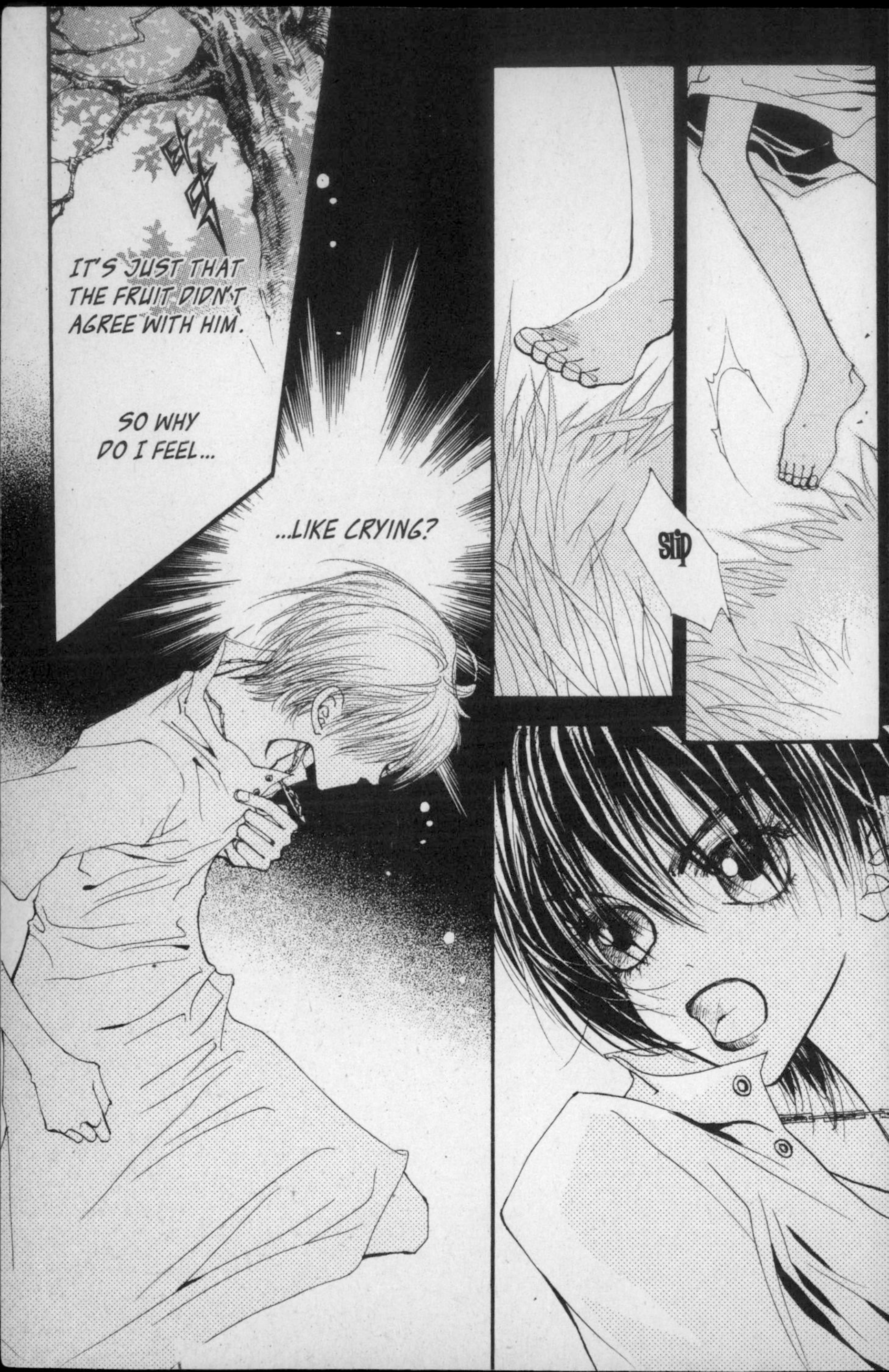
SLIP
IT'S JUST THAT THE FRUIT DIDN'T AGREE WITH HIM.
SO WHY DO I FEEL...
...LIKE CRYING?

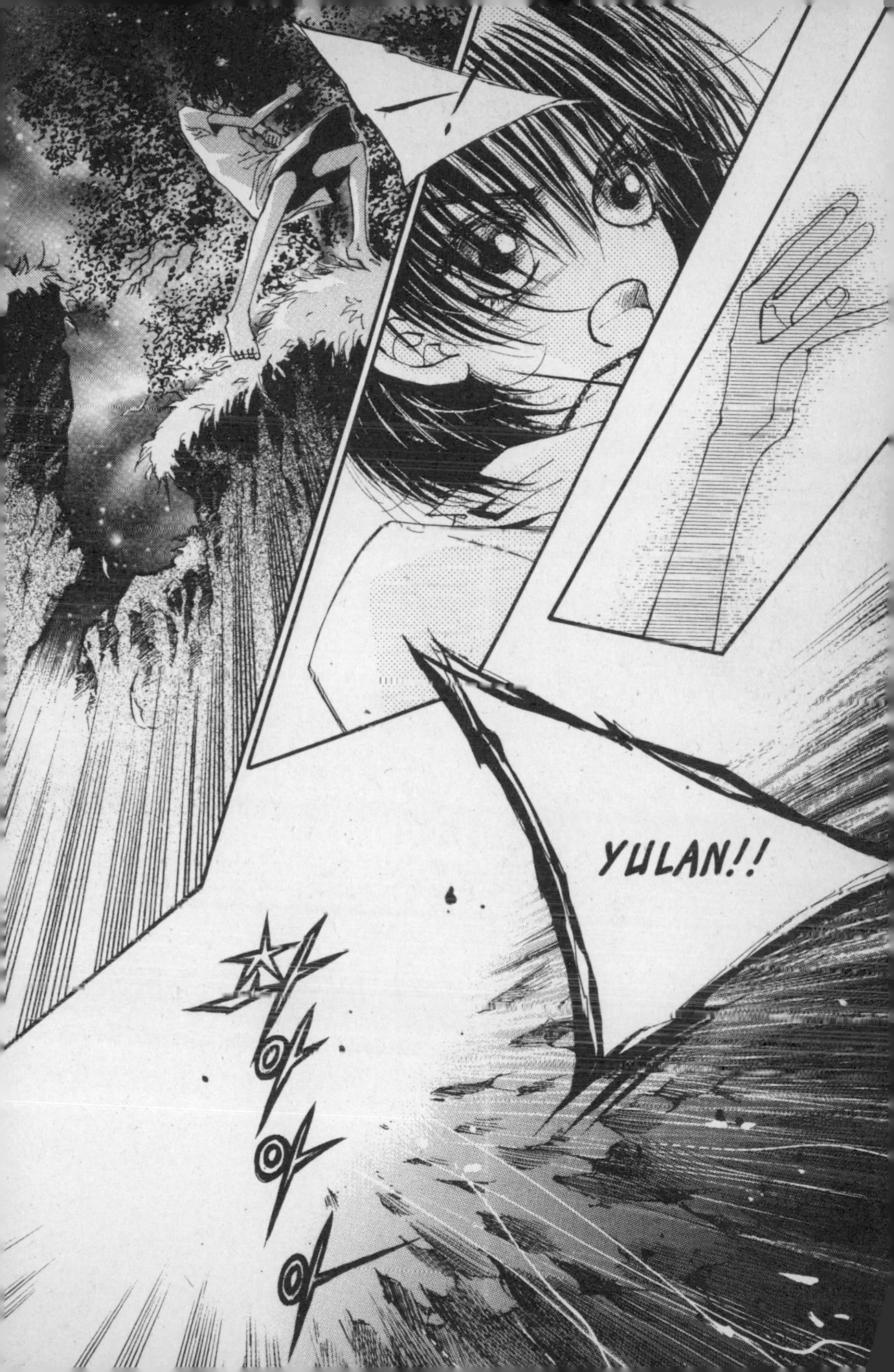
YULAN!!

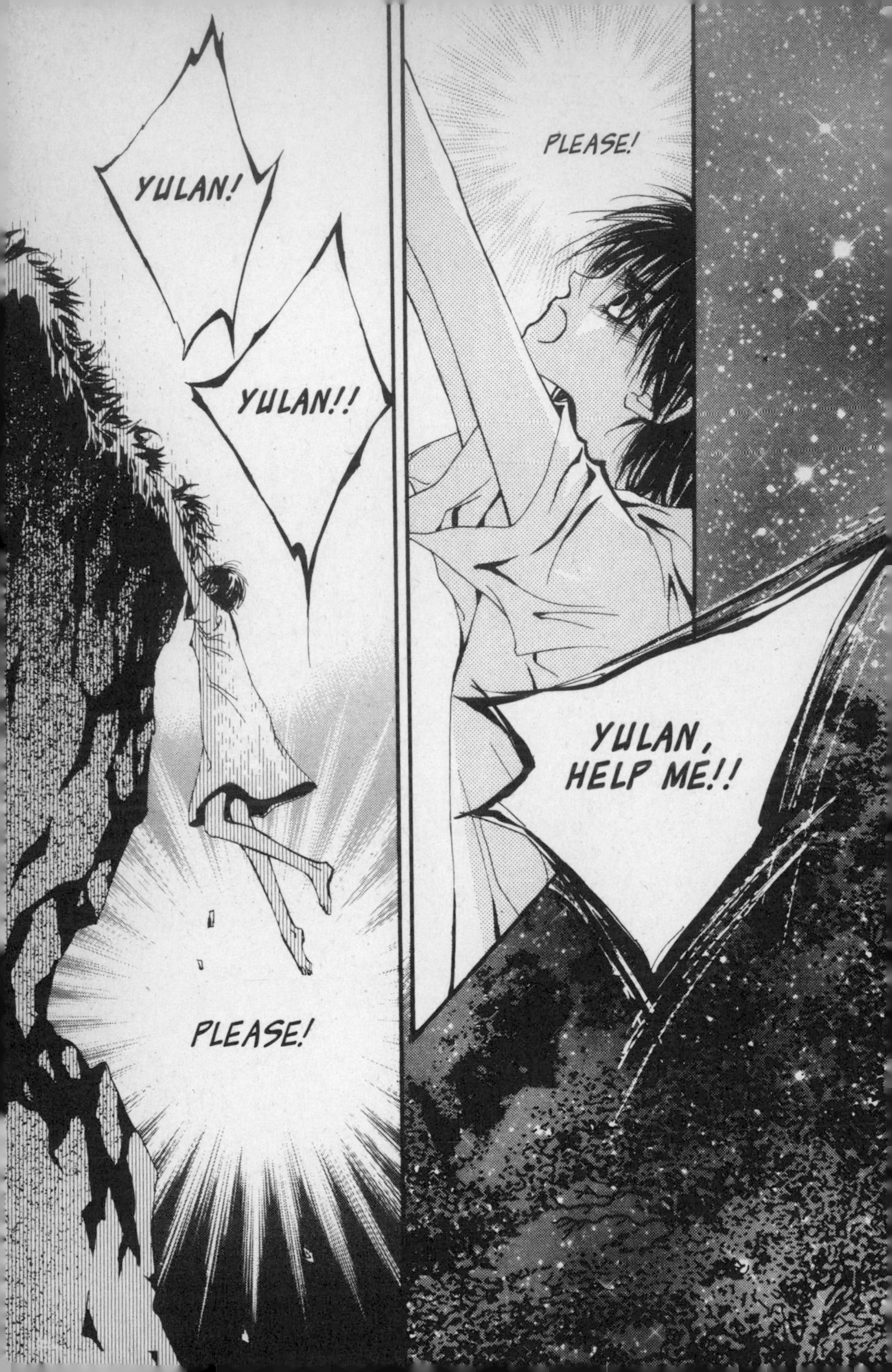
PLEASE!
YULAN, HELP ME!!
YULAN!
YULAN!!
PLEASE!

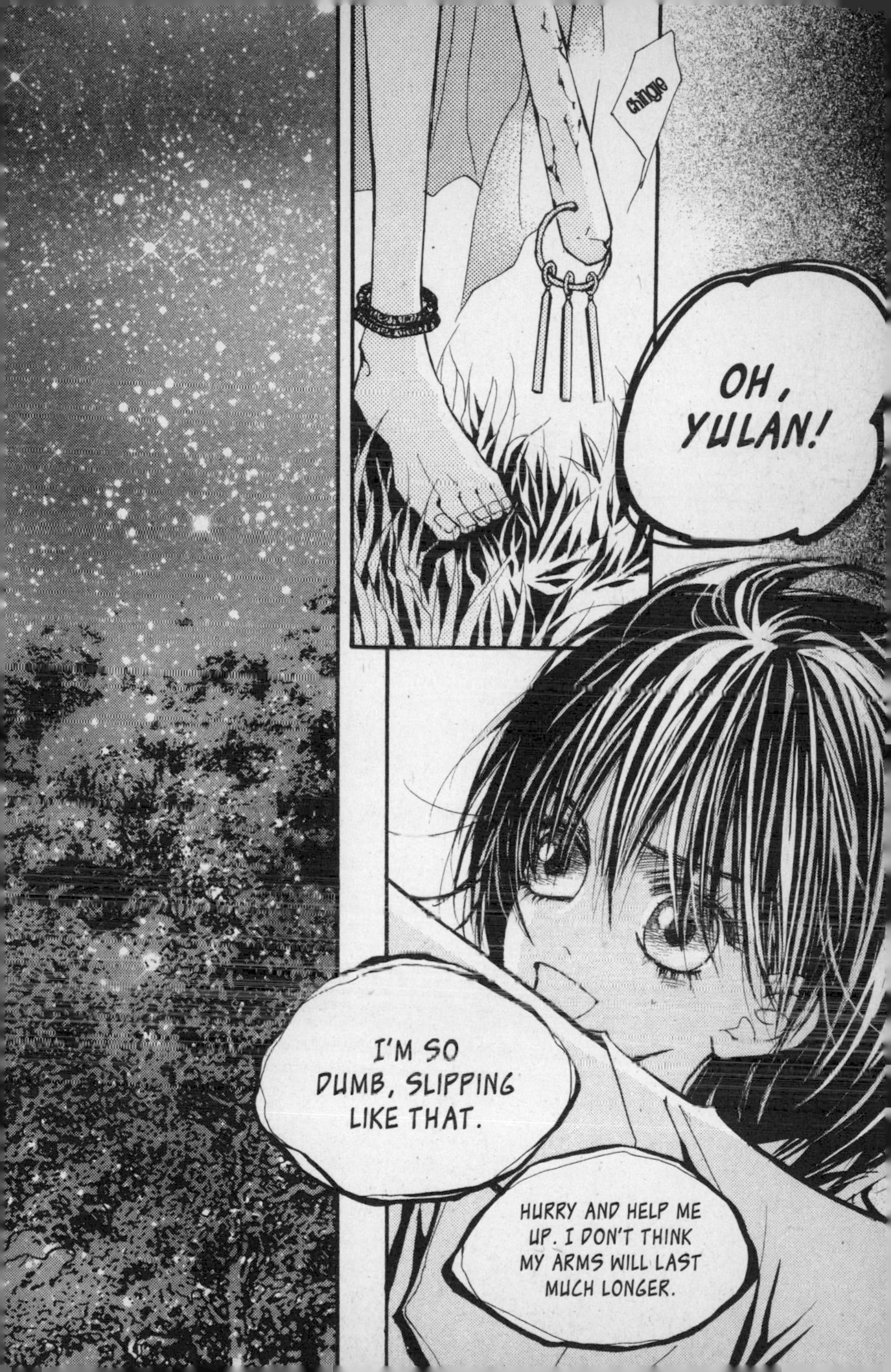
chingle
OH, YULAN!
I'M SO DUMB, SLIPPING LIKE THAT.
HURRY AND HELP ME UP. I DON'T THINK MY ARMS WILL LAST MUCH LONGER.

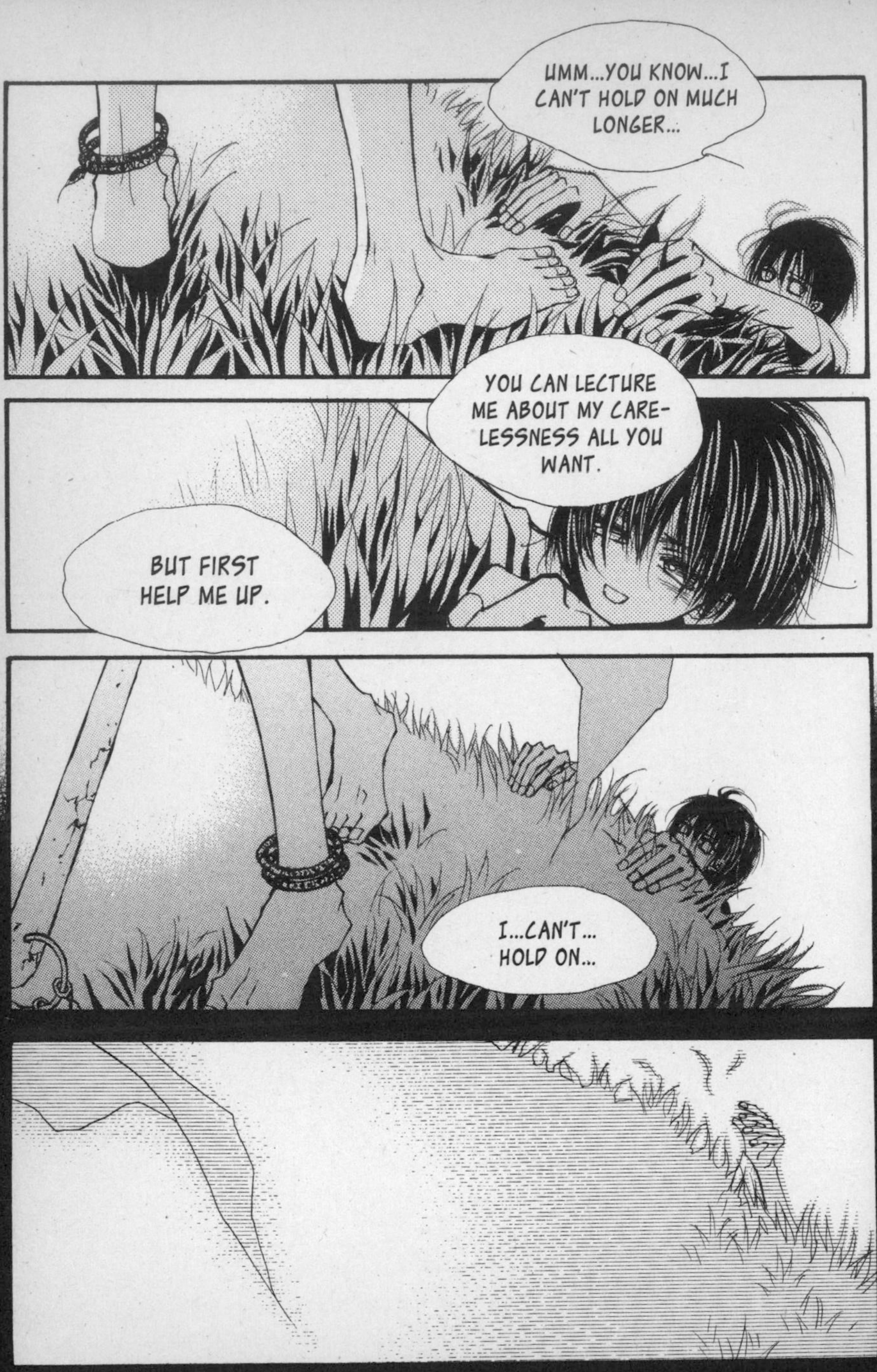
UMM...YOU KNOW...I CAN'T HOLD ON MUCH LONGER...
YOU CAN LECTURE ME ABOUT MY CARE-LESSNESS ALL YOU WANT.
BUT FIRST HELP ME UP.
I...CAN'T... HOLD ON...

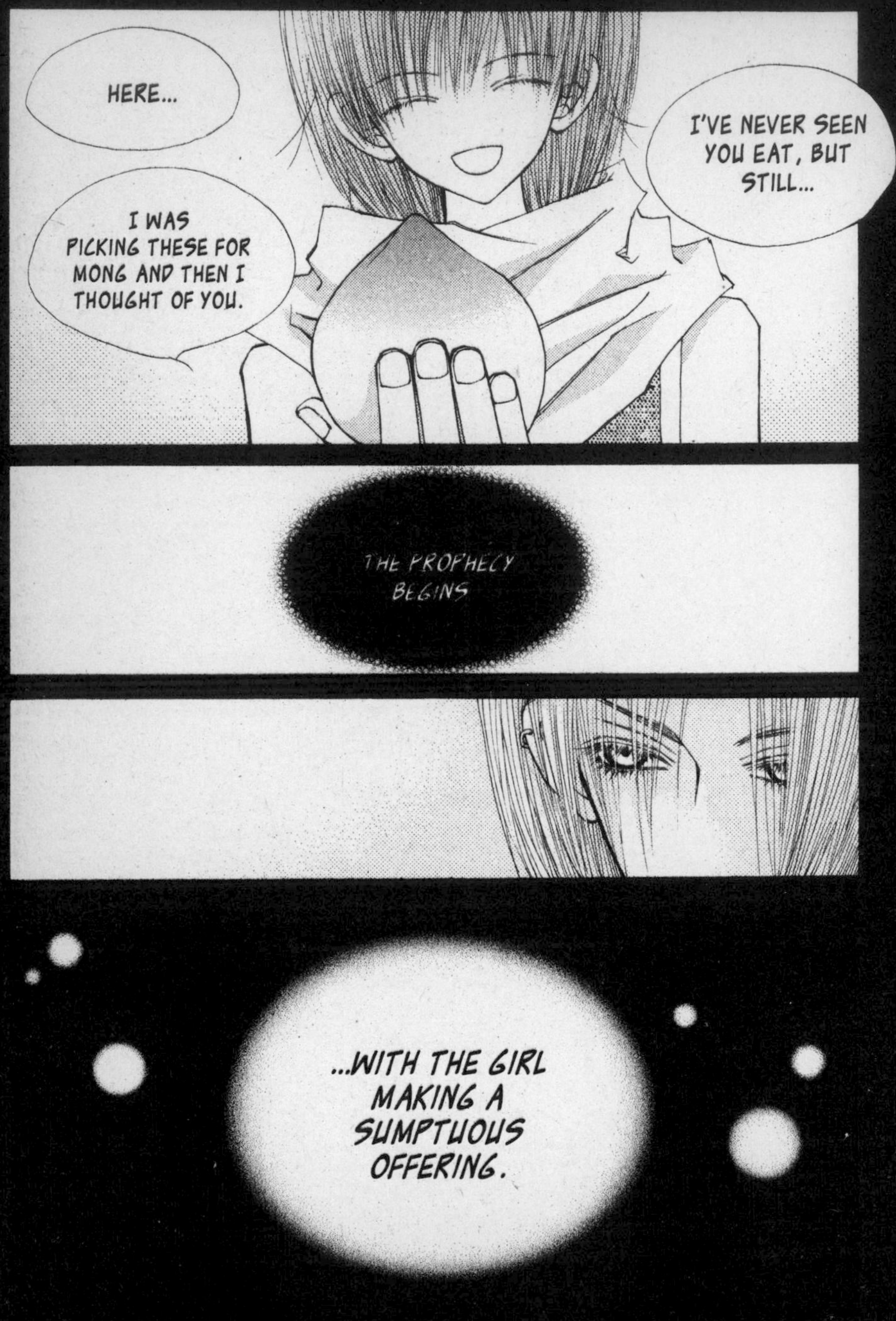
I'VE NEVER SEEN YOU EAT, BUT STILL...
HERE...
I WAS PICKING THESE FOR MONG AND THEN I THOUGHT OF YOU.
THE PROPHECY BEGINS
...WITH THE GIRL MAKING A SUMPTUOUS OFFERING.

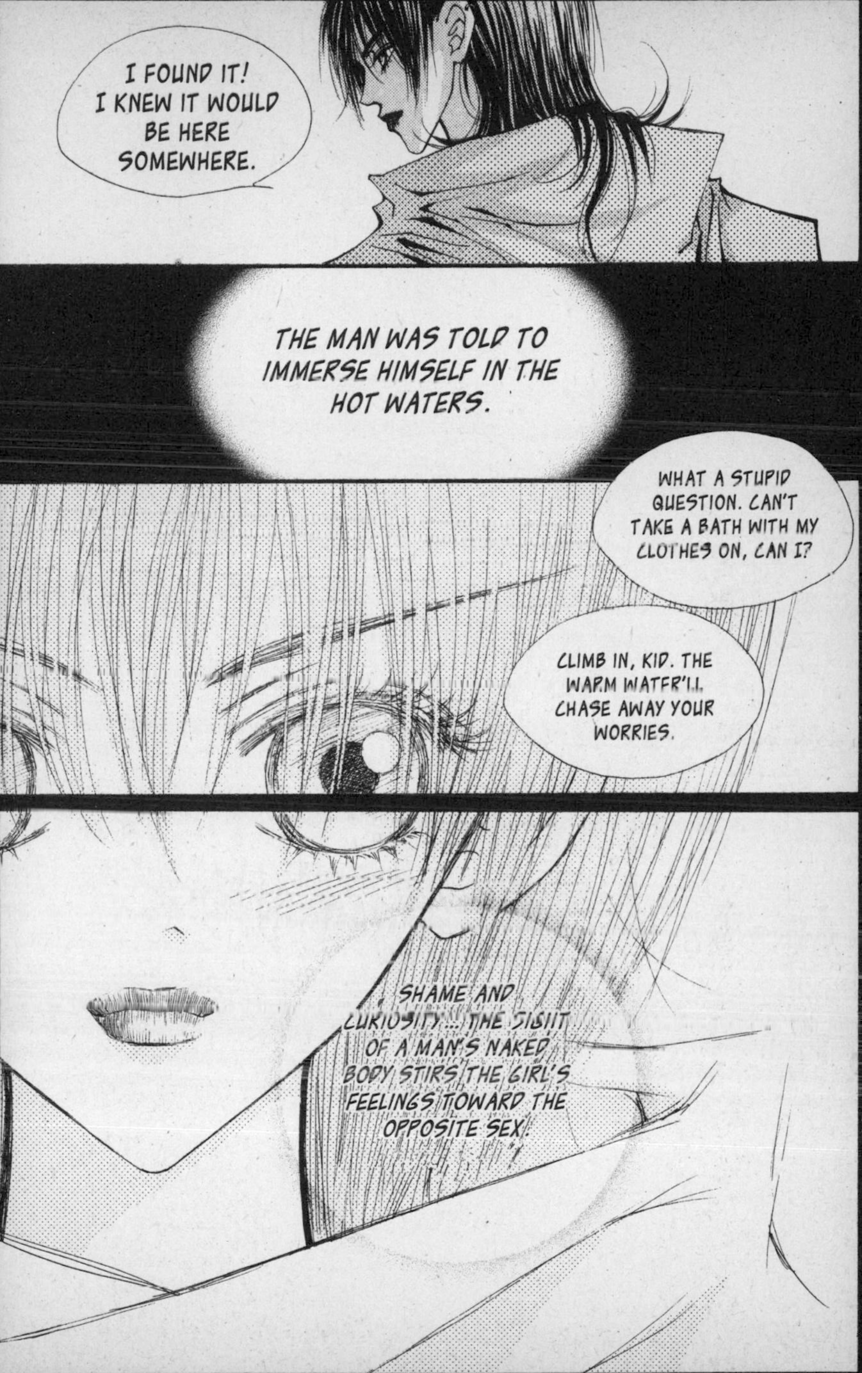
I FOUND IT! I KNEW IT WOULD BE HERE SOMEWHERE.
THE MAN WAS TOLD TO IMMERSE HIMSELF IN THE HOT WATERS.
WHAT A STUPID QUESTION. CAN'T TAKE A BATH WITH MY CLOTHES ON, CAN I?
CLIMB IN, KID. THE WARM WATER'LL CHASE AWAY YOUR WORRIES.
SHAME AND CURIOSITY... THE SIGHT OF A MAN'S NAKED BODY STIRS THE GIRL'S FEELINGS TOWARD THE OPPOSITE SEX.

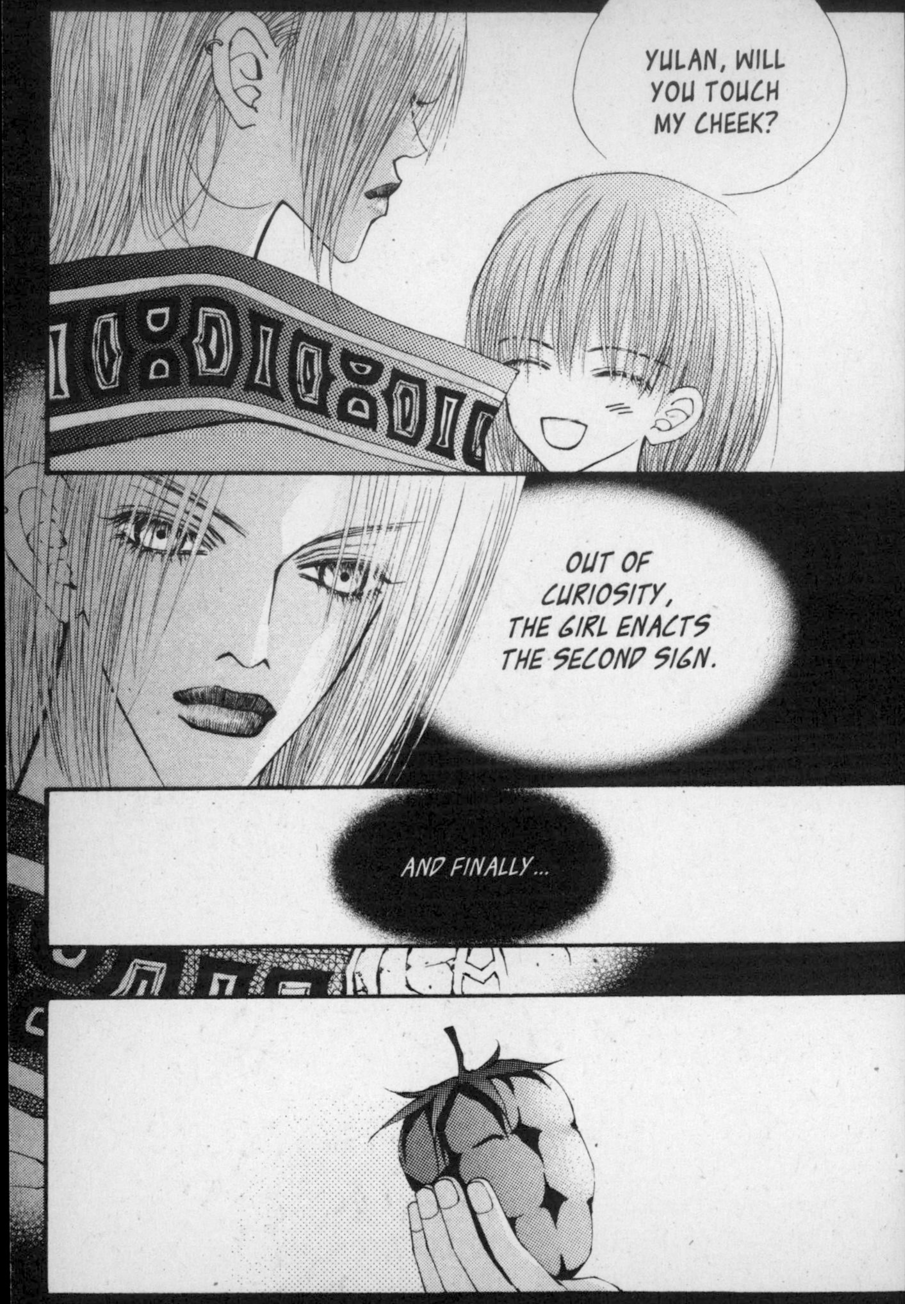
YULAN, WILL YOU TOUCH MY CHEEK?
OUT OF CURIOSITY, THE GIRL ENACTS THE SECOND SIGN.
AND FINALLY...

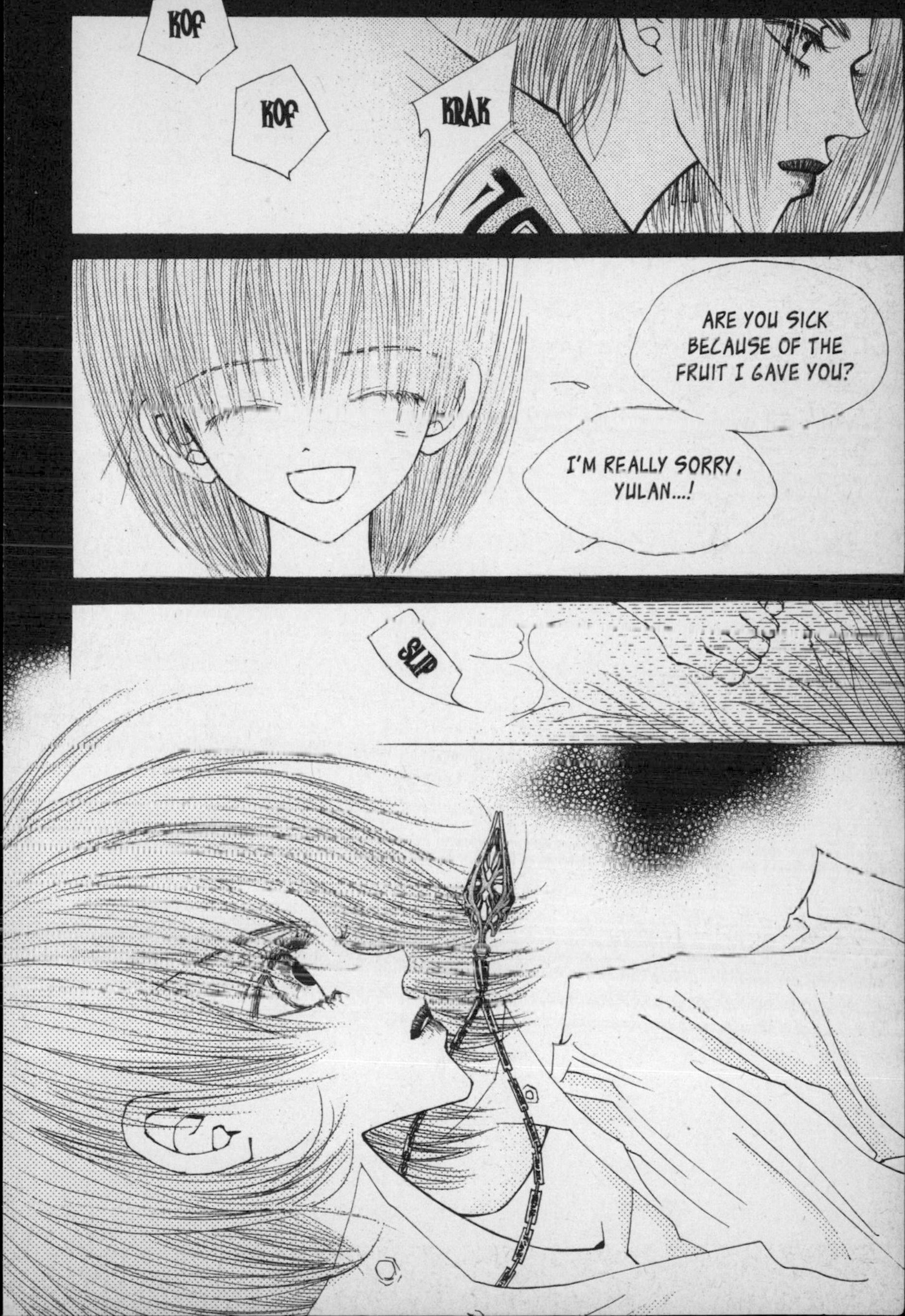
KOF
KOF
KRAK
ARE YOU SICK BECAUSE OF THE FRUIT I GAVE YOU?
I'M REALLY SORRY, YULAN...!
SLIP

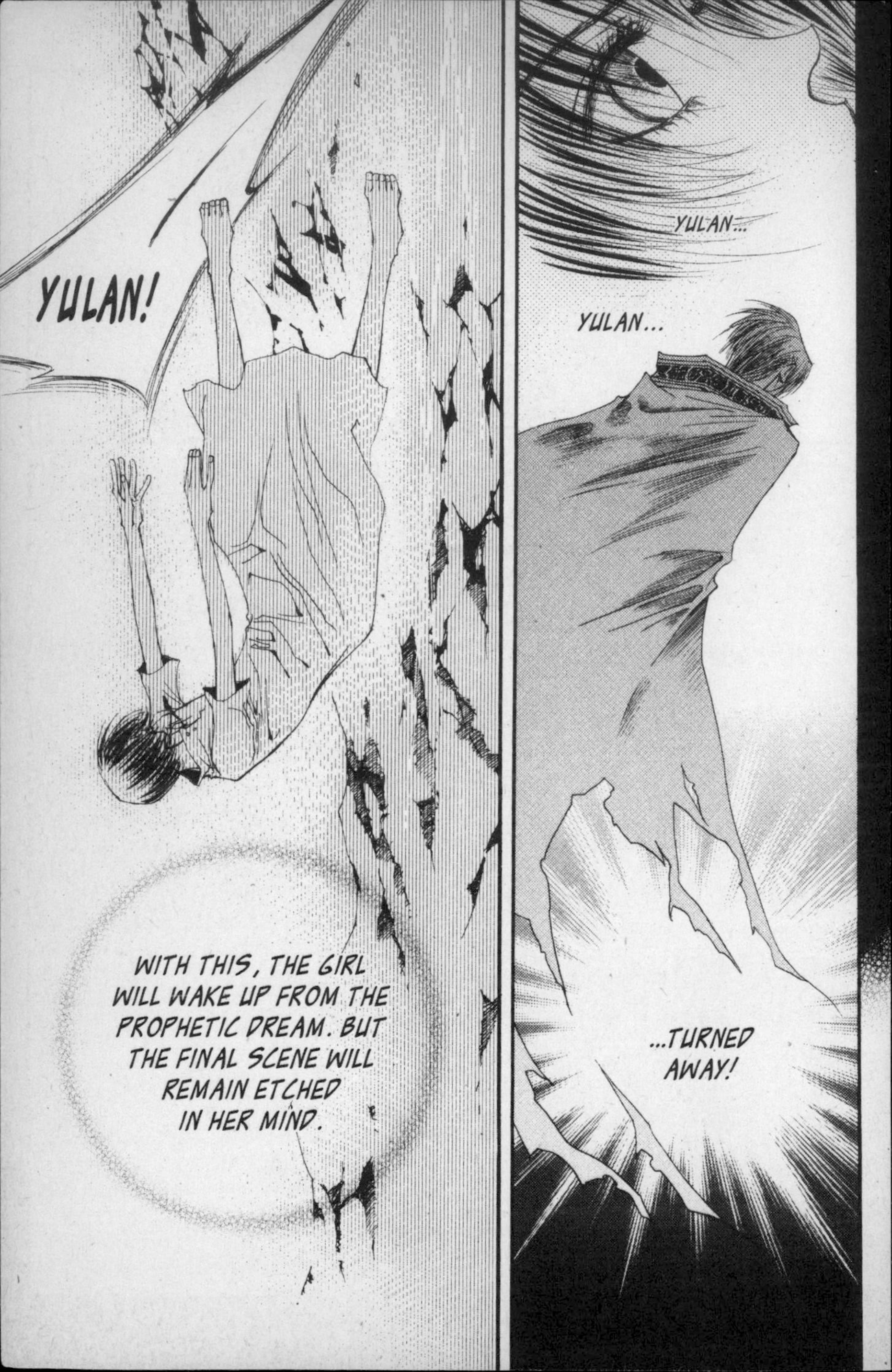
YULAN...
YULAN...
...TURNED AWAY!
YULAN!
WITH THIS, THE GIRL WILL WAKE UP FROM THE PROPHETIC DREAM. BUT THE FINAL SCENE WILL REMAIN ETCHED IN HER MIND.

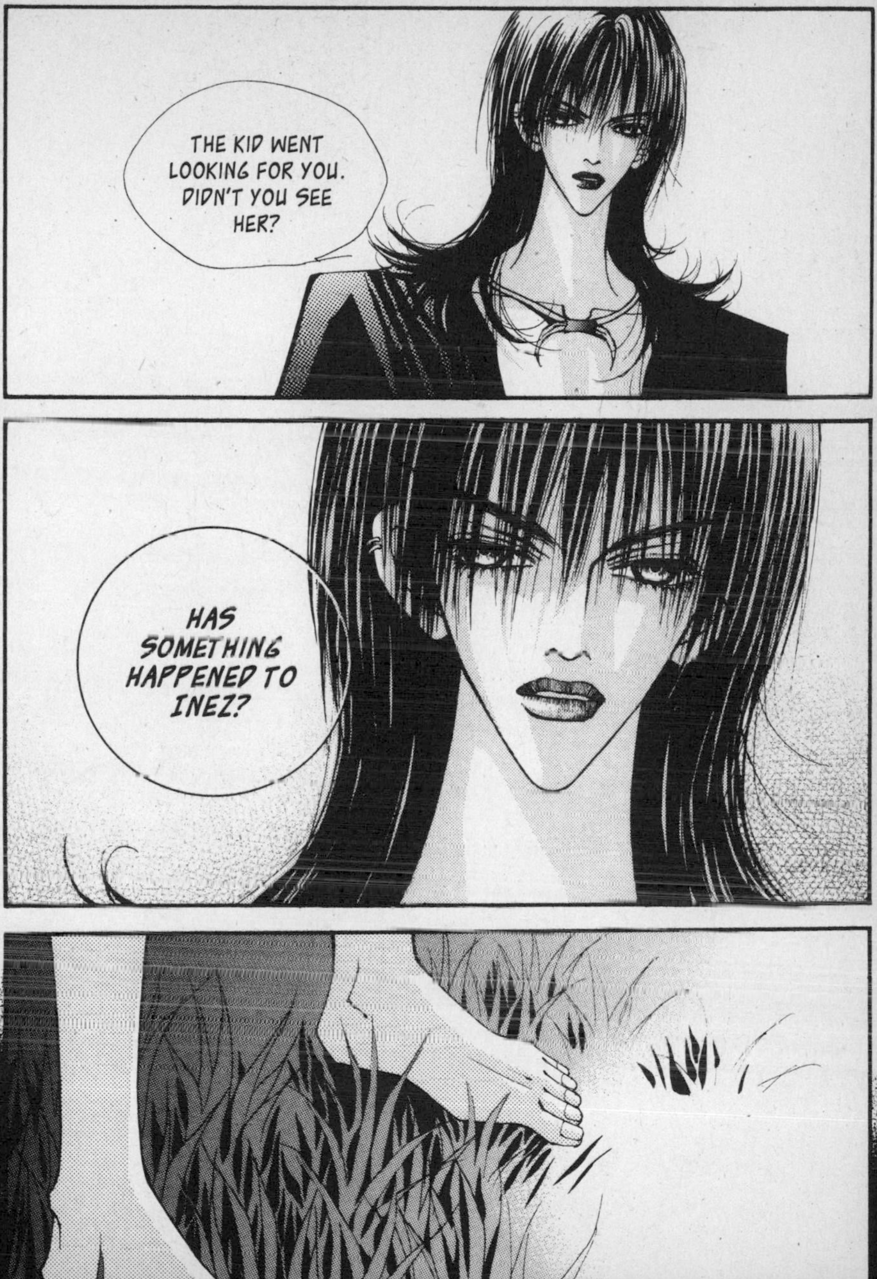
THE KID WENT LOOKING FOR YOU. DIDN'T YOU SEE HER?
HAS SOMETHING HAPPENED TO INEZ?

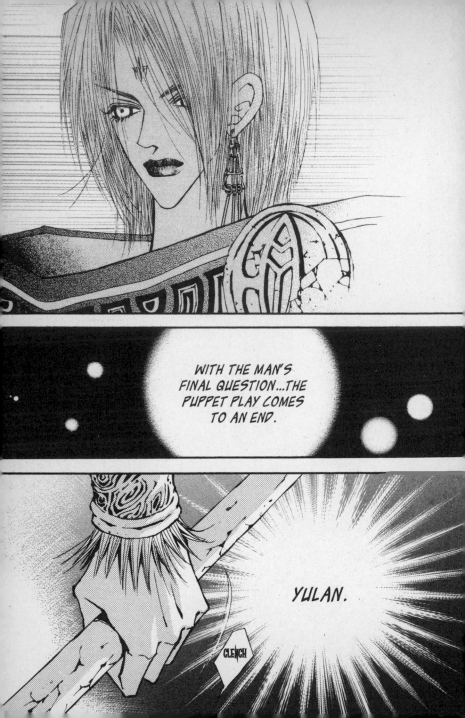

WITH THE MAN'S
FINAL QUESTION...THE
PUPPET PLAY COMES
TO AN END.

YULAN.

CLENCH

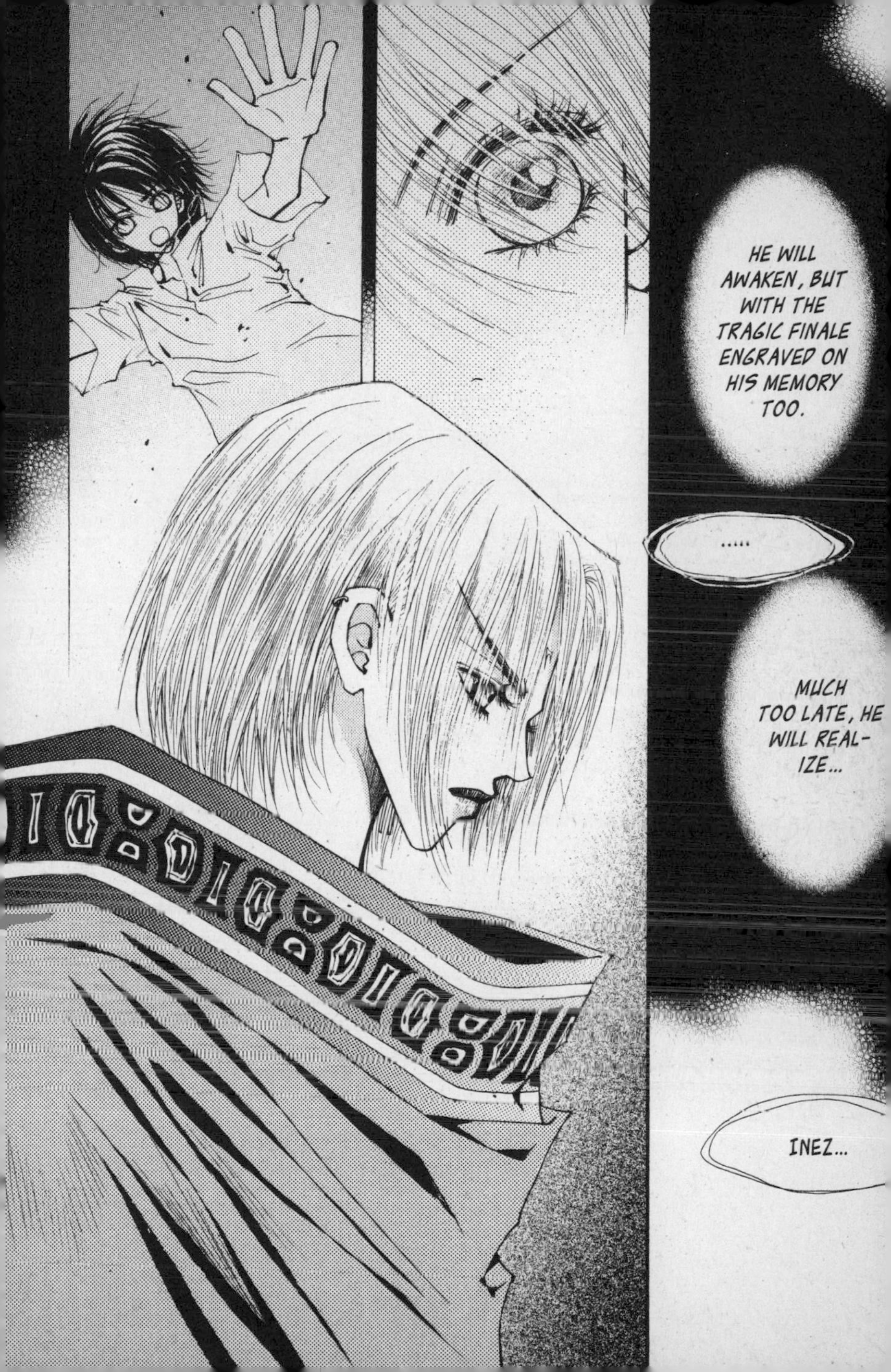
HE WILL AWAKEN, BUT WITH THE TRAGIC FINALE ENGRAVED ON HIS MEMORY TOO.
.....
MUCH TOO LATE, HE WILL REAL-IZE...
INEZ...

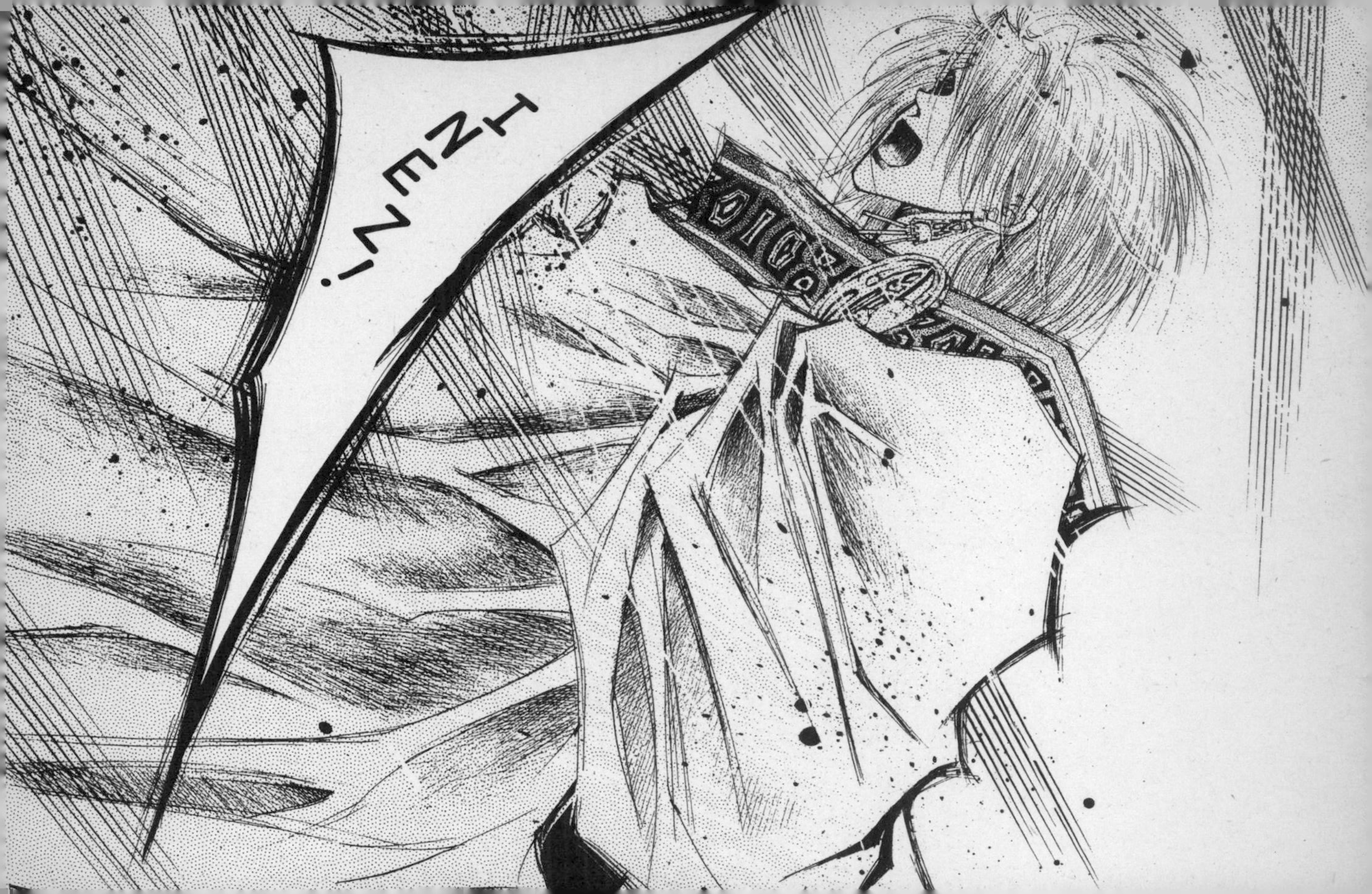
IZEN!

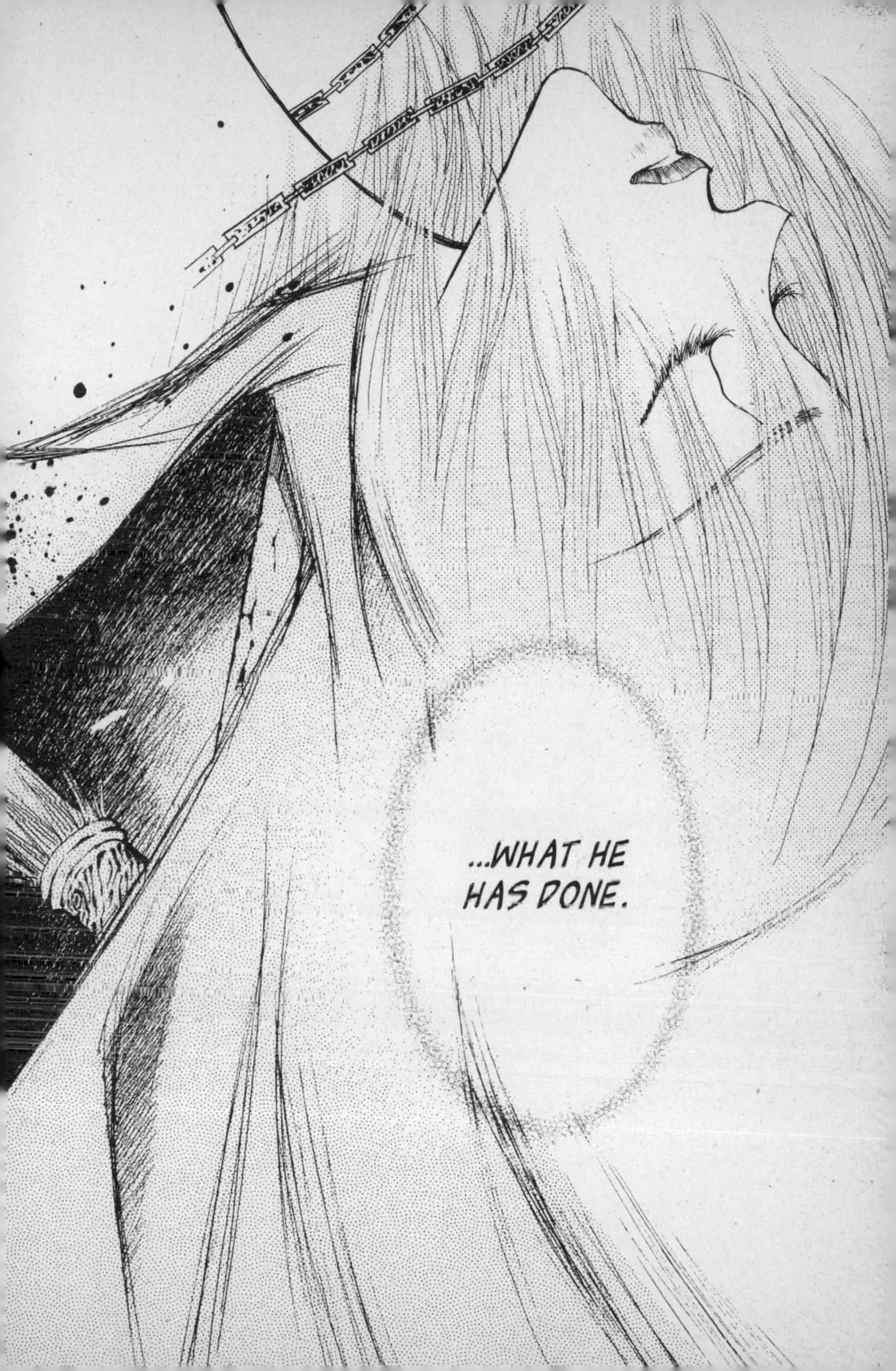
...WHAT HE HAS DONE.

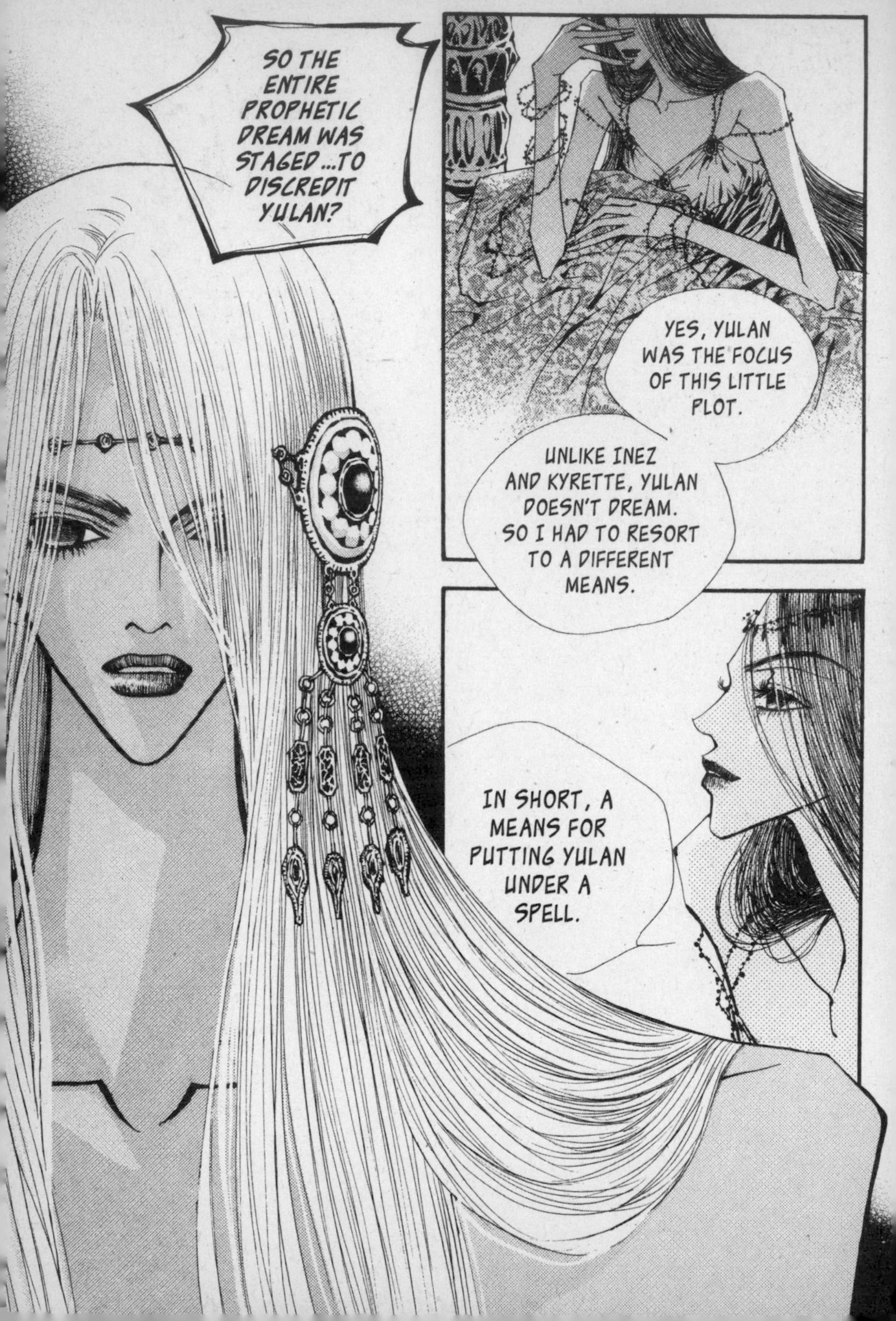
SO THE ENTIRE PROPHETIC DREAM WAS STAGED...TO DISCREDIT YULAN?
YES, YULAN WAS THE FOCUS OF THIS LITTLE PLOT.
UNLIKE INEZ AND KYRETTE, YULAN DOESN'T DREAM. SO I HAD TO RESORT TO A DIFFERENT MEANS.
IN SHORT, A MEANS FOR PUTTING YULAN UNDER A SPELL.

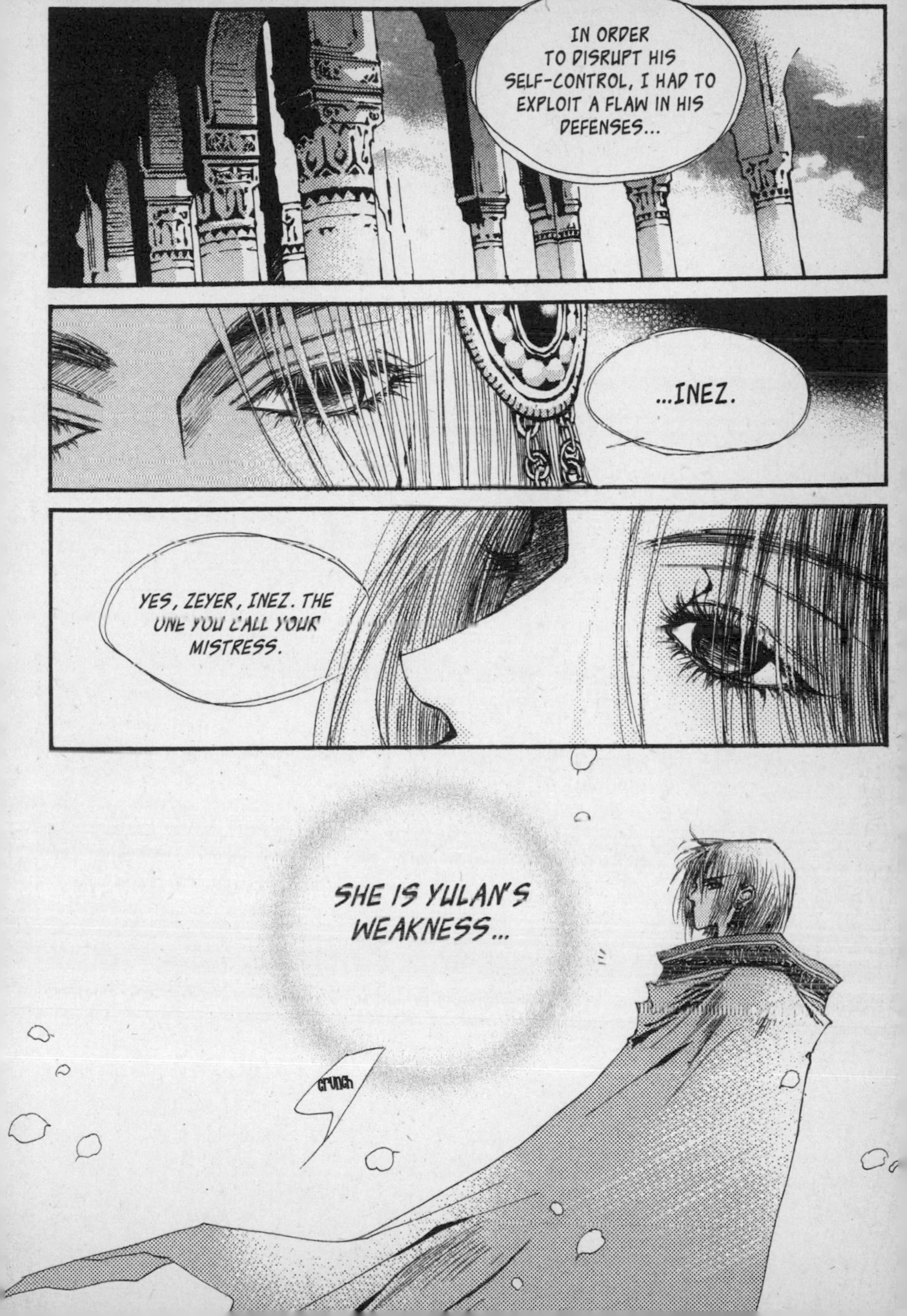
IN ORDER TO DISRUPT HIS SELF-CONTROL, I HAD TO EXPLOIT A FLAW IN HIS DEFENSES...
...INEZ.
YES, ZEYER, INEZ. THE ONE YOU CALL YOUR MISTRESS.
SHE IS YULAN'S WEAKNESS...
crunch

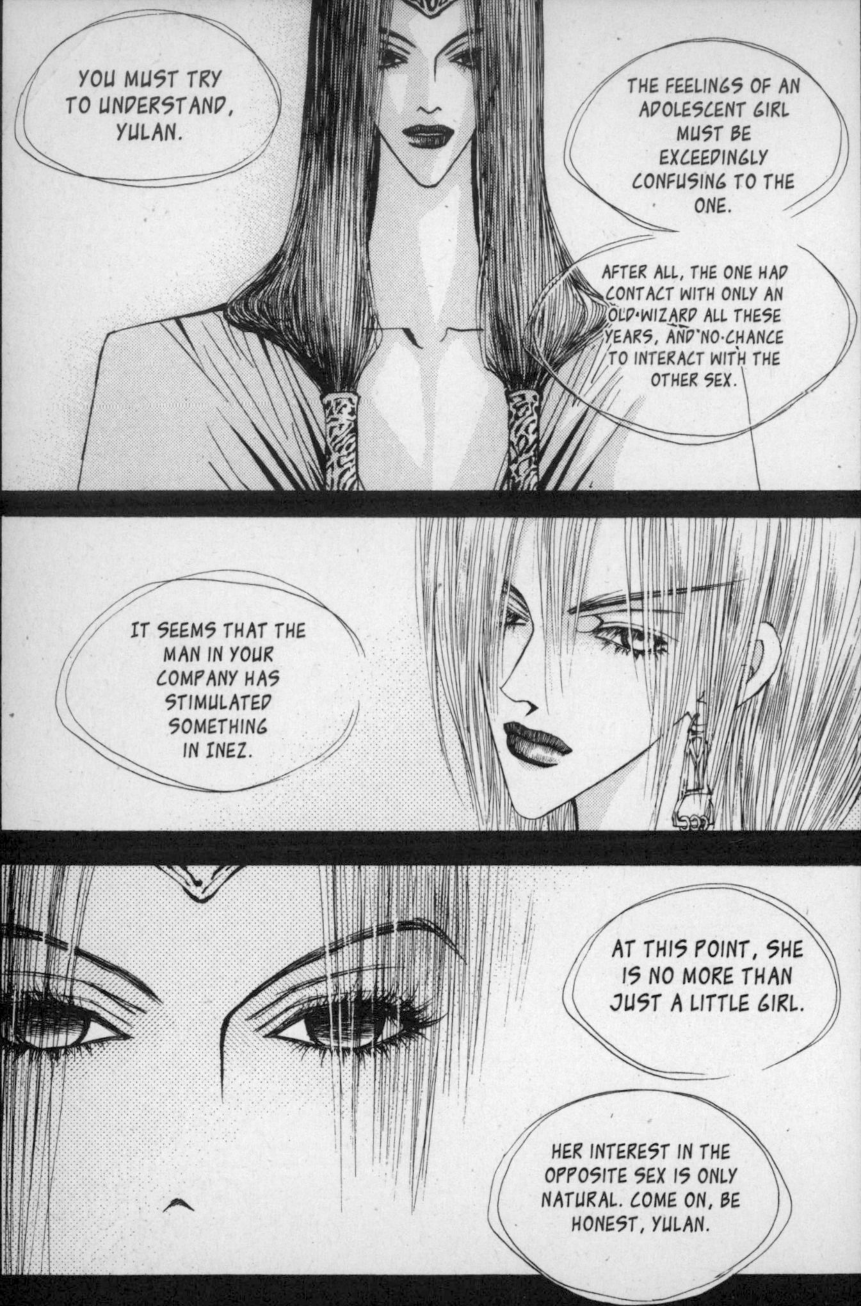
YOU MUST TRY TO UNDERSTAND, YULAN.
THE FEELINGS OF AN ADOLESCENT GIRL MUST BE EXCEEDINGLY CONFUSING TO THE ONE.
AFTER ALL, THE ONE HAD CONTACT WITH ONLY AN OLD WIZARD ALL THESE YEARS, AND NO CHANCE TO INTERACT WITH THE OTHER SEX.
IT SEEMS THAT THE MAN IN YOUR COMPANY HAS STIMULATED SOMETHING IN INEZ.
AT THIS POINT, SHE IS NO MORE THAN JUST A LITTLE GIRL.
HER INTEREST IN THE OPPOSITE SEX IS ONLY NATURAL. COME ON, BE HONEST, YULAN.

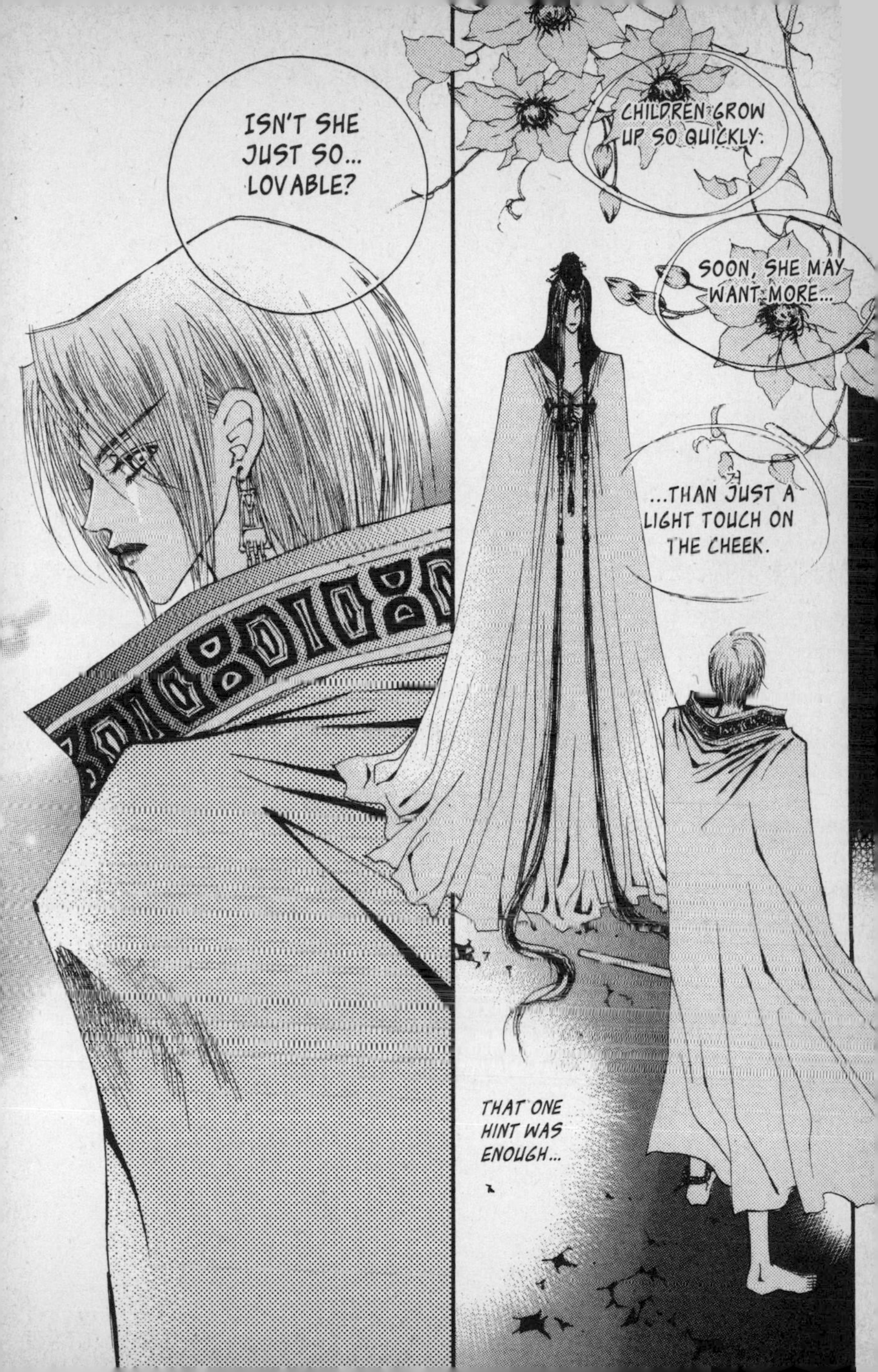
CHILDREN GROW UP SO QUICKLY.
SOON, SHE MAY WANT MORE...
...THAN JUST A LIGHT TOUCH ON THE CHEEK.
THAT ONE HINT WAS ENOUGH...
ISN'T SHE JUST SO... LOVABLE?

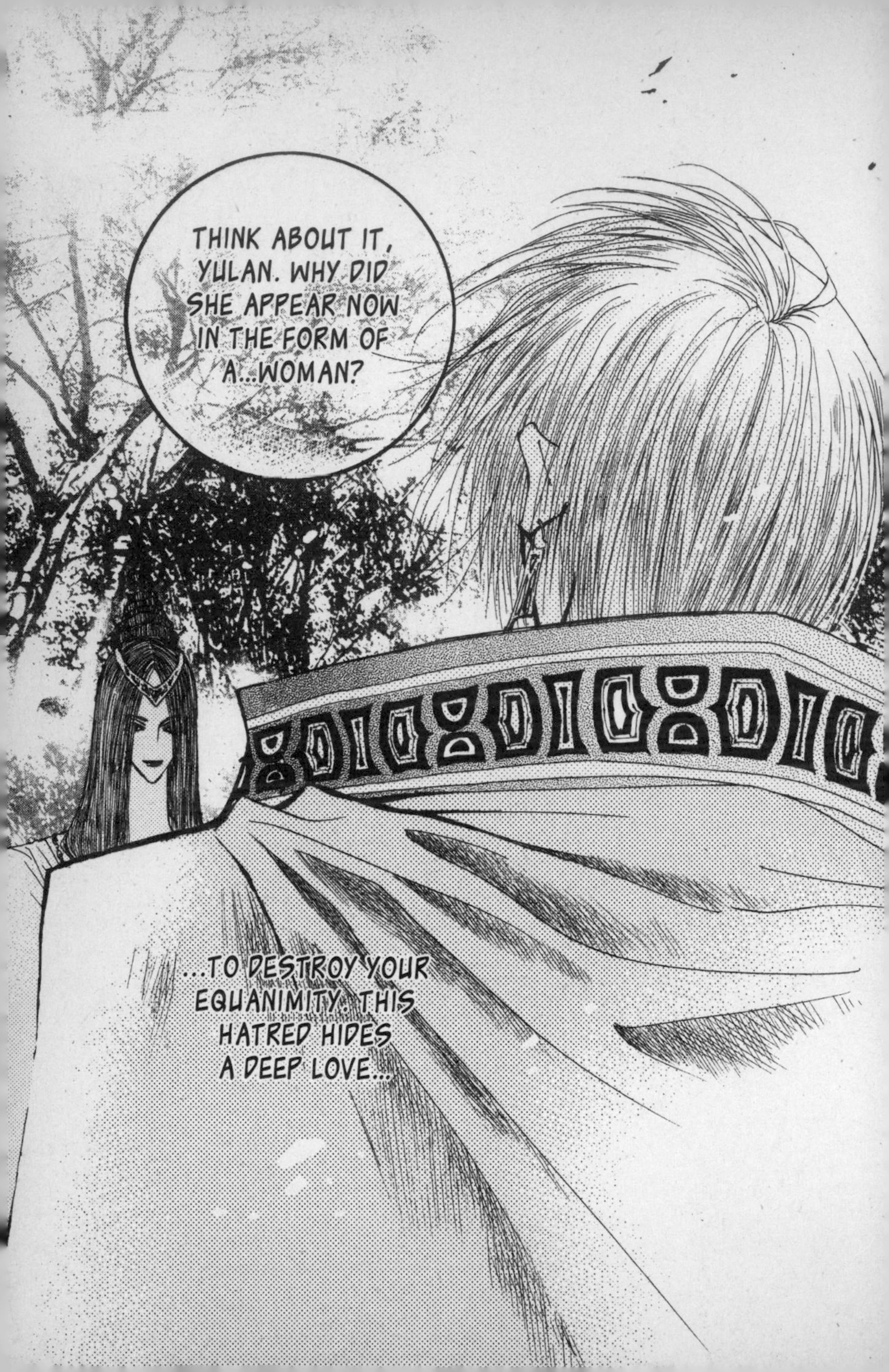
THINK ABOUT IT, YULAN. WHY DID SHE APPEAR NOW IN THE FORM OF A...WOMAN?
...TO DESTROY YOUR EQUANIMITY. THIS HATRED HIDES A DEEP LOVE...

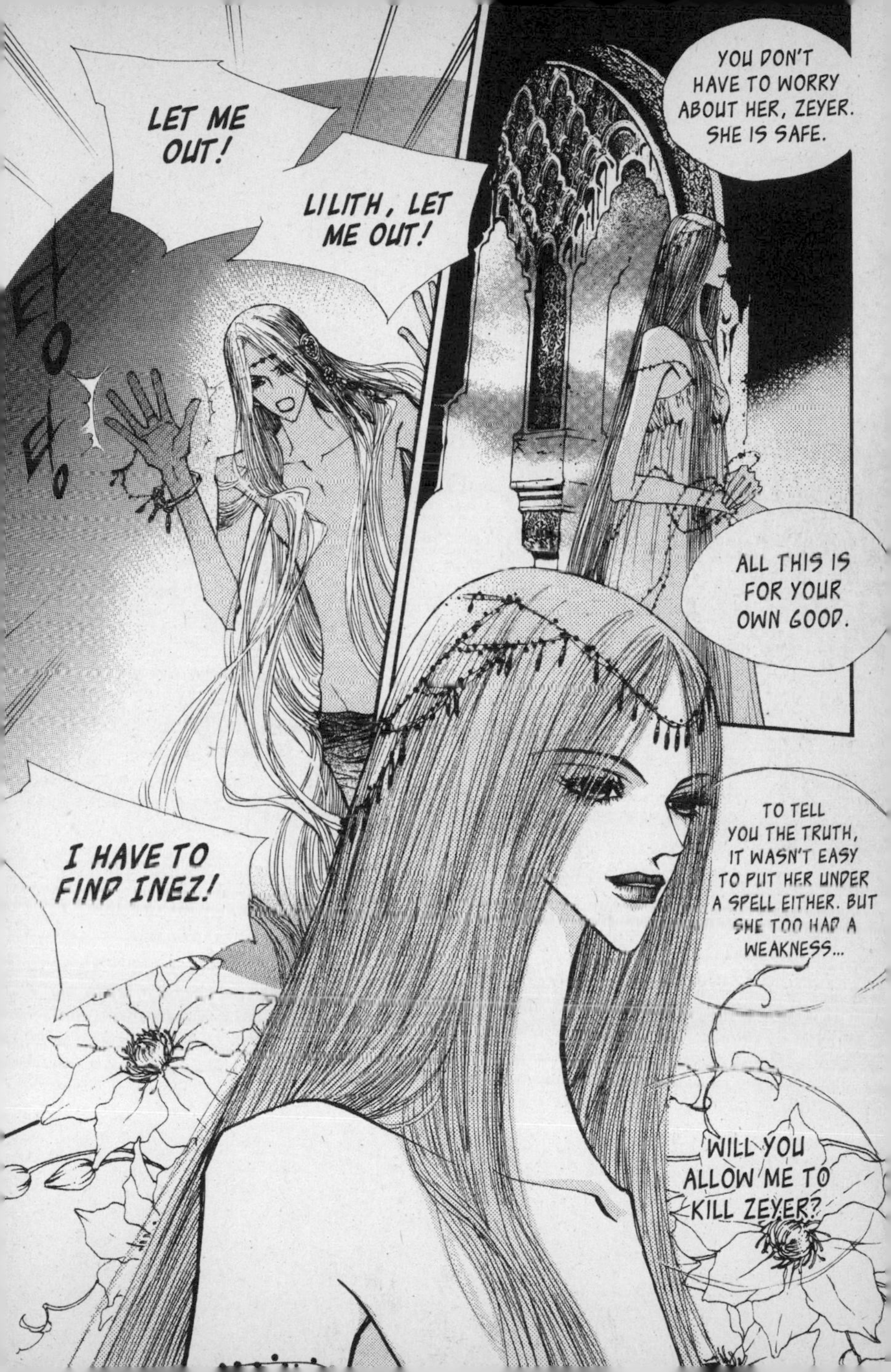
LET ME OUT!
LILITH, LET ME OUT!
I HAVE TO FIND INEZ!
YOU DON'T HAVE TO WORRY ABOUT HER, ZEYER. SHE IS SAFE.
ALL THIS IS FOR YOUR OWN GOOD.
TO TELL YOU THE TRUTH, IT WASN'T EASY TO PUT HER UNDER A SPELL EITHER. BUT SHE TOO HAD A WEAKNESS...
WILL YOU ALLOW ME TO KILL ZEYER?

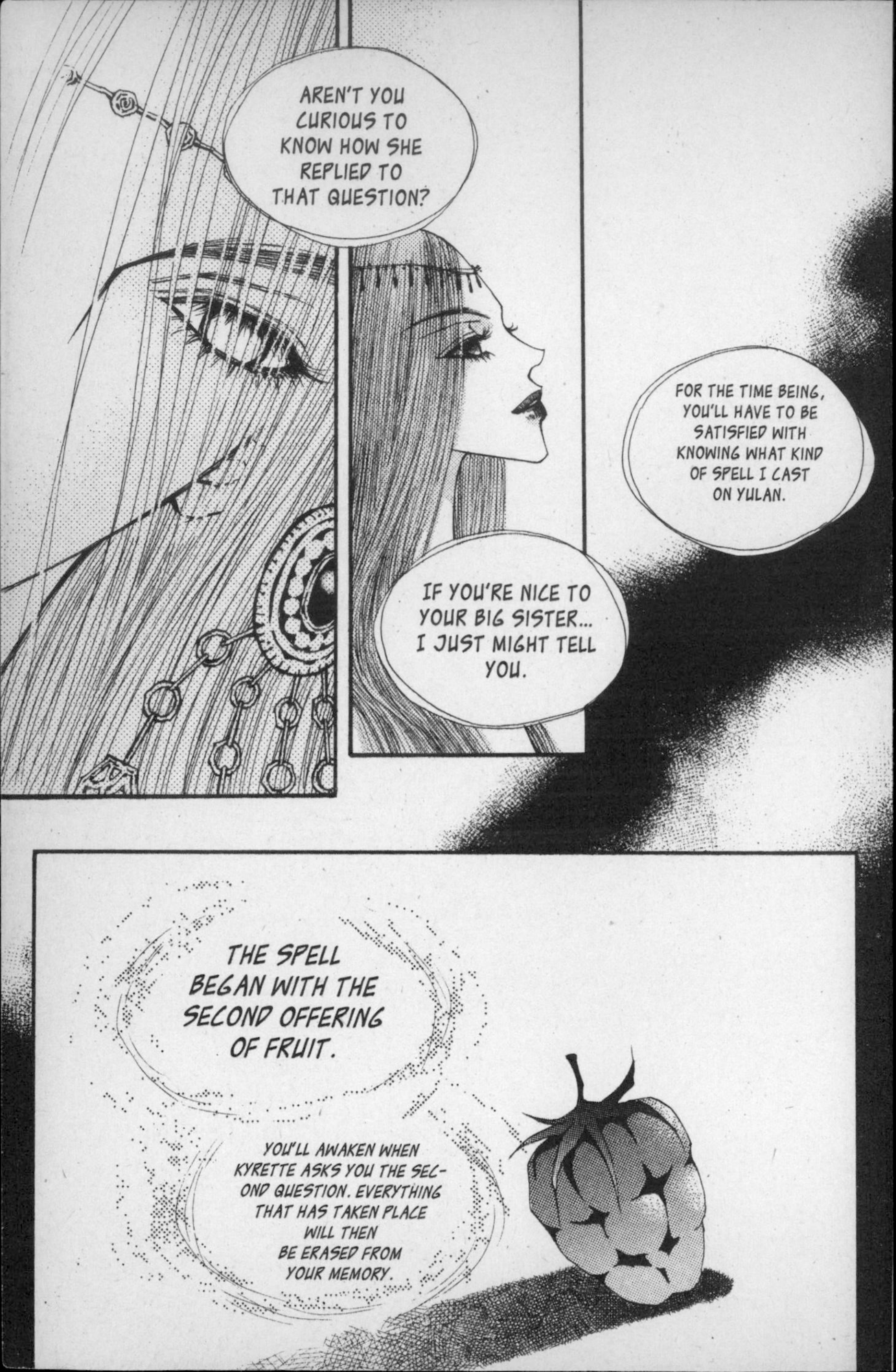
AREN'T YOU CURIOUS TO KNOW HOW SHE REPLIED TO THAT QUESTION?
FOR THE TIME BEING, YOU'LL HAVE TO BE SATISFIED WITH KNOWING WHAT KIND OF SPELL I CAST ON YULAN.
IF YOU'RE NICE TO YOUR BIG SISTER... I JUST MIGHT TELL YOU.
THE SPELL BEGAN WITH THE SECOND OFFERING OF FRUIT.
YOU'LL AWAKEN WHEN KYRETTE ASKS YOU THE SEC-OND QUESTION. EVERYTHING THAT HAS TAKEN PLACE WILL THEN BE ERASED FROM YOUR MEMORY.

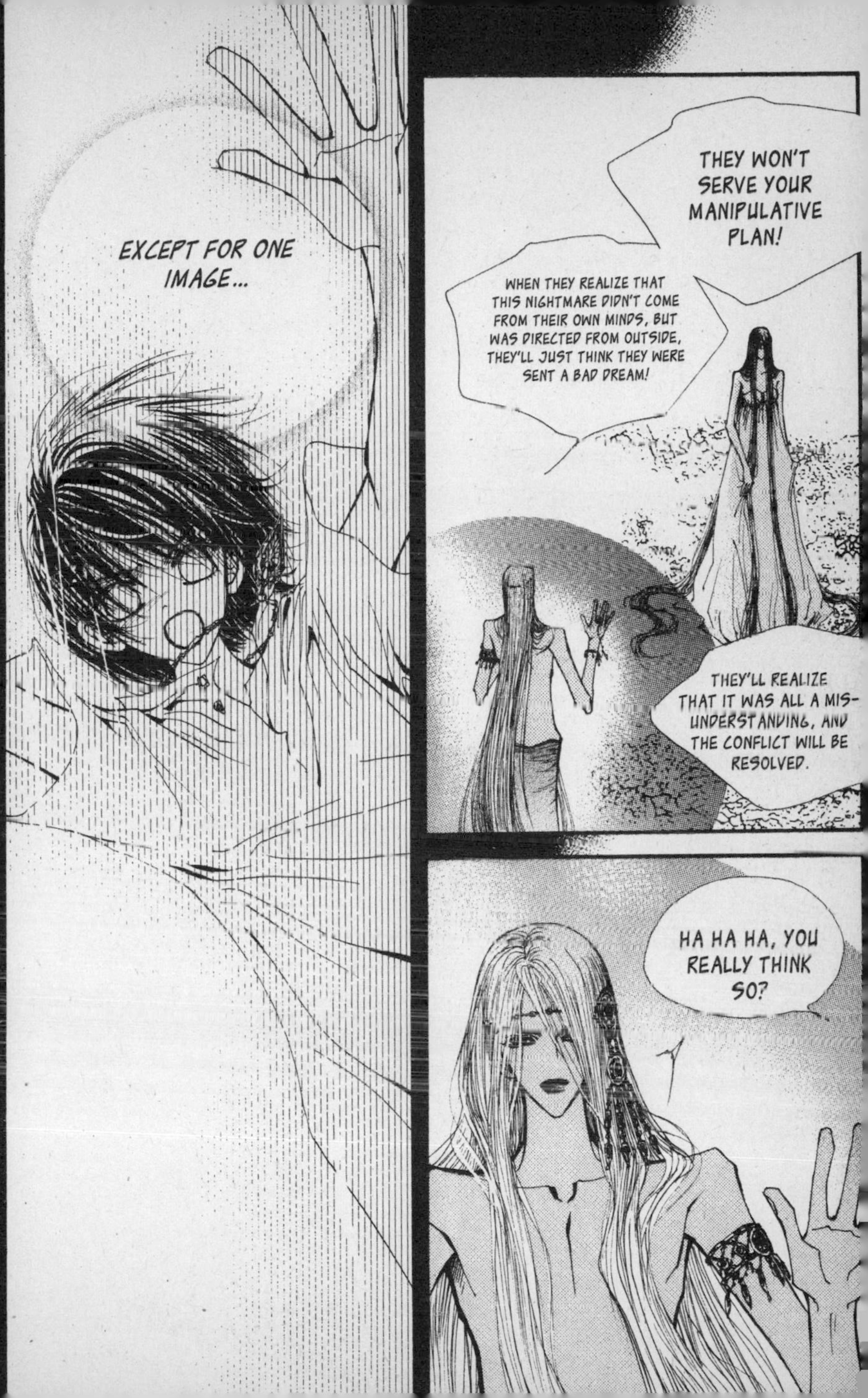
THEY WON'T SERVE YOUR MANIPULATIVE PLAN!
WHEN THEY REALIZE THAT THIS NIGHTMARE DIDN'T COME FROM THEIR OWN MINDS, BUT WAS DIRECTED FROM OUTSIDE, THEY'LL JUST THINK THEY WERE SENT A BAD DREAM!
THEY'LL REALIZE THAT IT WAS ALL A MIS-UNDERSTANDING, AND THE CONFLICT WILL BE RESOLVED.
HA HA HA, YOU REALLY THINK SO?
EXCEPT FOR ONE IMAGE...

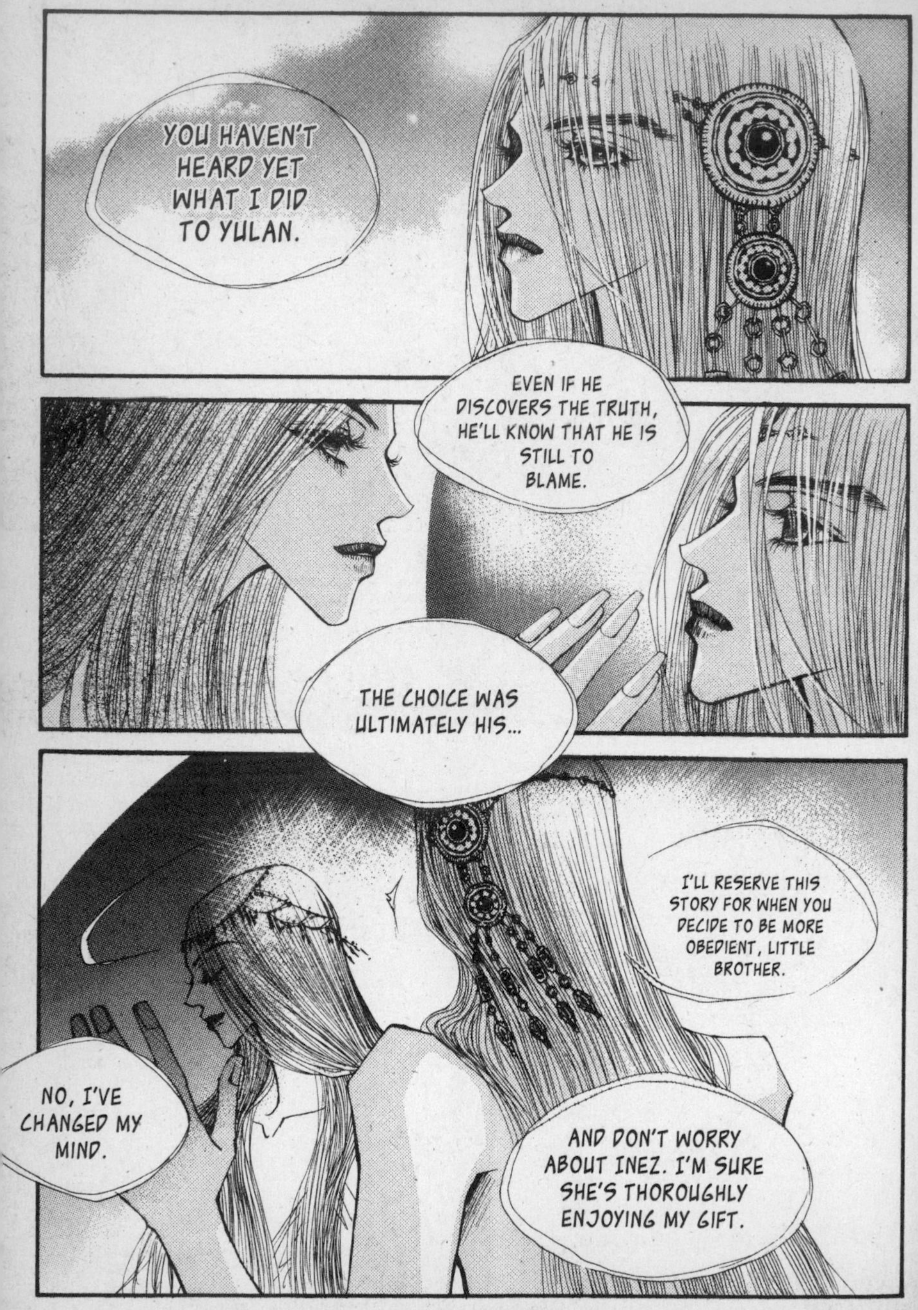
YOU HAVEN'T HEARD YET WHAT I DID TO YULAN.
EVEN IF HE DISCOVERS THE TRUTH, HE'LL KNOW THAT HE IS STILL TO BLAME.
THE CHOICE WAS ULTIMATELY HIS...
I'LL RESERVE THIS STORY FOR WHEN YOU DECIDE TO BE MORE OBEDIENT, LITTLE BROTHER.
AND DON'T WORRY ABOUT INEZ. I'M SURE SHE'S THOROUGHLY ENJOYING MY GIFT.
NO, I'VE CHANGED MY MIND.

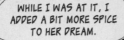

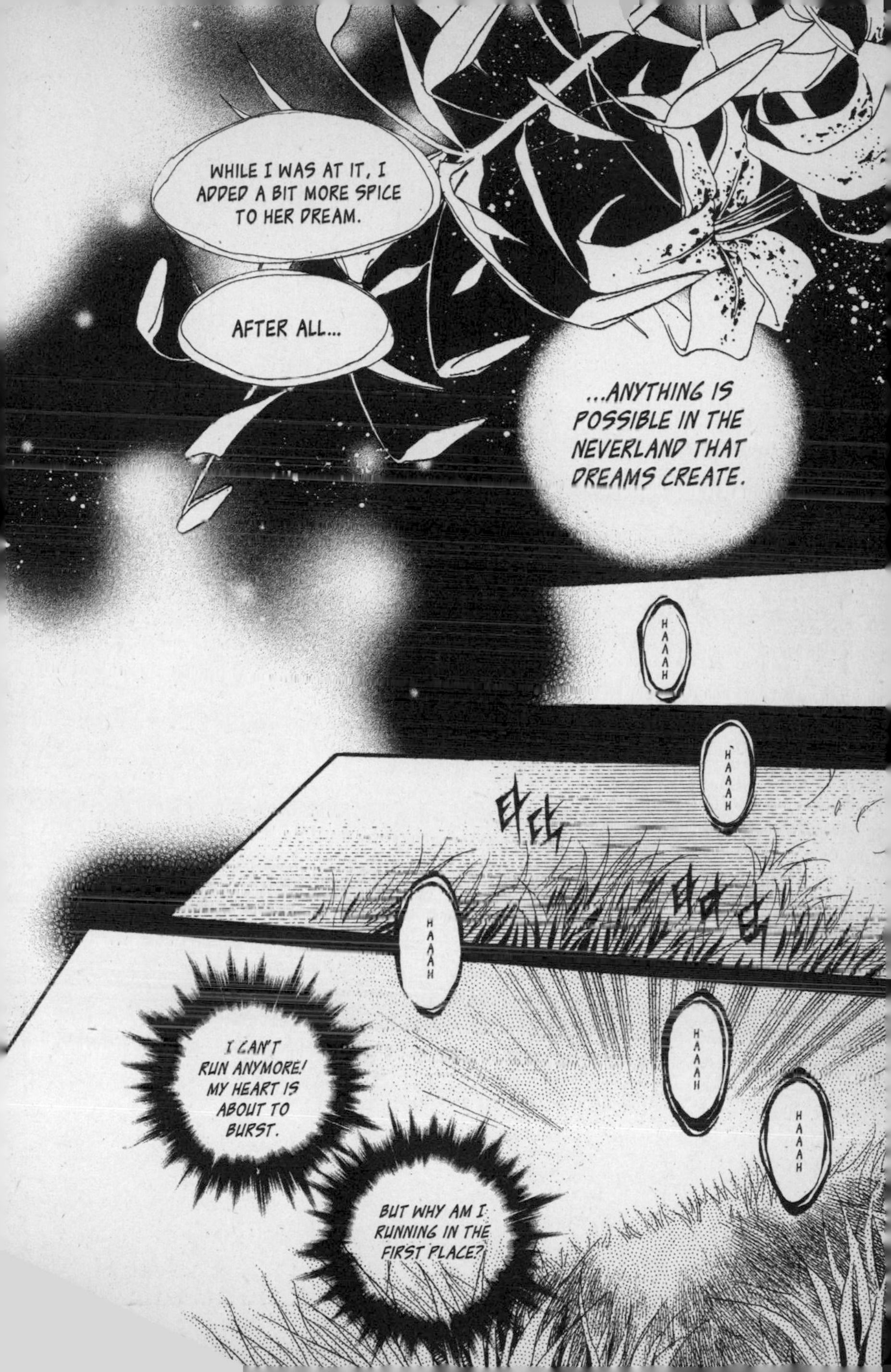

WHILE I WAS AT IT, I ADDED A BIT MORE SPICE TO HER DREAM.

AFTER ALL...

...ANYTHING IS POSSIBLE IN THE NEVERLAND THAT DREAMS CREATE.

HAAAH

HAAAH

HAAAH

I CAN'T RUN ANYMORE! MY HEART IS ABOUT TO BURST.

HAAAH

HAAAH

BUT WHY AM I RUNNING IN THE FIRST PLACE?

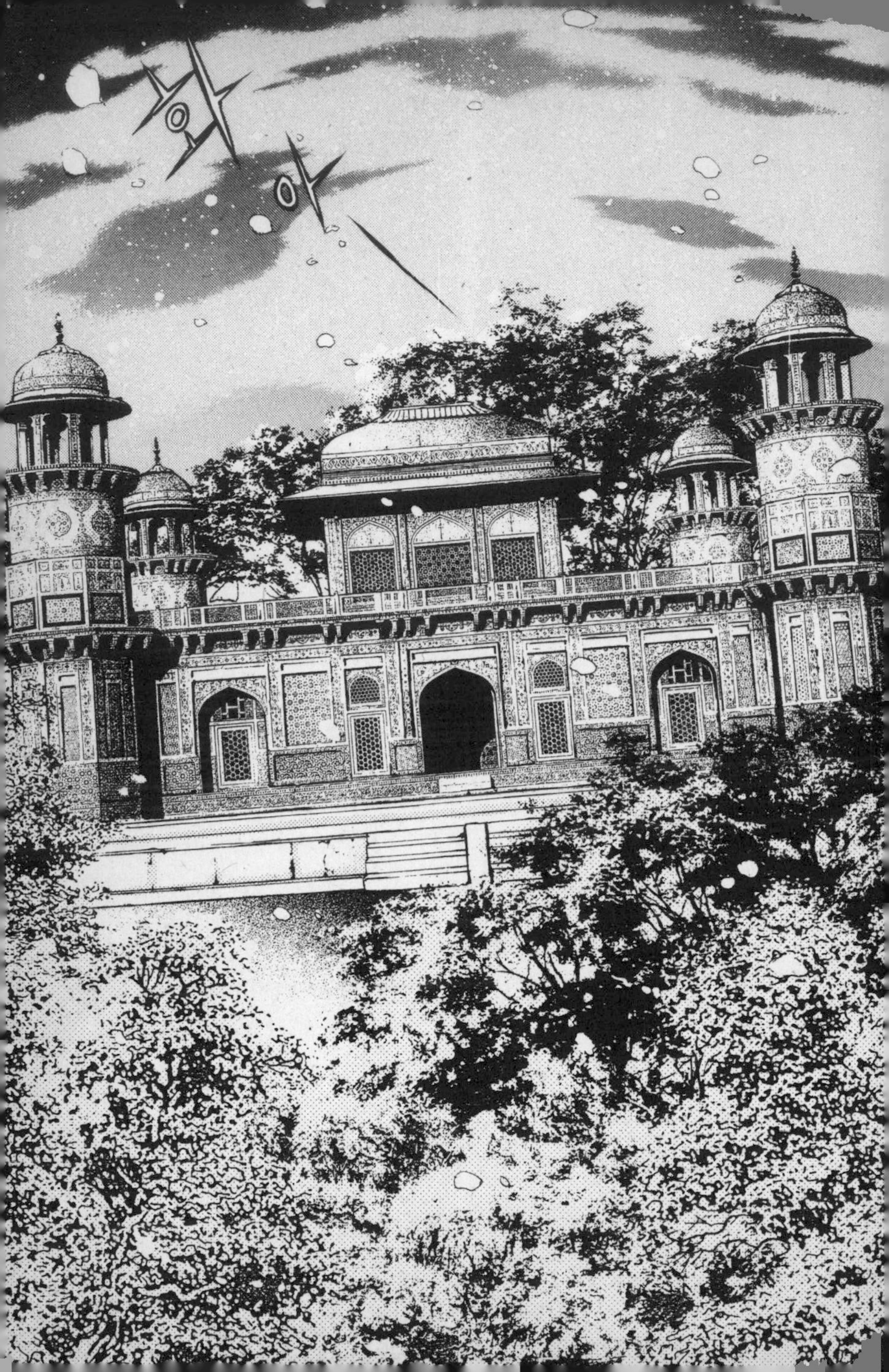
와아

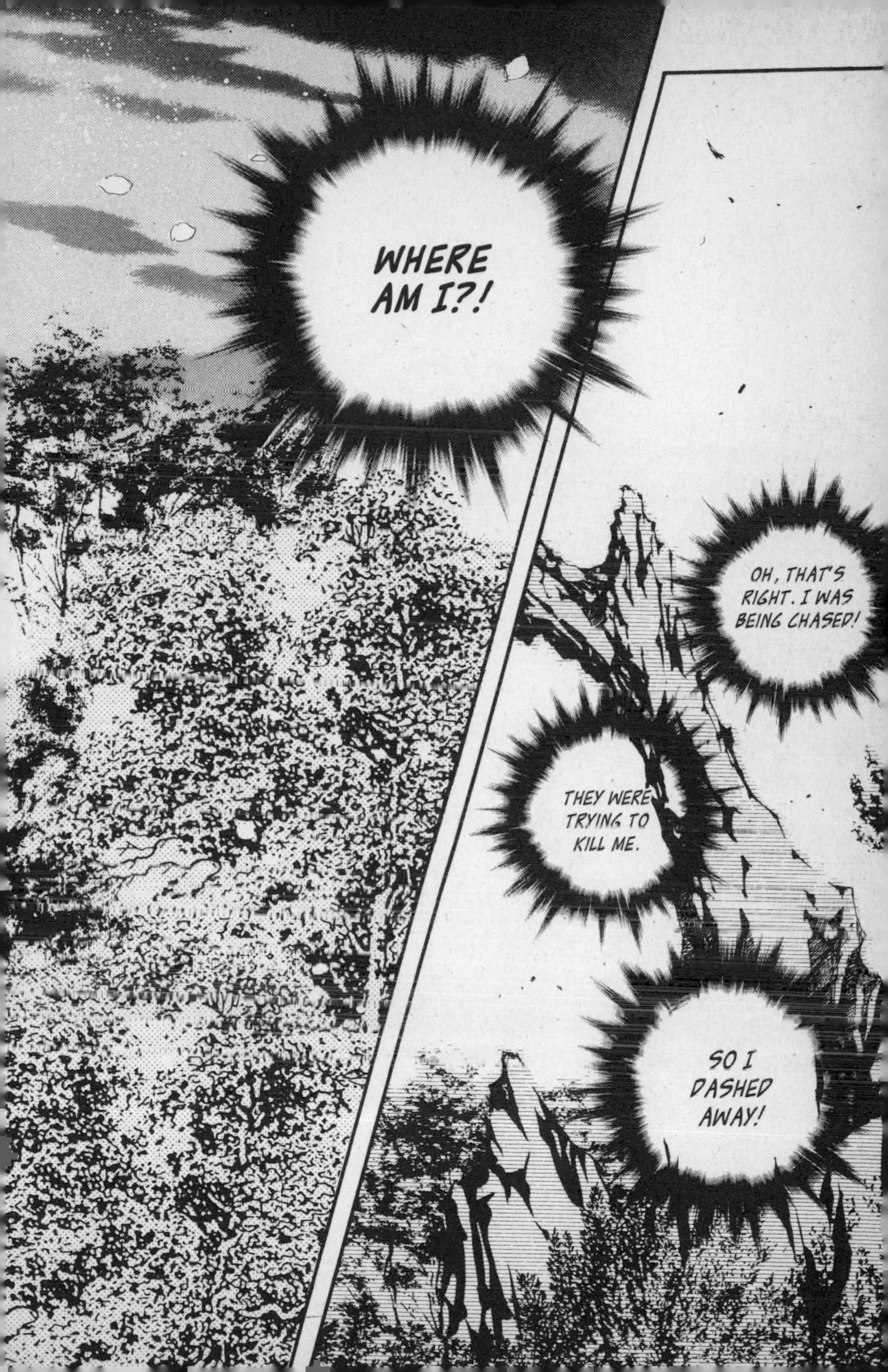
WHERE AM I?!
OH, THAT'S RIGHT. I WAS BEING CHASED!
THEY WERE TRYING TO KILL ME.
SO I DASHED AWAY!

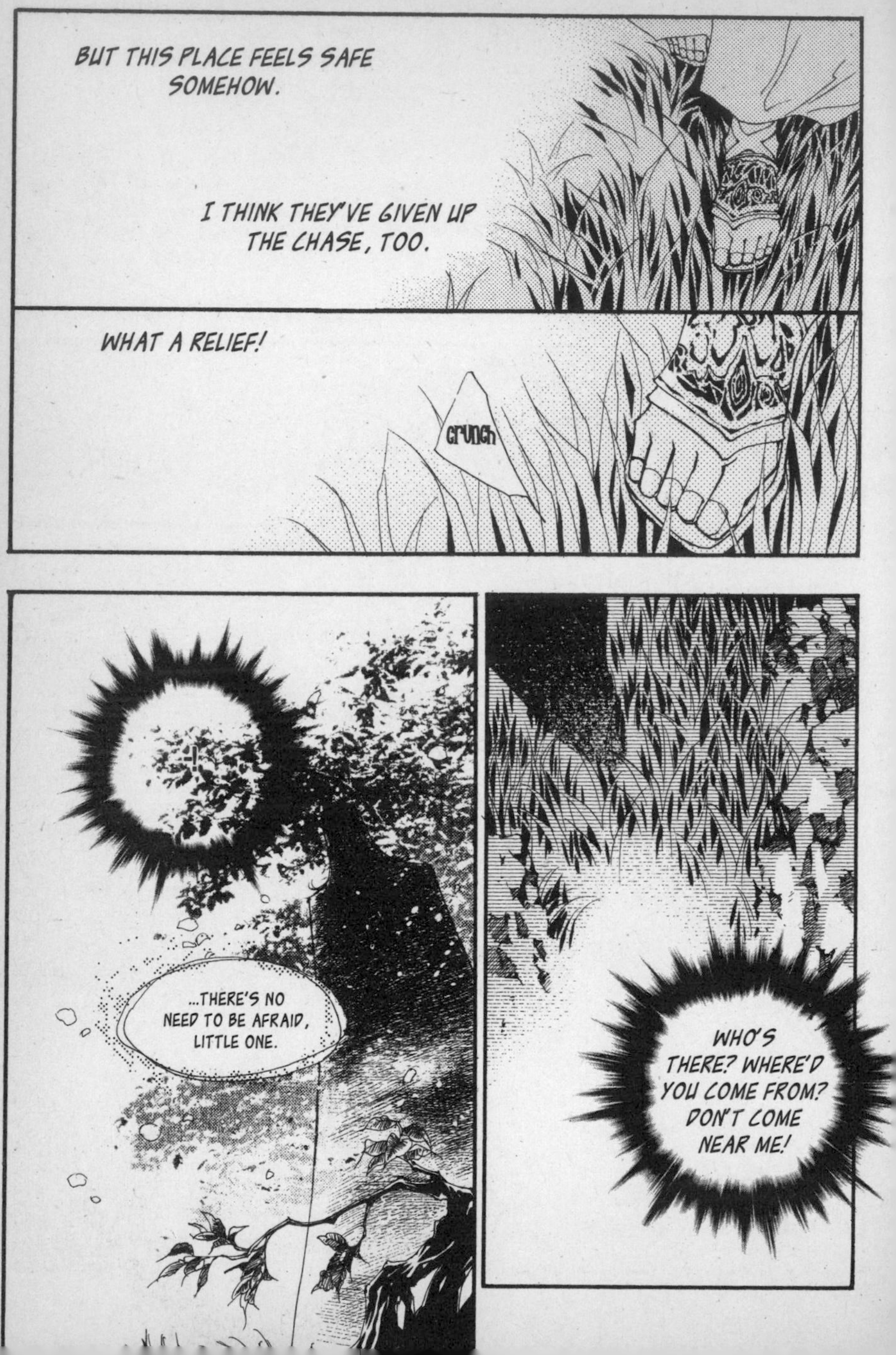
BUT THIS PLACE FEELS SAFE SOMEHOW.
I THINK THEY'VE GIVEN UP THE CHASE, TOO.
WHAT A RELIEF!
CRUNCH
WHO'S THERE? WHERE'D YOU COME FROM? DON'T COME NEAR ME!
!
...THERE'S NO NEED TO BE AFRAID, LITTLE ONE.

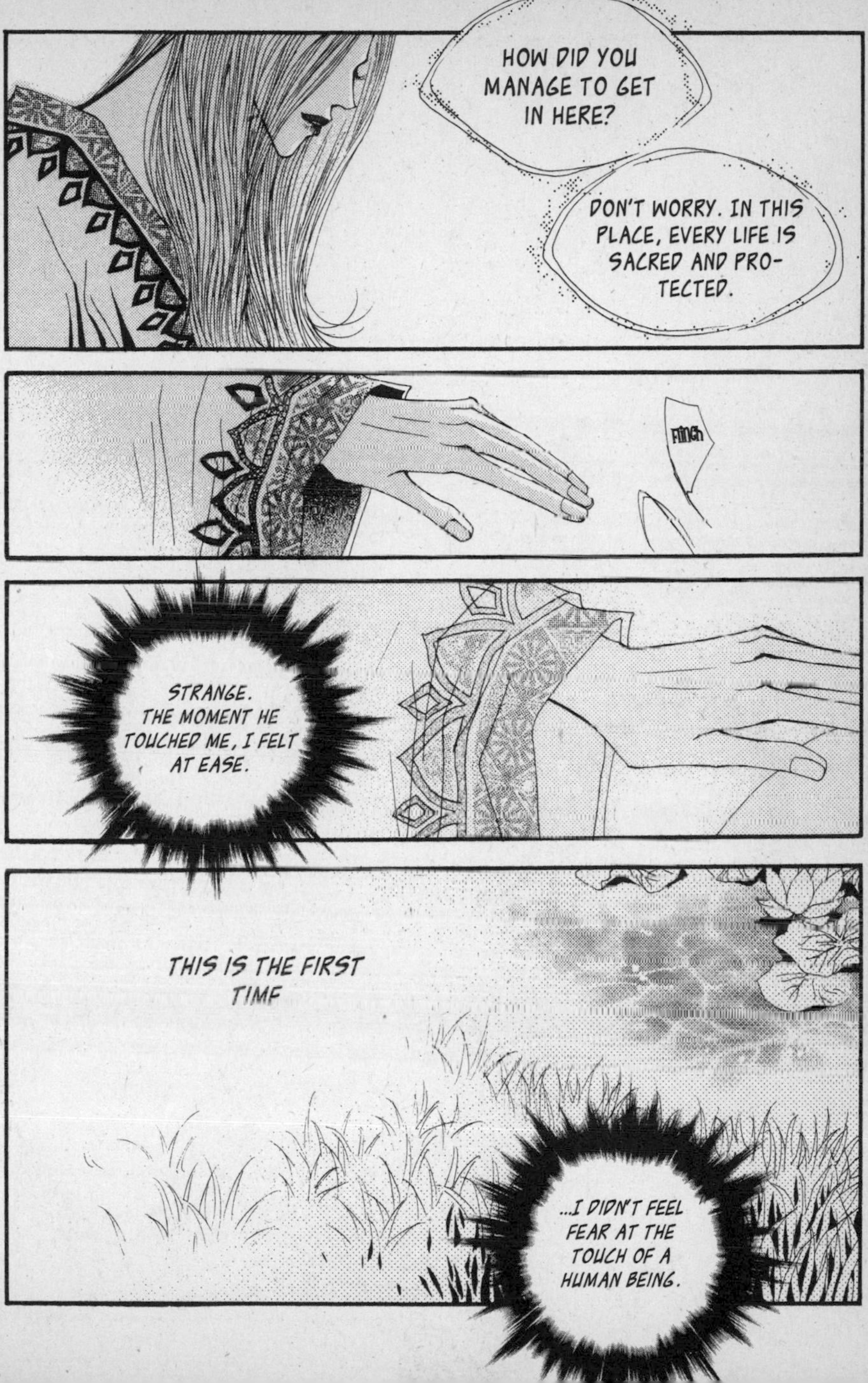
HOW DID YOU MANAGE TO GET IN HERE?
DON'T WORRY. IN THIS PLACE, EVERY LIFE IS SACRED AND PRO-TECTED.
Flinch
STRANGE. THE MOMENT HE TOUCHED ME, I FELT AT EASE.
THIS IS THE FIRST TIME
...I DIDN'T FEEL FEAR AT THE TOUCH OF A HUMAN BEING.

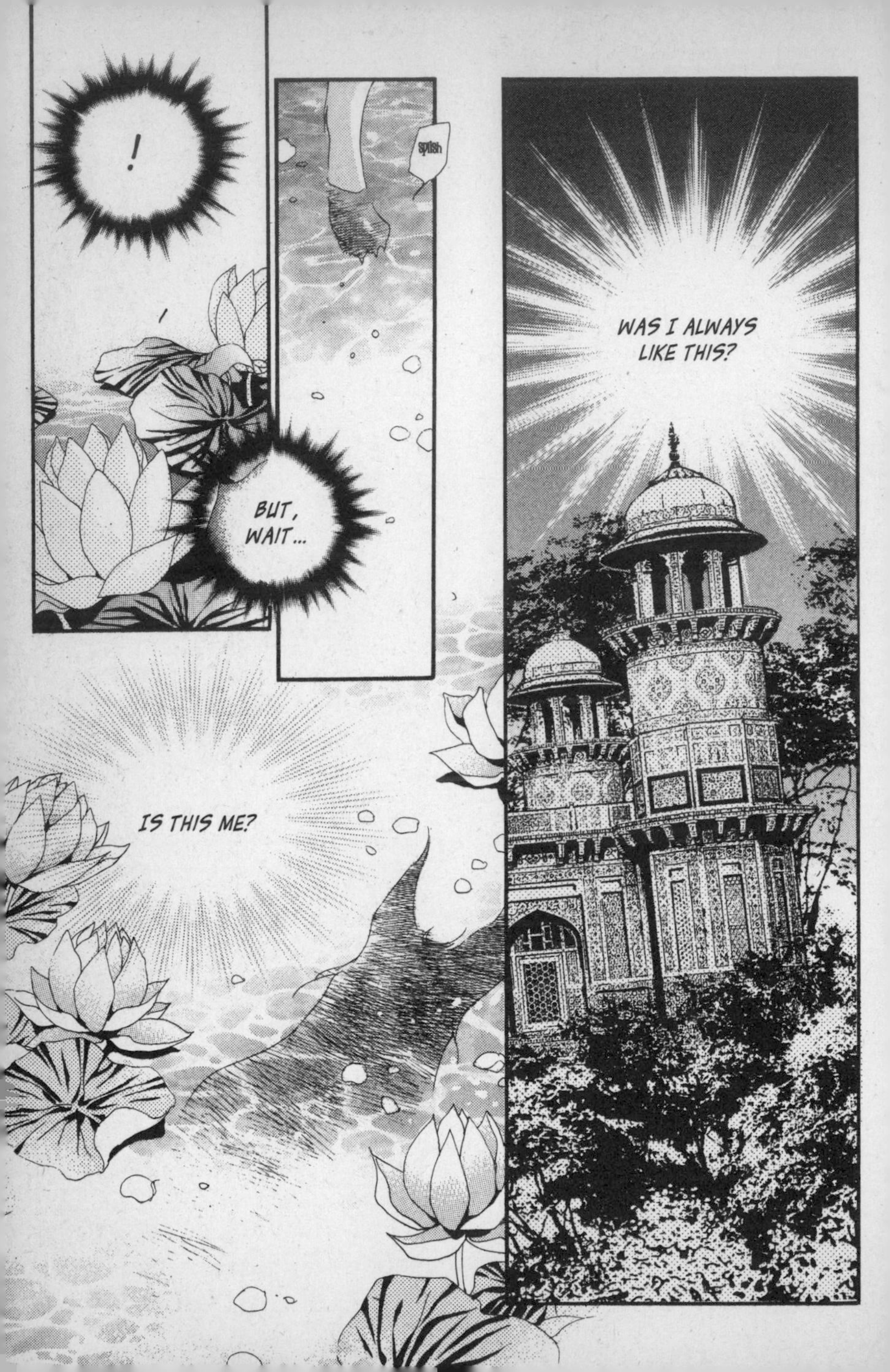
!
splish
BUT, WAIT...
IS THIS ME?
WAS I ALWAYS LIKE THIS?

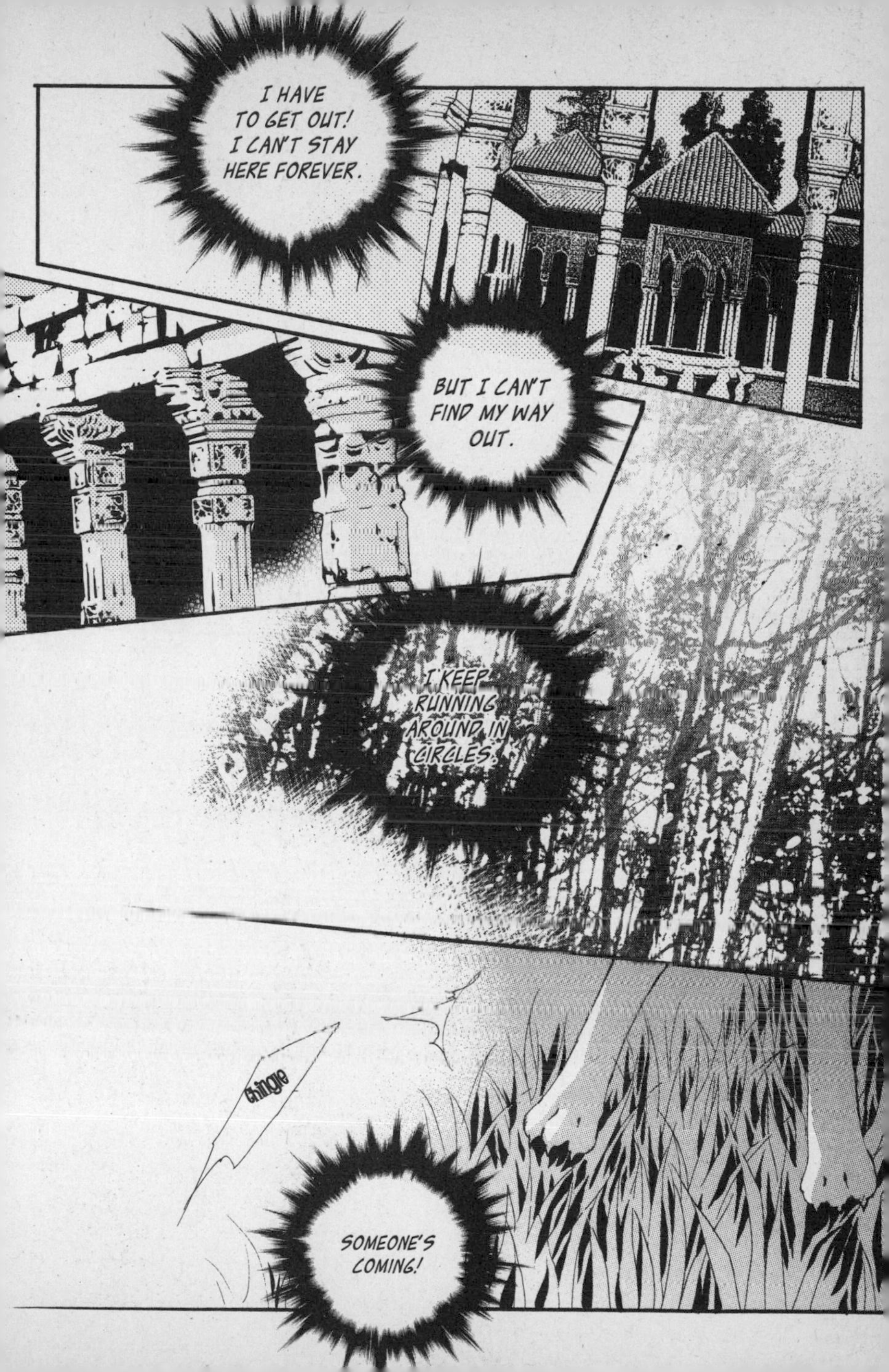
I HAVE TO GET OUT! I CAN'T STAY HERE FOREVER.
BUT I CAN'T FIND MY WAY OUT.
I KEEP RUNNING AROUND IN CIRCLES.
Chingle
SOMEONE'S COMING!

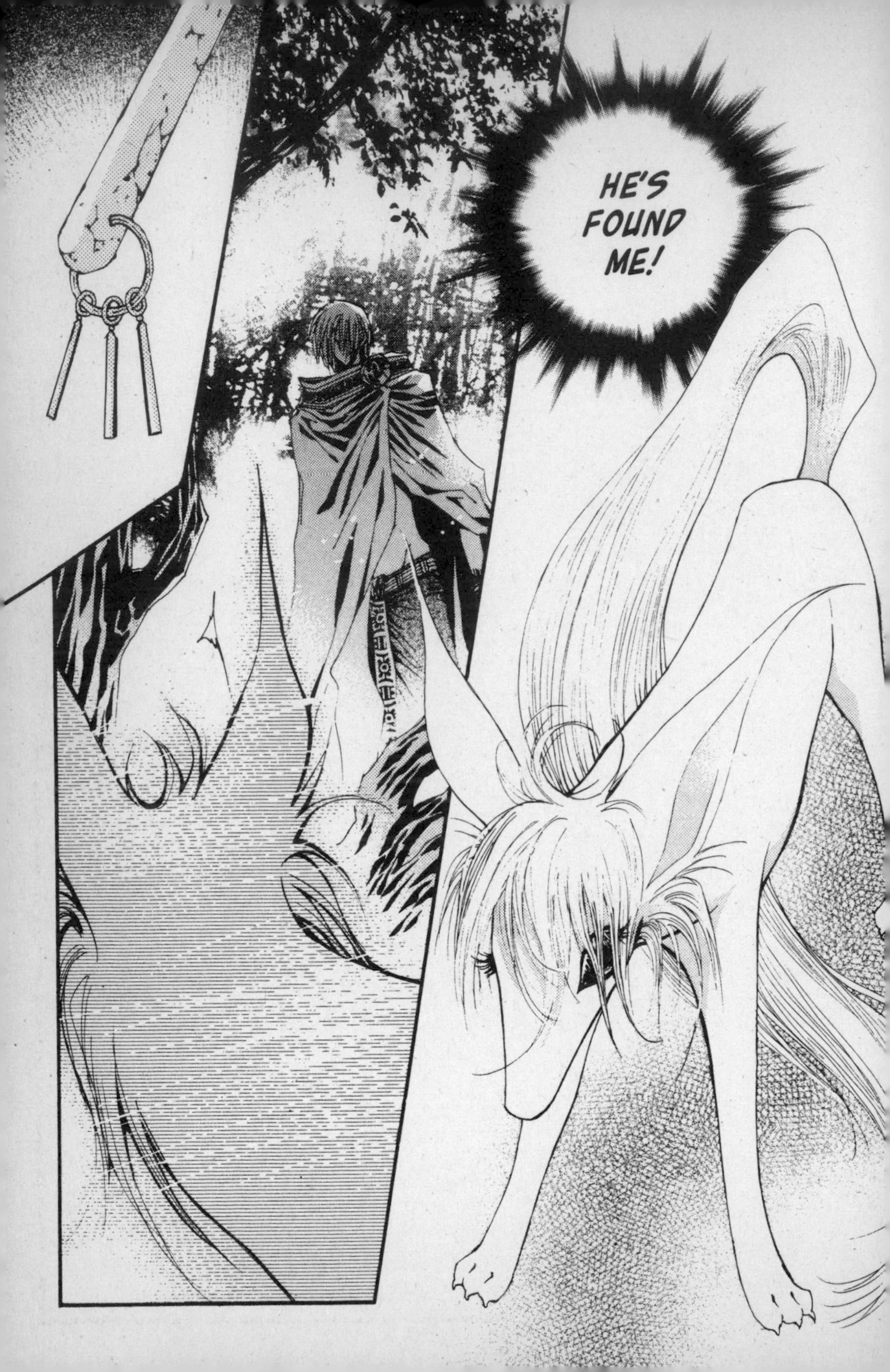
HE'S FOUND ME!

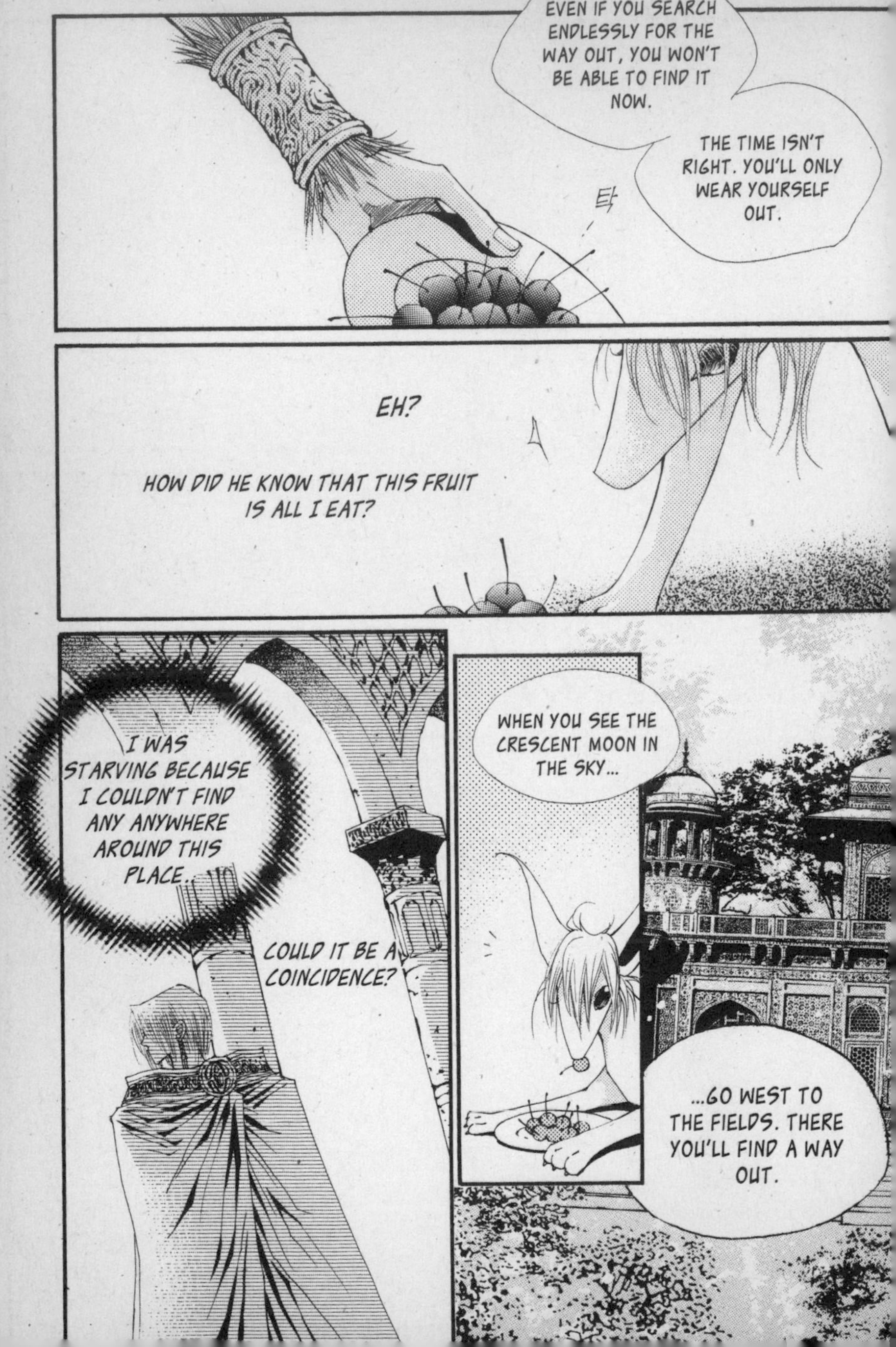
EVEN IF YOU SEARCH ENDLESSLY FOR THE WAY OUT, YOU WON'T BE ABLE TO FIND IT NOW.
THE TIME ISN'T RIGHT. YOU'LL ONLY WEAR YOURSELF OUT.
탁
EH?
HOW DID HE KNOW THAT THIS FRUIT IS ALL I EAT?
I WAS STARVING BECAUSE I COULDN'T FIND ANY ANYWHERE AROUND THIS PLACE...
COULD IT BE A COINCIDENCE?
WHEN YOU SEE THE CRESCENT MOON IN THE SKY...
...GO WEST TO THE FIELDS. THERE YOU'LL FIND A WAY OUT.

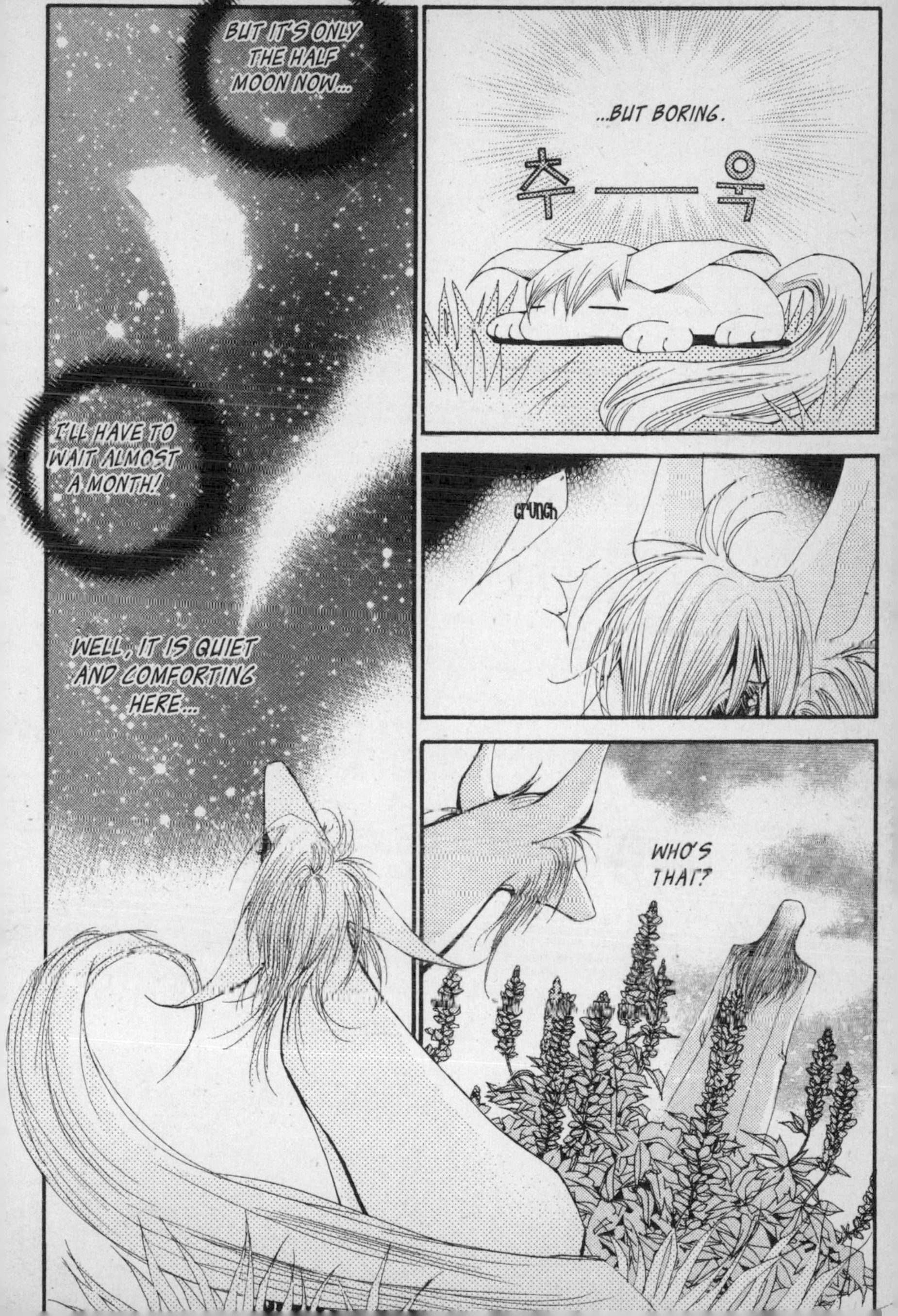
BUT IT'S ONLY THE HALF MOON NOW...
I'LL HAVE TO WAIT ALMOST A MONTH!
WELL, IT IS QUIET AND COMFORTING HERE...
...BUT BORING.
추ㅡ욱
CRUNCH
WHO'S THAT?

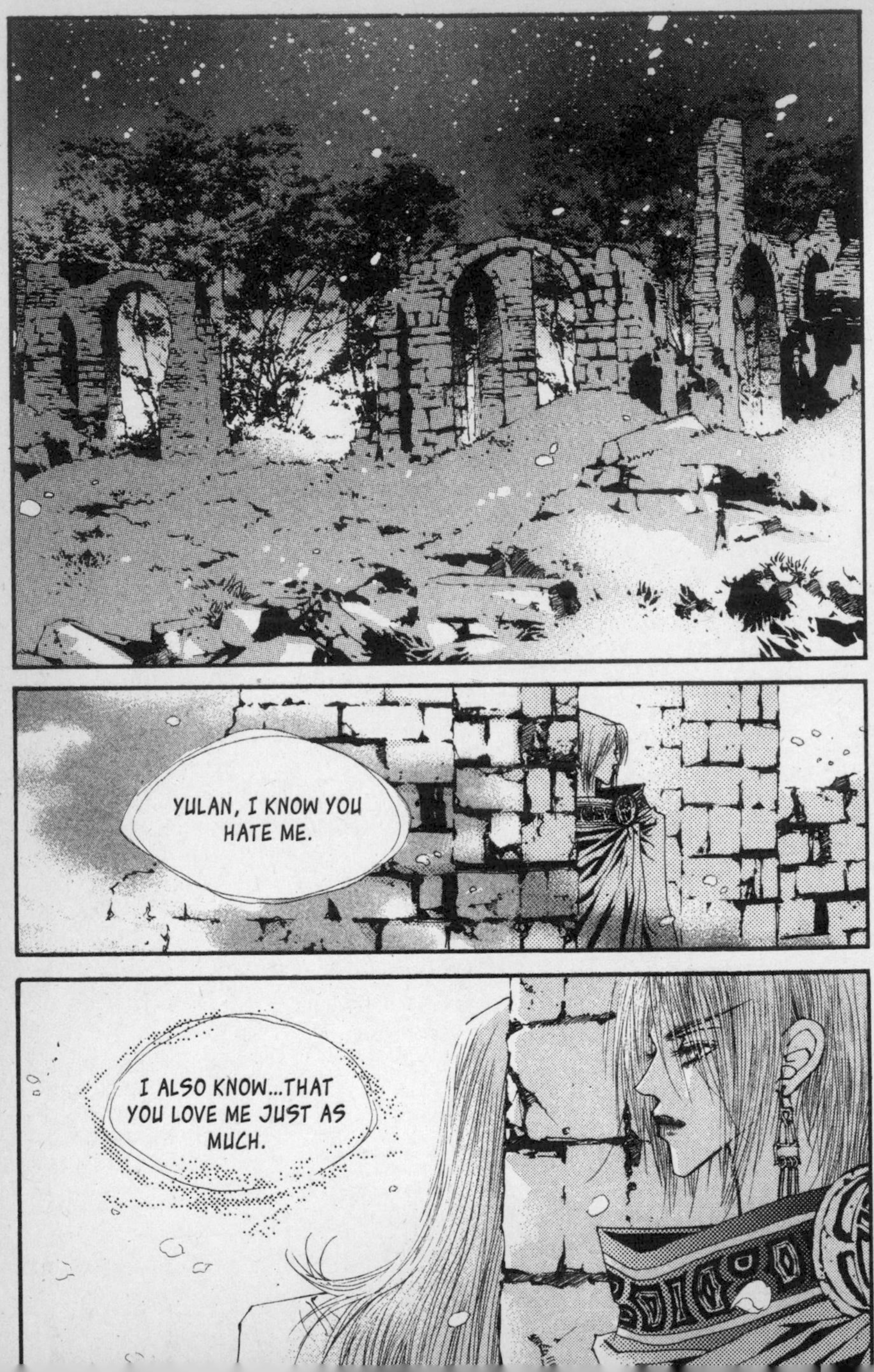
YULAN, I KNOW YOU HATE ME.
I ALSO KNOW...THAT YOU LOVE ME JUST AS MUCH.

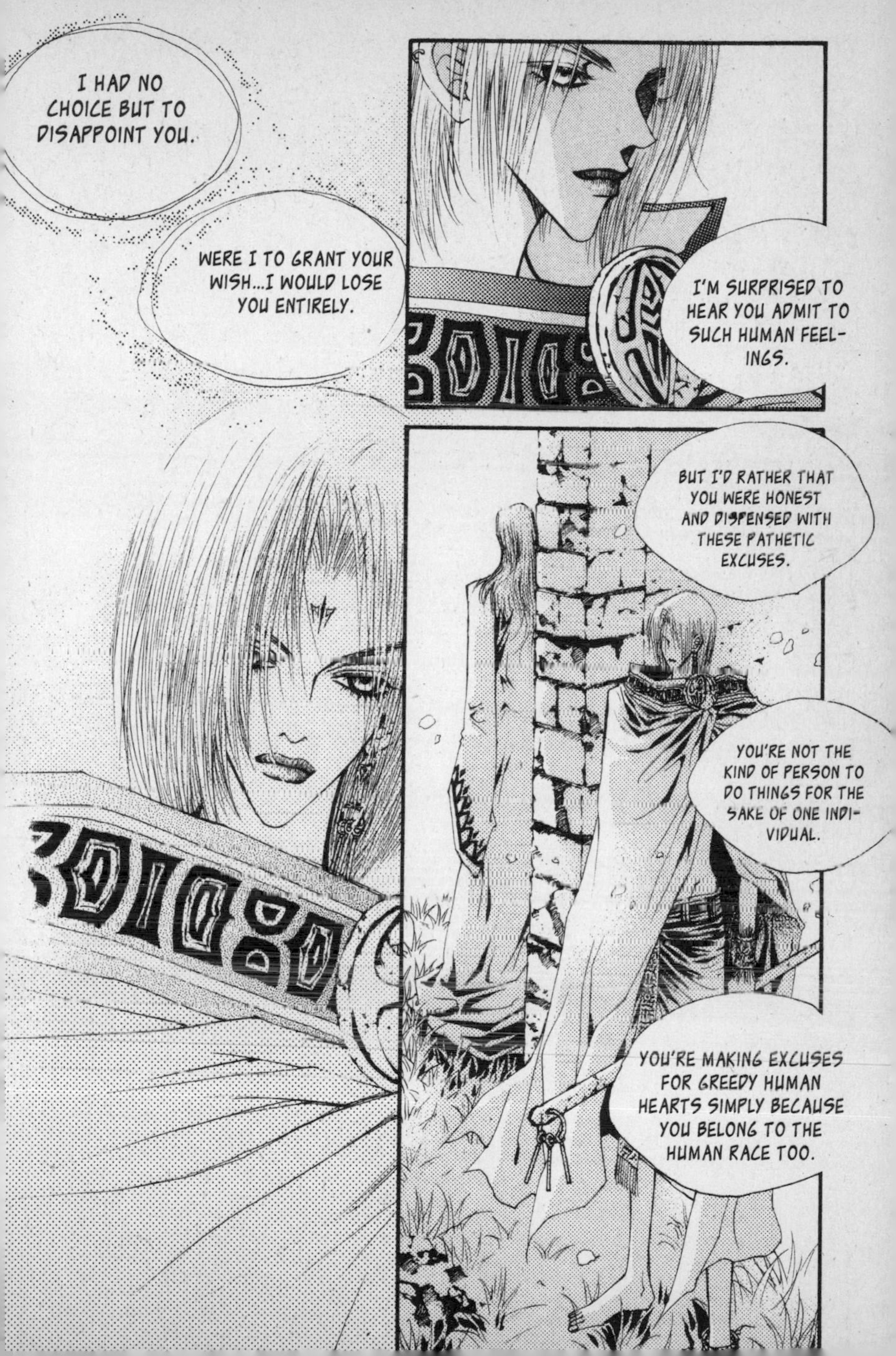
I HAD NO CHOICE BUT TO DISAPPOINT YOU.
WERE I TO GRANT YOUR WISH...I WOULD LOSE YOU ENTIRELY.
I'M SURPRISED TO HEAR YOU ADMIT TO SUCH HUMAN FEEL-INGS.
BUT I'D RATHER THAT YOU WERE HONEST AND DISPENSED WITH THESE PATHETIC EXCUSES.
YOU'RE NOT THE KIND OF PERSON TO DO THINGS FOR THE SAKE OF ONE INDI-VIDUAL.
YOU'RE MAKING EXCUSES FOR GREEDY HUMAN HEARTS SIMPLY BECAUSE YOU BELONG TO THE HUMAN RACE TOO.

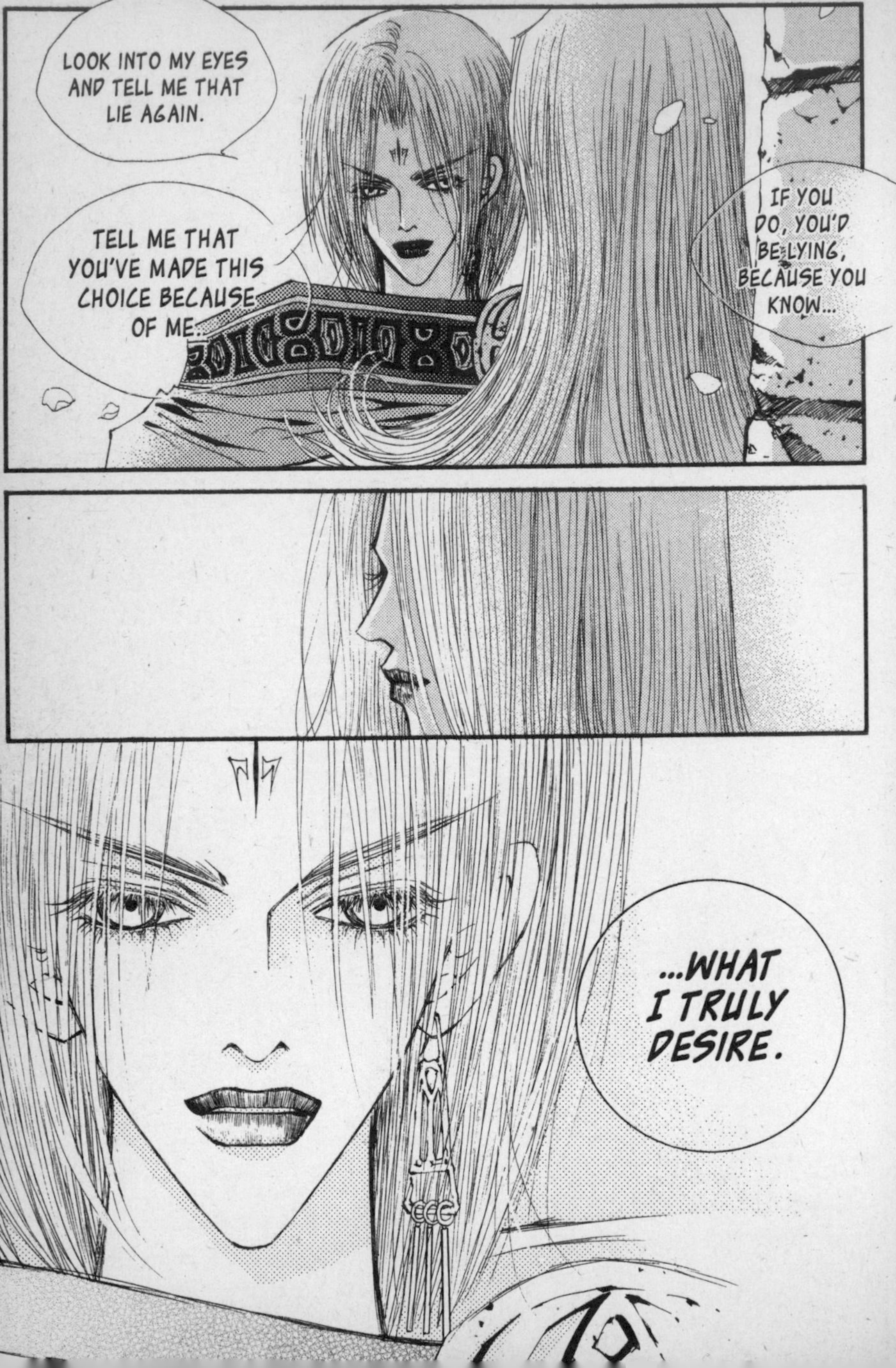
LOOK INTO MY EYES AND TELL ME THAT LIE AGAIN.
TELL ME THAT YOU'VE MADE THIS CHOICE BECAUSE OF ME.
IF YOU DO, YOU'D BE LYING, BECAUSE YOU KNOW...
...WHAT I TRULY DESIRE.

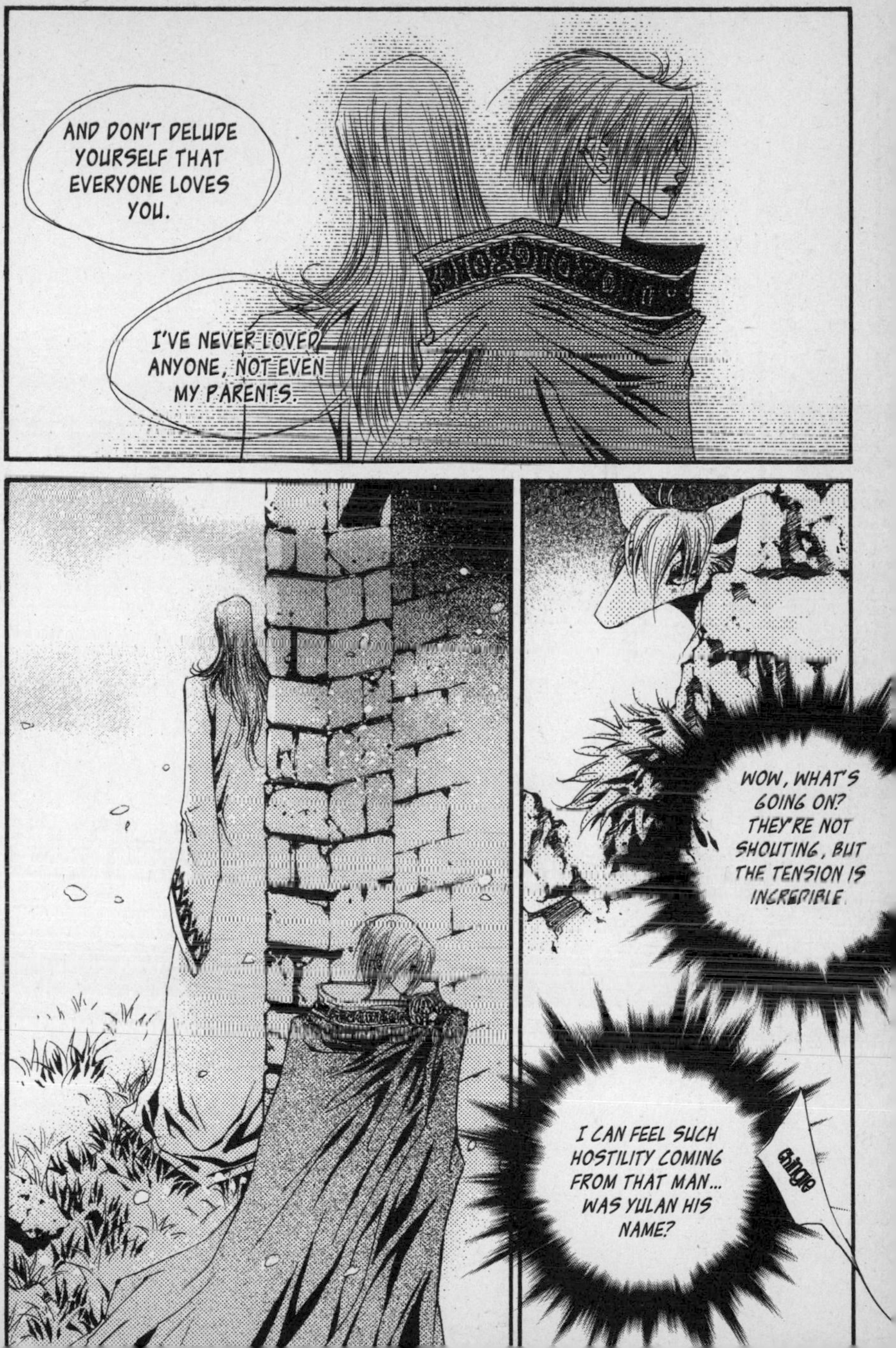
AND DON'T DELUDE YOURSELF THAT EVERYONE LOVES YOU.
I'VE NEVER LOVED ANYONE, NOT EVEN MY PARENTS.
WOW, WHAT'S GOING ON? THEY'RE NOT SHOUTING, BUT THE TENSION IS INCREDIBLE.
I CAN FEEL SUCH HOSTILITY COMING FROM THAT MAN... WAS YULAN HIS NAME?
cringe

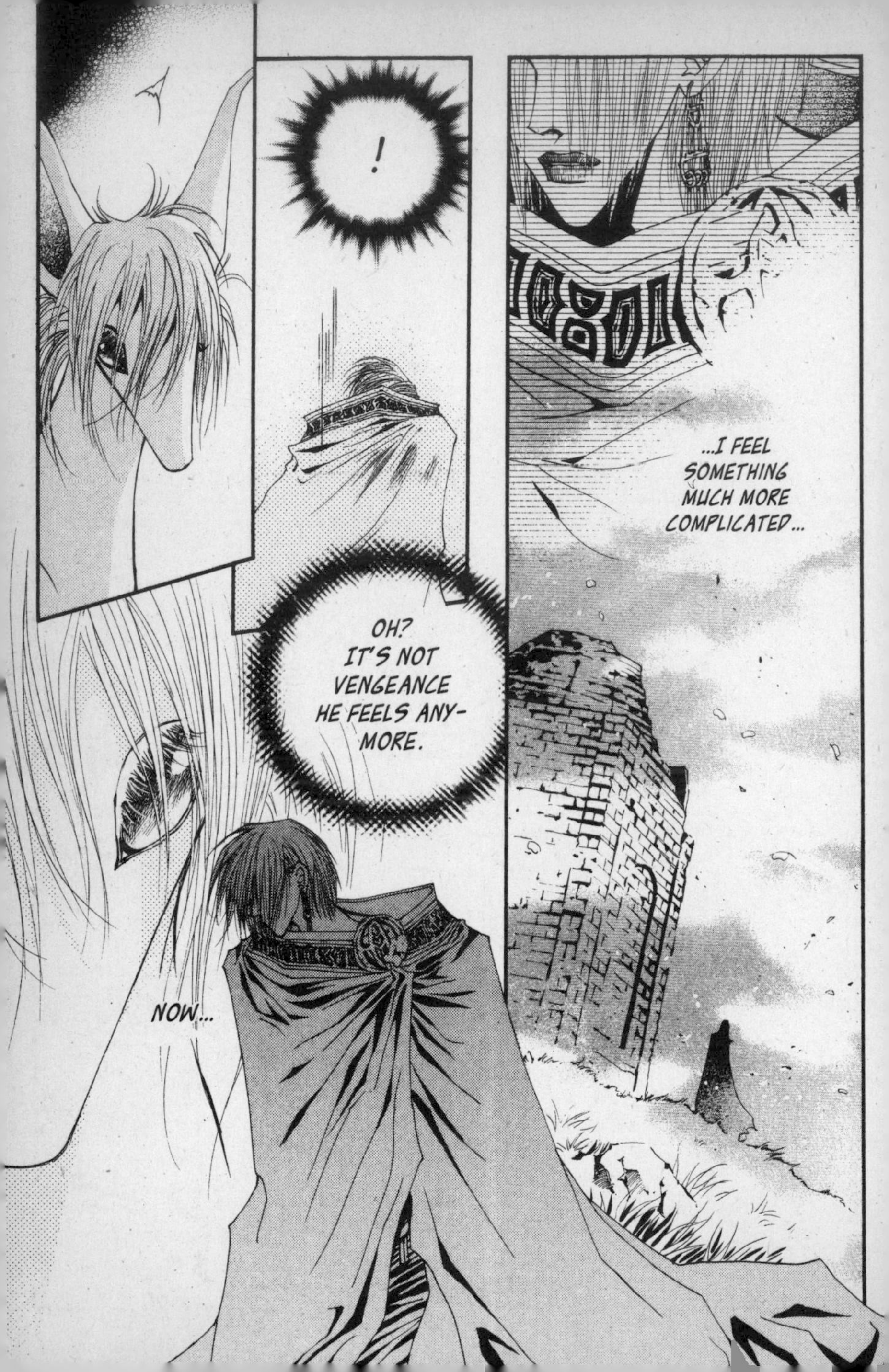
...I FEEL SOMETHING MUCH MORE COMPLICATED...
!
OH? IT'S NOT VENGEANCE HE FEELS ANY-MORE.
NOW...

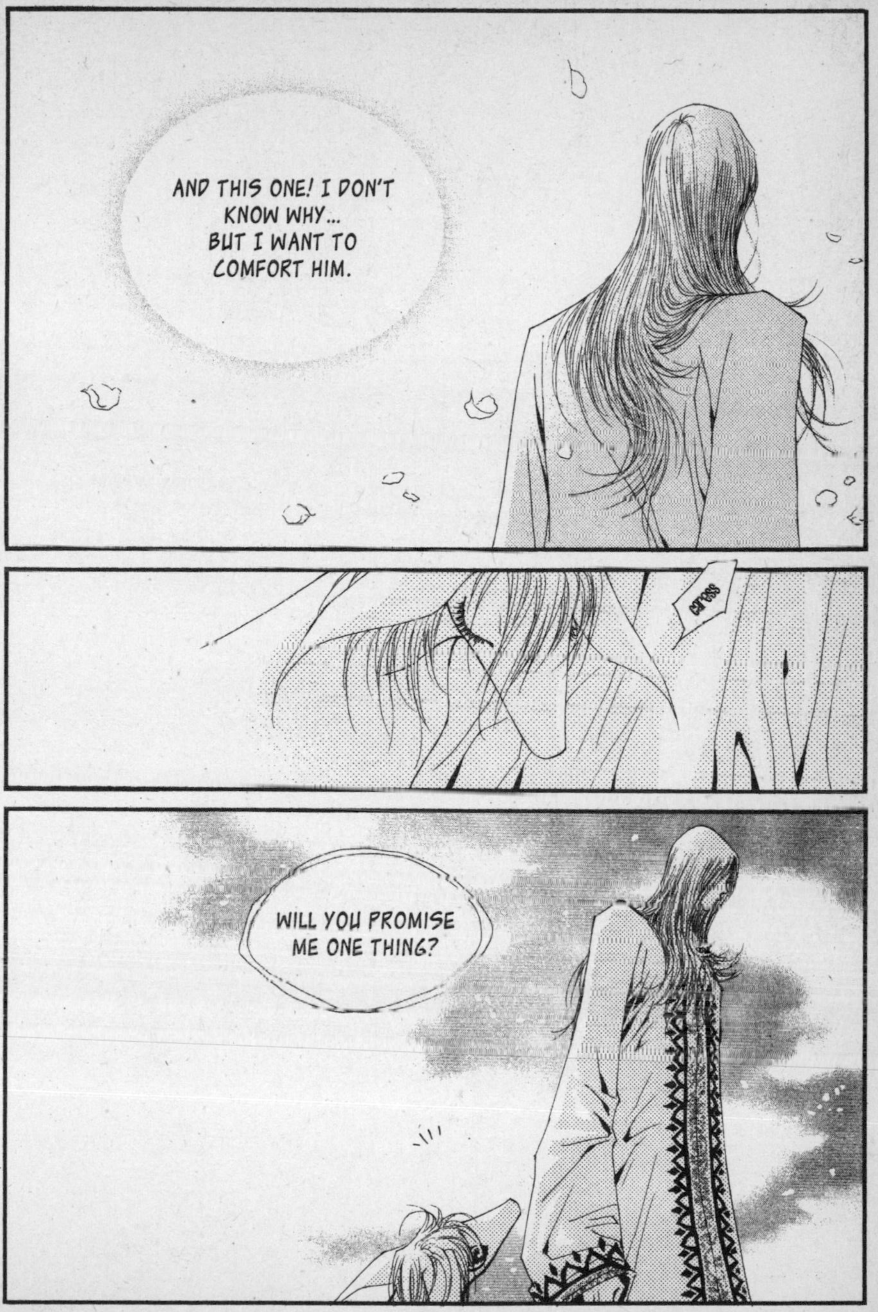
AND THIS ONE! I DON'T KNOW WHY... BUT I WANT TO COMFORT HIM.
caress
WILL YOU PROMISE ME ONE THING?

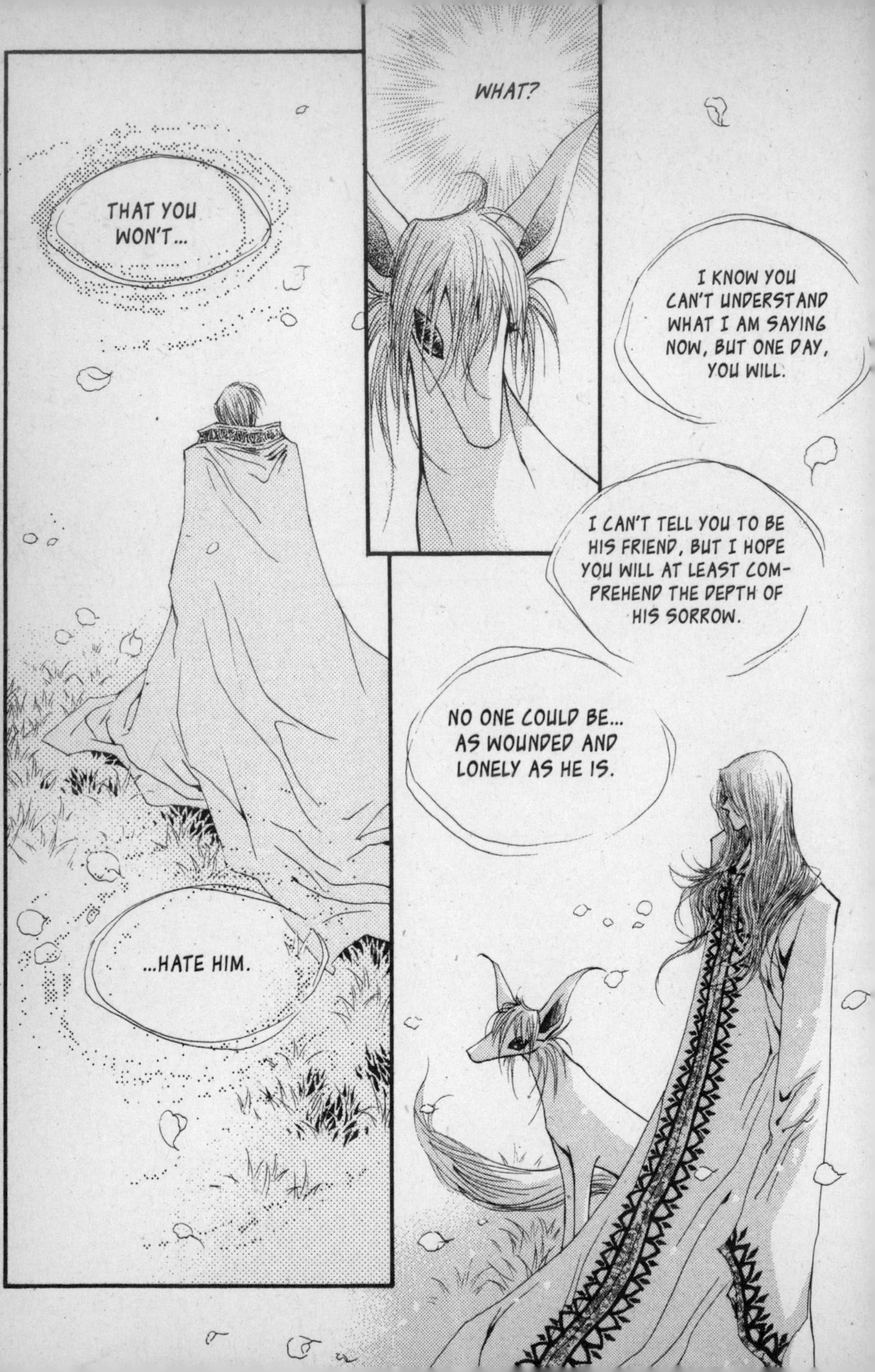
THAT YOU WON'T...
...HATE HIM.
WHAT?
I KNOW YOU CAN'T UNDERSTAND WHAT I AM SAYING NOW, BUT ONE DAY, YOU WILL.
I CAN'T TELL YOU TO BE HIS FRIEND, BUT I HOPE YOU WILL AT LEAST COMPREHEND THE DEPTH OF HIS SORROW.
NO ONE COULD BE... AS WOUNDED AND LONELY AS HE IS.

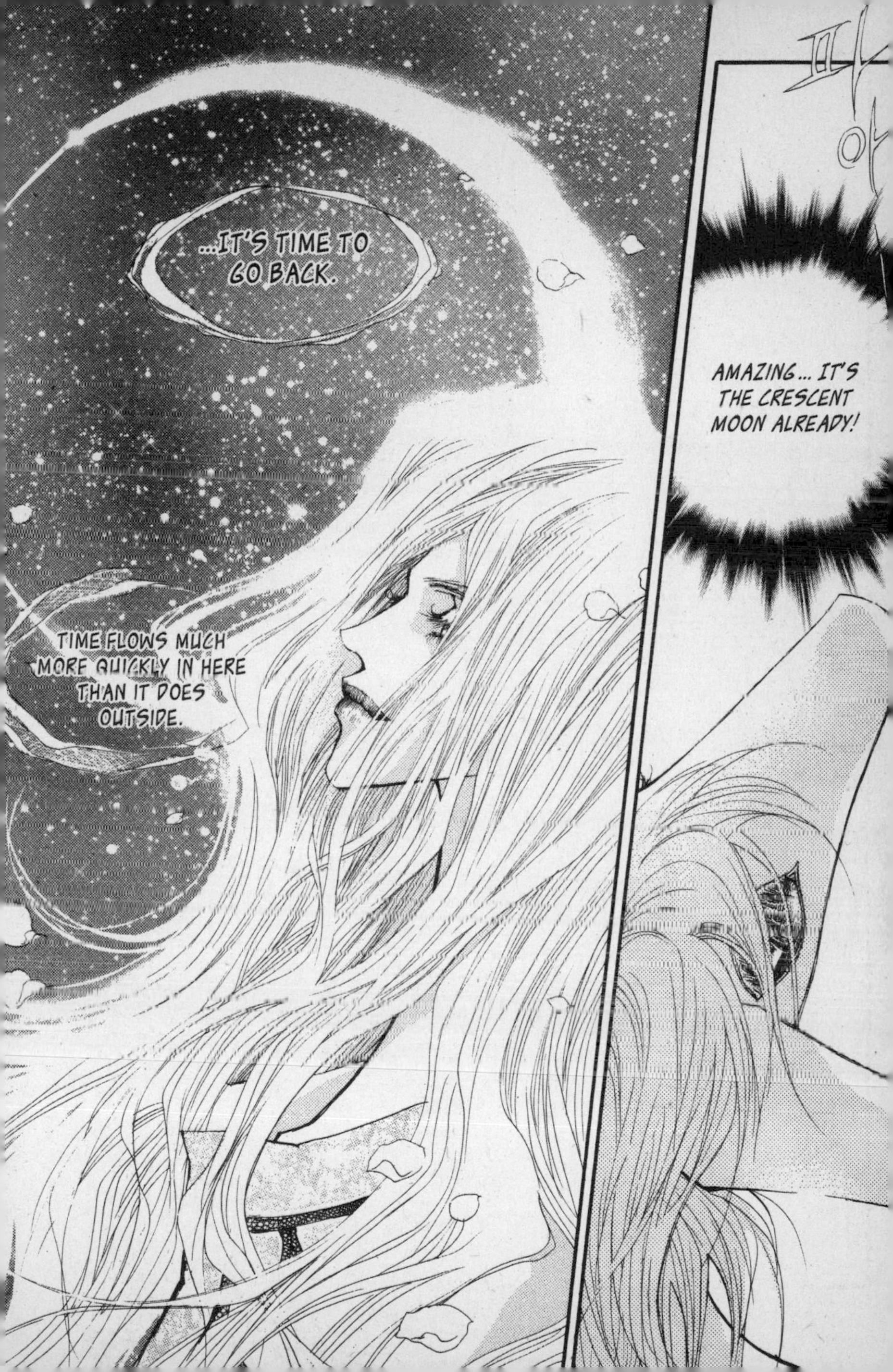
AMAZING... IT'S THE CRESCENT MOON ALREADY!
...IT'S TIME TO GO BACK.
TIME FLOWS MUCH MORE QUICKLY IN HERE THAN IT DOES OUTSIDE.

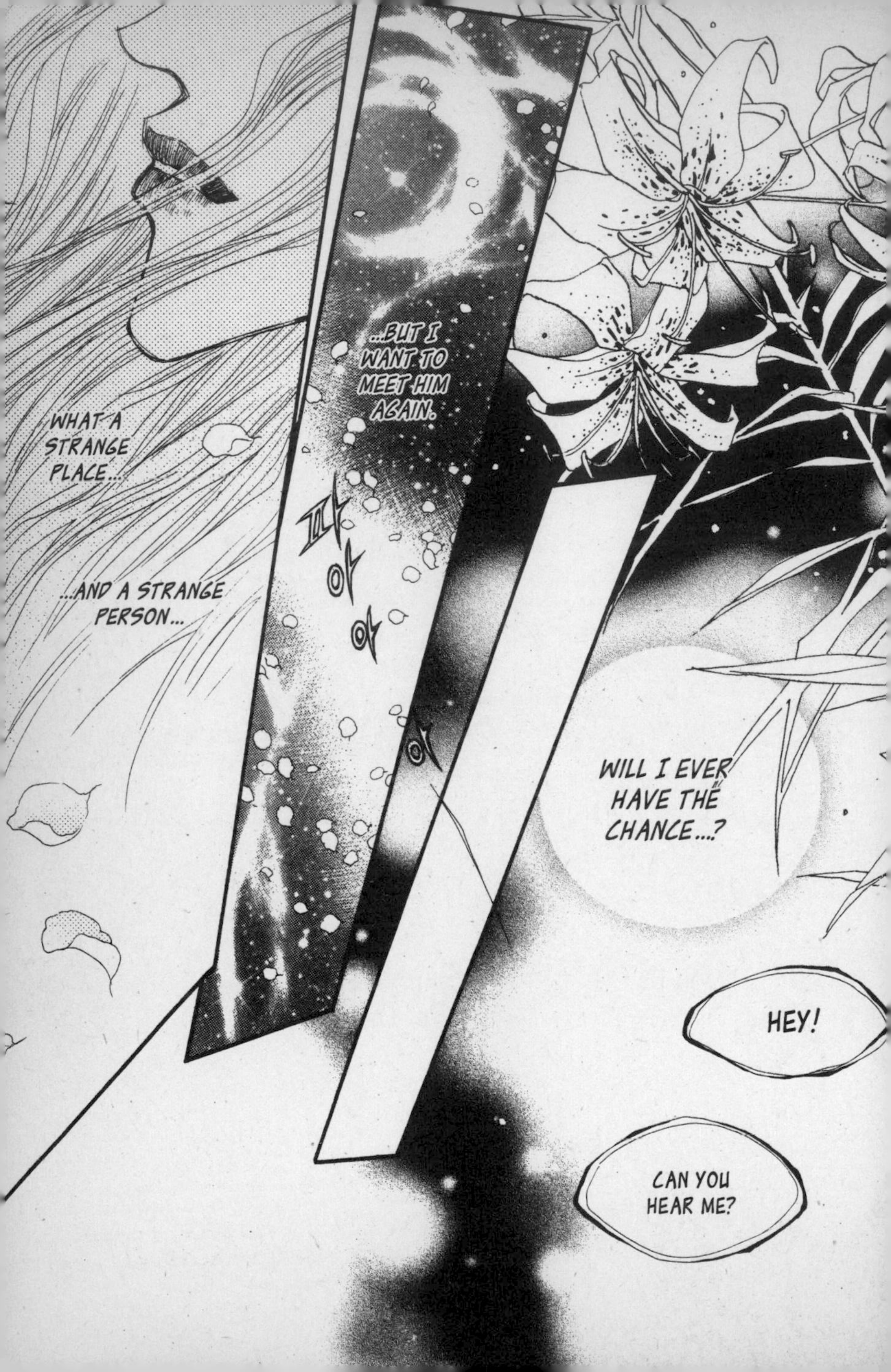
WHAT A STRANGE PLACE...
...AND A STRANGE PERSON...
...BUT I WANT TO MEET HIM AGAIN.
WILL I EVER HAVE THE CHANCE...?
HEY!
CAN YOU HEAR ME?

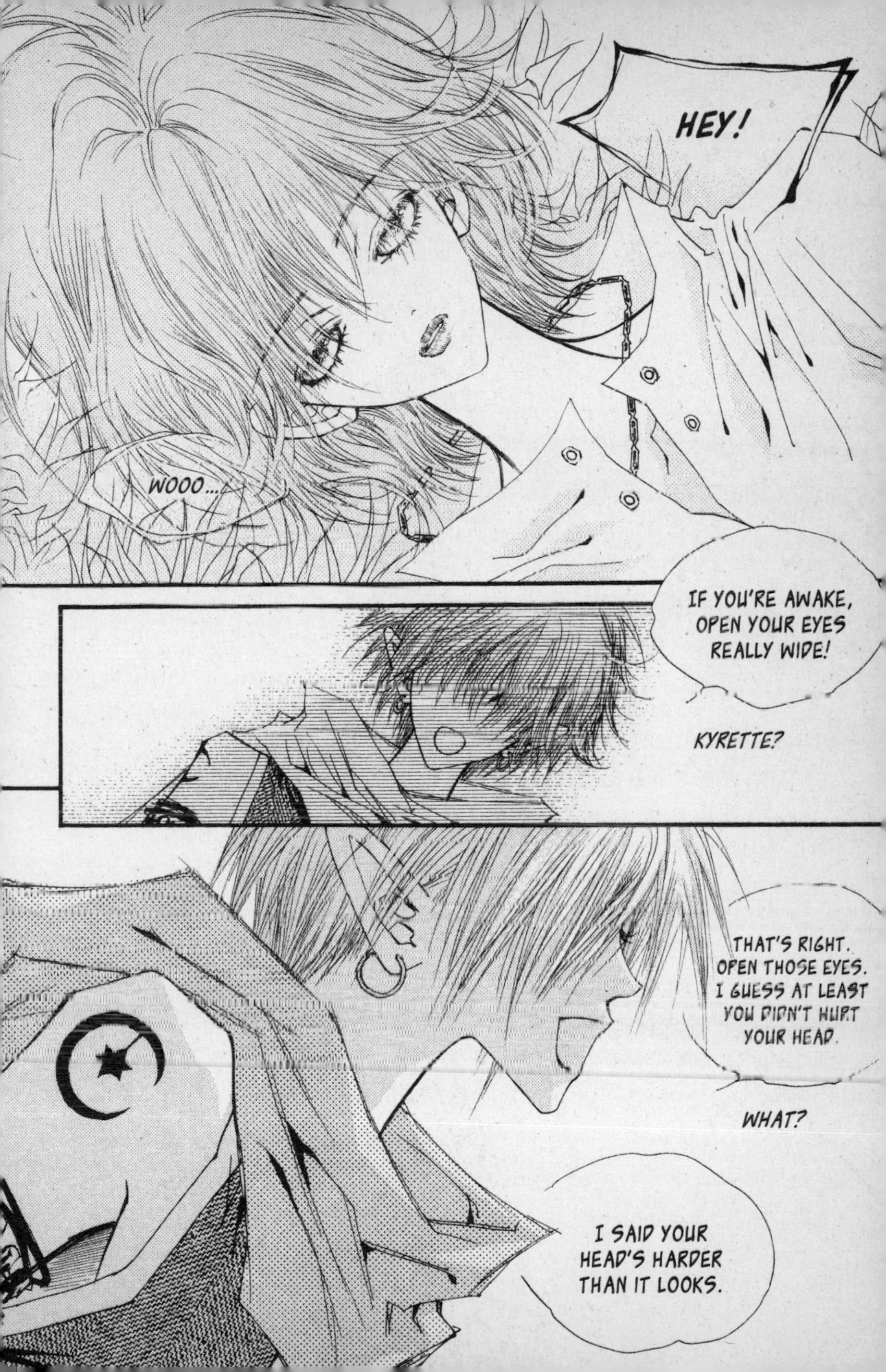
HEY!
WOOO...
IF YOU'RE AWAKE, OPEN YOUR EYES REALLY WIDE!
KYRETTE?
THAT'S RIGHT. OPEN THOSE EYES. I GUESS AT LEAST YOU DIDN'T HURT YOUR HEAD.
WHAT?
I SAID YOUR HEAD'S HARDER THAN IT LOOKS.

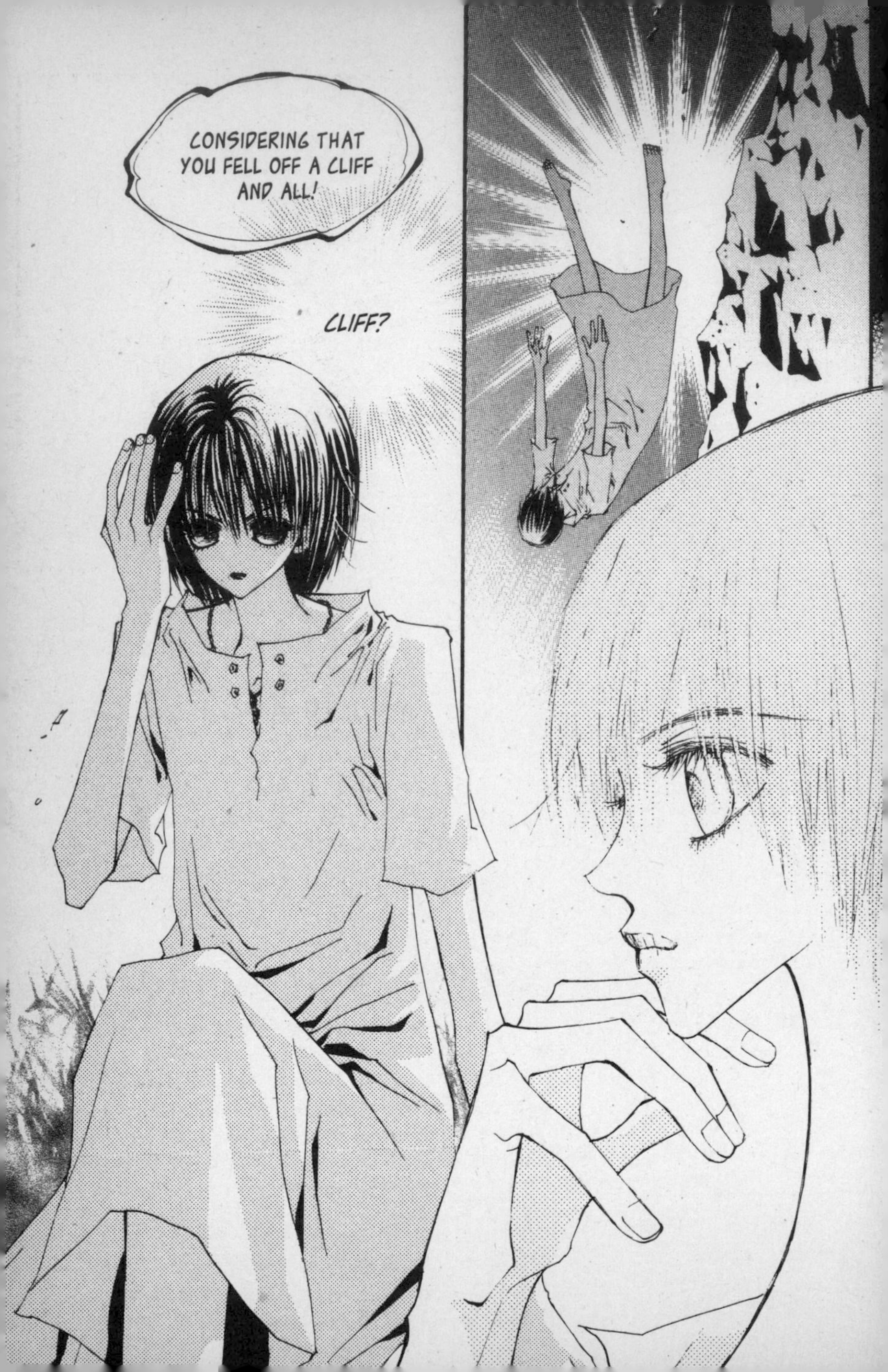
CONSIDERING THAT YOU FELL OFF A CLIFF AND ALL!
CLIFF?

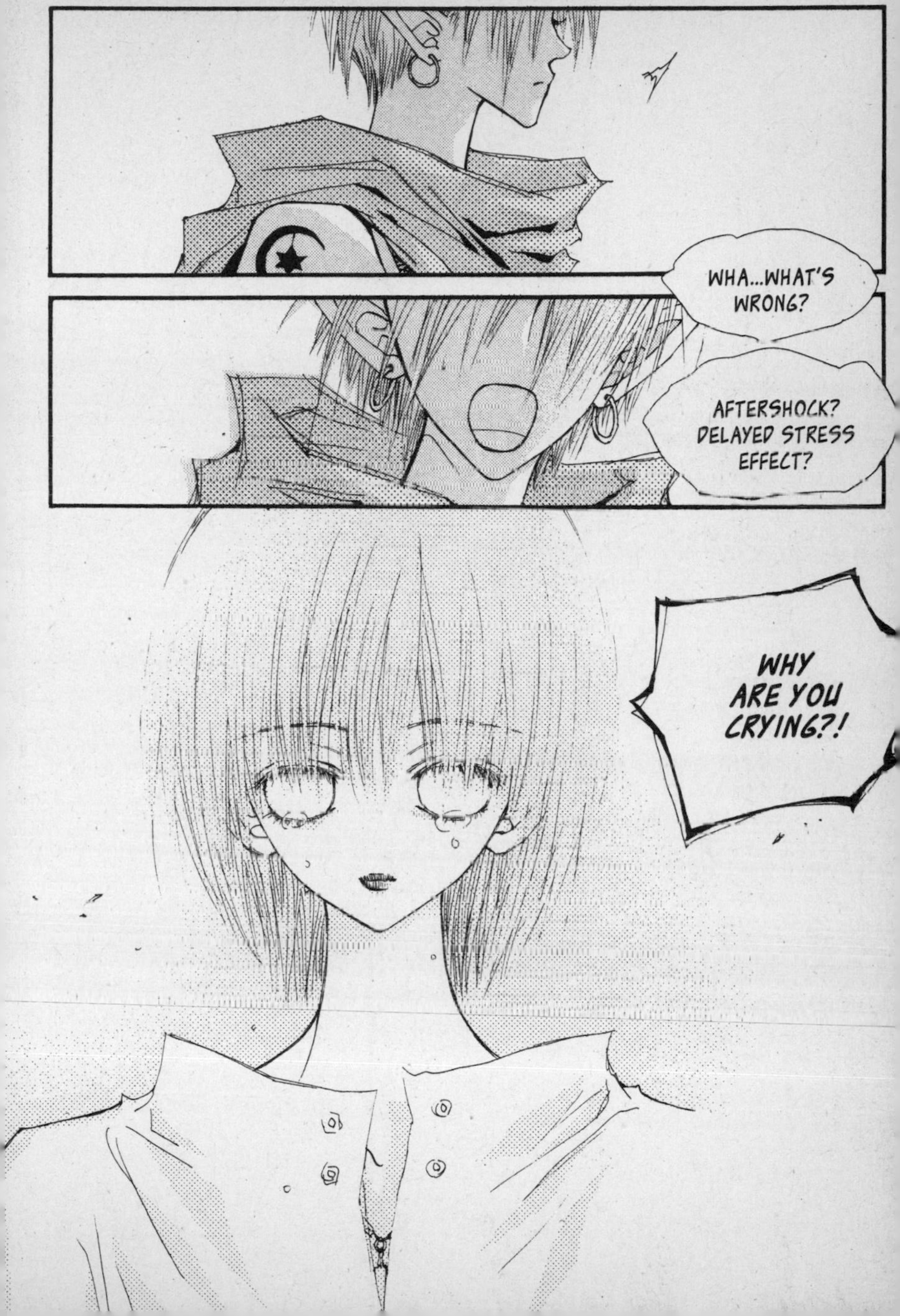
WHA...WHAT'S WRONG?
AFTERSHOCK? DELAYED STRESS EFFECT?
WHY ARE YOU CRYING?!

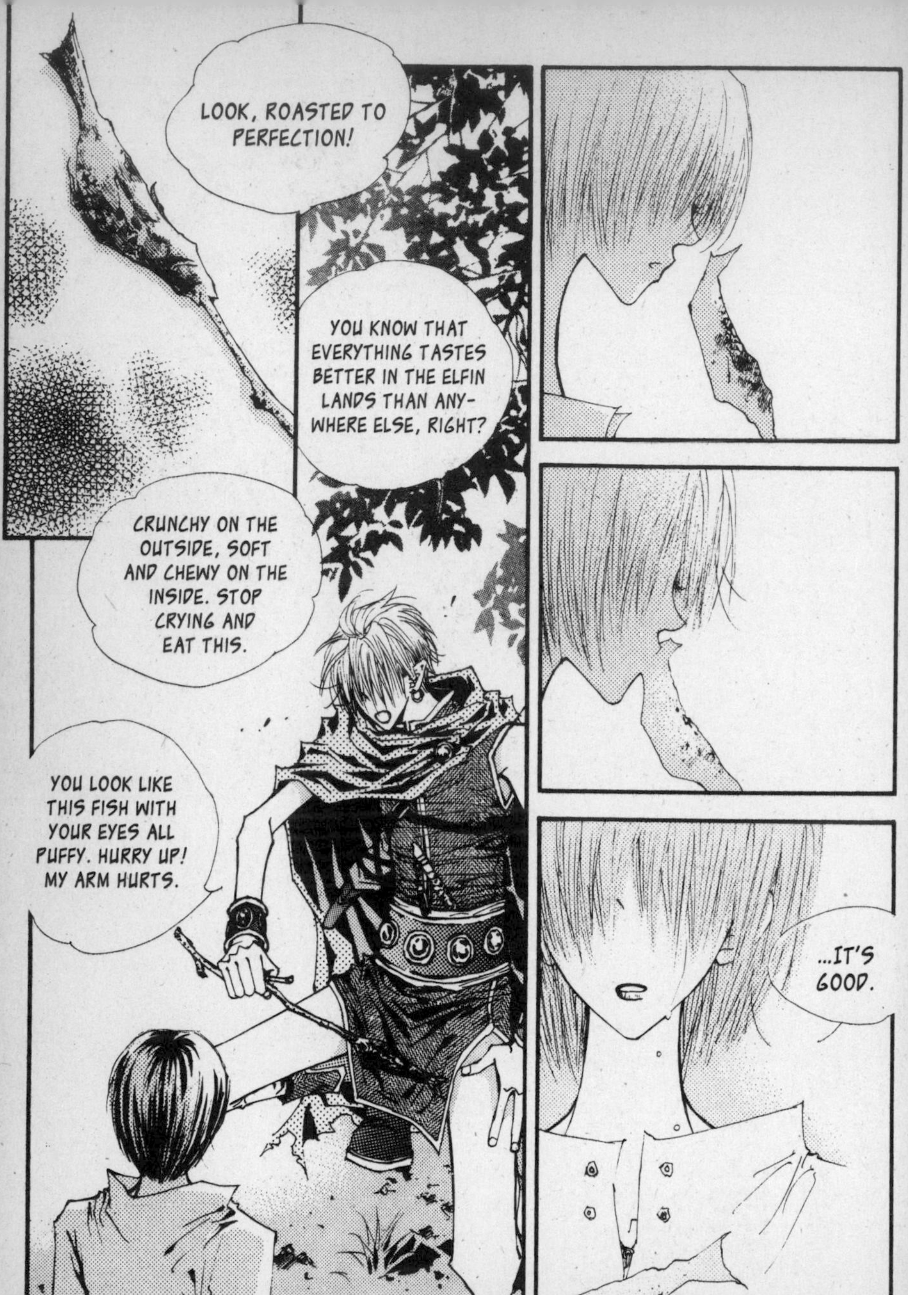
LOOK, ROASTED TO PERFECTION!
YOU KNOW THAT EVERYTHING TASTES BETTER IN THE ELFIN LANDS THAN ANY-WHERE ELSE, RIGHT?
CRUNCHY ON THE OUTSIDE, SOFT AND CHEWY ON THE INSIDE. STOP CRYING AND EAT THIS.
YOU LOOK LIKE THIS FISH WITH YOUR EYES ALL PUFFY. HURRY UP! MY ARM HURTS.
...IT'S GOOD.

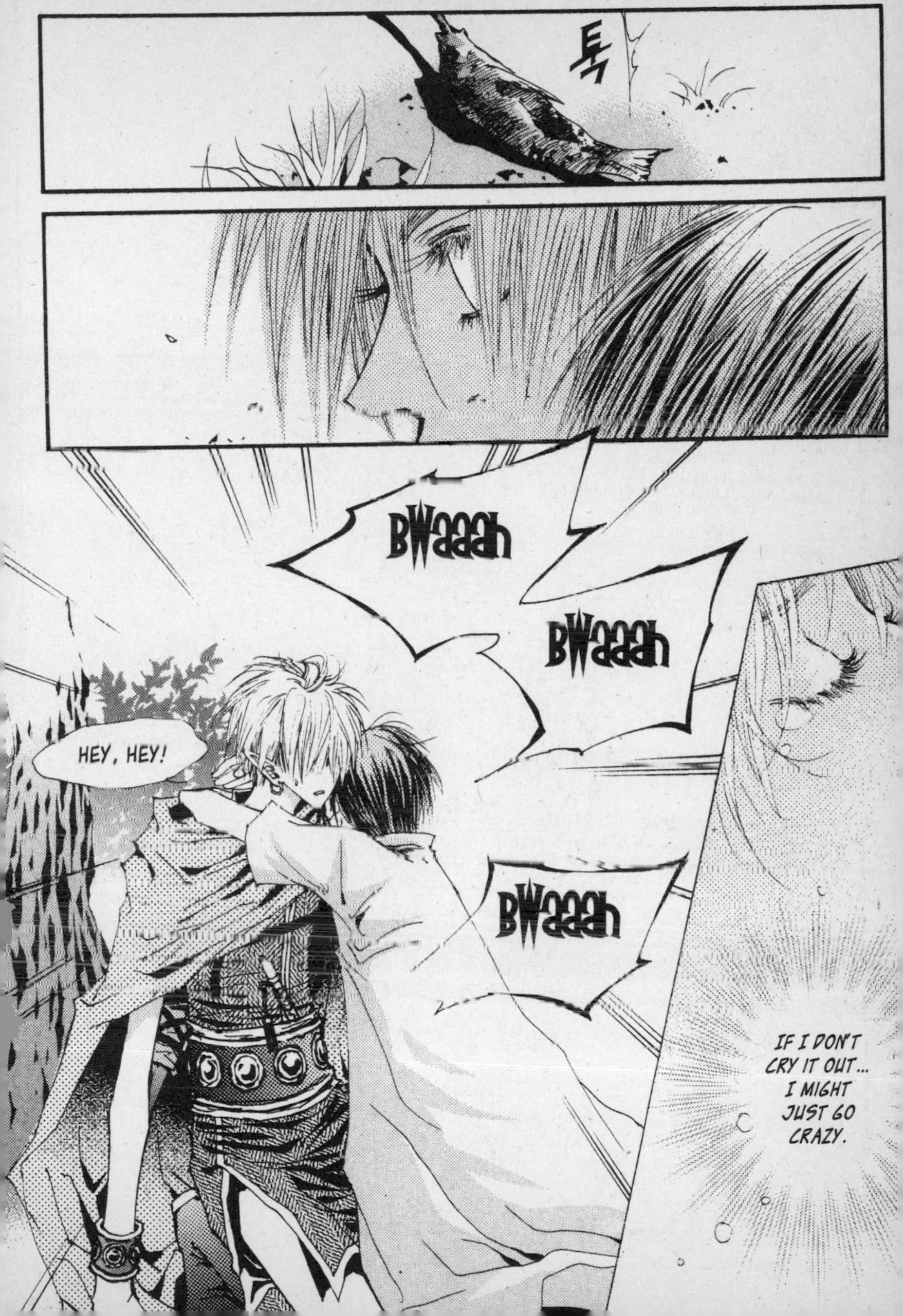
톡
BWAAAH
BWAAAH
HEY, HEY!
BWAAAH
IF I DON'T CRY IT OUT... I MIGHT JUST GO CRAZY.

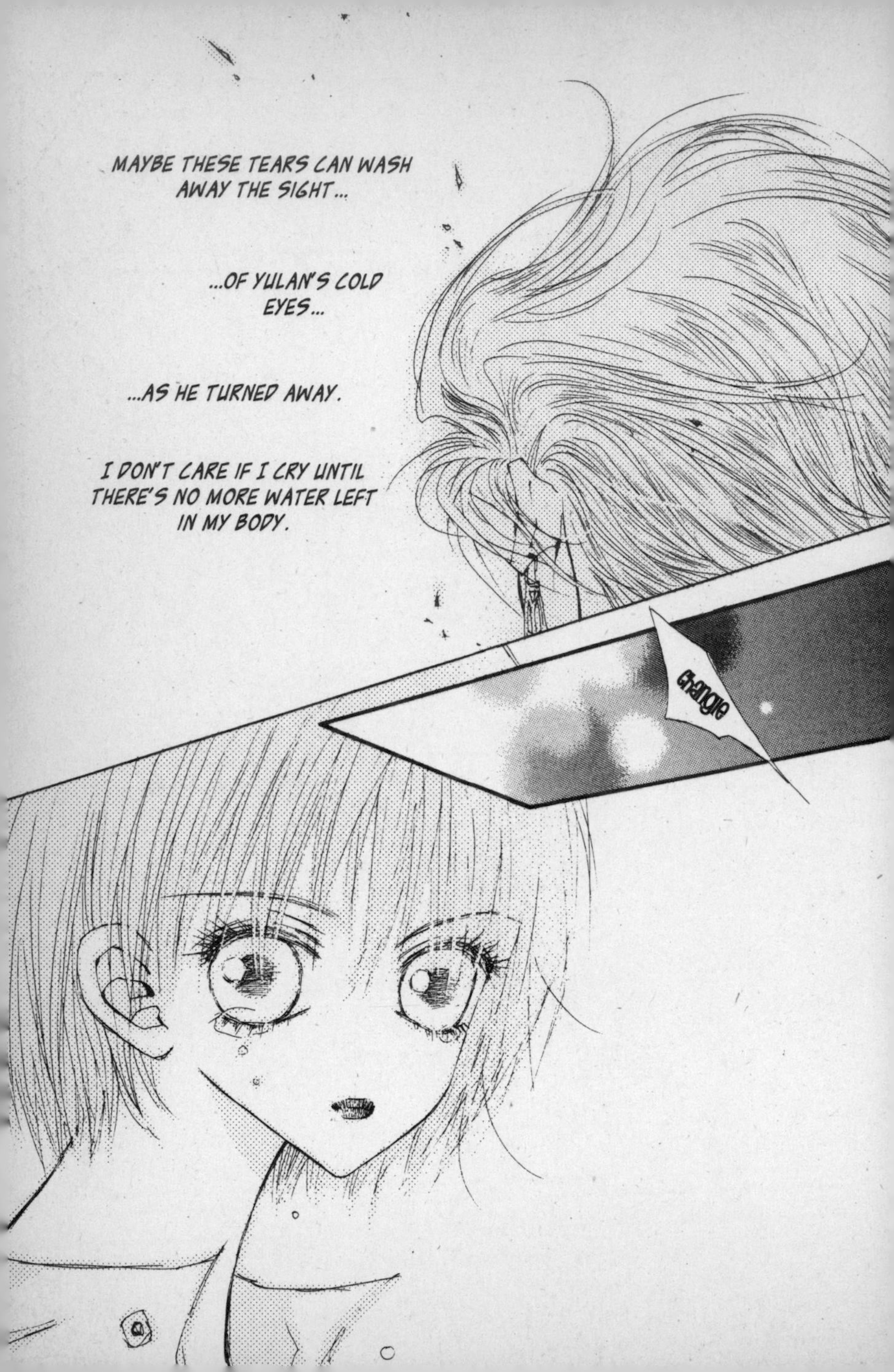
MAYBE THESE TEARS CAN WASH AWAY THE SIGHT...
...OF YULAN'S COLD EYES...
...AS HE TURNED AWAY.
I DON'T CARE IF I CRY UNTIL THERE'S NO MORE WATER LEFT IN MY BODY.
changle

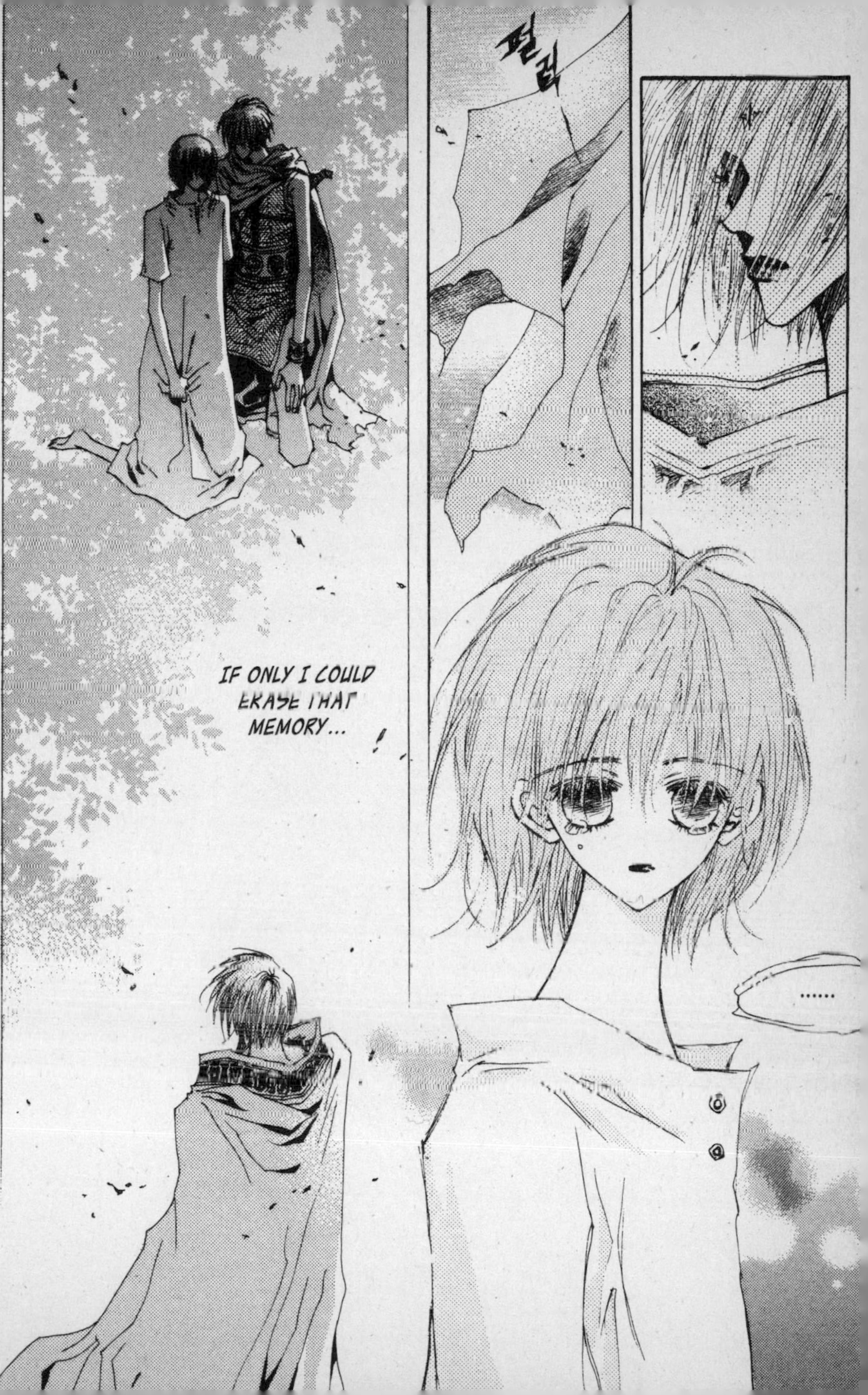
펄럭
IF ONLY I COULD ERASE THAT MEMORY...
......

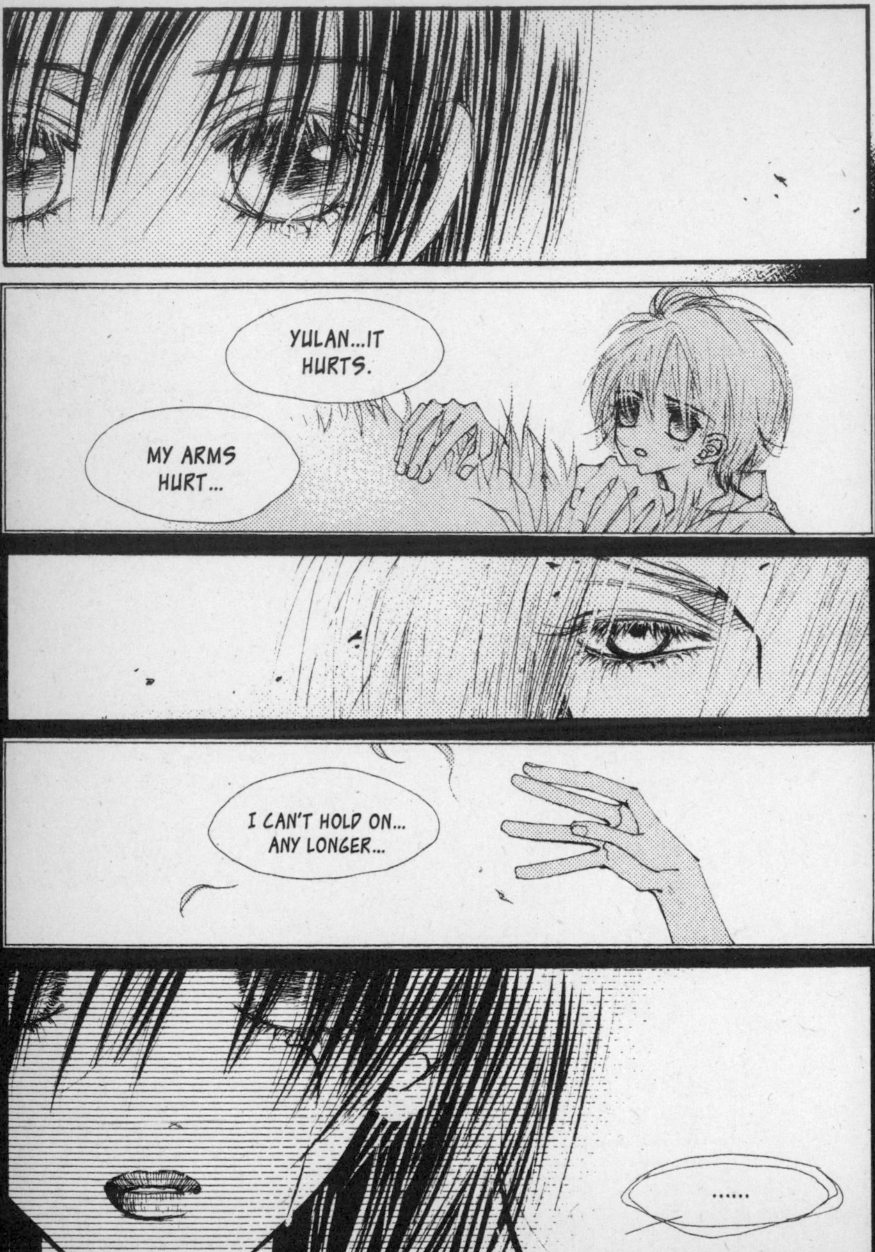
YULAN...IT HURTS.
MY ARMS HURT...
I CAN'T HOLD ON... ANY LONGER...
......

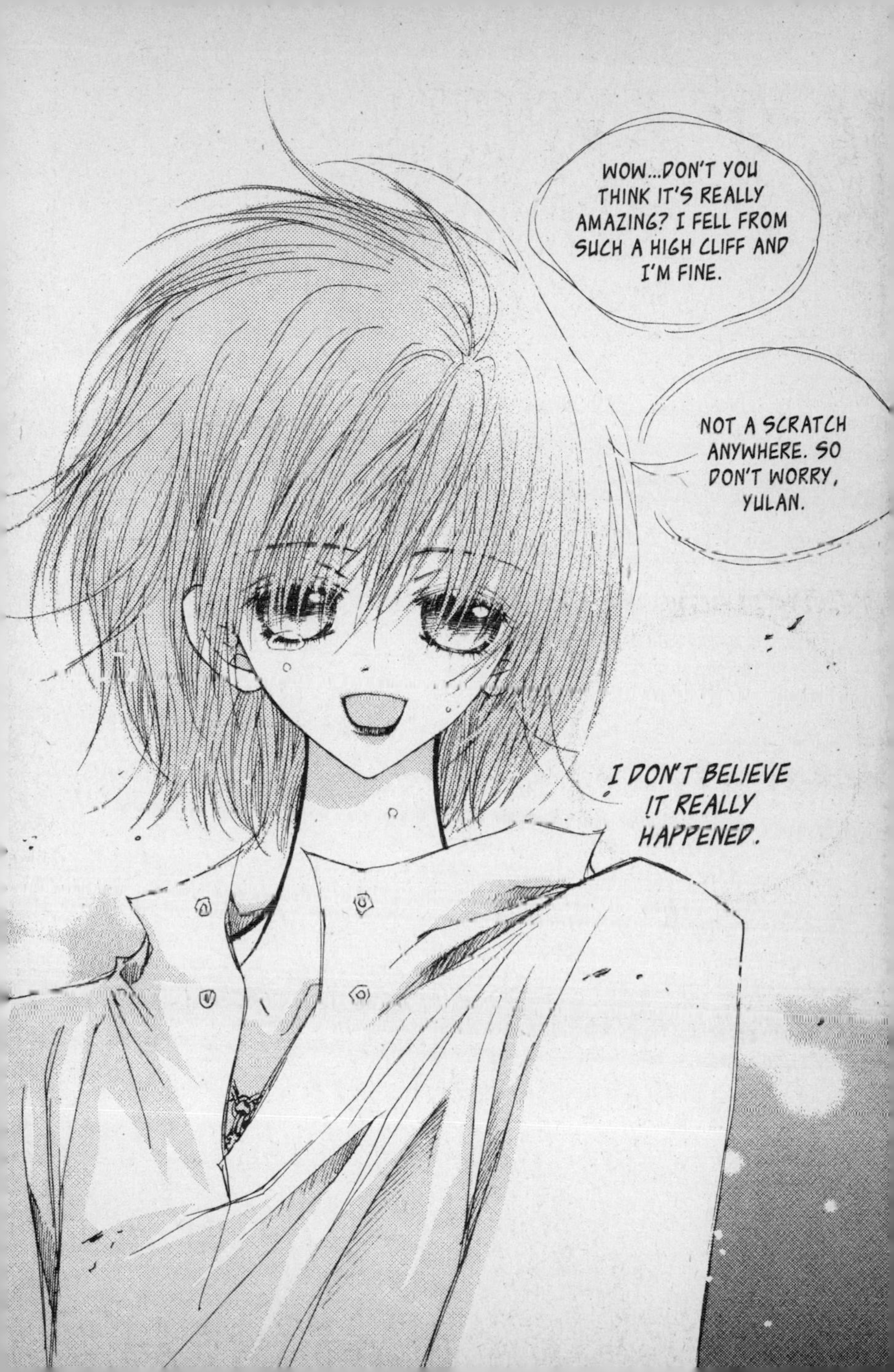
WOW...DON'T YOU THINK IT'S REALLY AMAZING? I FELL FROM SUCH A HIGH CLIFF AND I'M FINE.
NOT A SCRATCH ANYWHERE. SO DON'T WORRY, YULAN.
I DON'T BELIEVE IT REALLY HAPPENED.

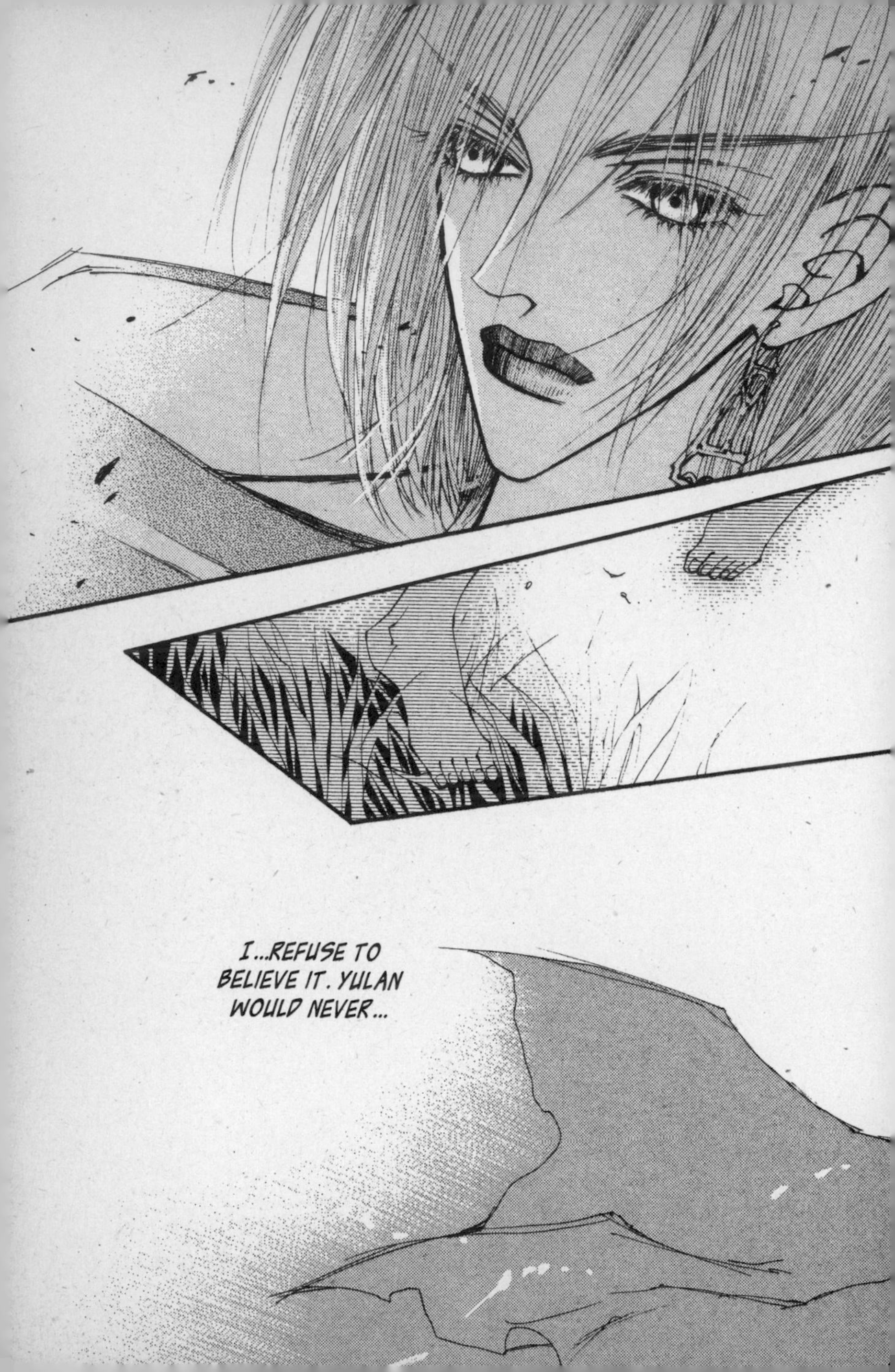
F..
I...REFUSE TO BELIEVE IT. YULAN WOULD NEVER...

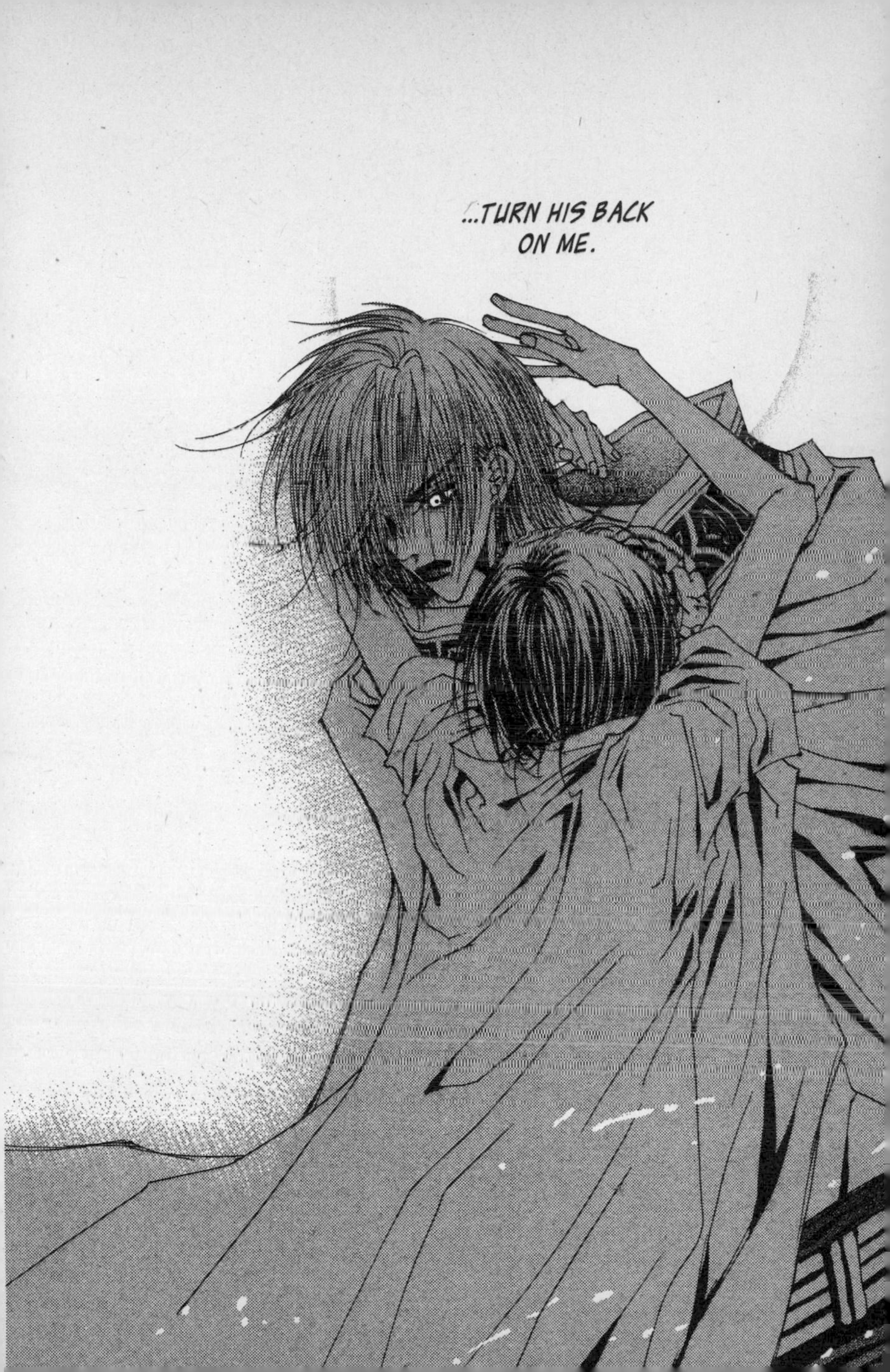
...TURN HIS BACK ON ME.

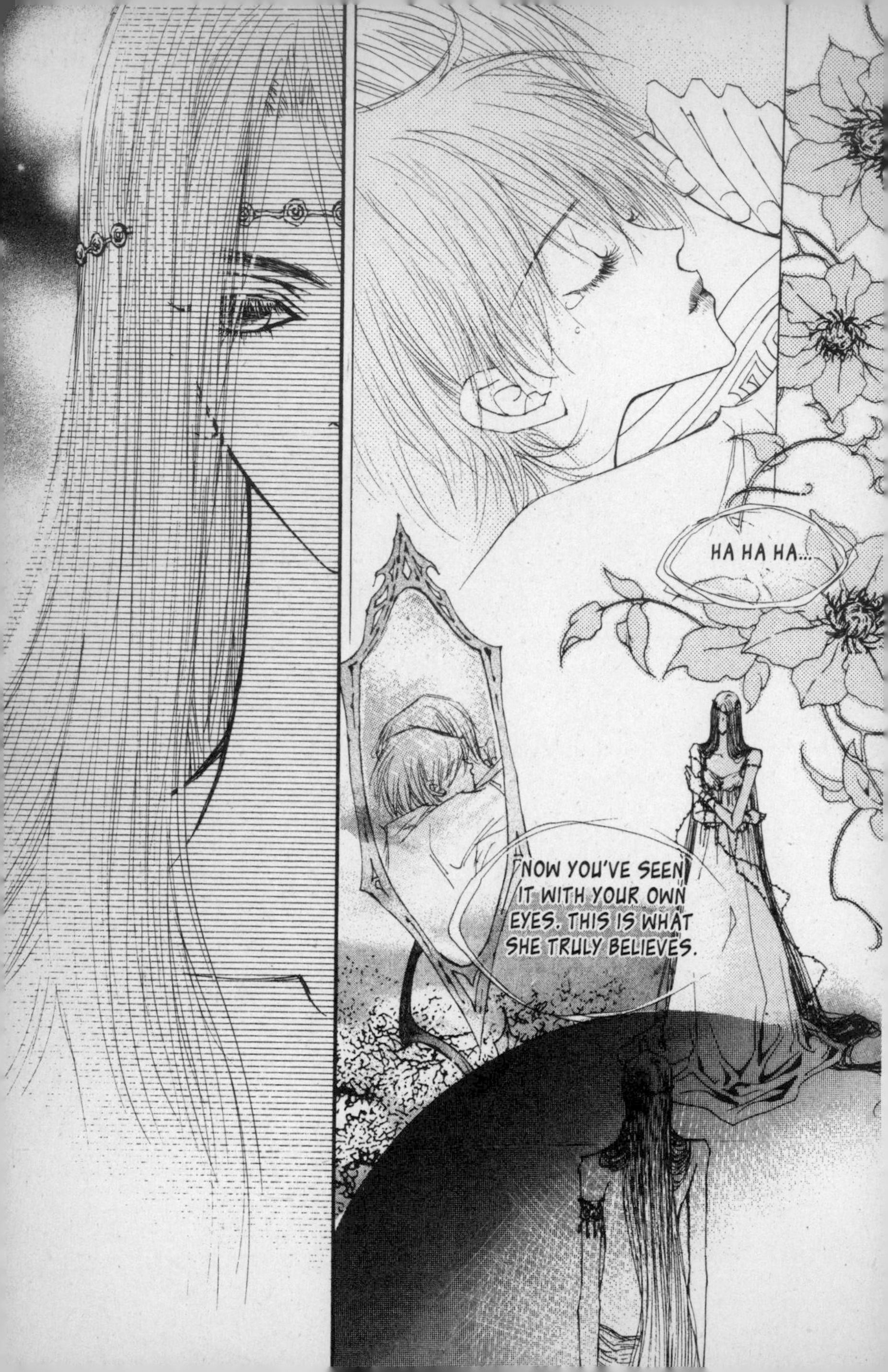
HA HA HA...
NOW YOU'VE SEEN IT WITH YOUR OWN EYES. THIS IS WHAT SHE TRULY BELIEVES.

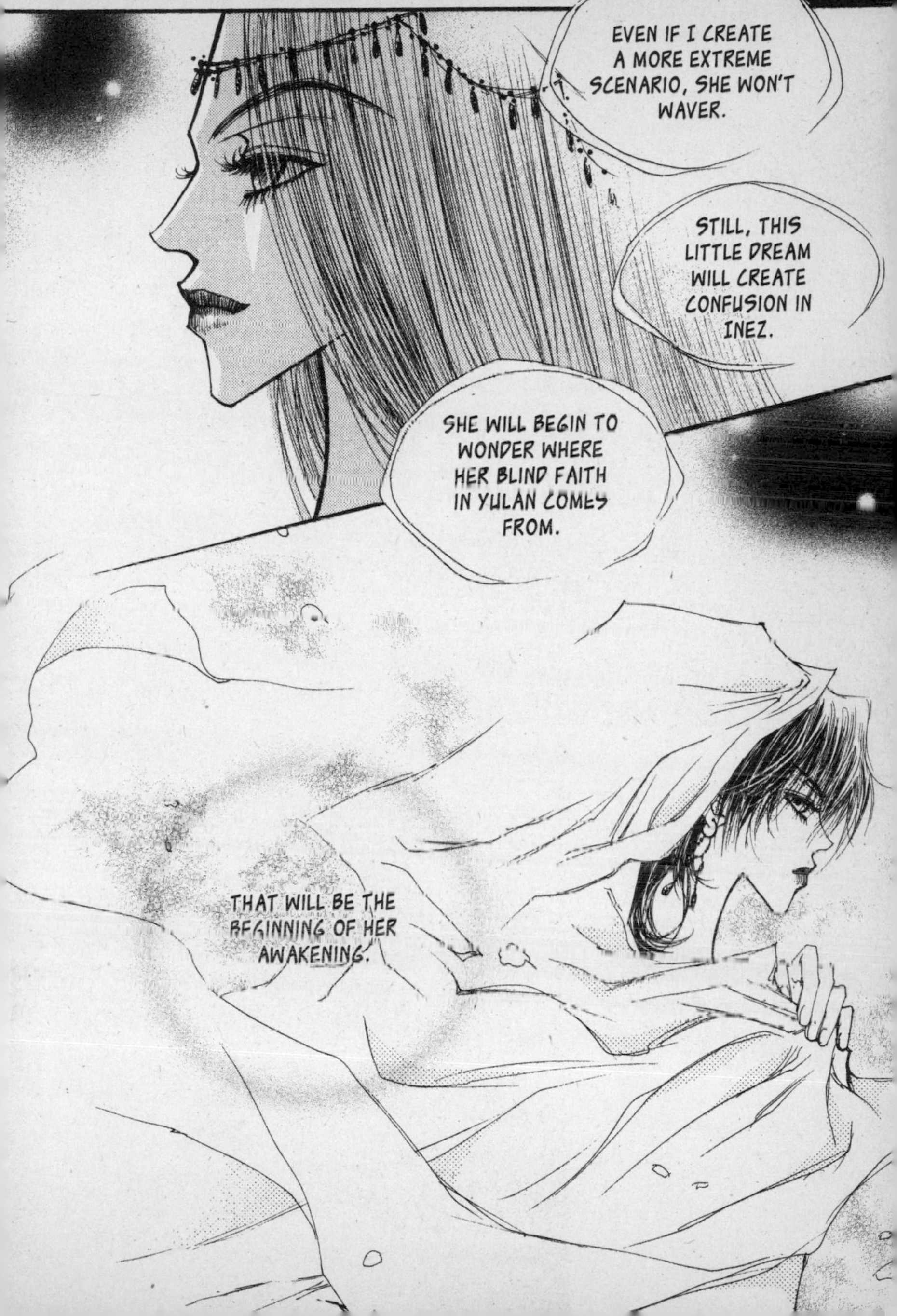
EVEN IF I CREATE A MORE EXTREME SCENARIO, SHE WON'T WAVER.
STILL, THIS LITTLE DREAM WILL CREATE CONFUSION IN INEZ.
SHE WILL BEGIN TO WONDER WHERE HER BLIND FAITH IN YULAN COMES FROM.
THAT WILL BE THE BEGINNING OF HER AWAKENING.

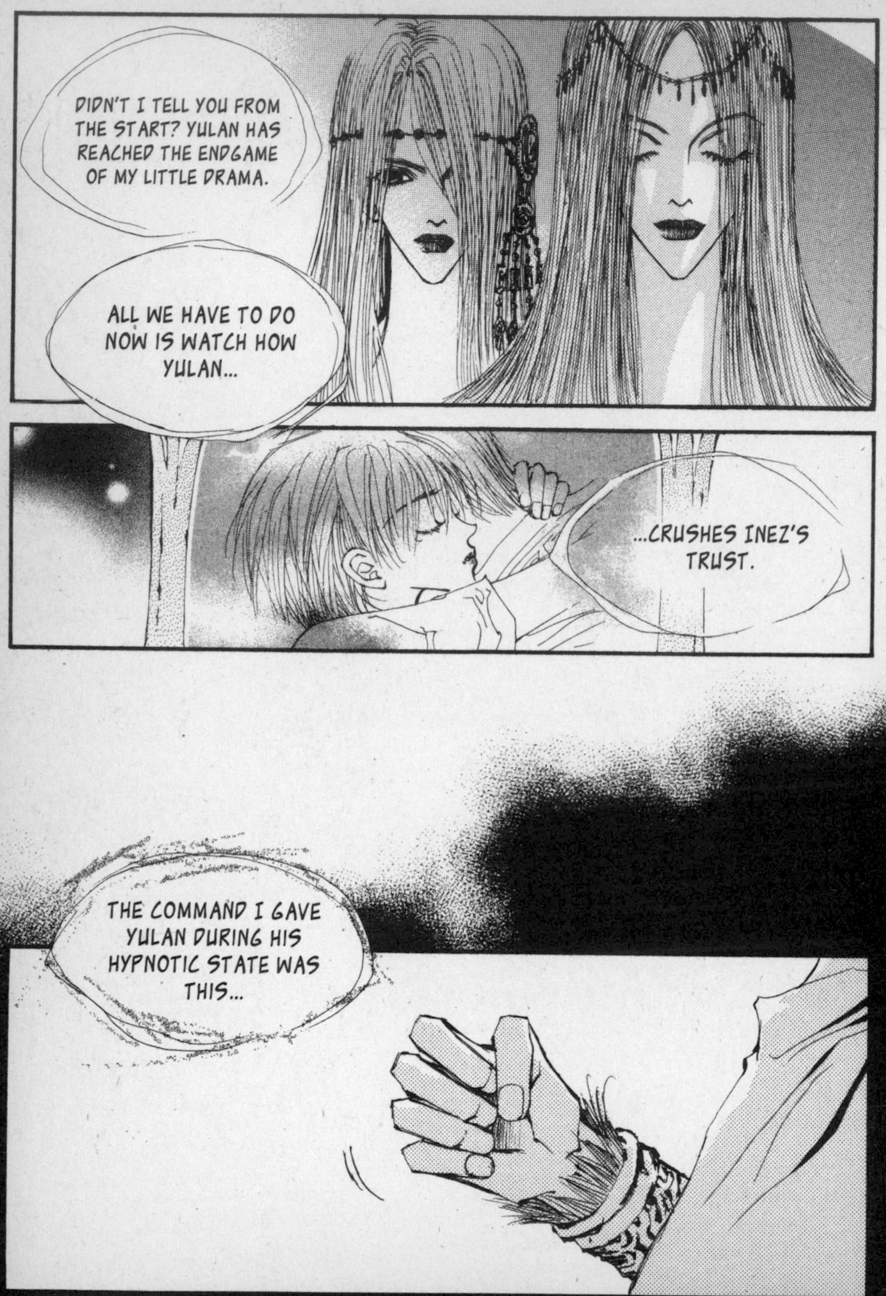
DIDN'T I TELL YOU FROM THE START? YULAN HAS REACHED THE ENDGAME OF MY LITTLE DRAMA.
ALL WE HAVE TO DO NOW IS WATCH HOW YULAN...
...CRUSHES INEZ'S TRUST.
THE COMMAND I GAVE YULAN DURING HIS HYPNOTIC STATE WAS THIS...

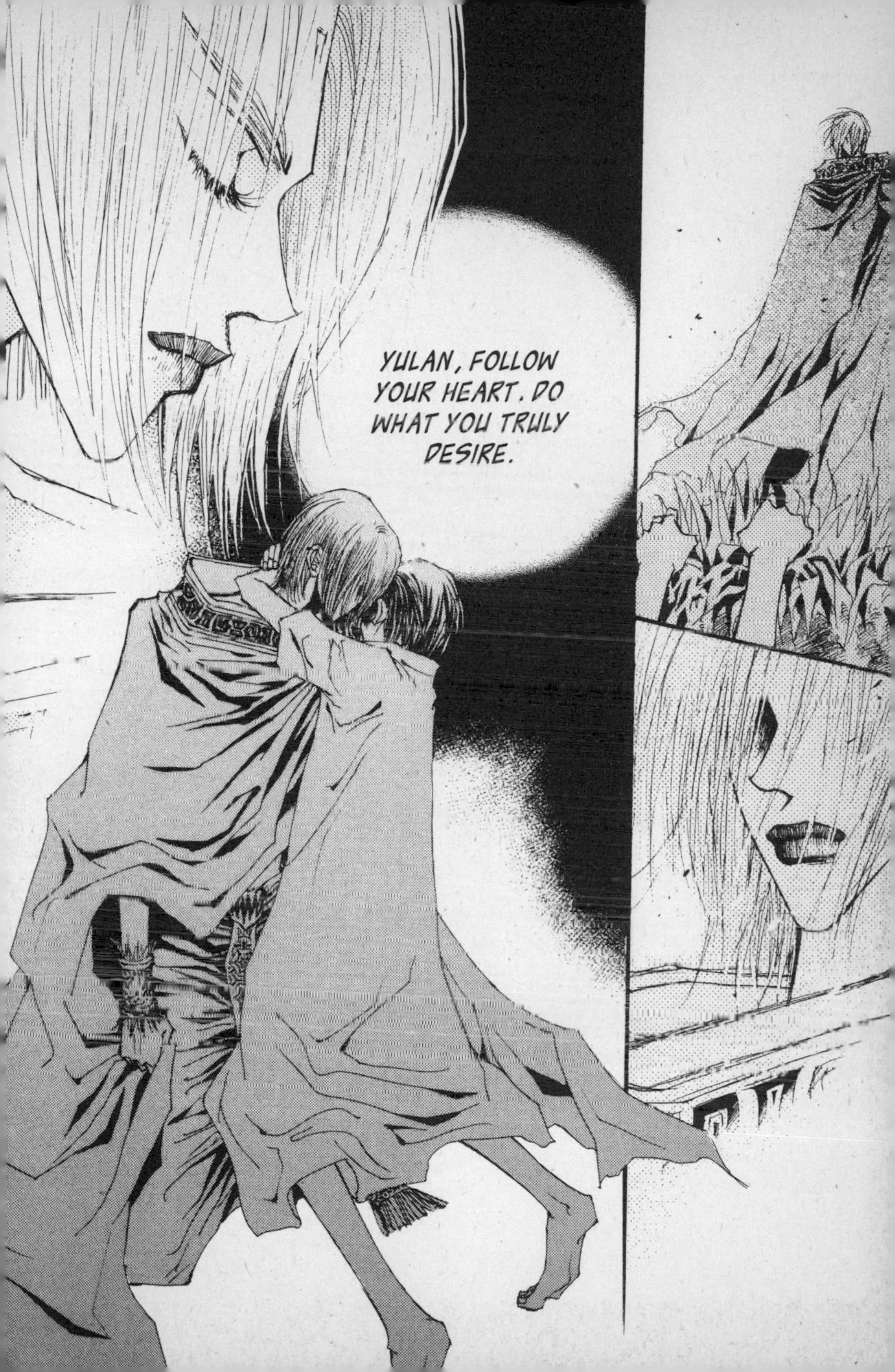
YULAN, FOLLOW YOUR HEART. DO WHAT YOU TRULY DESIRE.

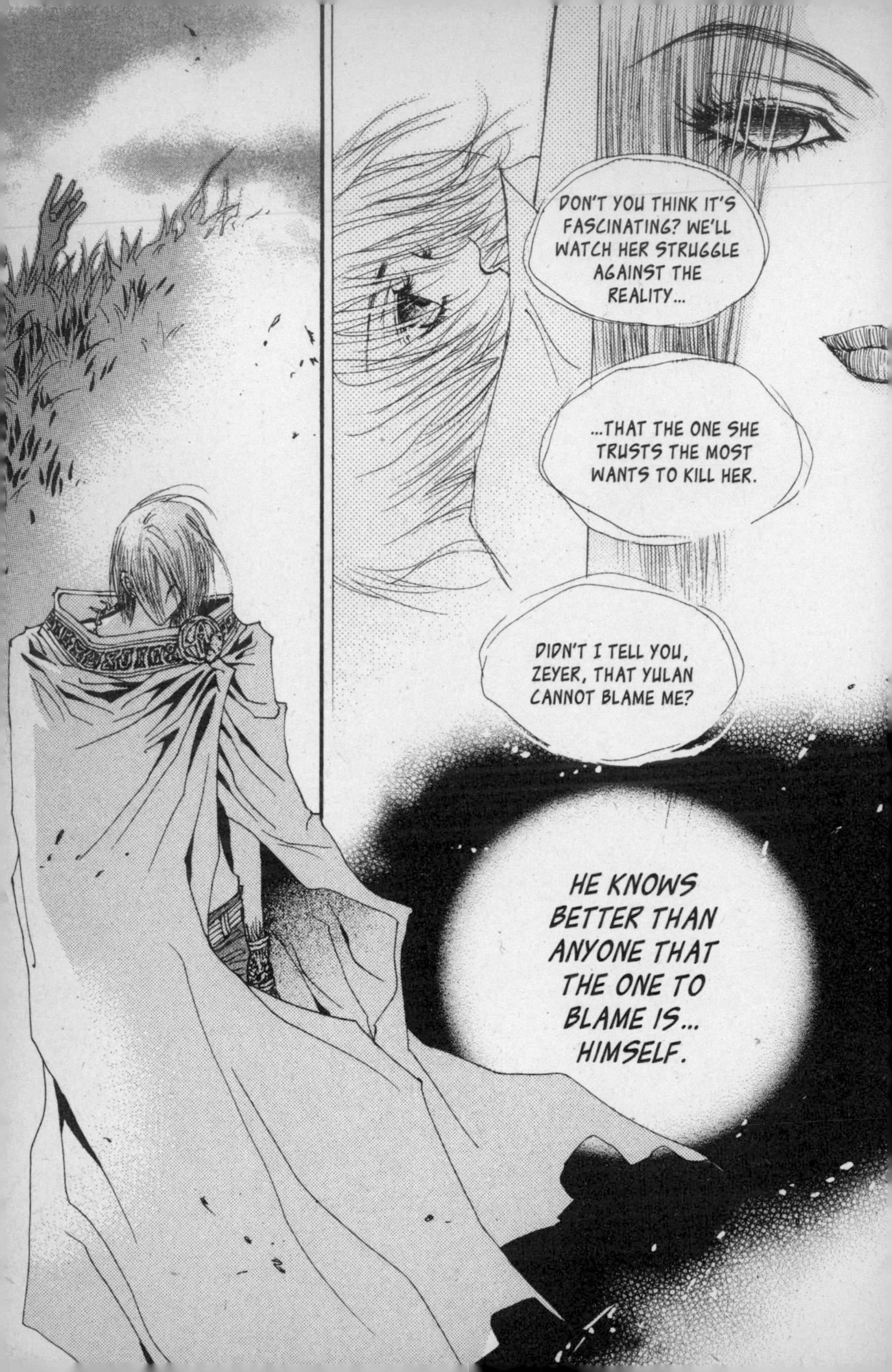
DON'T YOU THINK IT'S FASCINATING? WE'LL WATCH HER STRUGGLE AGAINST THE REALITY...
...THAT THE ONE SHE TRUSTS THE MOST WANTS TO KILL HER.
DIDN'T I TELL YOU, ZEYER, THAT YULAN CANNOT BLAME ME?
HE KNOWS BETTER THAN ANYONE THAT THE ONE TO BLAME IS... HIMSELF.

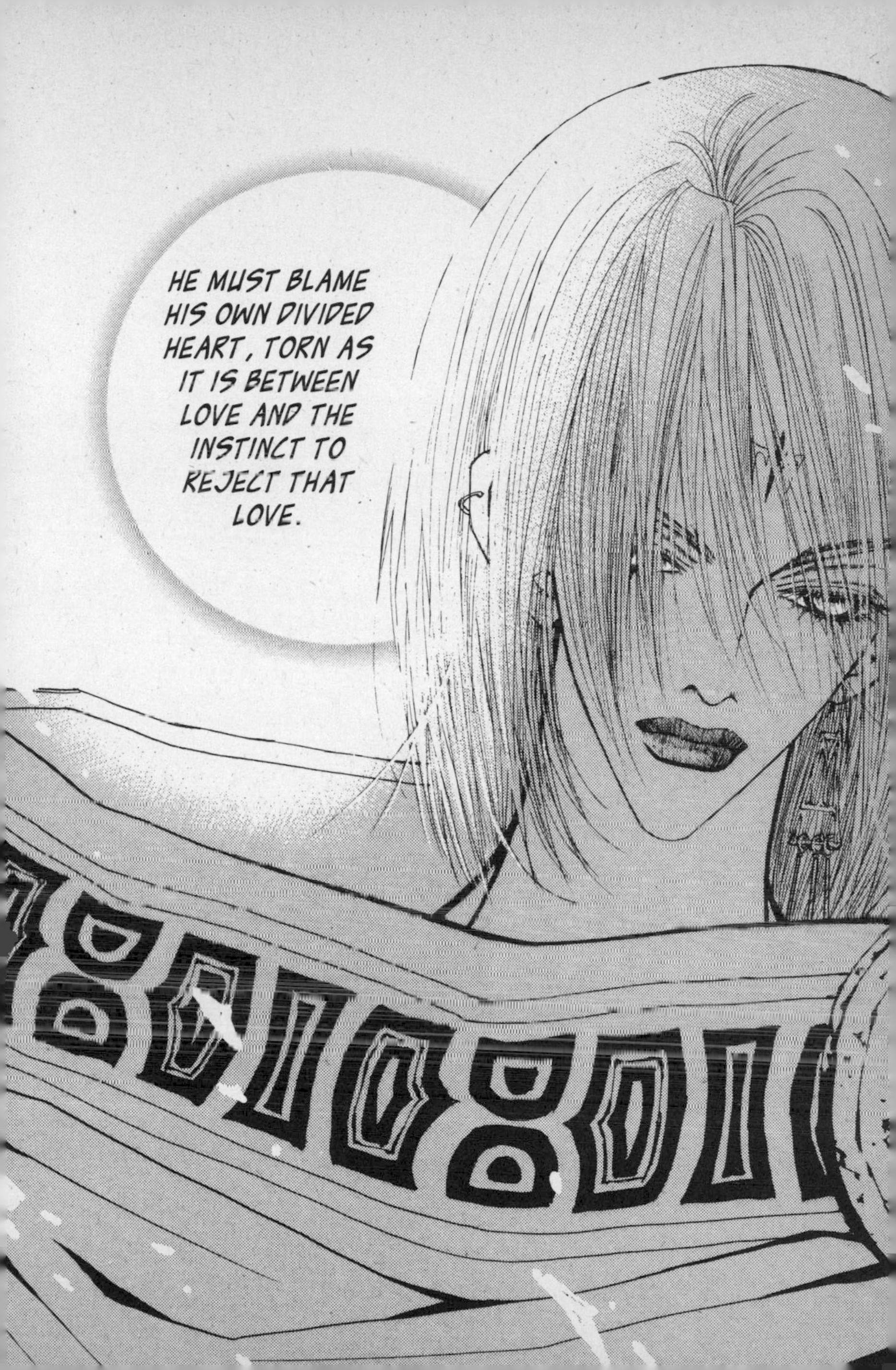
HE MUST BLAME HIS OWN DIVIDED HEART, TORN AS IT IS BETWEEN LOVE AND THE INSTINCT TO REJECT THAT LOVE.

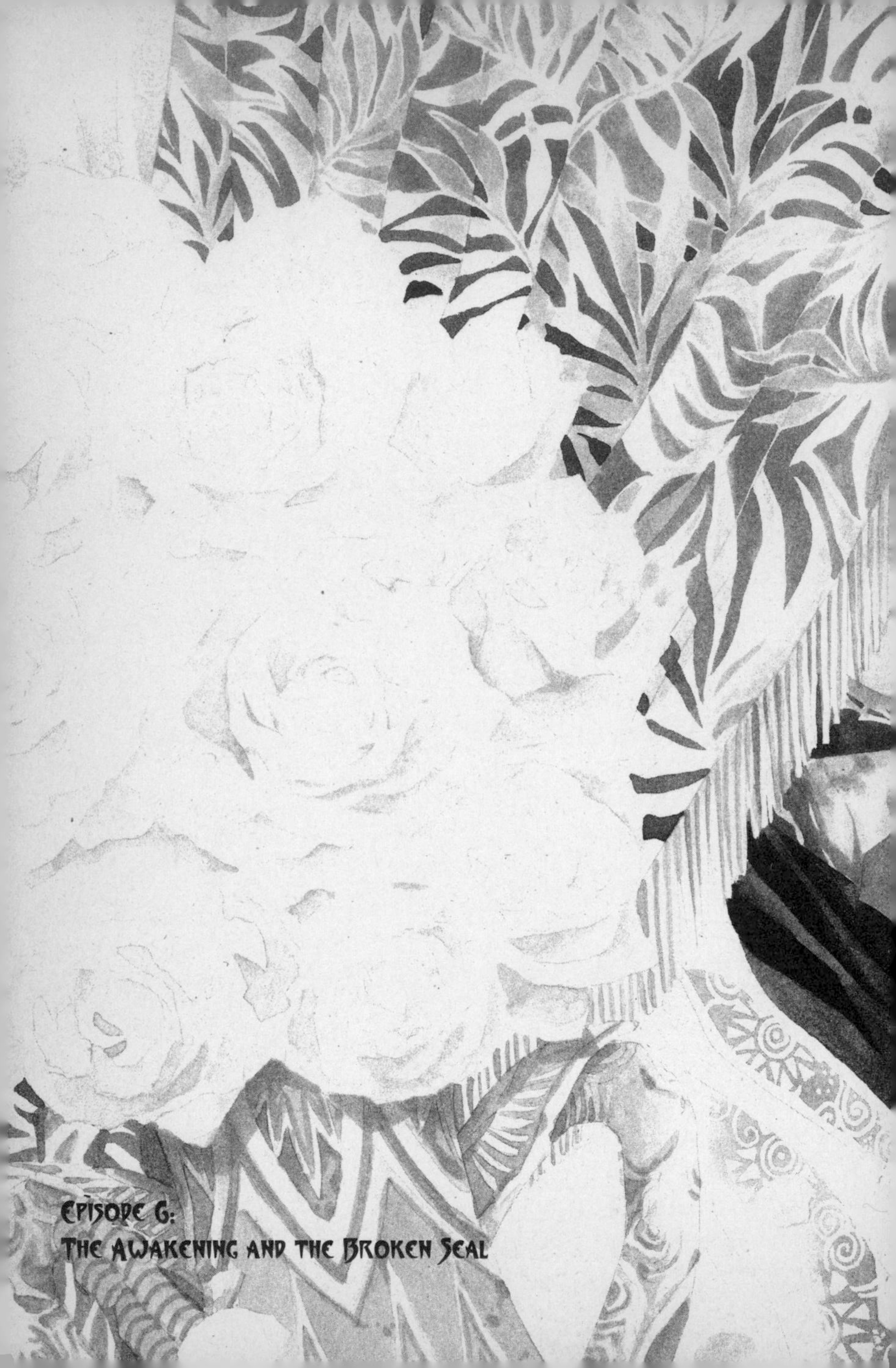

Episode 6:
The Awakening and the Broken Seal

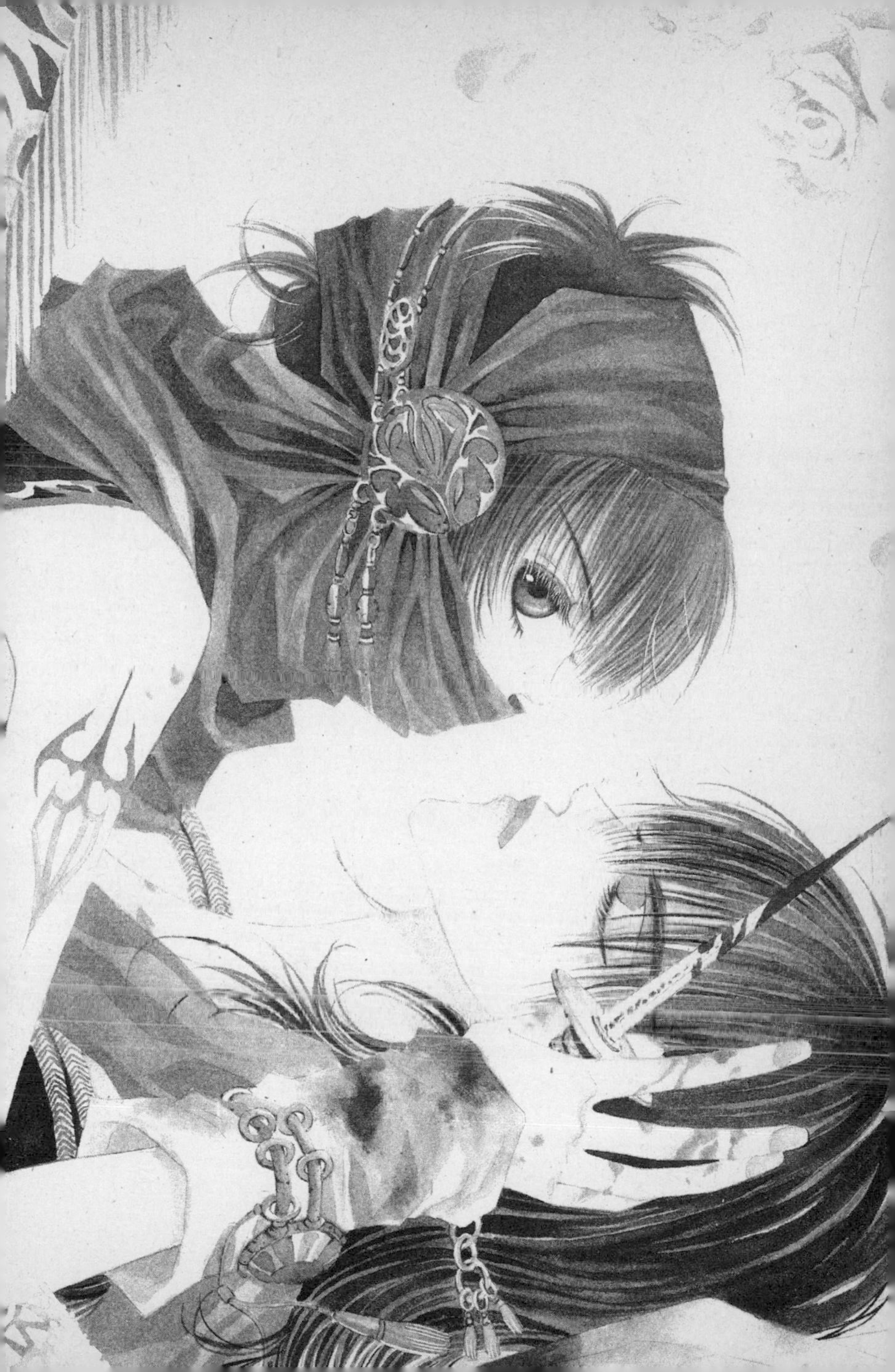

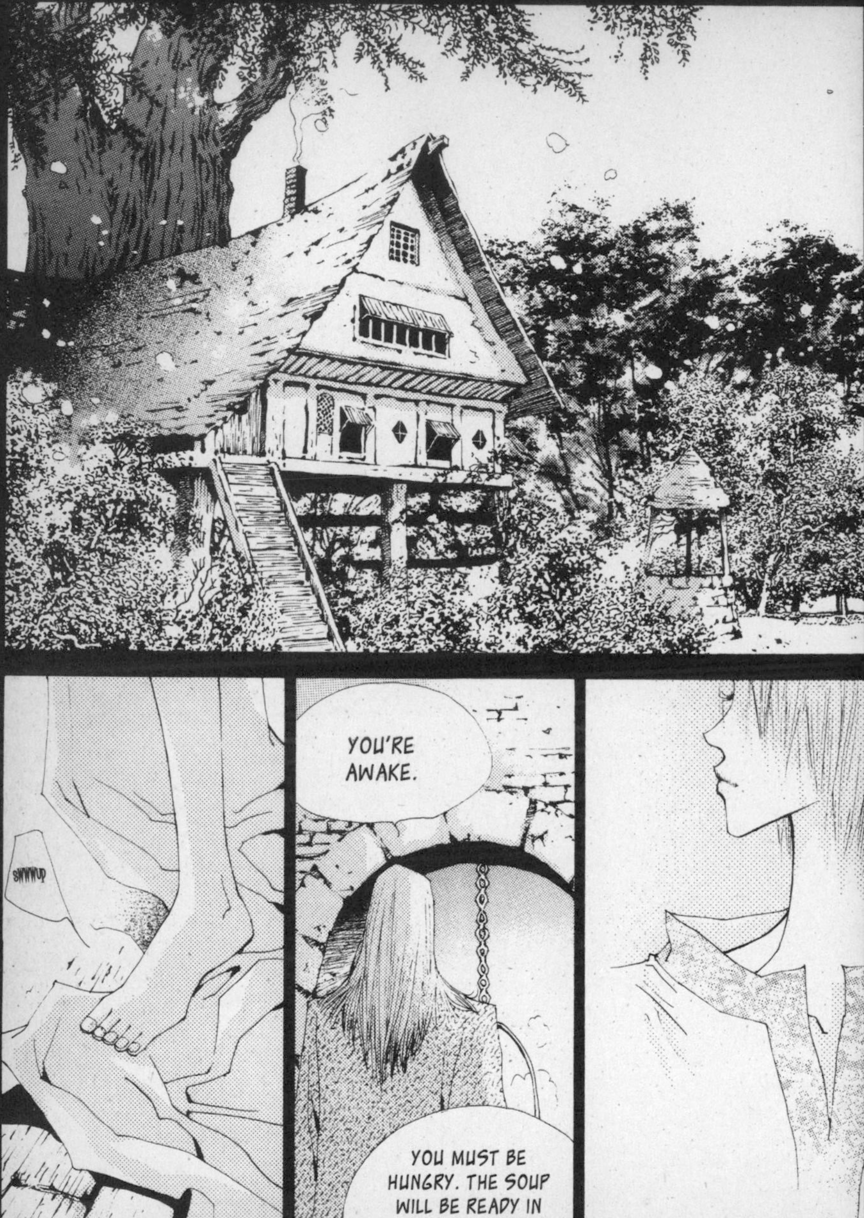
YOU'RE AWAKE.
YOU MUST BE HUNGRY. THE SOUP WILL BE READY IN JUST A MINUTE.
SWWWUP

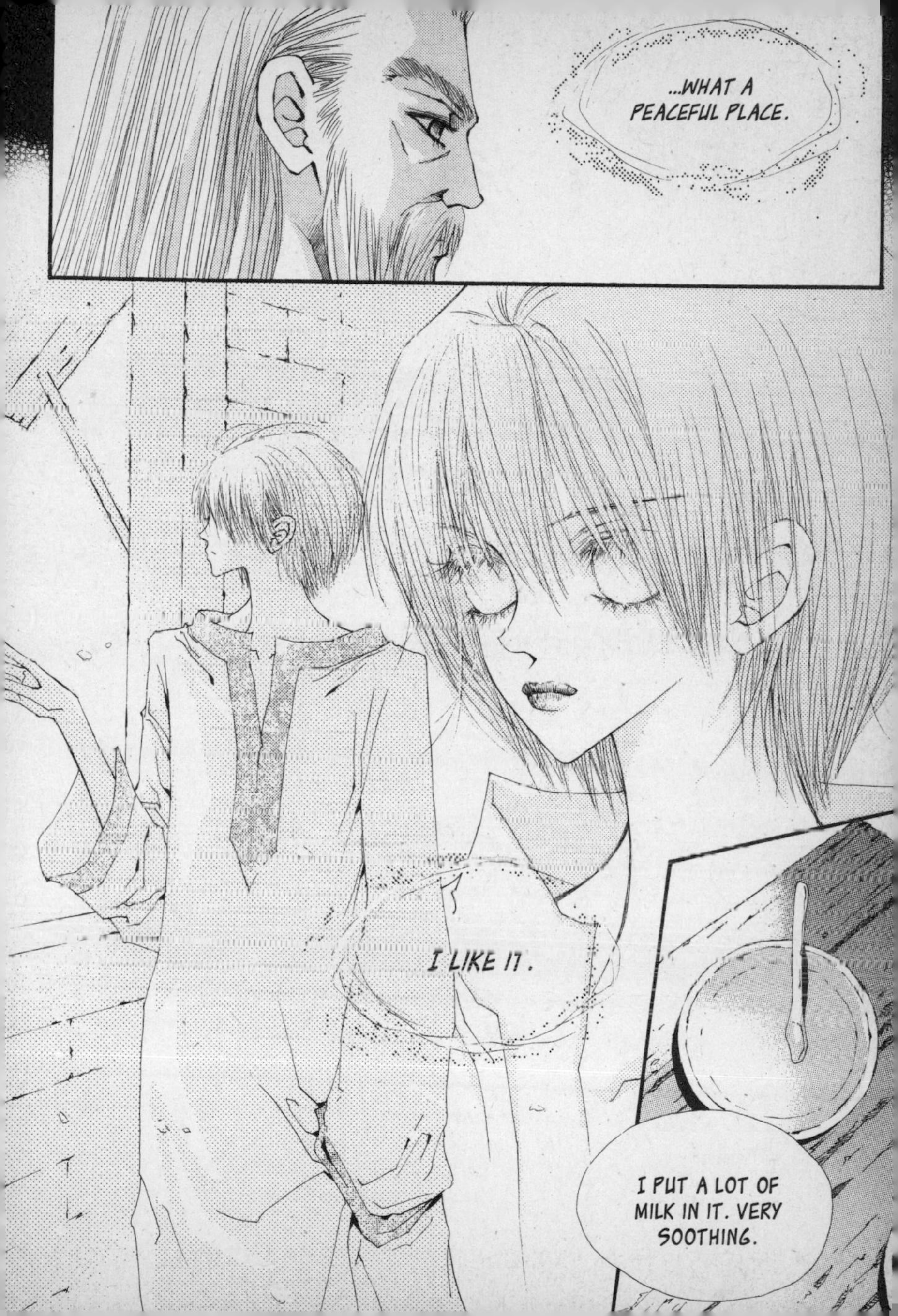
...WHAT A PEACEFUL PLACE.
I LIKE IT.
I PUT A LOT OF MILK IN IT. VERY SOOTHING.

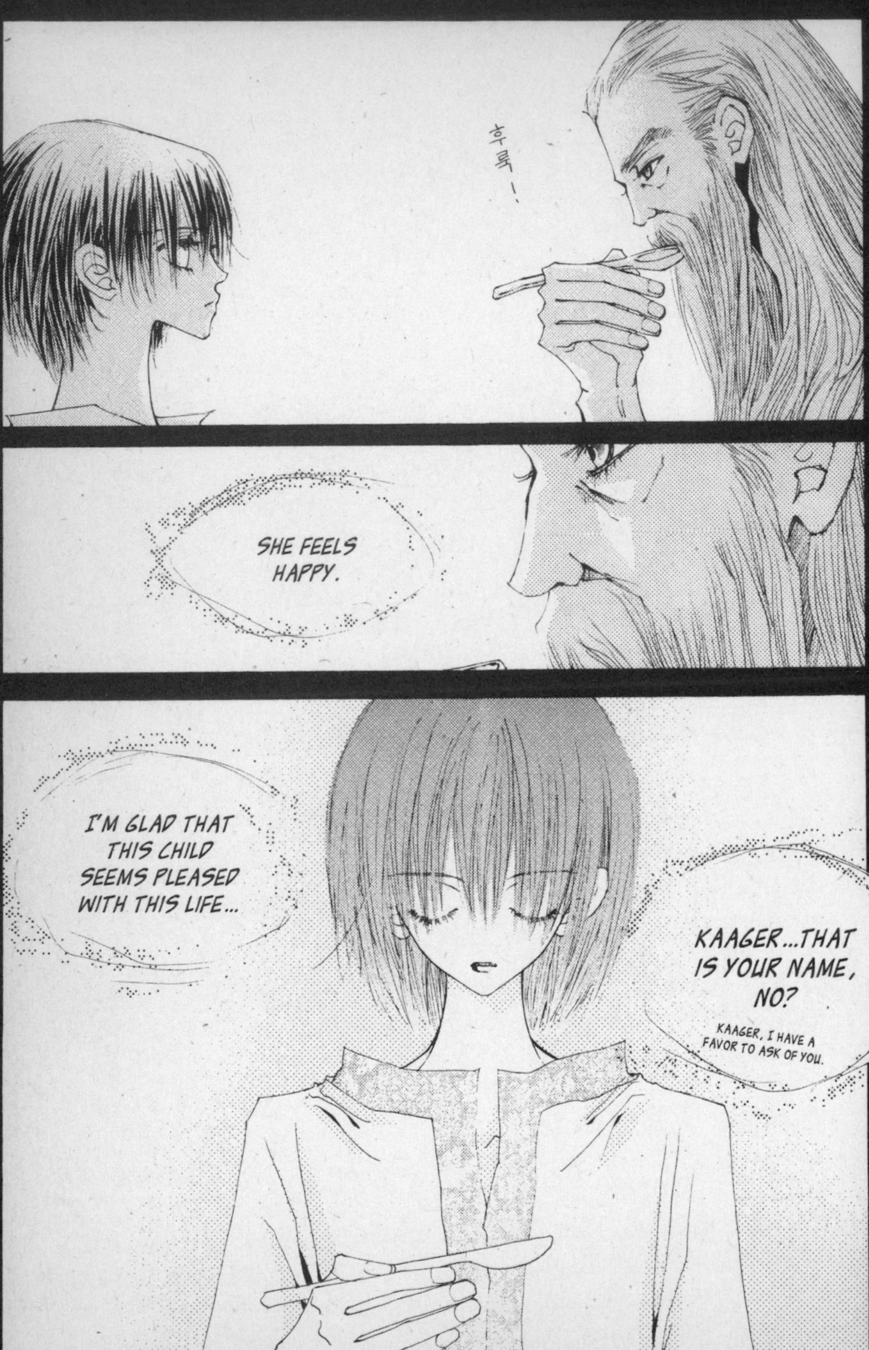
후룩…
SHE FEELS HAPPY.
KAAGER...THAT IS YOUR NAME, NO?
KAAGER, I HAVE A FAVOR TO ASK OF YOU.
I'M GLAD THAT THIS CHILD SEEMS PLEASED WITH THIS LIFE...

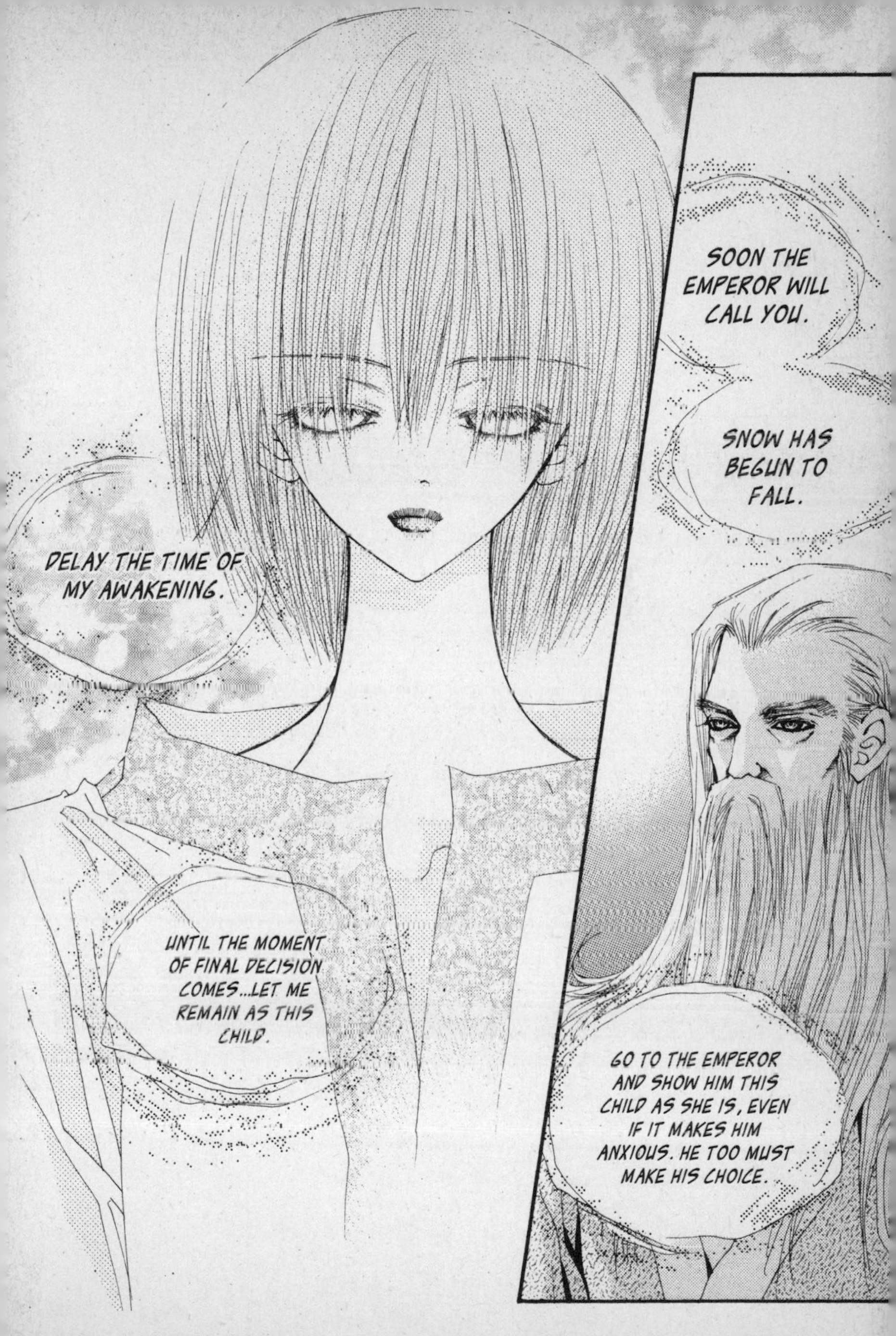
SOON THE EMPEROR WILL CALL YOU.
SNOW HAS BEGUN TO FALL.
GO TO THE EMPEROR AND SHOW HIM THIS CHILD AS SHE IS, EVEN IF IT MAKES HIM ANXIOUS. HE TOO MUST MAKE HIS CHOICE.
DELAY THE TIME OF MY AWAKENING.
UNTIL THE MOMENT OF FINAL DECISION COMES...LET ME REMAIN AS THIS CHILD.

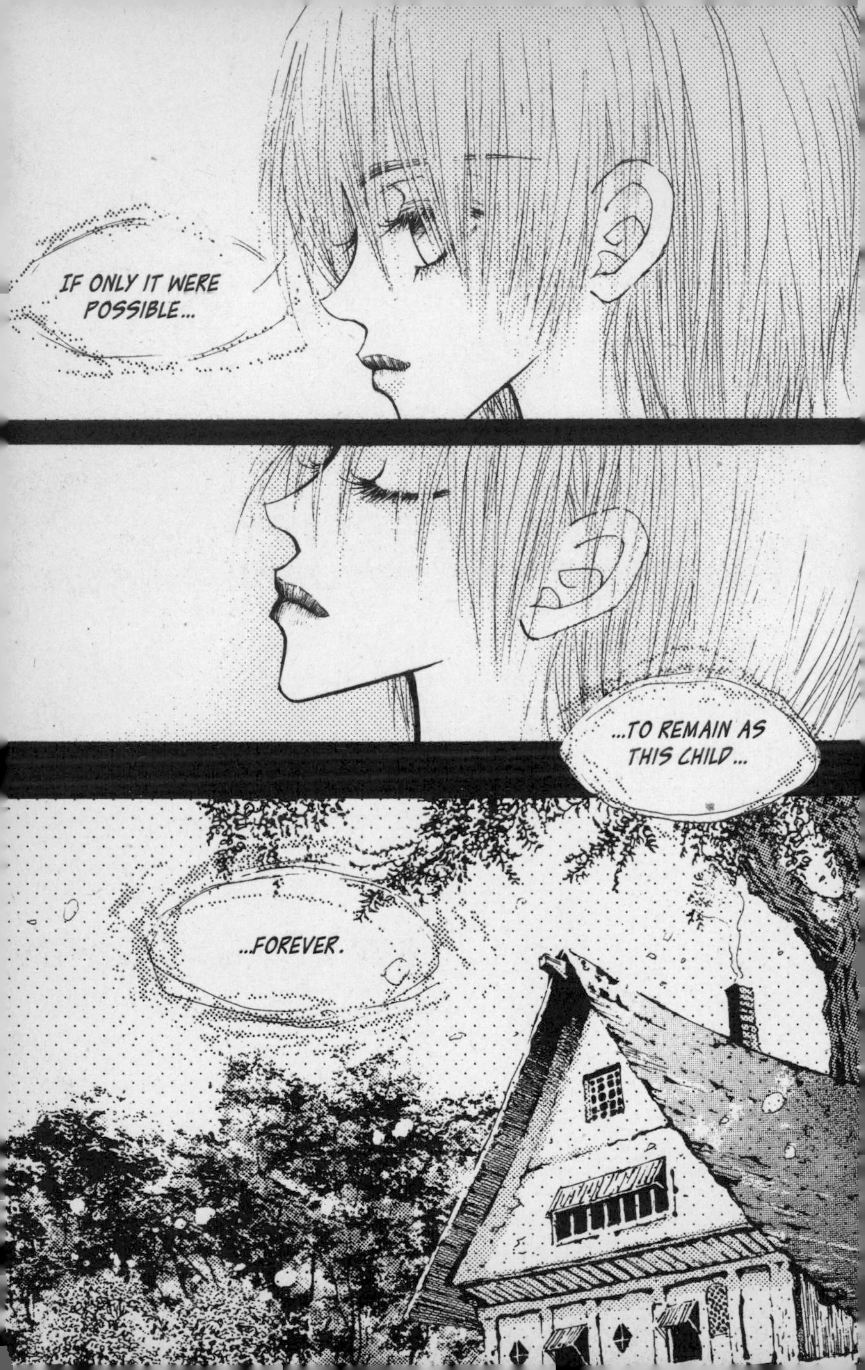
IF ONLY IT WERE POSSIBLE...
...TO REMAIN AS THIS CHILD...
...FOREVER.

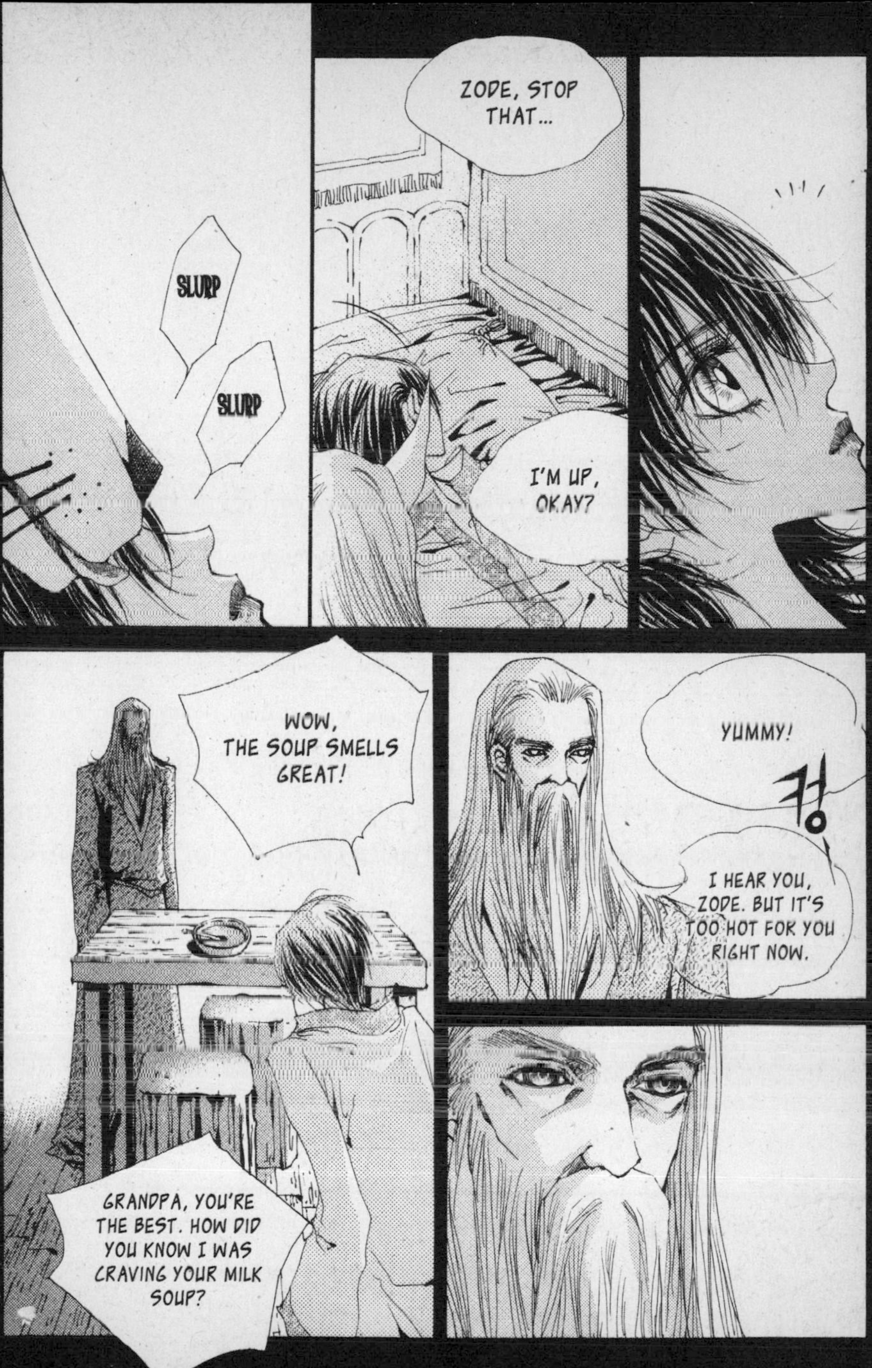
SLURP
SLURP
ZODE, STOP THAT...
I'M UP, OKAY?
WOW, THE SOUP SMELLS GREAT!
GRANDPA, YOU'RE THE BEST. HOW DID YOU KNOW I WAS CRAVING YOUR MILK SOUP?
YUMMY!
쾅
I HEAR YOU, ZODE. BUT IT'S TOO HOT FOR YOU RIGHT NOW.

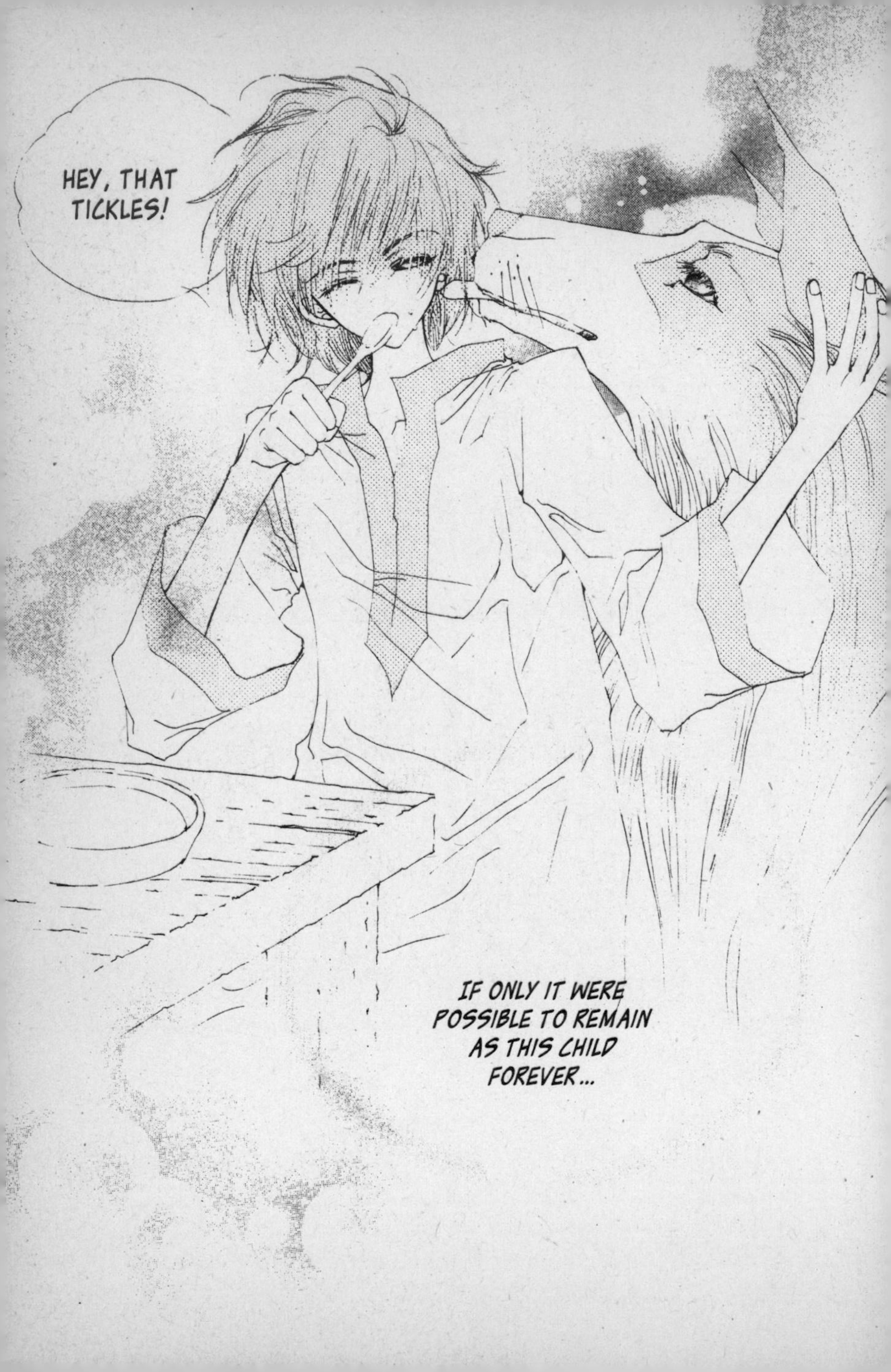
HEY, THAT TICKLES!
IF ONLY IT WERE POSSIBLE TO REMAIN AS THIS CHILD FOREVER...

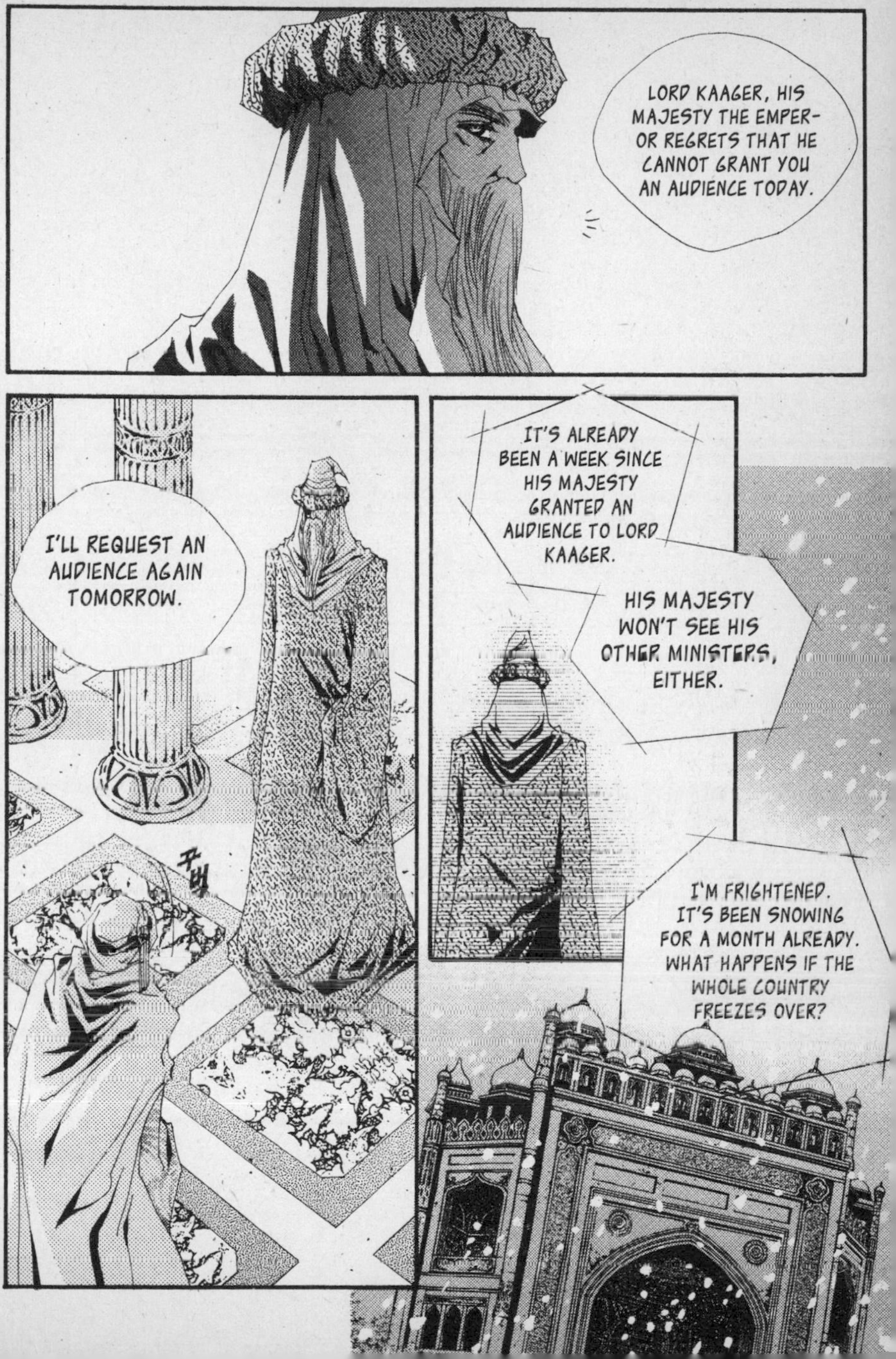
LORD KAAGER, HIS MAJESTY THE EMPER-OR REGRETS THAT HE CANNOT GRANT YOU AN AUDIENCE TODAY.
I'LL REQUEST AN AUDIENCE AGAIN TOMORROW.
꾸벅
IT'S ALREADY BEEN A WEEK SINCE HIS MAJESTY GRANTED AN AUDIENCE TO LORD KAAGER.
HIS MAJESTY WON'T SEE HIS OTHER MINISTERS, EITHER.
I'M FRIGHTENED. IT'S BEEN SNOWING FOR A MONTH ALREADY. WHAT HAPPENS IF THE WHOLE COUNTRY FREEZES OVER?

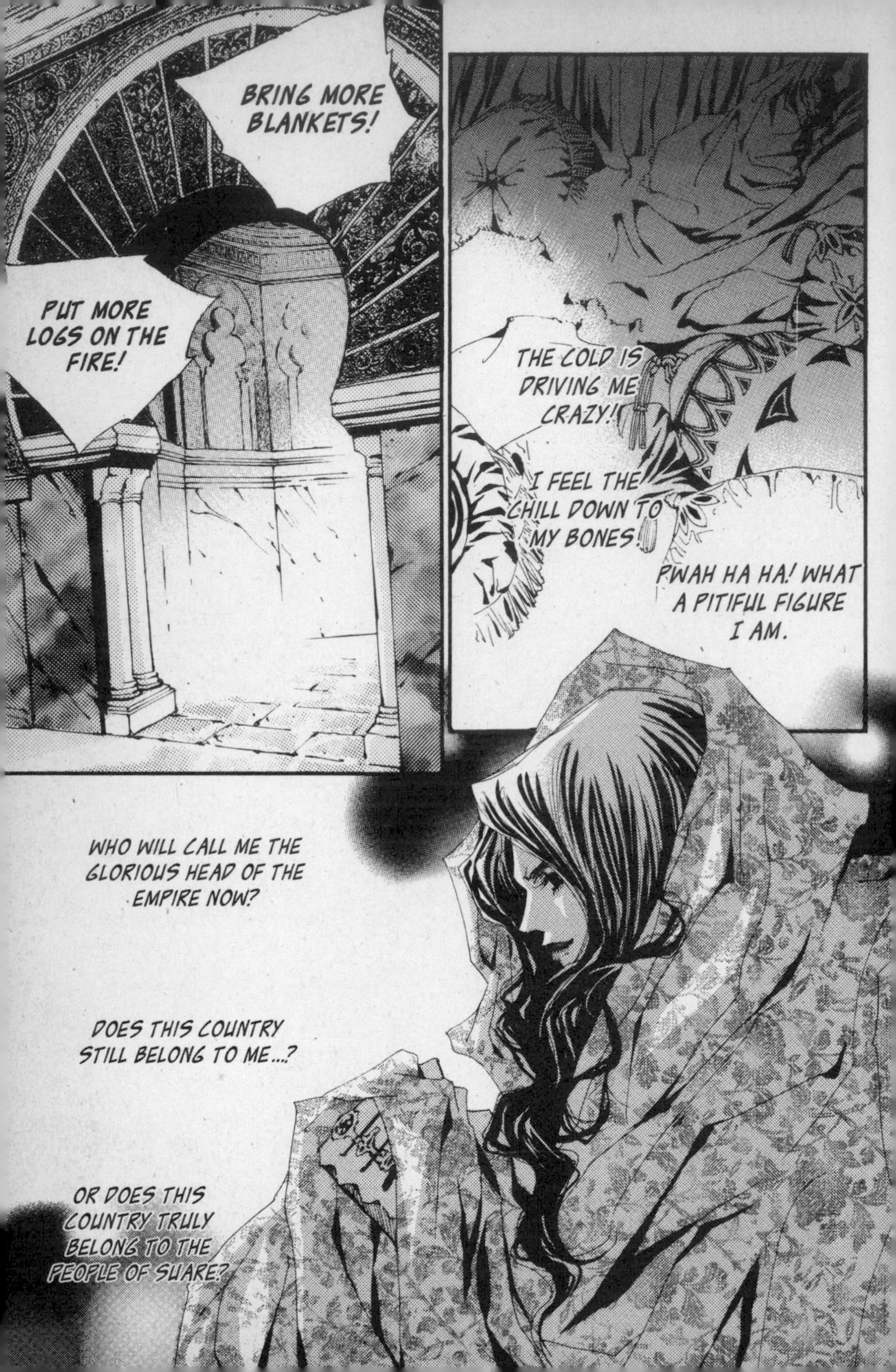
BRING MORE BLANKETS!
PUT MORE LOGS ON THE FIRE!
THE COLD IS DRIVING ME CRAZY!
I FEEL THE CHILL DOWN TO MY BONES!
PWAH HA HA! WHAT A PITIFUL FIGURE I AM.
WHO WILL CALL ME THE GLORIOUS HEAD OF THE EMPIRE NOW?
DOES THIS COUNTRY STILL BELONG TO ME...?
OR DOES THIS COUNTRY TRULY BELONG TO THE PEOPLE OF SUARE?

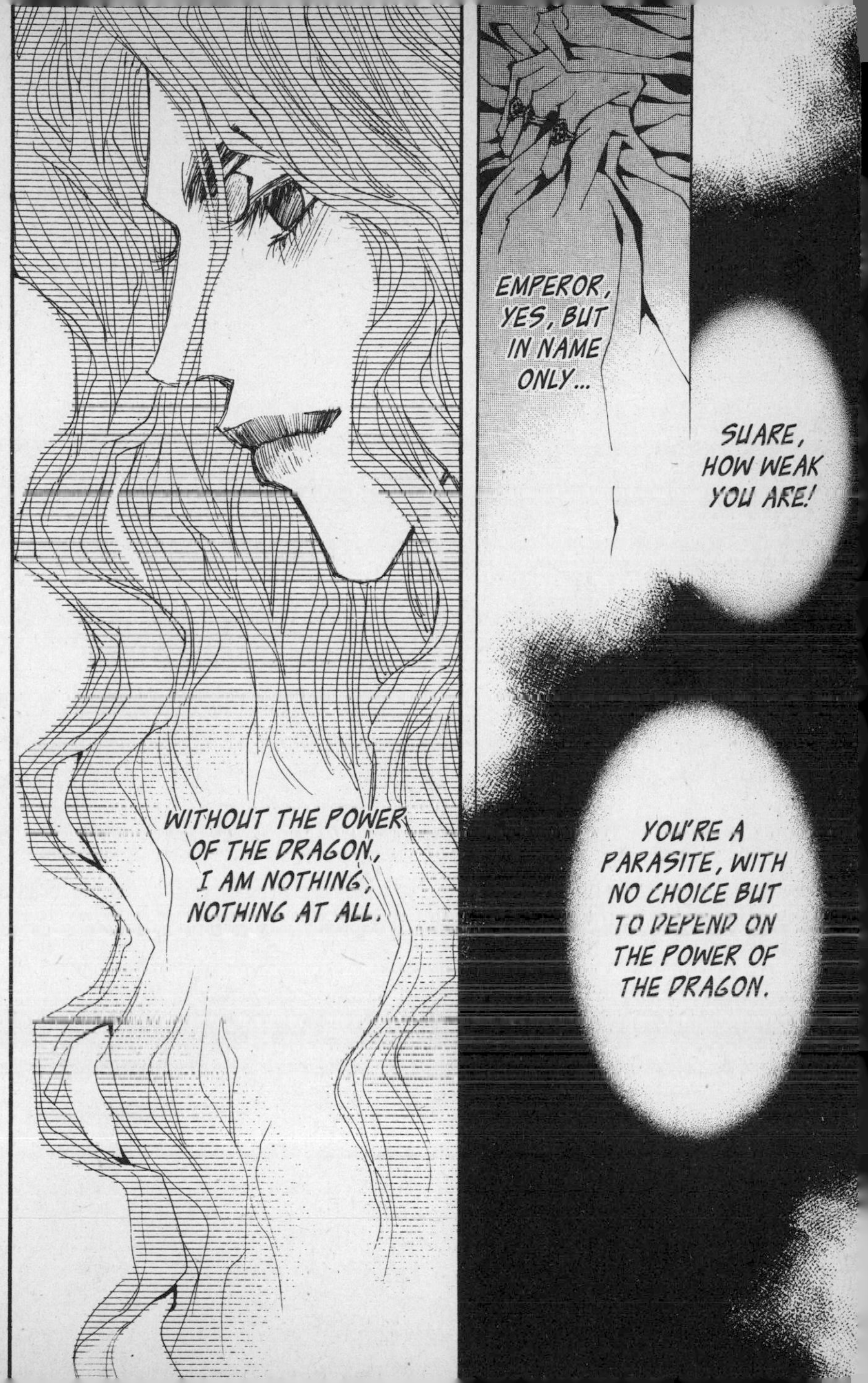
SUARE, HOW WEAK YOU ARE!
YOU'RE A PARASITE, WITH NO CHOICE BUT TO DEPEND ON THE POWER OF THE DRAGON.
EMPEROR, YES, BUT IN NAME ONLY...
WITHOUT THE POWER OF THE DRAGON, I AM NOTHING, NOTHING AT ALL.

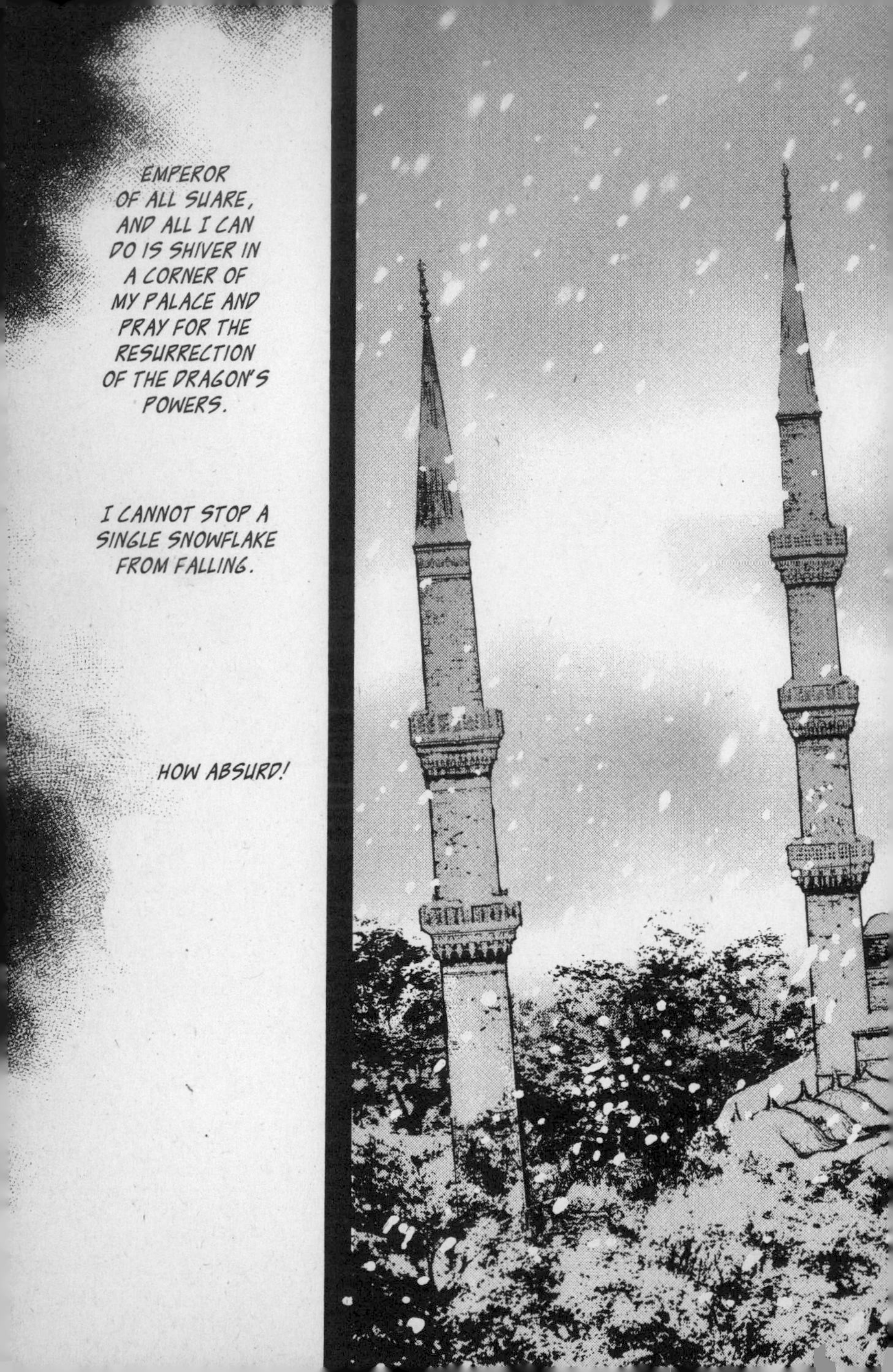
EMPEROR OF ALL SUARE, AND ALL I CAN DO IS SHIVER IN A CORNER OF MY PALACE AND PRAY FOR THE RESURRECTION OF THE DRAGON'S POWERS.
I CANNOT STOP A SINGLE SNOWFLAKE FROM FALLING.
HOW ABSURD!

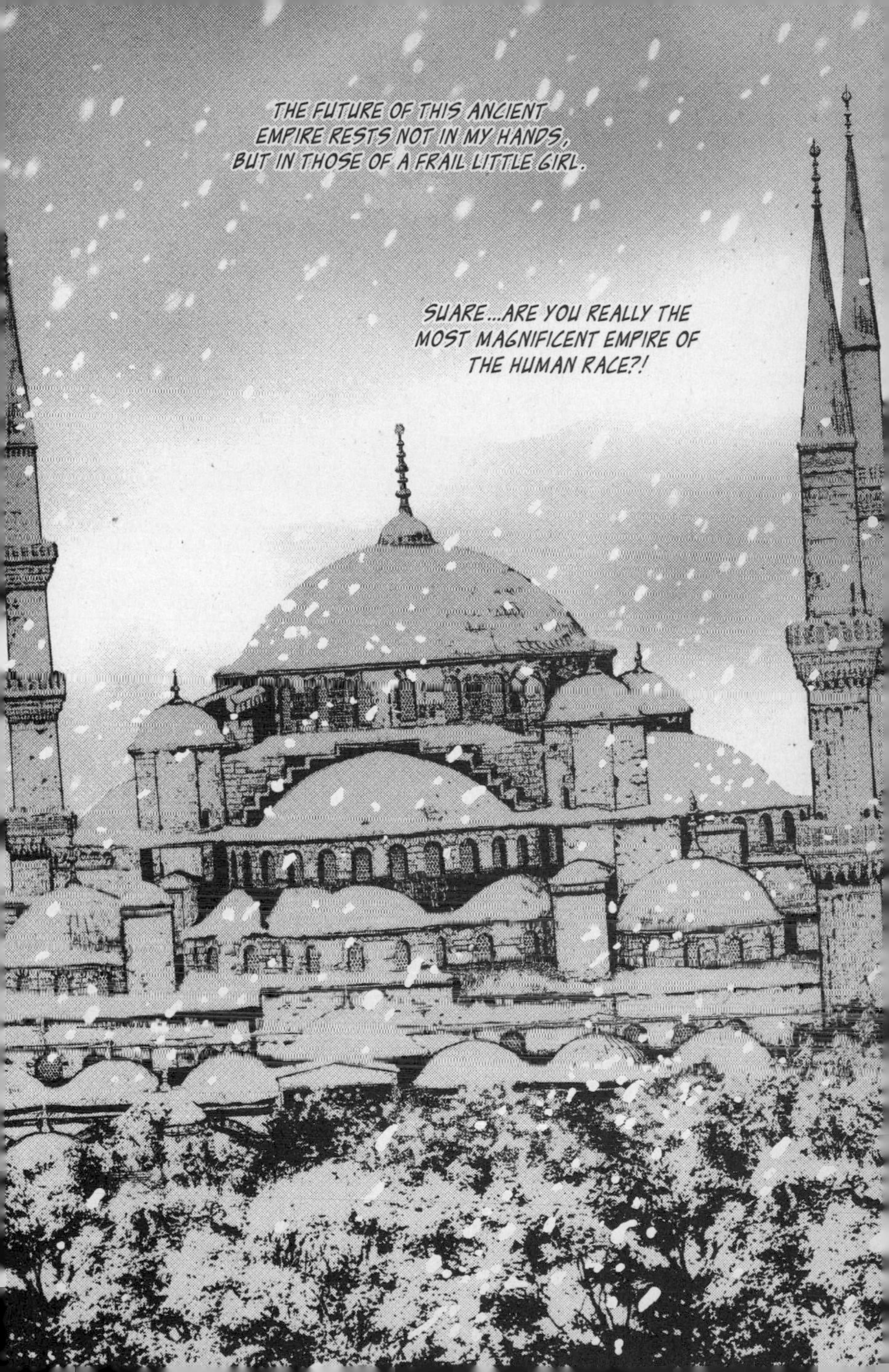
THE FUTURE OF THIS ANCIENT EMPIRE RESTS NOT IN MY HANDS, BUT IN THOSE OF A FRAIL LITTLE GIRL.
SUARE...ARE YOU REALLY THE MOST MAGNIFICENT EMPIRE OF THE HUMAN RACE?!

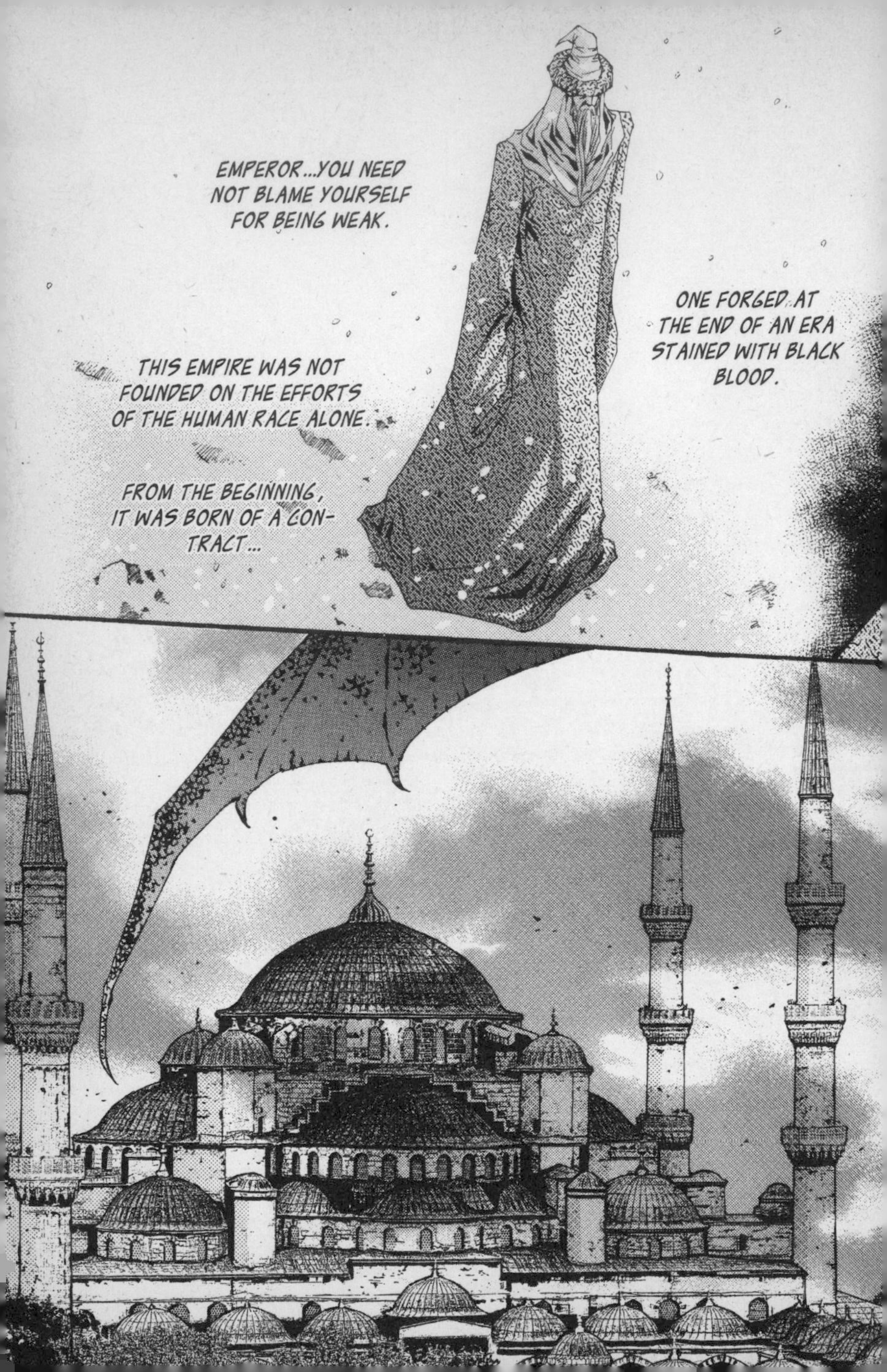
EMPEROR...YOU NEED NOT BLAME YOURSELF FOR BEING WEAK.
THIS EMPIRE WAS NOT FOUNDED ON THE EFFORTS OF THE HUMAN RACE ALONE.
FROM THE BEGINNING, IT WAS BORN OF A CON-TRACT...
ONE FORGED AT THE END OF AN ERA STAINED WITH BLACK BLOOD.

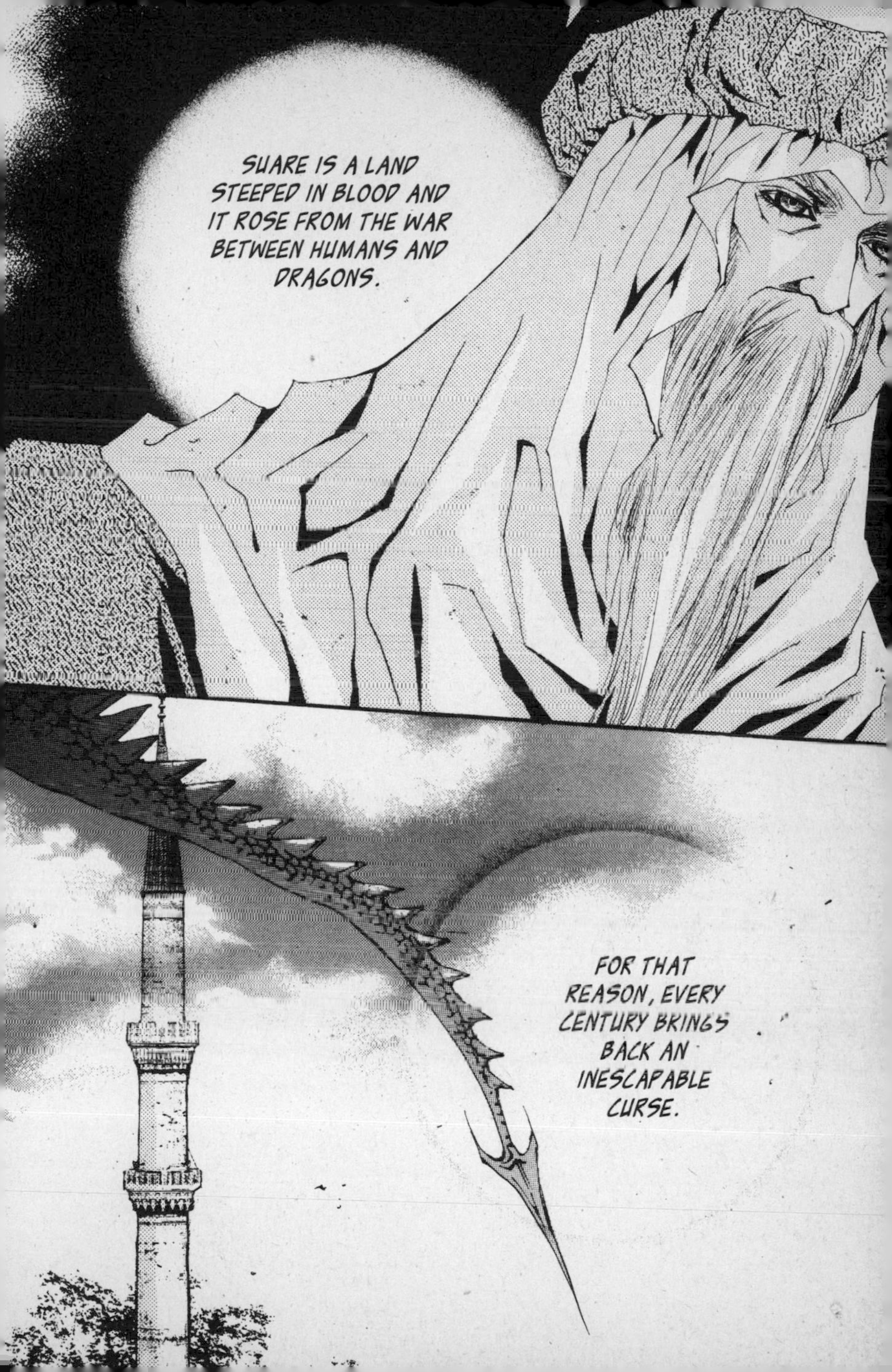
SUARE IS A LAND STEEPED IN BLOOD AND IT ROSE FROM THE WAR BETWEEN HUMANS AND DRAGONS.
FOR THAT REASON, EVERY CENTURY BRINGS BACK AN INESCAPABLE CURSE.

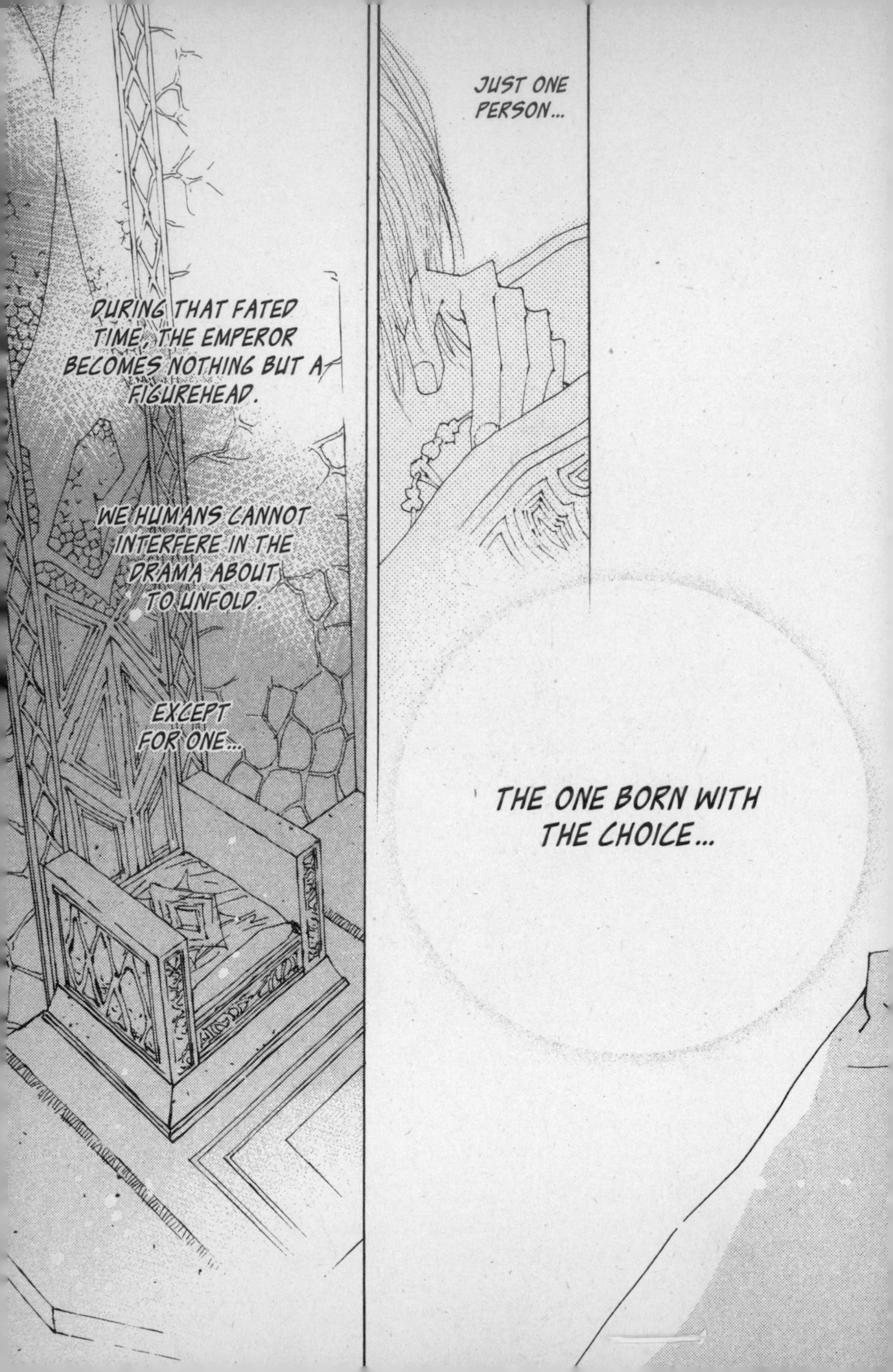
DURING THAT FATED TIME, THE EMPEROR BECOMES NOTHING BUT A FIGUREHEAD.
WE HUMANS CANNOT INTERFERE IN THE DRAMA ABOUT TO UNFOLD.
EXCEPT FOR ONE...
JUST ONE PERSON...
THE ONE BORN WITH THE CHOICE...

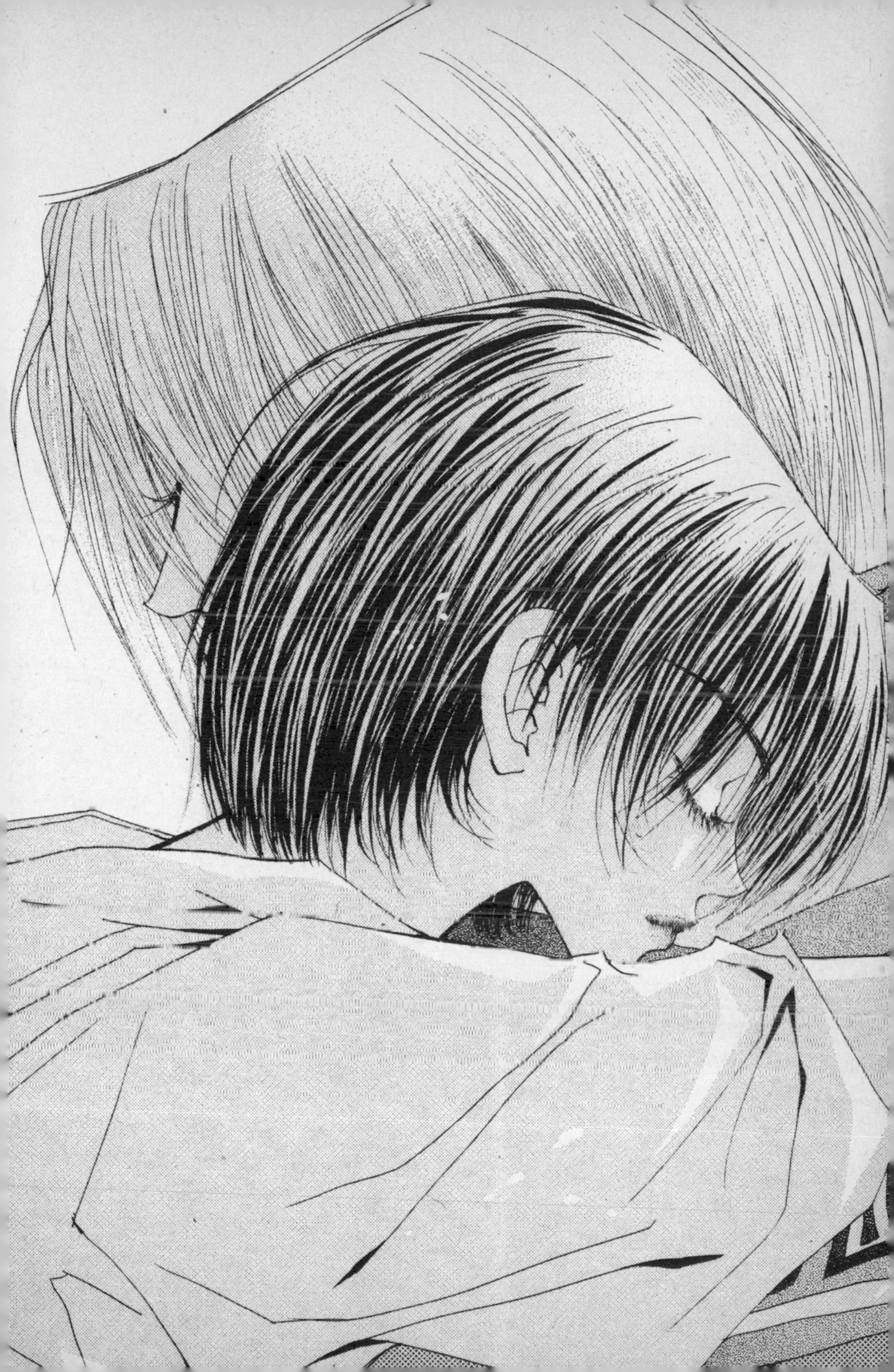

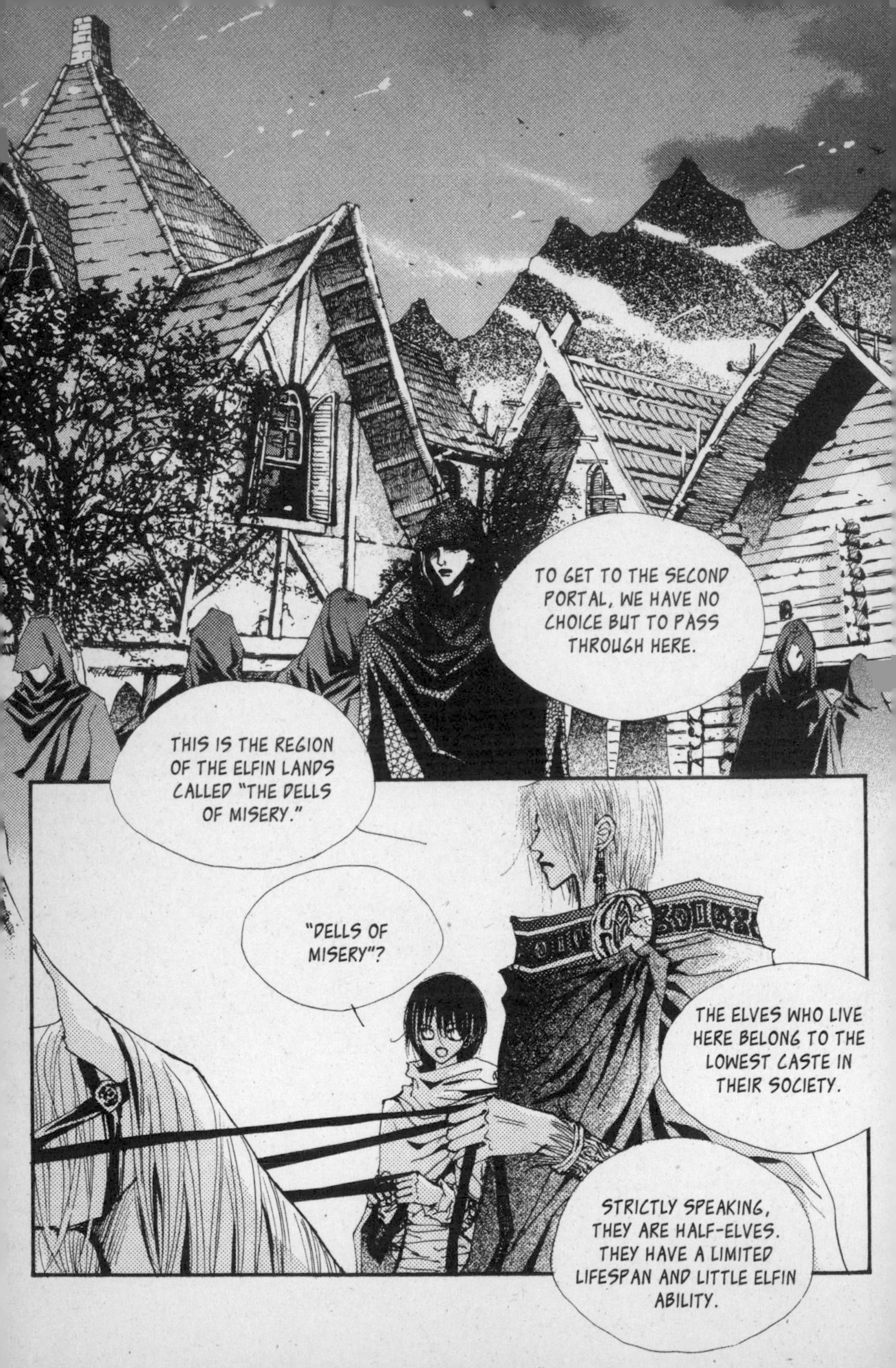
TO GET TO THE SECOND PORTAL, WE HAVE NO CHOICE BUT TO PASS THROUGH HERE.
THIS IS THE REGION OF THE ELFIN LANDS CALLED "THE DELLS OF MISERY."
"DELLS OF MISERY"?
THE ELVES WHO LIVE HERE BELONG TO THE LOWEST CASTE IN THEIR SOCIETY.
STRICTLY SPEAKING, THEY ARE HALF-ELVES. THEY HAVE A LIMITED LIFESPAN AND LITTLE ELFIN ABILITY.

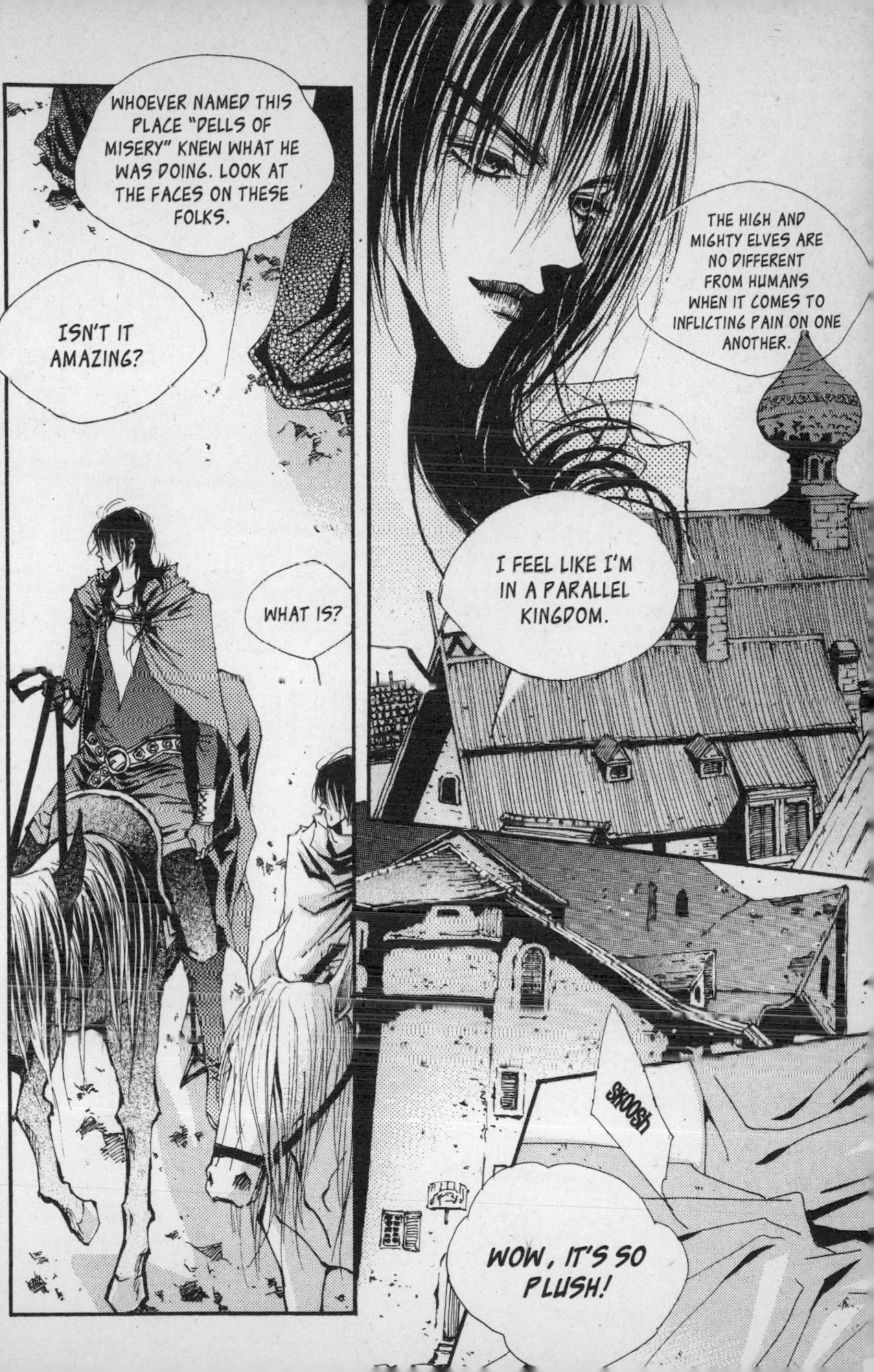
WHOEVER NAMED THIS PLACE "DELLS OF MISERY" KNEW WHAT HE WAS DOING. LOOK AT THE FACES ON THESE FOLKS.
ISN'T IT AMAZING?
WHAT IS?
THE HIGH AND MIGHTY ELVES ARE NO DIFFERENT FROM HUMANS WHEN IT COMES TO INFLICTING PAIN ON ONE ANOTHER.
I FEEL LIKE I'M IN A PARALLEL KINGDOM.
SKOOSH
WOW, IT'S SO PLUSH!

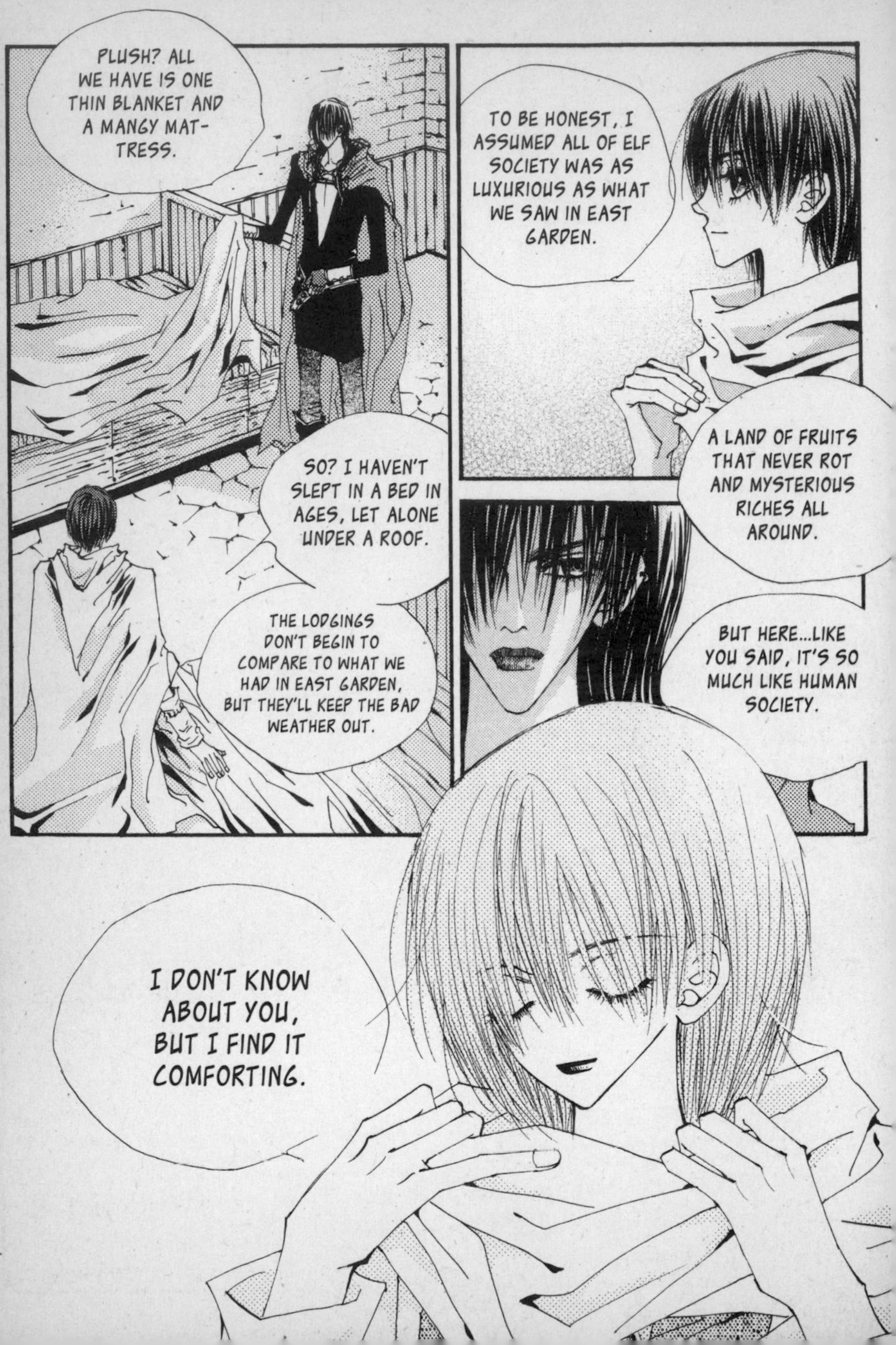
PLUSH? ALL WE HAVE IS ONE THIN BLANKET AND A MANGY MAT-TRESS.
SO? I HAVEN'T SLEPT IN A BED IN AGES, LET ALONE UNDER A ROOF.
THE LODGINGS DON'T BEGIN TO COMPARE TO WHAT WE HAD IN EAST GARDEN, BUT THEY'LL KEEP THE BAD WEATHER OUT.
TO BE HONEST, I ASSUMED ALL OF ELF SOCIETY WAS AS LUXURIOUS AS WHAT WE SAW IN EAST GARDEN.
A LAND OF FRUITS THAT NEVER ROT AND MYSTERIOUS RICHES ALL AROUND.
BUT HERE...LIKE YOU SAID, IT'S SO MUCH LIKE HUMAN SOCIETY.
I DON'T KNOW ABOUT YOU, BUT I FIND IT COMFORTING.

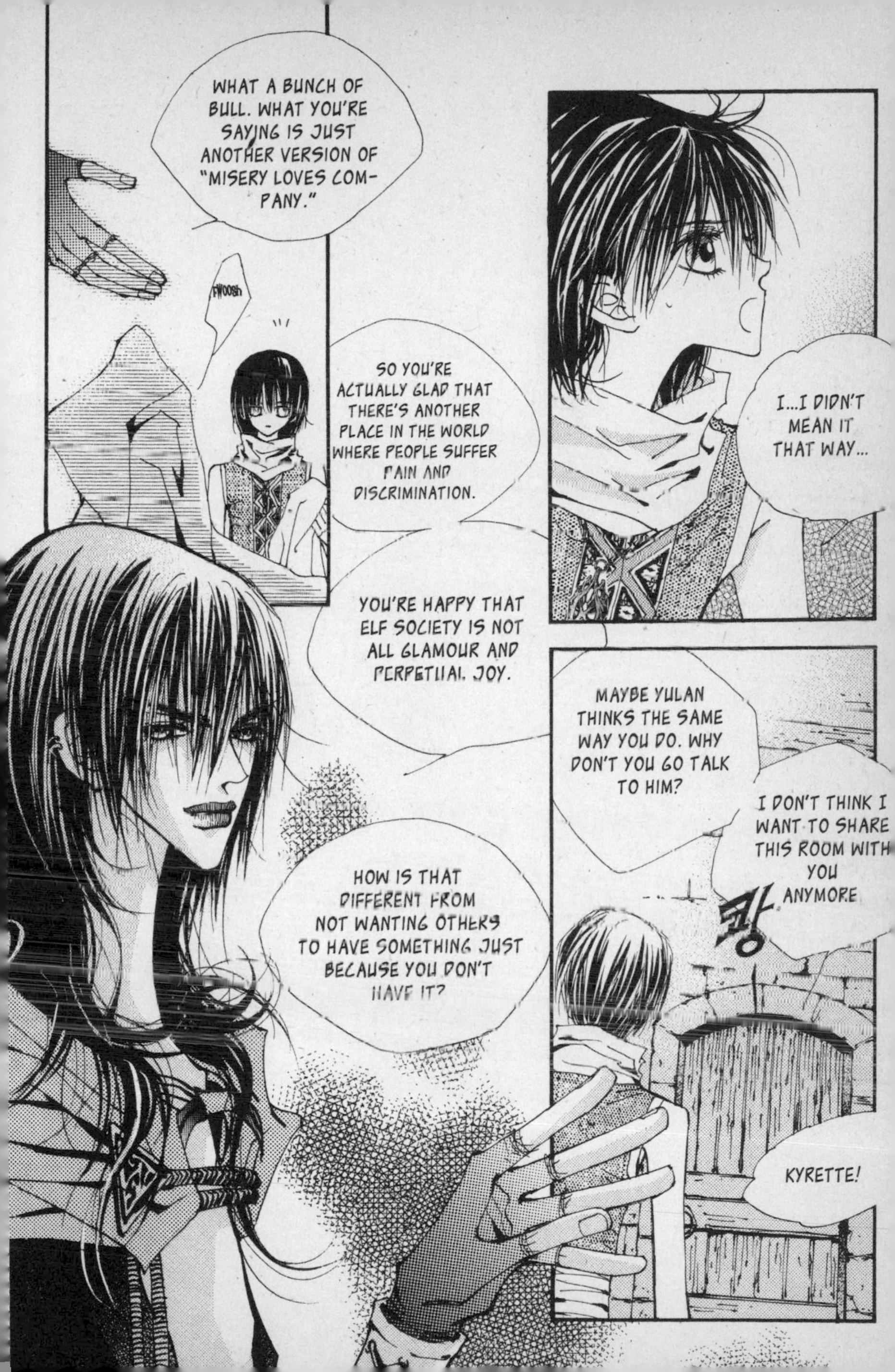

WHAT A BUNCH OF BULL. WHAT YOU'RE SAYING IS JUST ANOTHER VERSION OF "MISERY LOVES COM-PANY."
FWOOSH
SO YOU'RE ACTUALLY GLAD THAT THERE'S ANOTHER PLACE IN THE WORLD WHERE PEOPLE SUFFER PAIN AND DISCRIMINATION.
I...I DIDN'T MEAN IT THAT WAY...
YOU'RE HAPPY THAT ELF SOCIETY IS NOT ALL GLAMOUR AND PERPETUAL JOY.
HOW IS THAT DIFFERENT FROM NOT WANTING OTHERS TO HAVE SOMETHING JUST BECAUSE YOU DON'T HAVE IT?
MAYBE YULAN THINKS THE SAME WAY YOU DO. WHY DON'T YOU GO TALK TO HIM?
I DON'T THINK I WANT TO SHARE THIS ROOM WITH YOU ANYMORE
쾅
KYRETTE!

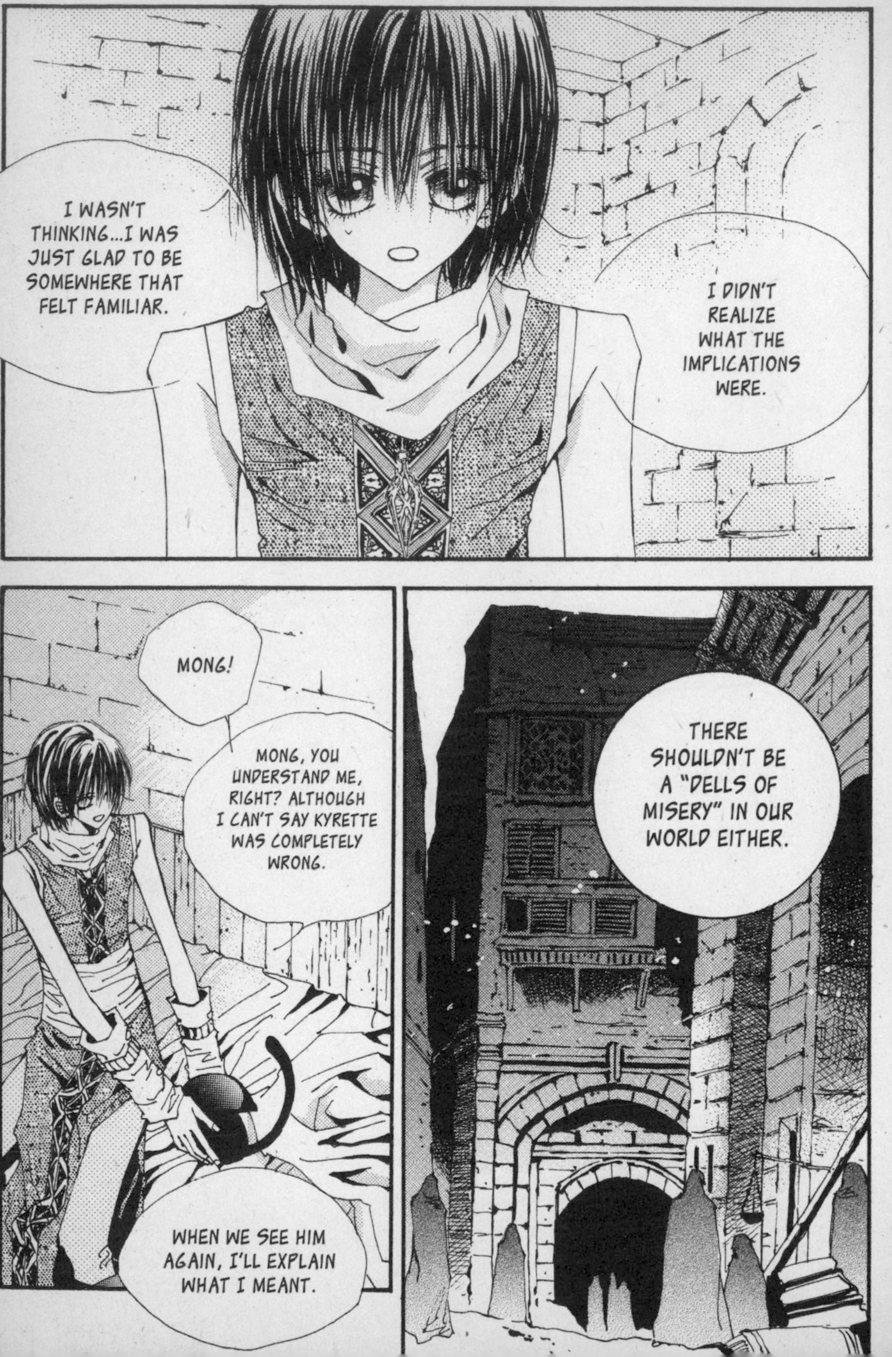
I WASN'T THINKING...I WAS JUST GLAD TO BE SOMEWHERE THAT FELT FAMILIAR.
I DIDN'T REALIZE WHAT THE IMPLICATIONS WERE.
MONG!
MONG, YOU UNDERSTAND ME, RIGHT? ALTHOUGH I CAN'T SAY KYRETTE WAS COMPLETELY WRONG.
WHEN WE SEE HIM AGAIN, I'LL EXPLAIN WHAT I MEANT.
THERE SHOULDN'T BE A "DELLS OF MISERY" IN OUR WORLD EITHER.

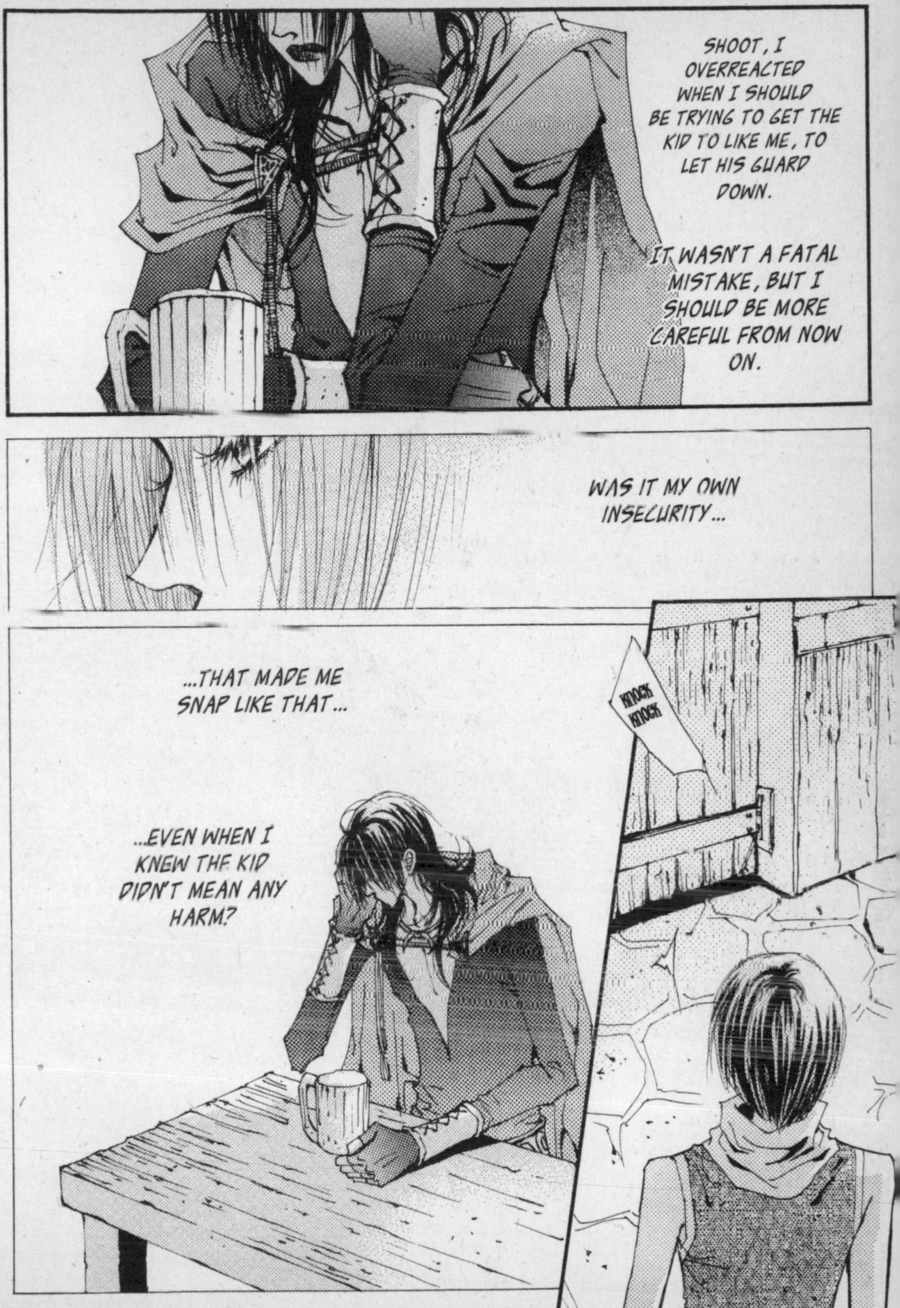
SHOOT, I OVERREACTED WHEN I SHOULD BE TRYING TO GET THE KID TO LIKE ME, TO LET HIS GUARD DOWN.
IT WASN'T A FATAL MISTAKE, BUT I SHOULD BE MORE CAREFUL FROM NOW ON.
WAS IT MY OWN INSECURITY...
KNOCK KNOCK
...THAT MADE ME SNAP LIKE THAT...
...EVEN WHEN I KNEW THE KID DIDN'T MEAN ANY HARM?

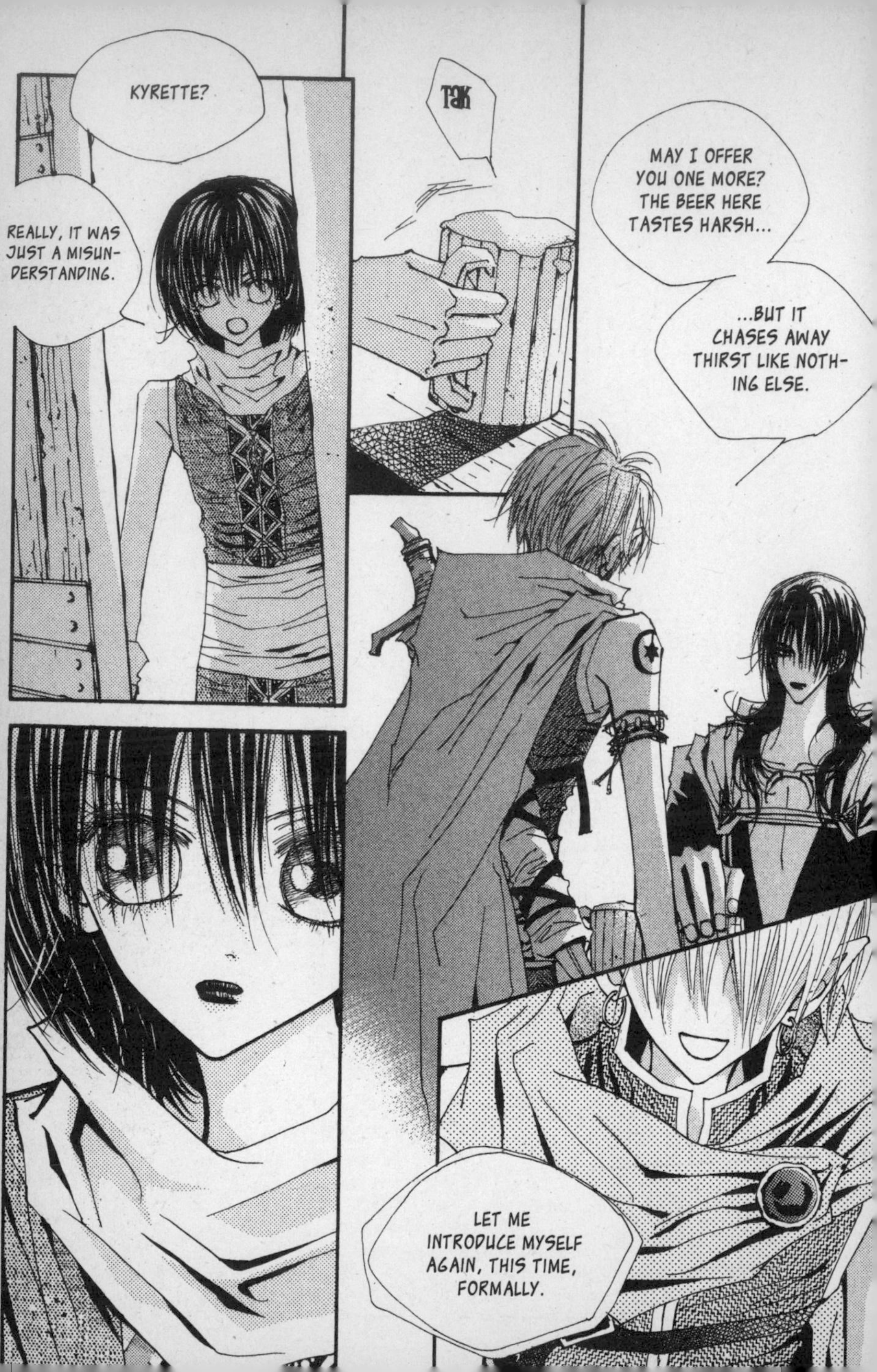
KYRETTE?
REALLY, IT WAS JUST A MISUNDERSTANDING.
TAK
MAY I OFFER YOU ONE MORE? THE BEER HERE TASTES HARSH...
...BUT IT CHASES AWAY THIRST LIKE NOTHING ELSE.
LET ME INTRODUCE MYSELF AGAIN, THIS TIME, FORMALLY.

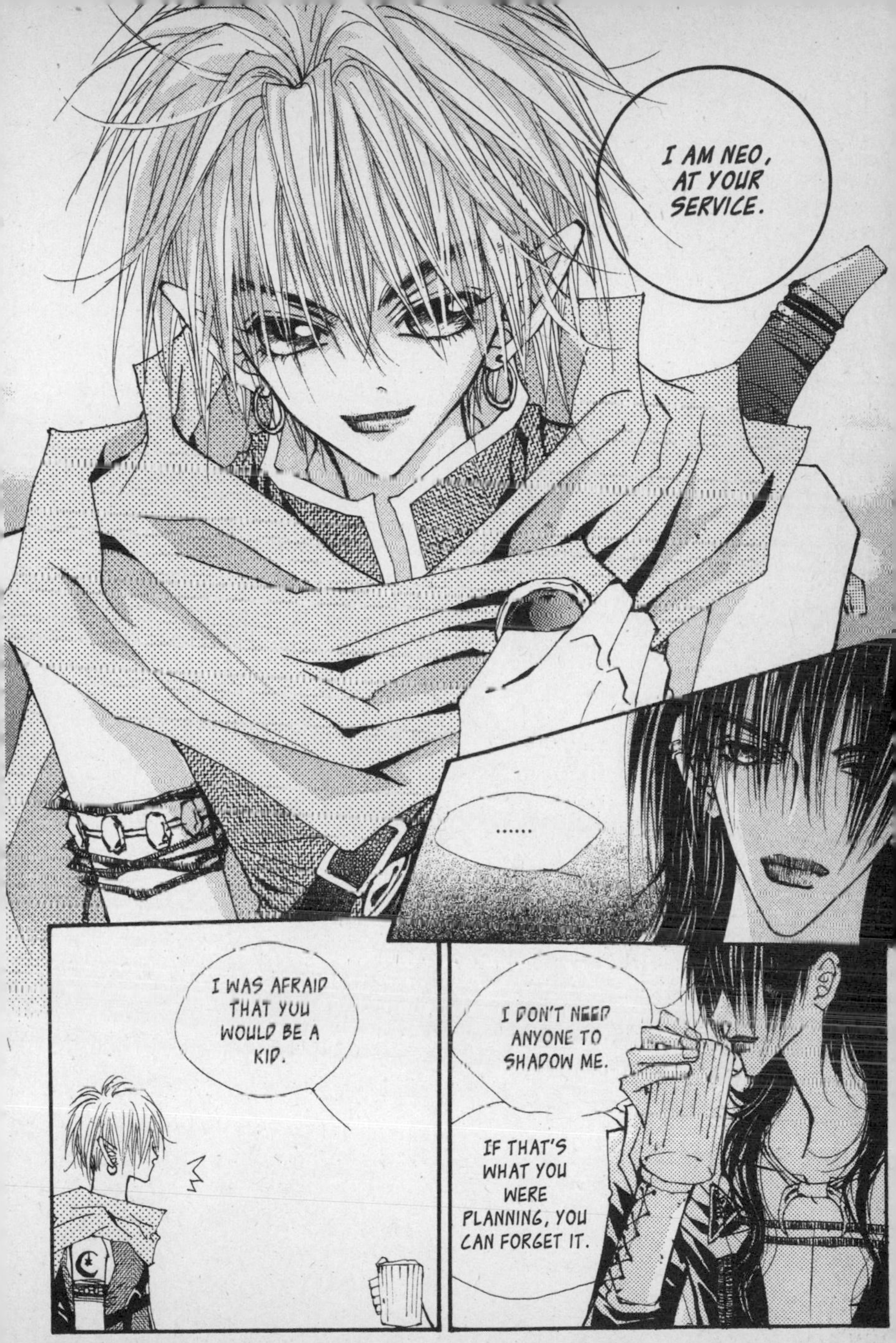
I AM NEO, AT YOUR SERVICE.
......
I WAS AFRAID THAT YOU WOULD BE A KID.
I DON'T NEED ANYONE TO SHADOW ME.
IF THAT'S WHAT YOU WERE PLANNING, YOU CAN FORGET IT.

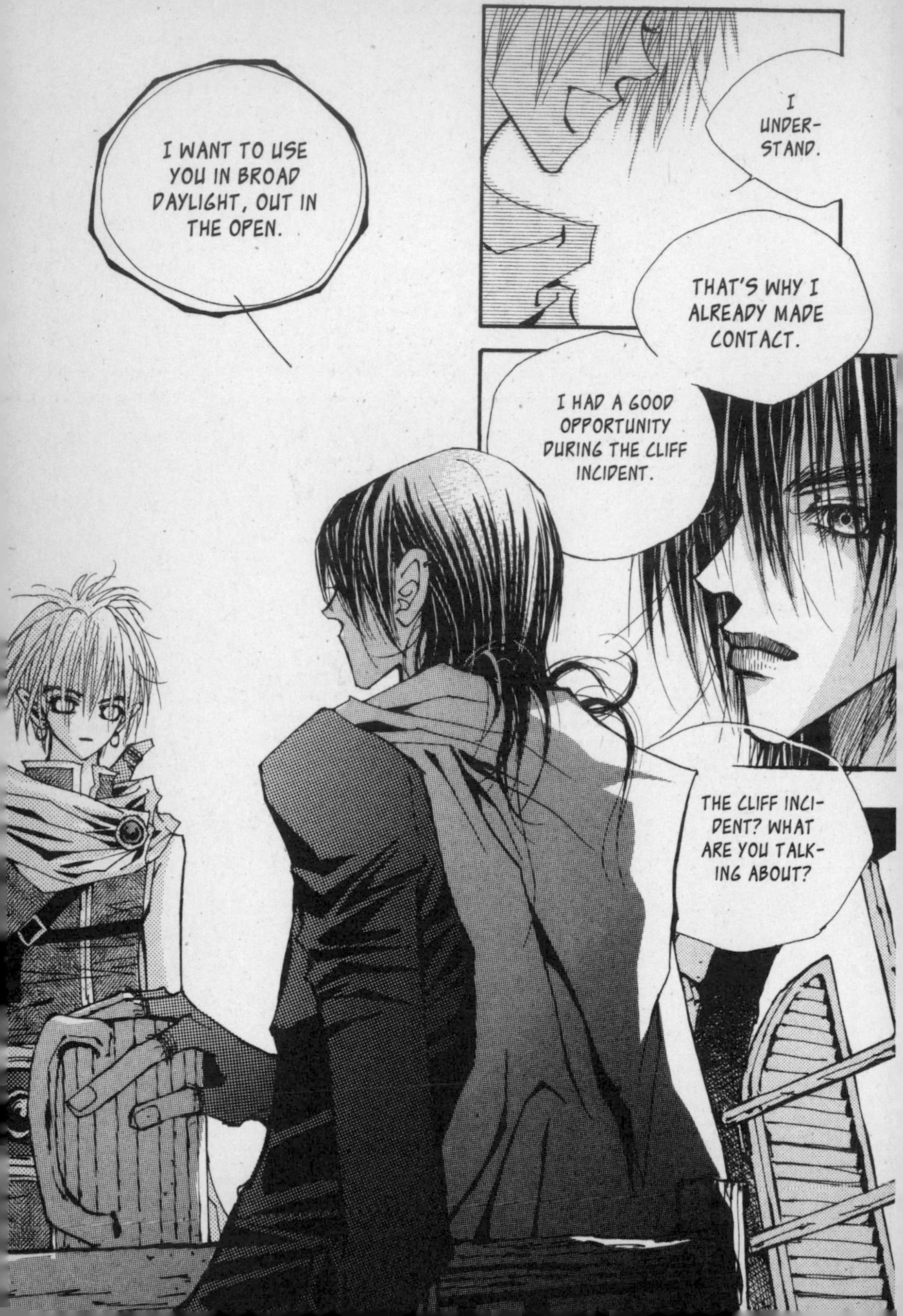
I WANT TO USE YOU IN BROAD DAYLIGHT, OUT IN THE OPEN.
I UNDER-STAND.
THAT'S WHY I ALREADY MADE CONTACT.
I HAD A GOOD OPPORTUNITY DURING THE CLIFF INCIDENT.
THE CLIFF INCI-DENT? WHAT ARE YOU TALK-ING ABOUT?

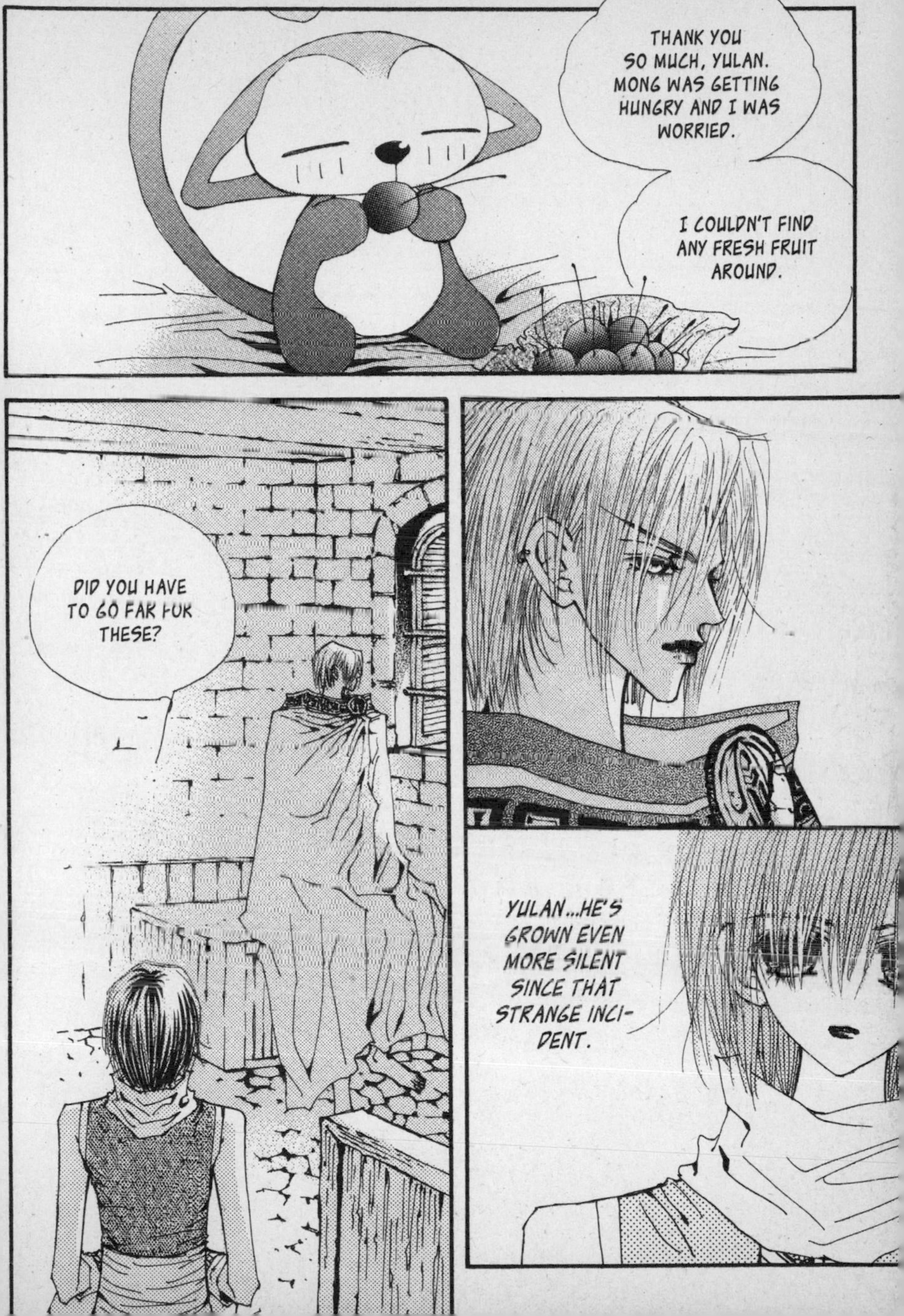
THANK YOU SO MUCH, YULAN. MONG WAS GETTING HUNGRY AND I WAS WORRIED.
I COULDN'T FIND ANY FRESH FRUIT AROUND.
DID YOU HAVE TO GO FAR FOR THESE?
YULAN...HE'S GROWN EVEN MORE SILENT SINCE THAT STRANGE INCI-DENT.

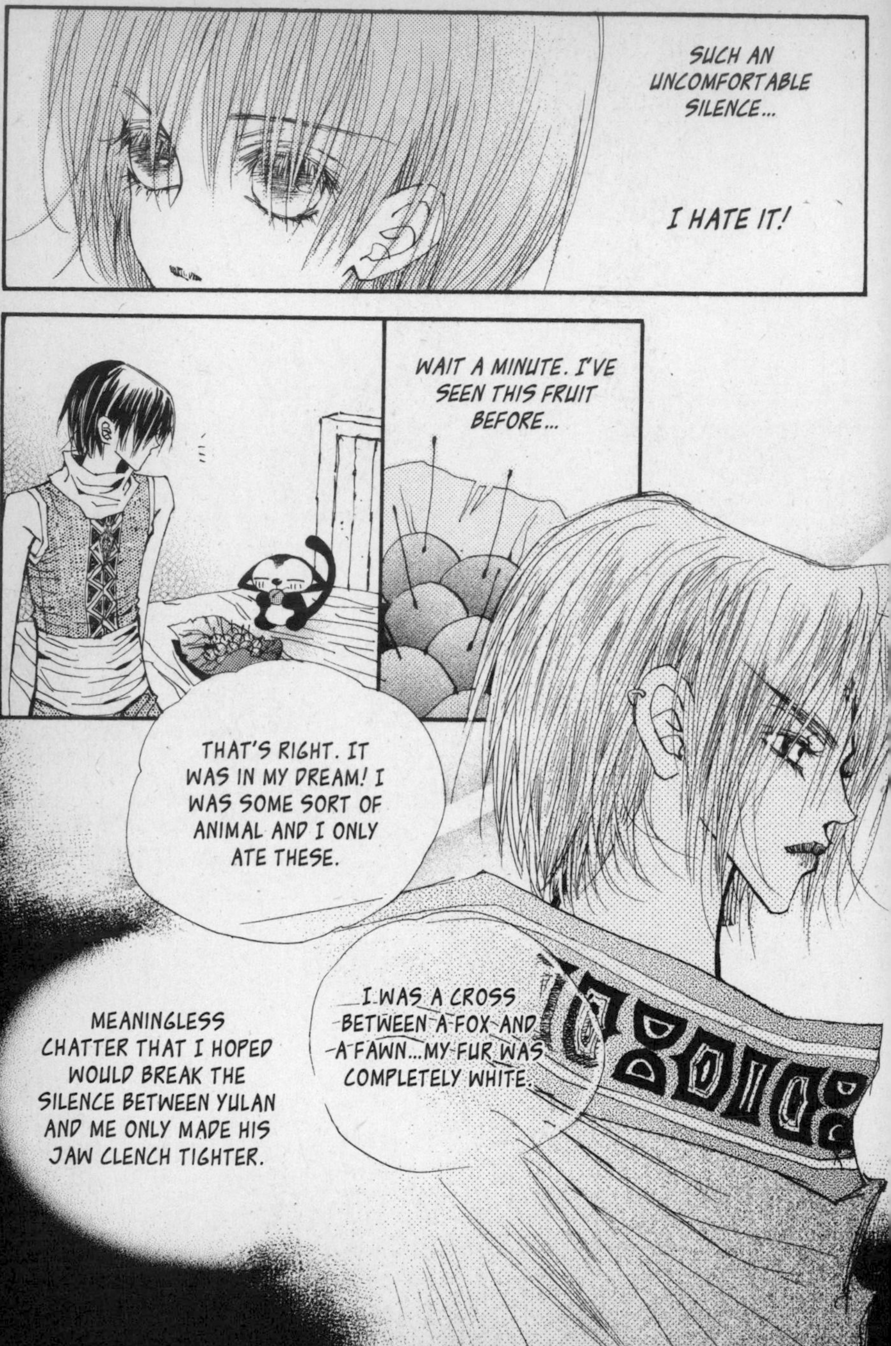
SUCH AN UNCOMFORTABLE SILENCE...
I HATE IT!
WAIT A MINUTE. I'VE SEEN THIS FRUIT BEFORE...
THAT'S RIGHT. IT WAS IN MY DREAM! I WAS SOME SORT OF ANIMAL AND I ONLY ATE THESE.
I WAS A CROSS BETWEEN A FOX AND A FAWN...MY FUR WAS COMPLETELY WHITE.
MEANINGLESS CHATTER THAT I HOPED WOULD BREAK THE SILENCE BETWEEN YULAN AND ME ONLY MADE HIS JAW CLENCH TIGHTER.

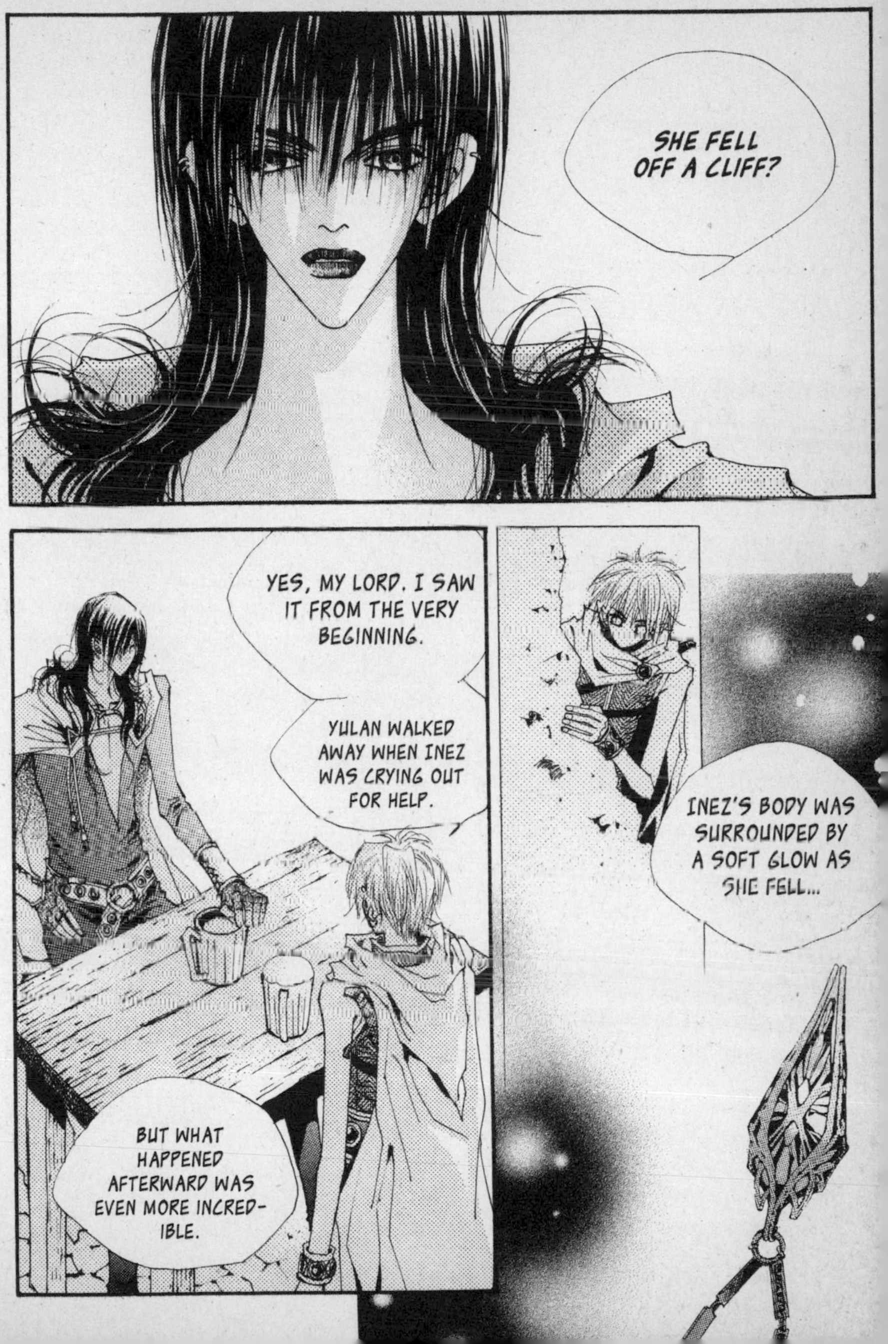
SHE FELL OFF A CLIFF?
YES, MY LORD. I SAW IT FROM THE VERY BEGINNING.
YULAN WALKED AWAY WHEN INEZ WAS CRYING OUT FOR HELP.
BUT WHAT HAPPENED AFTERWARD WAS EVEN MORE INCRED-IBLE.
INEZ'S BODY WAS SURROUNDED BY A SOFT GLOW AS SHE FELL...

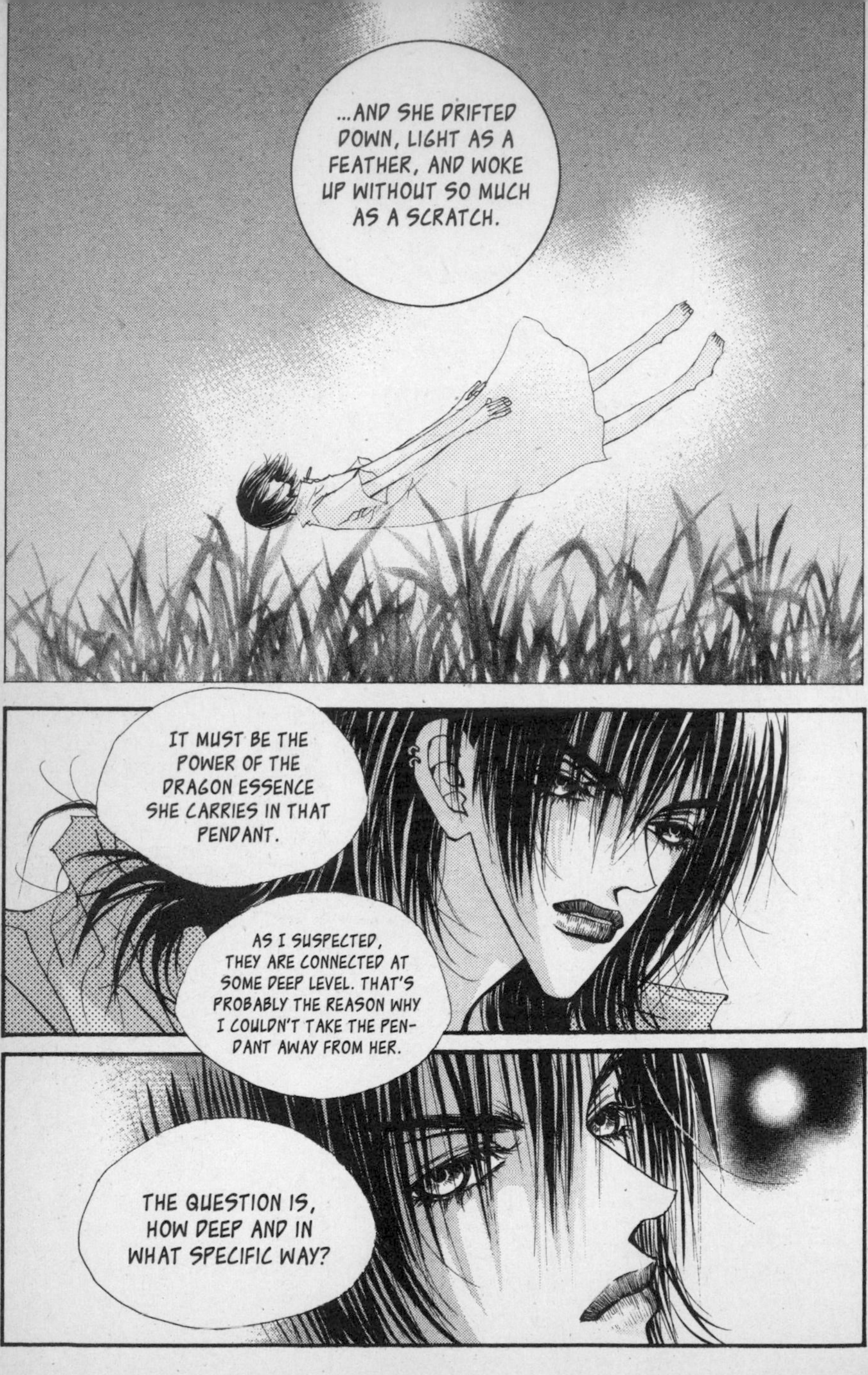
...AND SHE DRIFTED DOWN, LIGHT AS A FEATHER, AND WOKE UP WITHOUT SO MUCH AS A SCRATCH.
IT MUST BE THE POWER OF THE DRAGON ESSENCE SHE CARRIES IN THAT PENDANT.
AS I SUSPECTED, THEY ARE CONNECTED AT SOME DEEP LEVEL. THAT'S PROBABLY THE REASON WHY I COULDN'T TAKE THE PEN-DANT AWAY FROM HER.
THE QUESTION IS, HOW DEEP AND IN WHAT SPECIFIC WAY?

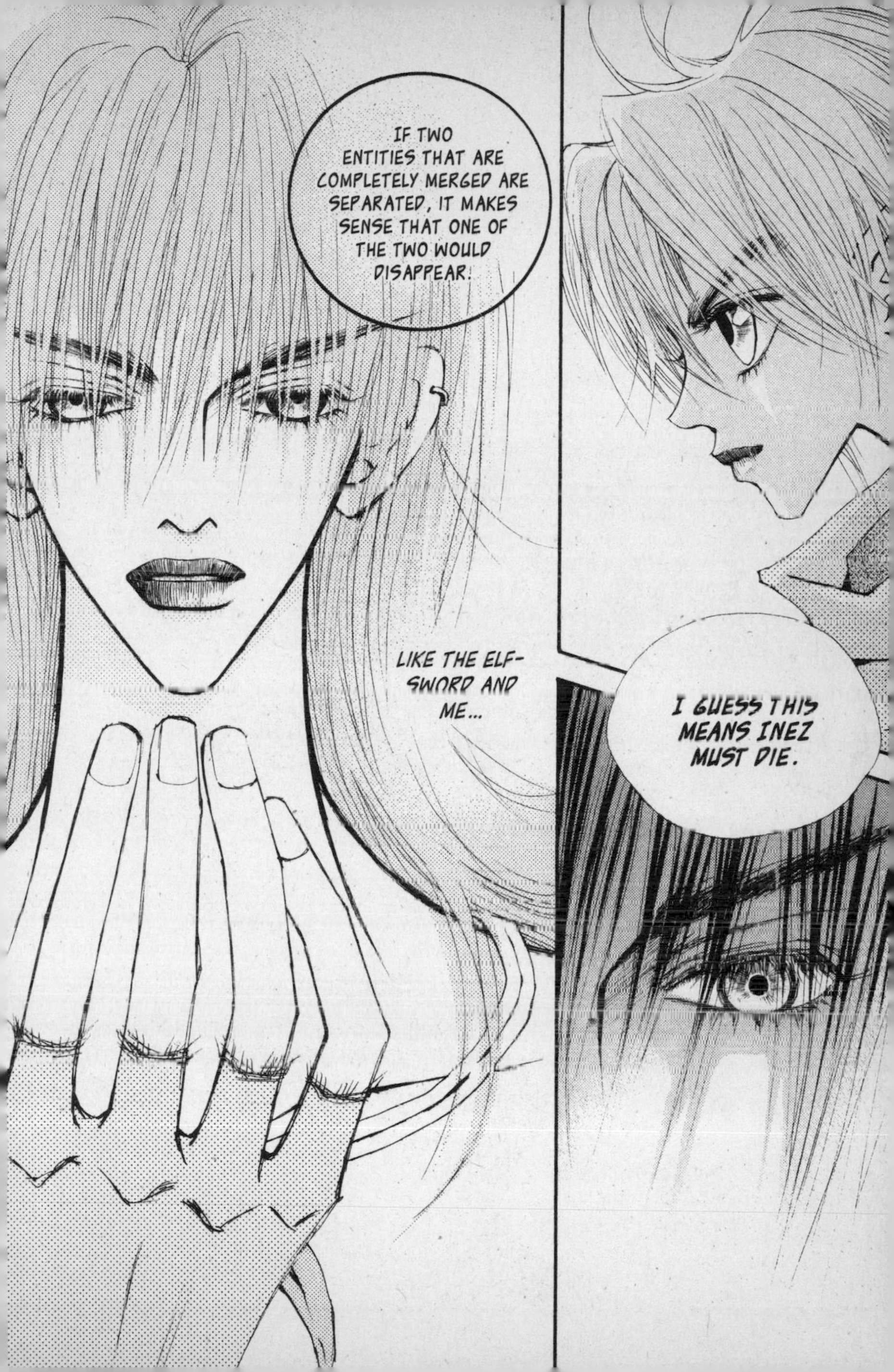
IF TWO ENTITIES THAT ARE COMPLETELY MERGED ARE SEPARATED, IT MAKES SENSE THAT ONE OF THE TWO WOULD DISAPPEAR.
LIKE THE ELF-SWORD AND ME...
I GUESS THIS MEANS INEZ MUST DIE.

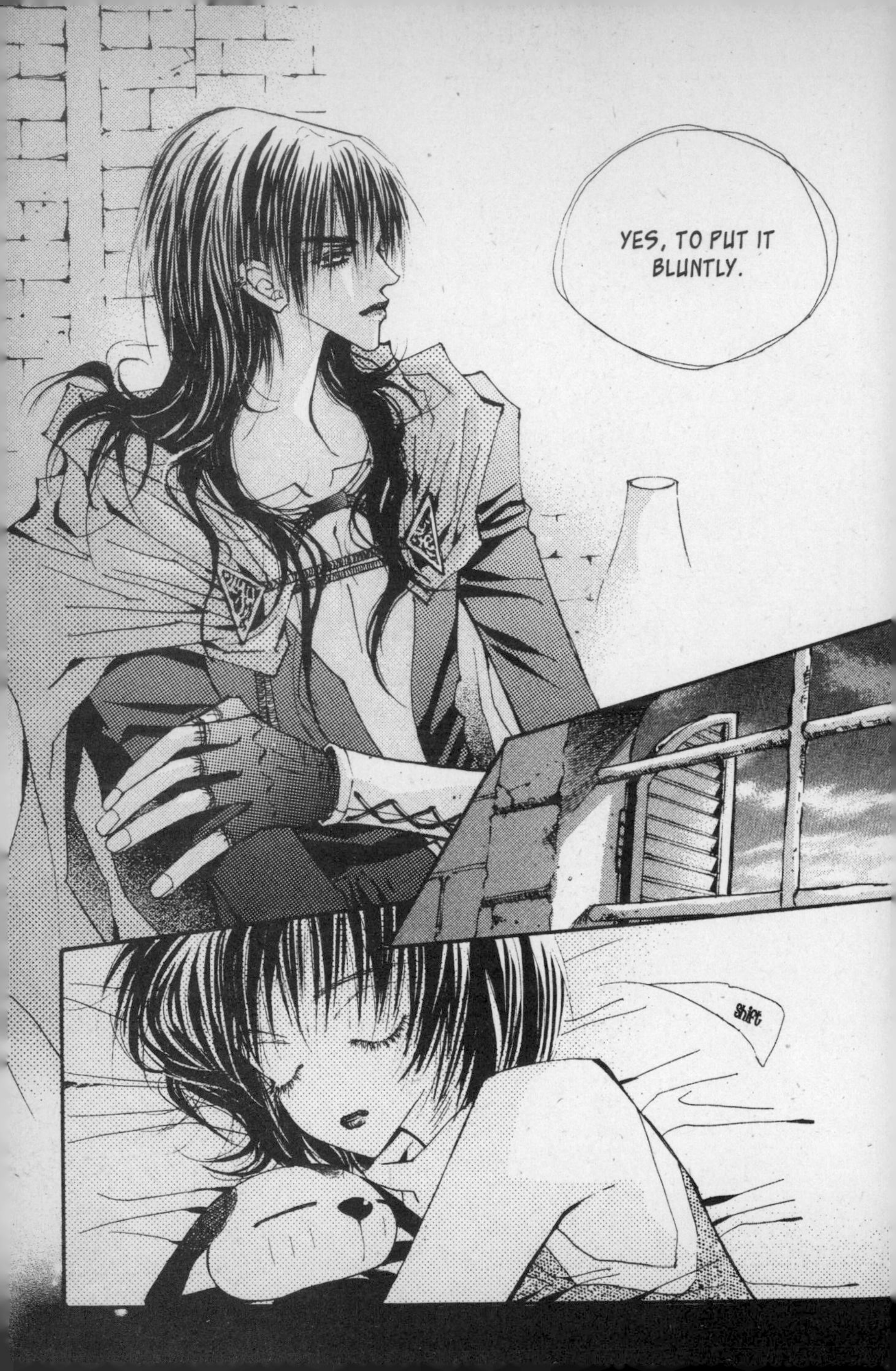
YES, TO PUT IT BLUNTLY.
SHIFT

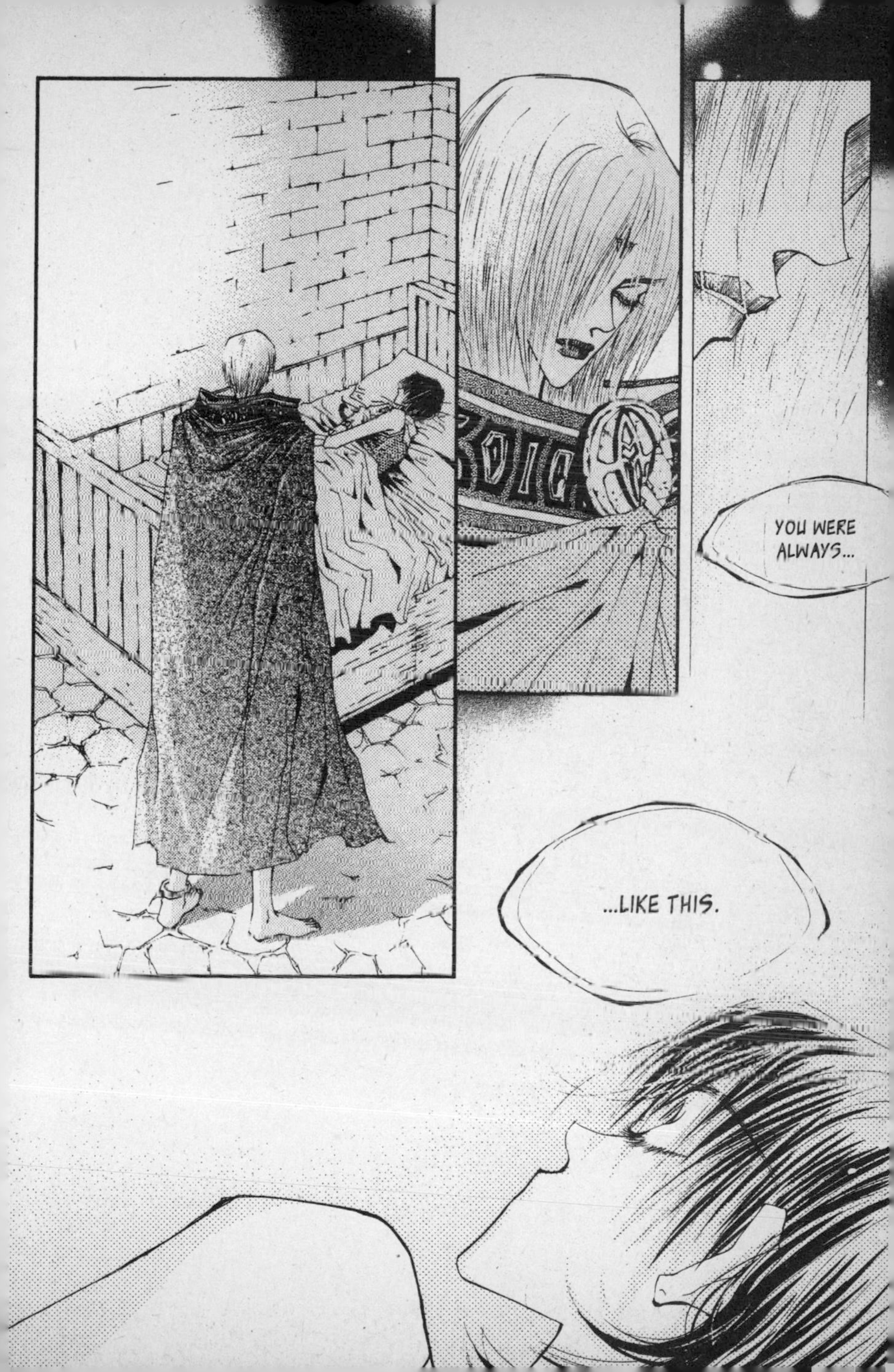
YOU WERE ALWAYS...
...LIKE THIS.

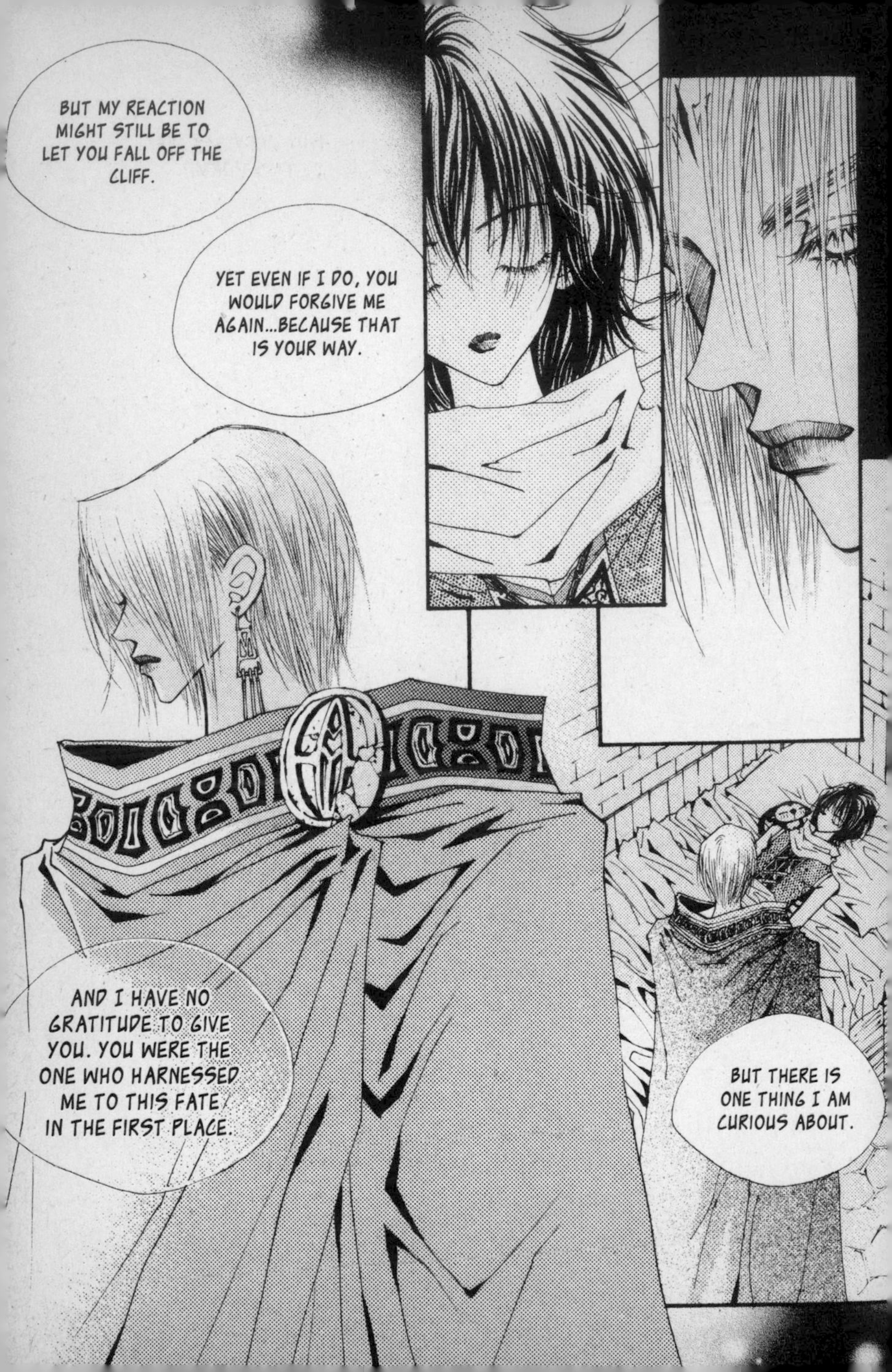
BUT MY REACTION MIGHT STILL BE TO LET YOU FALL OFF THE CLIFF.
YET EVEN IF I DO, YOU WOULD FORGIVE ME AGAIN...BECAUSE THAT IS YOUR WAY.
AND I HAVE NO GRATITUDE TO GIVE YOU. YOU WERE THE ONE WHO HARNESSED ME TO THIS FATE IN THE FIRST PLACE.
BUT THERE IS ONE THING I AM CURIOUS ABOUT.

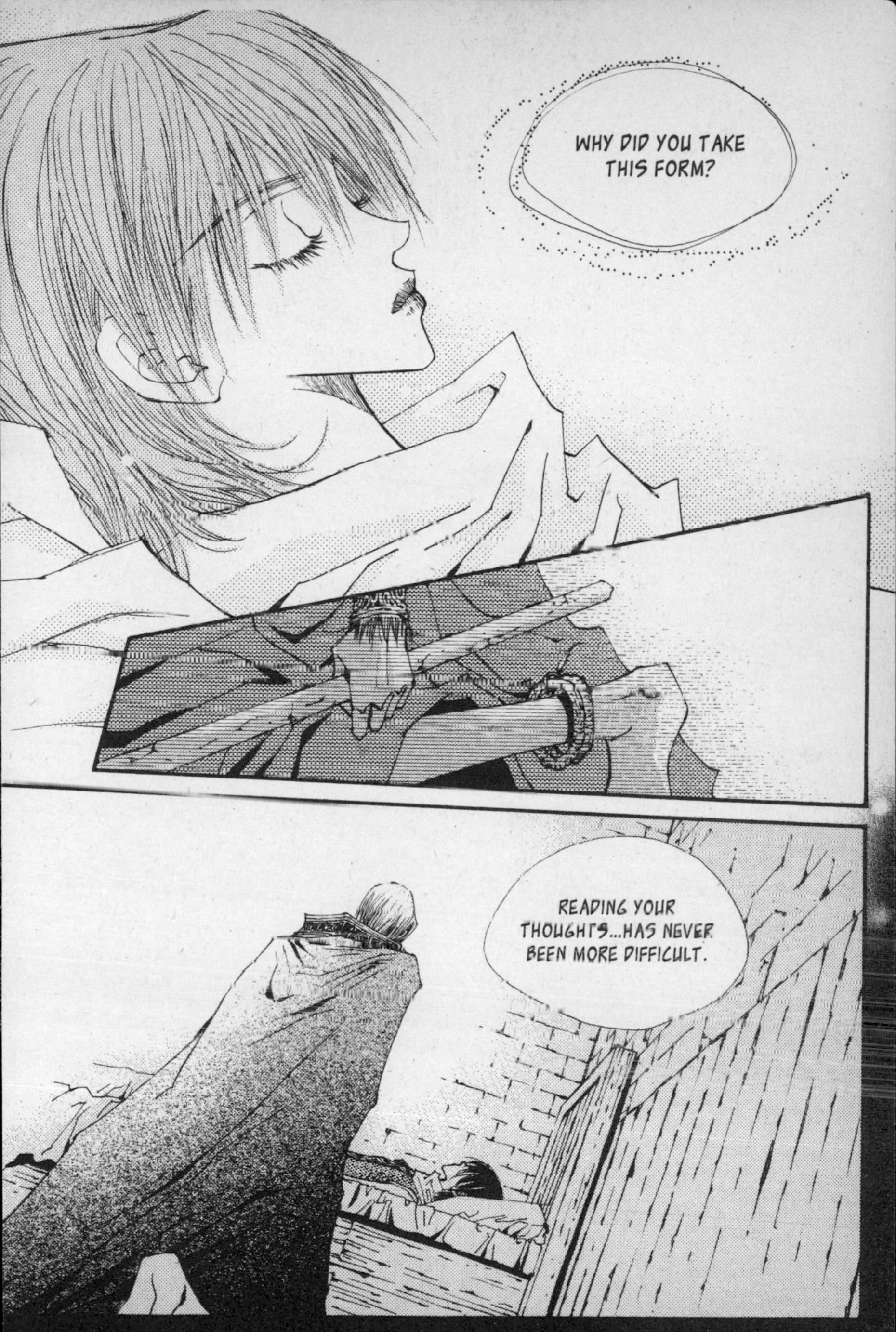
WHY DID YOU TAKE THIS FORM?
READING YOUR THOUGHTS...HAS NEVER BEEN MORE DIFFICULT.

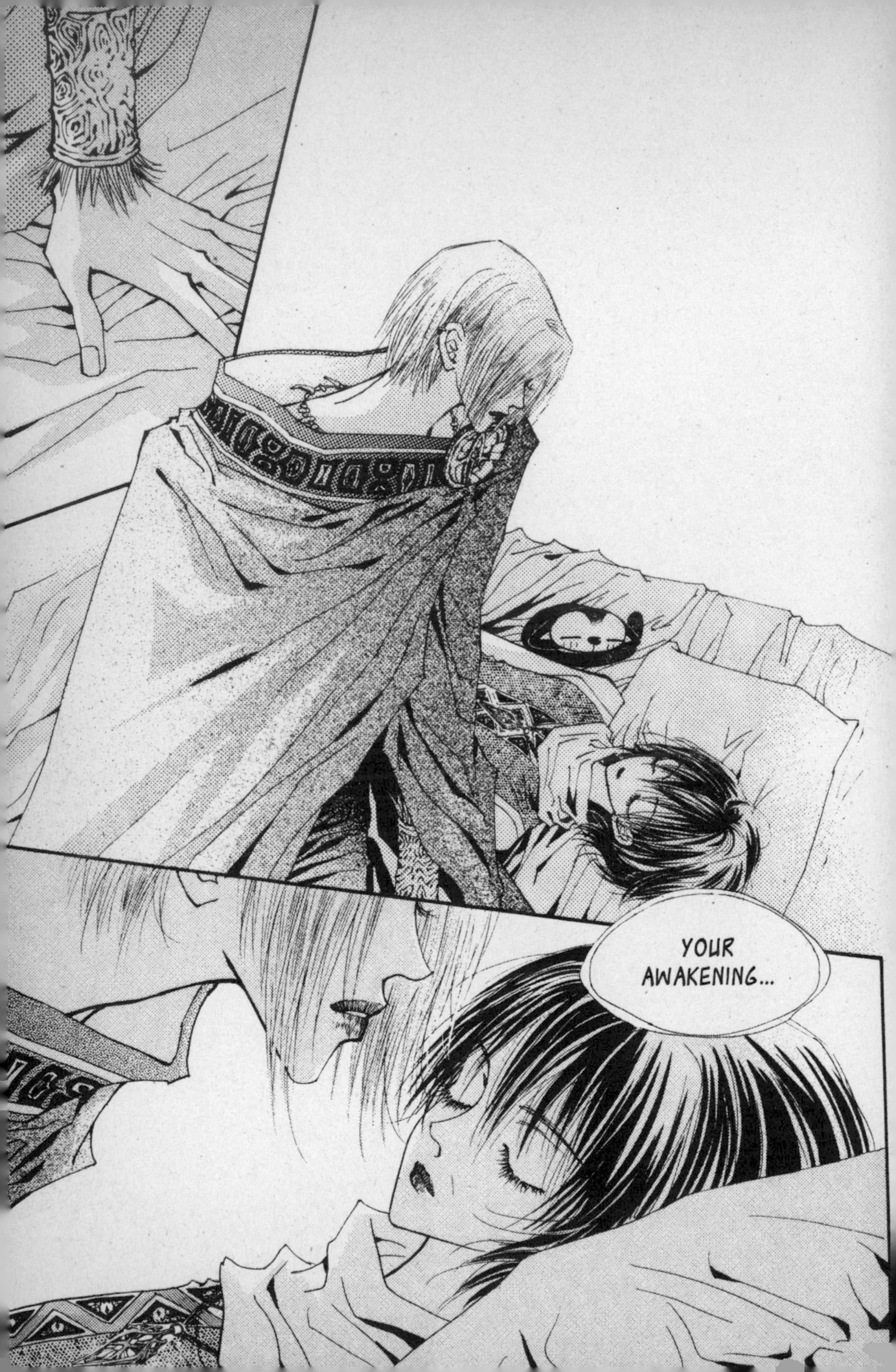
YOUR AWAKENING...

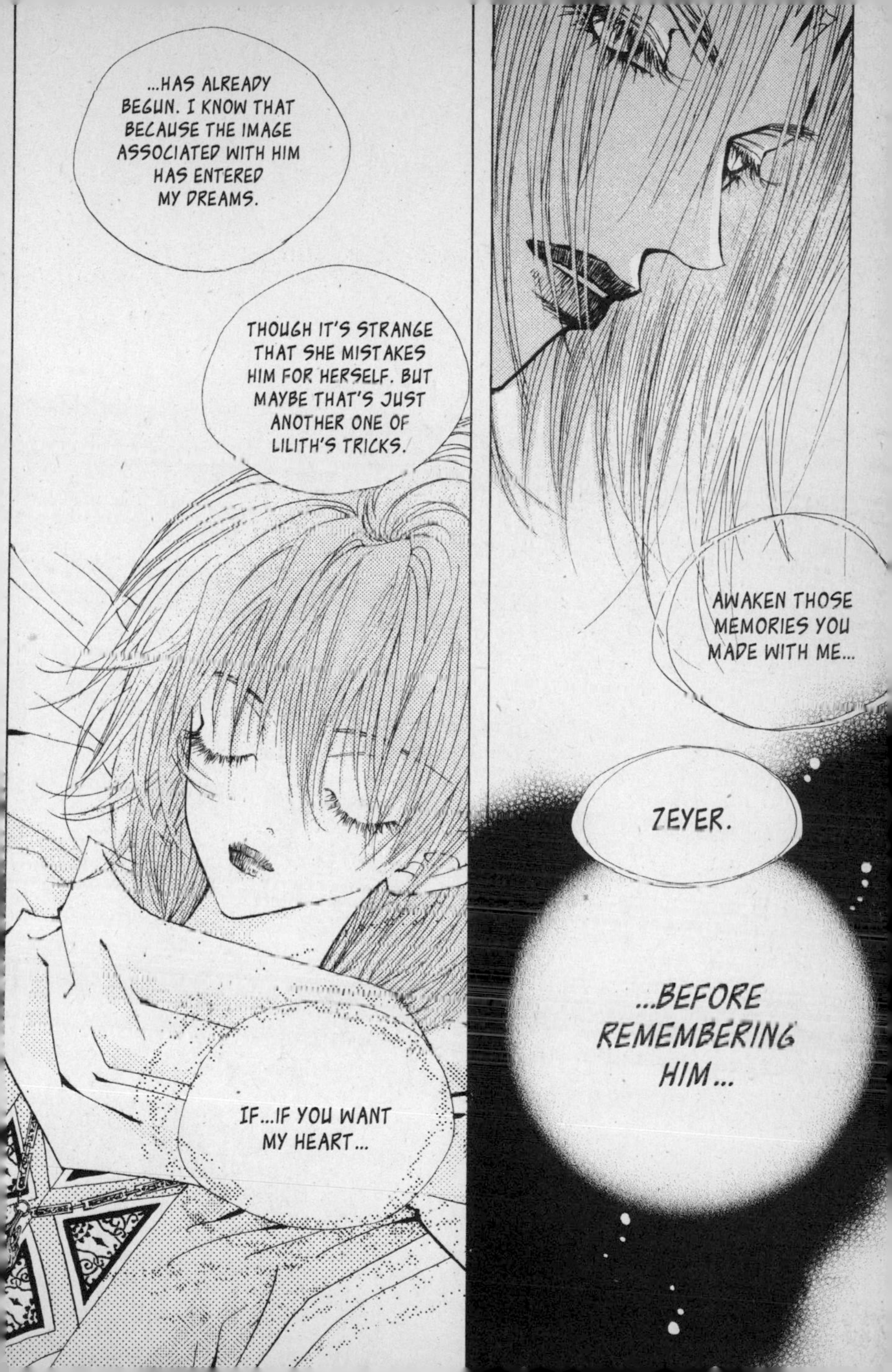
...HAS ALREADY BEGUN. I KNOW THAT BECAUSE THE IMAGE ASSOCIATED WITH HIM HAS ENTERED MY DREAMS.
THOUGH IT'S STRANGE THAT SHE MISTAKES HIM FOR HERSELF. BUT MAYBE THAT'S JUST ANOTHER ONE OF LILITH'S TRICKS.
IF...IF YOU WANT MY HEART...
AWAKEN THOSE MEMORIES YOU MADE WITH ME...
ZEYER.
...BEFORE REMEMBERING HIM...

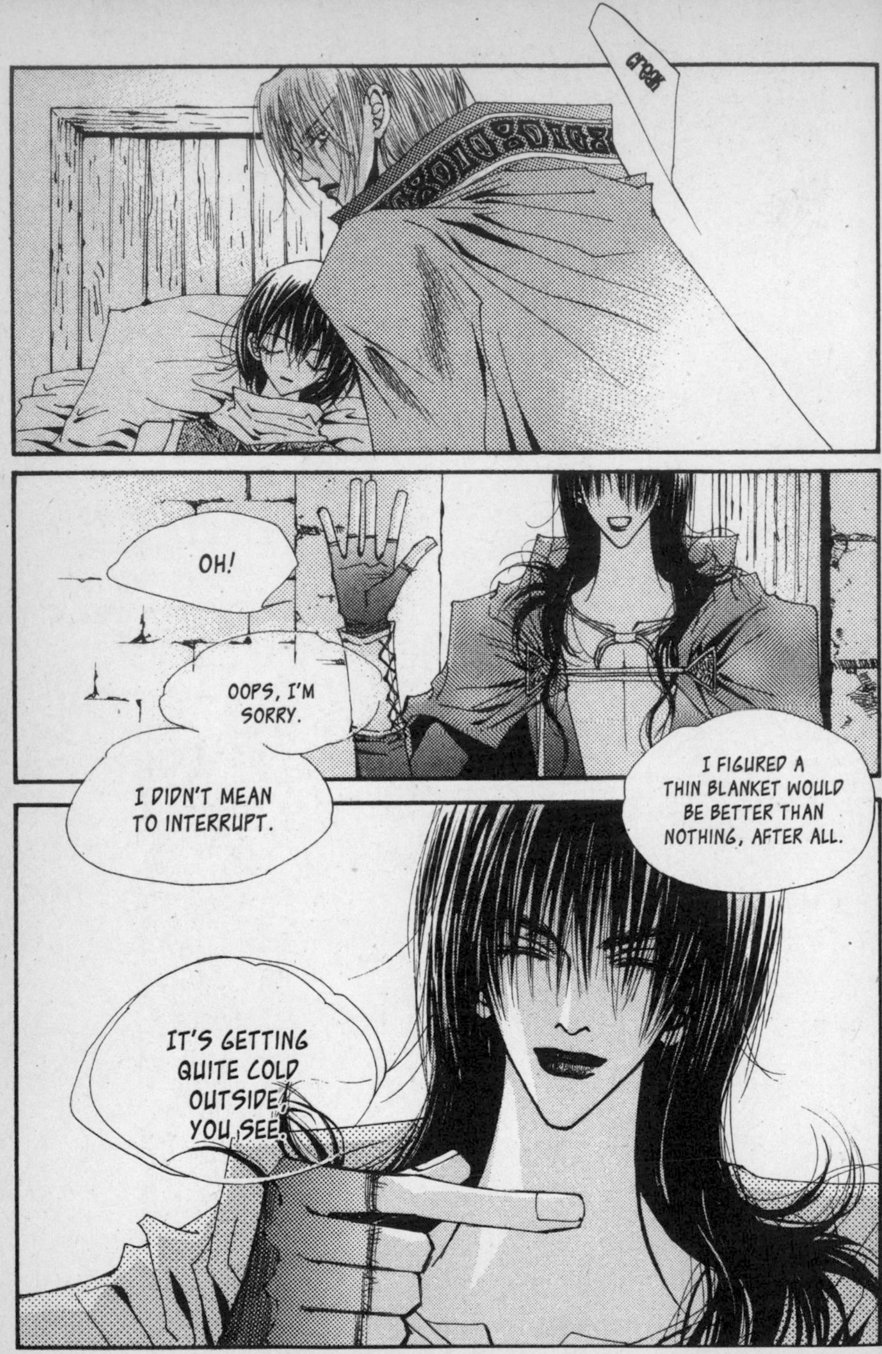
creak
OH!
OOPS, I'M SORRY.
I DIDN'T MEAN TO INTERRUPT.
I FIGURED A THIN BLANKET WOULD BE BETTER THAN NOTHING, AFTER ALL.
IT'S GETTING QUITE COLD OUTSIDE, YOU SEE.

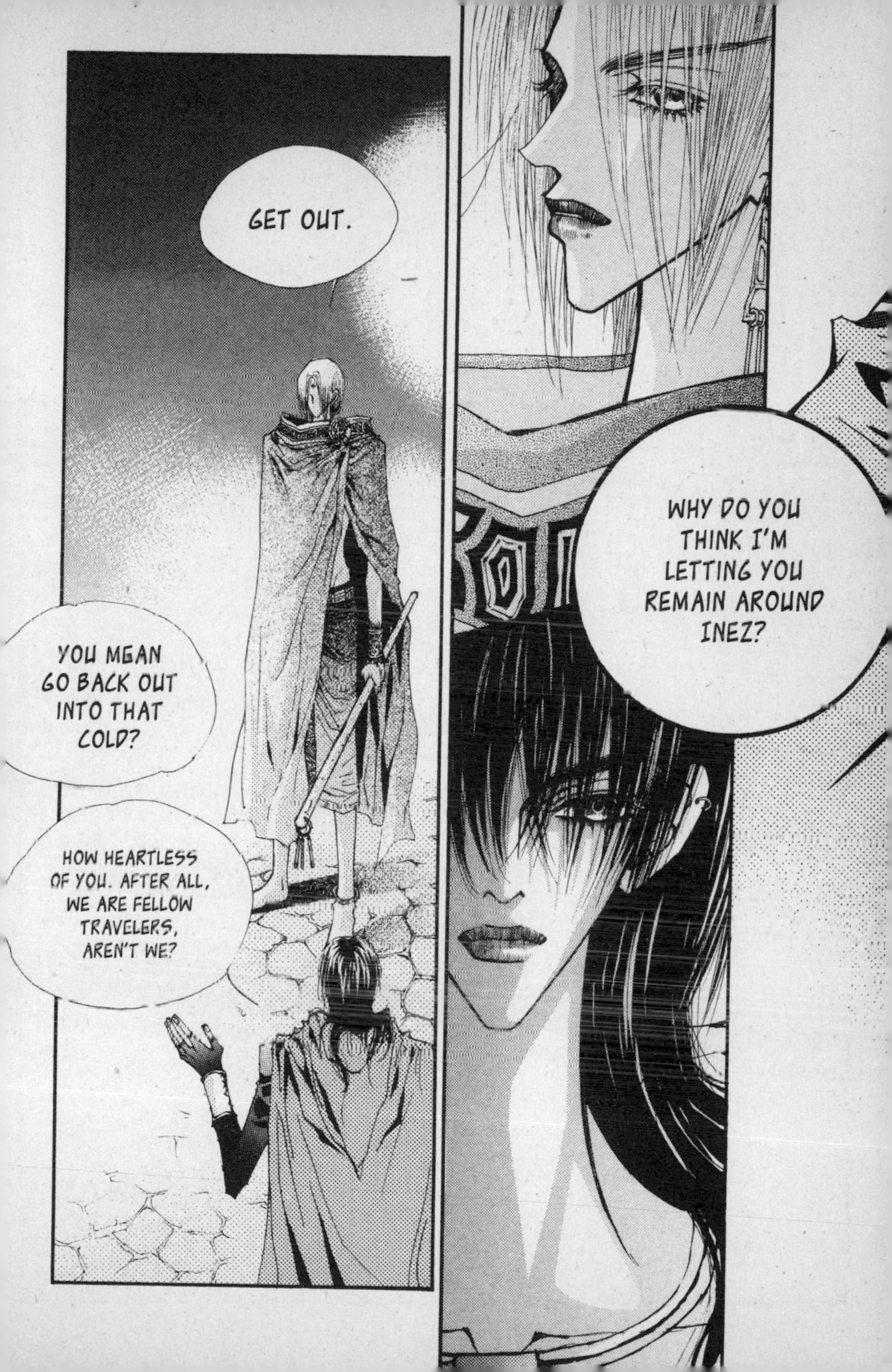
GET OUT.
YOU MEAN GO BACK OUT INTO THAT COLD?
HOW HEARTLESS OF YOU. AFTER ALL, WE ARE FELLOW TRAVELERS, AREN'T WE?
WHY DO YOU THINK I'M LETTING YOU REMAIN AROUND INEZ?

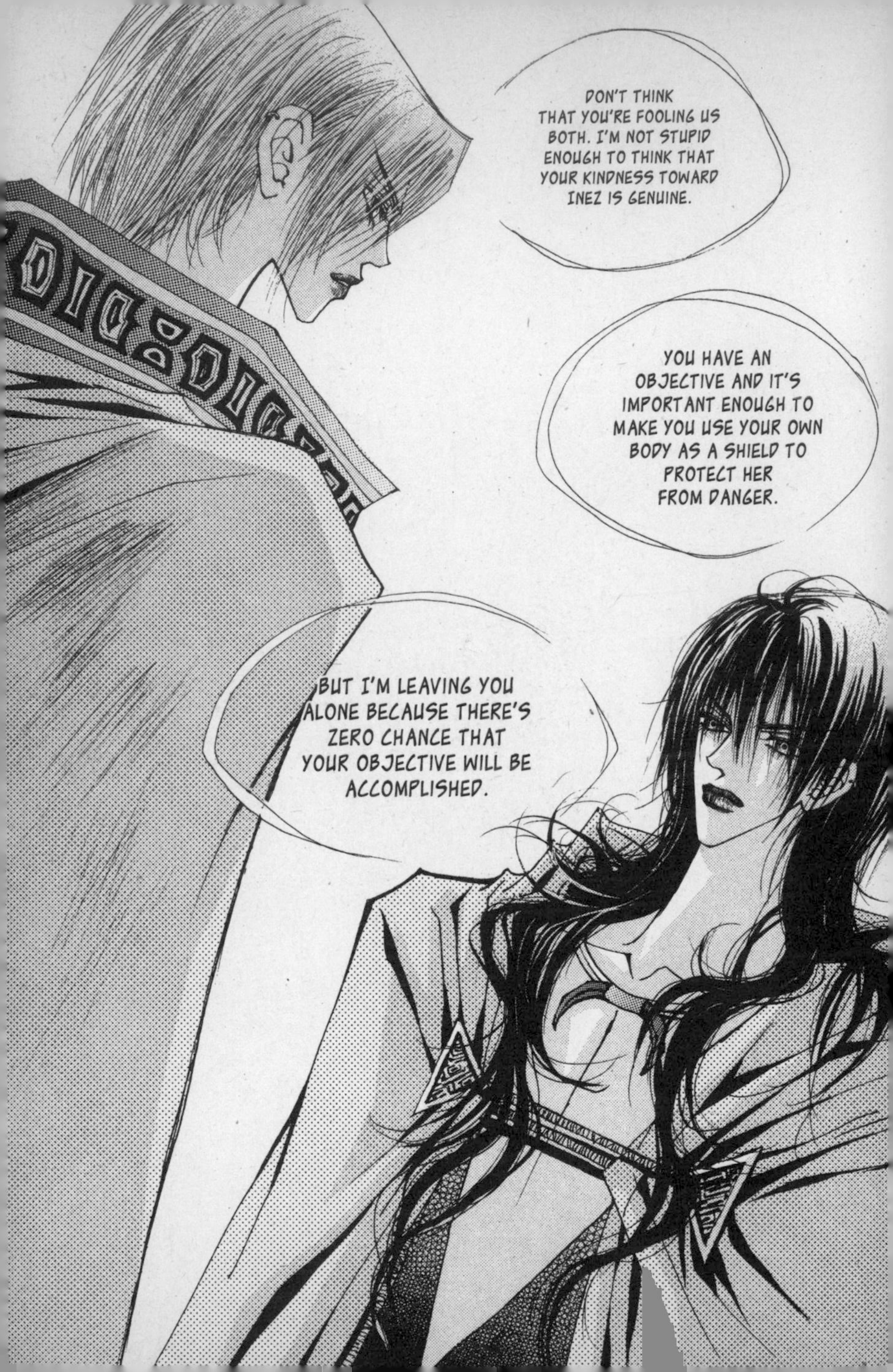
DON'T THINK THAT YOU'RE FOOLING US BOTH. I'M NOT STUPID ENOUGH TO THINK THAT YOUR KINDNESS TOWARD INEZ IS GENUINE.
YOU HAVE AN OBJECTIVE AND IT'S IMPORTANT ENOUGH TO MAKE YOU USE YOUR OWN BODY AS A SHIELD TO PROTECT HER FROM DANGER.
BUT I'M LEAVING YOU ALONE BECAUSE THERE'S ZERO CHANCE THAT YOUR OBJECTIVE WILL BE ACCOMPLISHED.

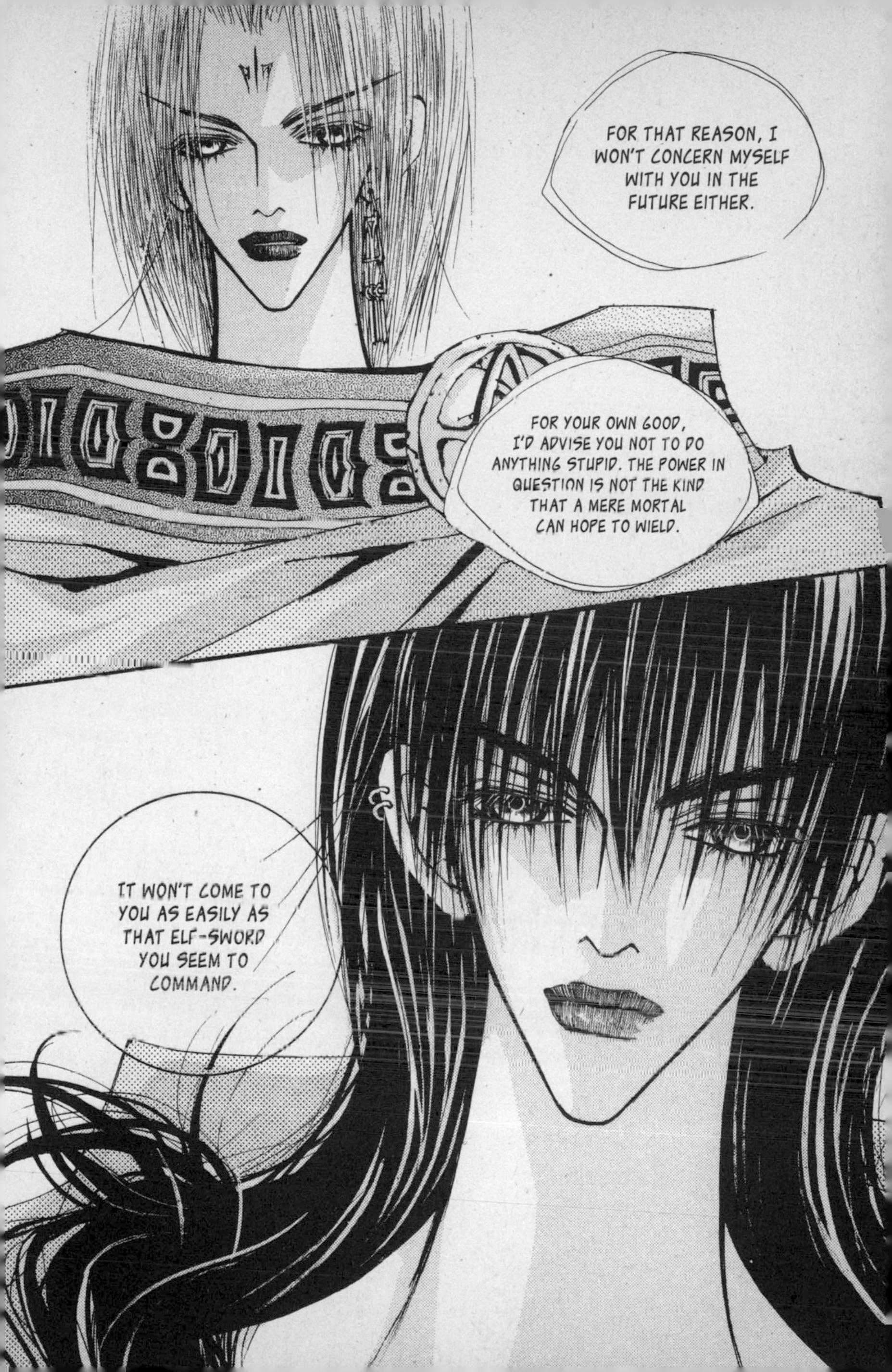
FOR THAT REASON, I WON'T CONCERN MYSELF WITH YOU IN THE FUTURE EITHER.
FOR YOUR OWN GOOD, I'D ADVISE YOU NOT TO DO ANYTHING STUPID. THE POWER IN QUESTION IS NOT THE KIND THAT A MERE MORTAL CAN HOPE TO WIELD.
IT WON'T COME TO YOU AS EASILY AS THAT ELF-SWORD YOU SEEM TO COMMAND.

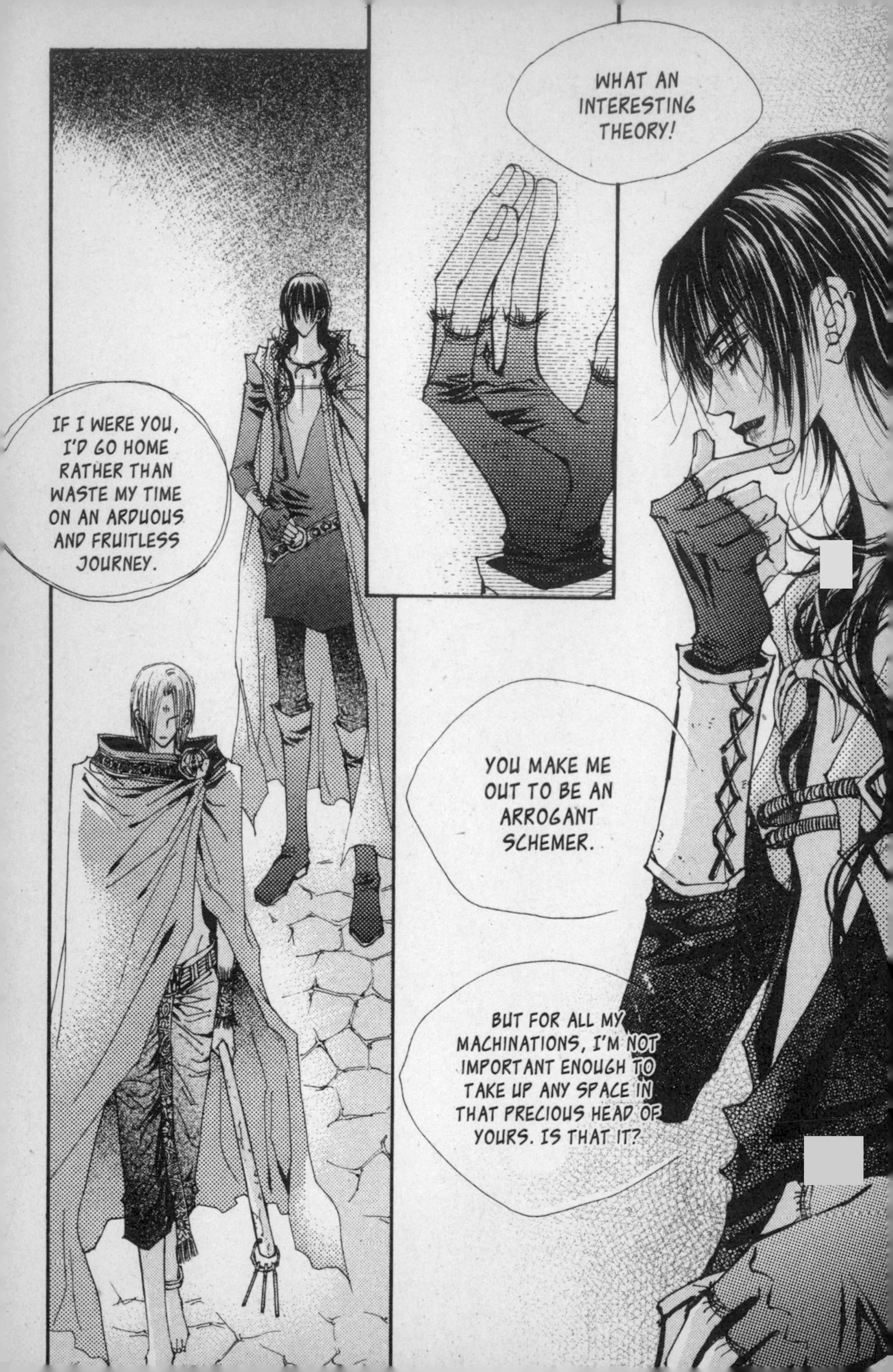
IF I WERE YOU, I'D GO HOME RATHER THAN WASTE MY TIME ON AN ARDUOUS AND FRUITLESS JOURNEY.
WHAT AN INTERESTING THEORY!
YOU MAKE ME OUT TO BE AN ARROGANT SCHEMER.
BUT FOR ALL MY MACHINATIONS, I'M NOT IMPORTANT ENOUGH TO TAKE UP ANY SPACE IN THAT PRECIOUS HEAD OF YOURS. IS THAT IT?

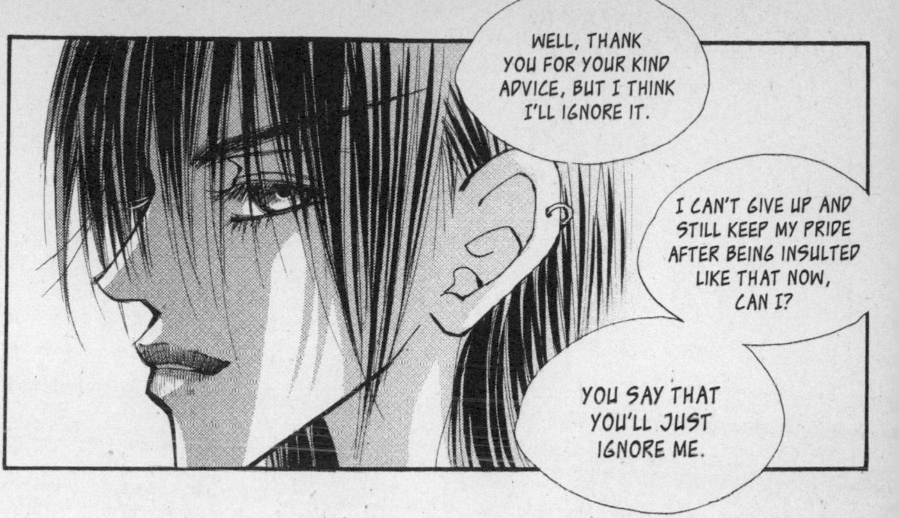
WELL, THANK YOU FOR YOUR KIND ADVICE, BUT I THINK I'LL IGNORE IT.
I CAN'T GIVE UP AND STILL KEEP MY PRIDE AFTER BEING INSULTED LIKE THAT NOW, CAN I?
YOU SAY THAT YOU'LL JUST IGNORE ME.

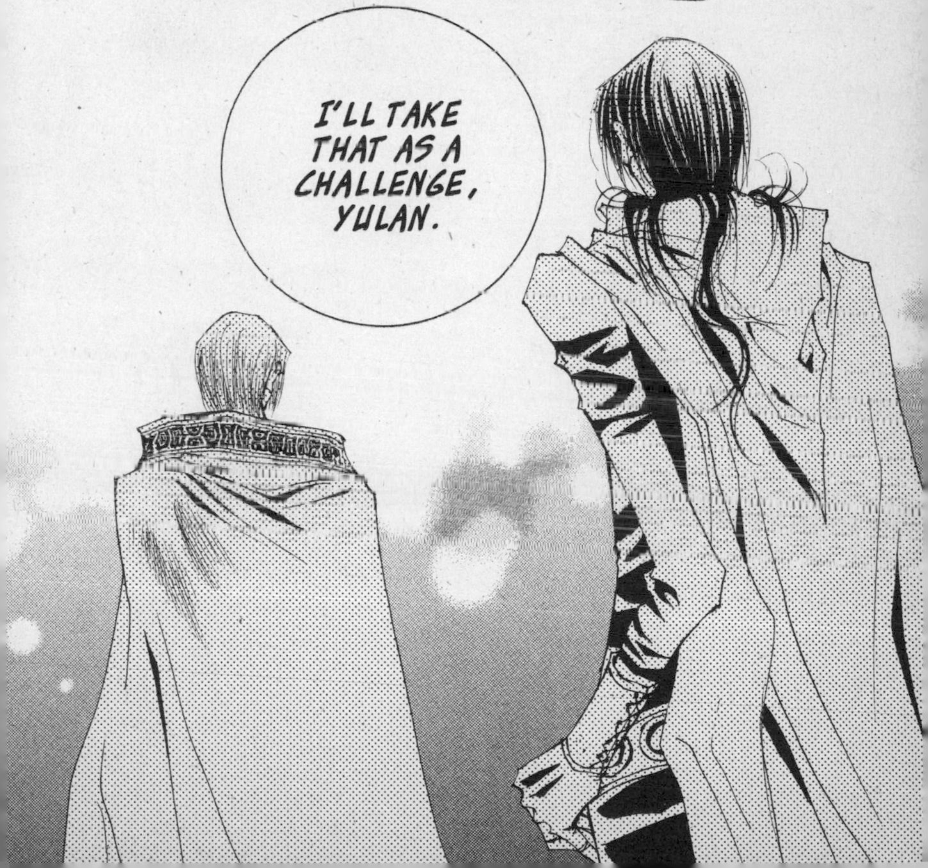
I'LL TAKE THAT AS A CHALLENGE, YULAN.

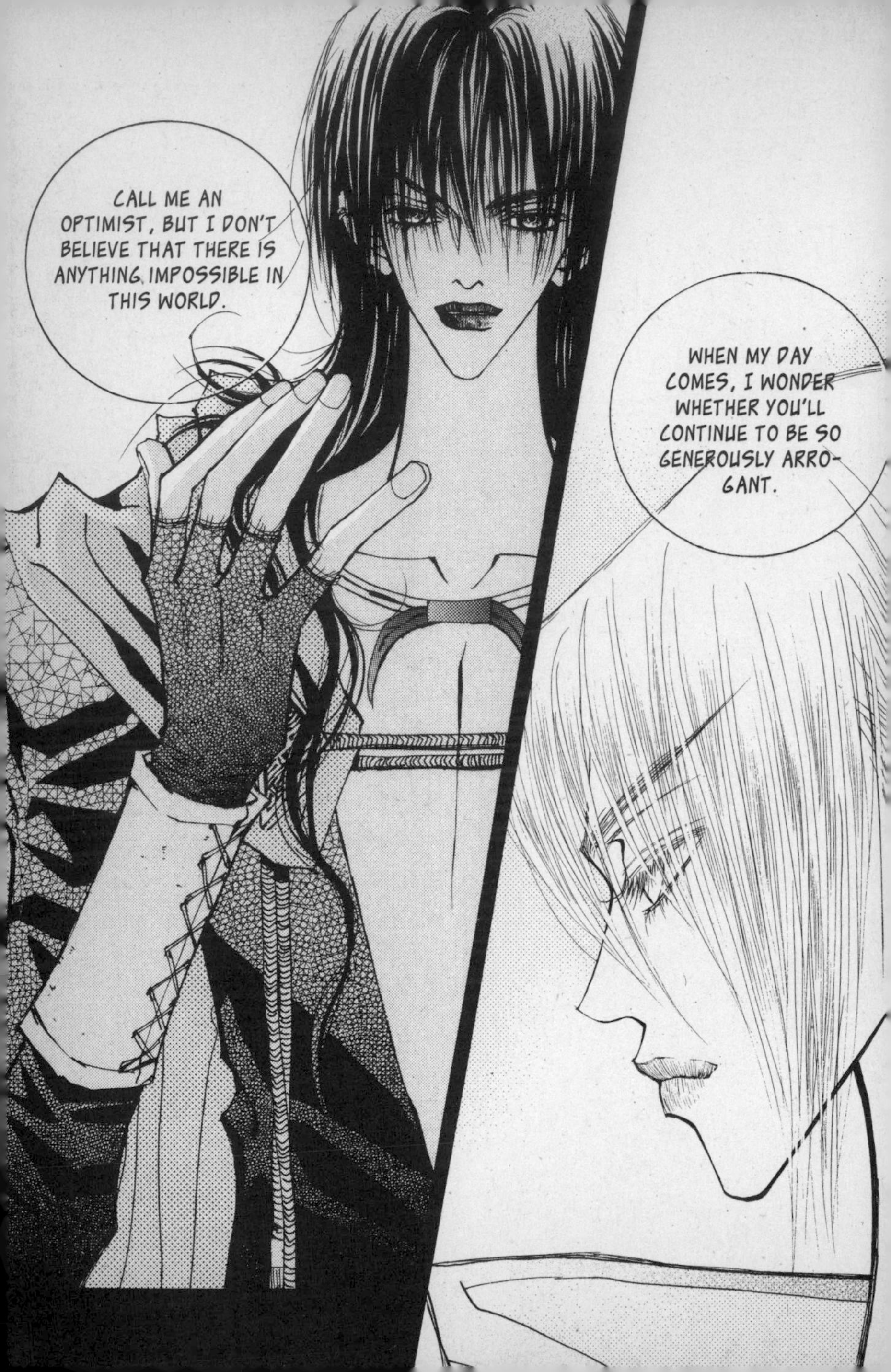
CALL ME AN OPTIMIST, BUT I DON'T BELIEVE THAT THERE IS ANYTHING IMPOSSIBLE IN THIS WORLD.
WHEN MY DAY COMES, I WONDER WHETHER YOU'LL CONTINUE TO BE SO GENEROUSLY ARRO-GANT.

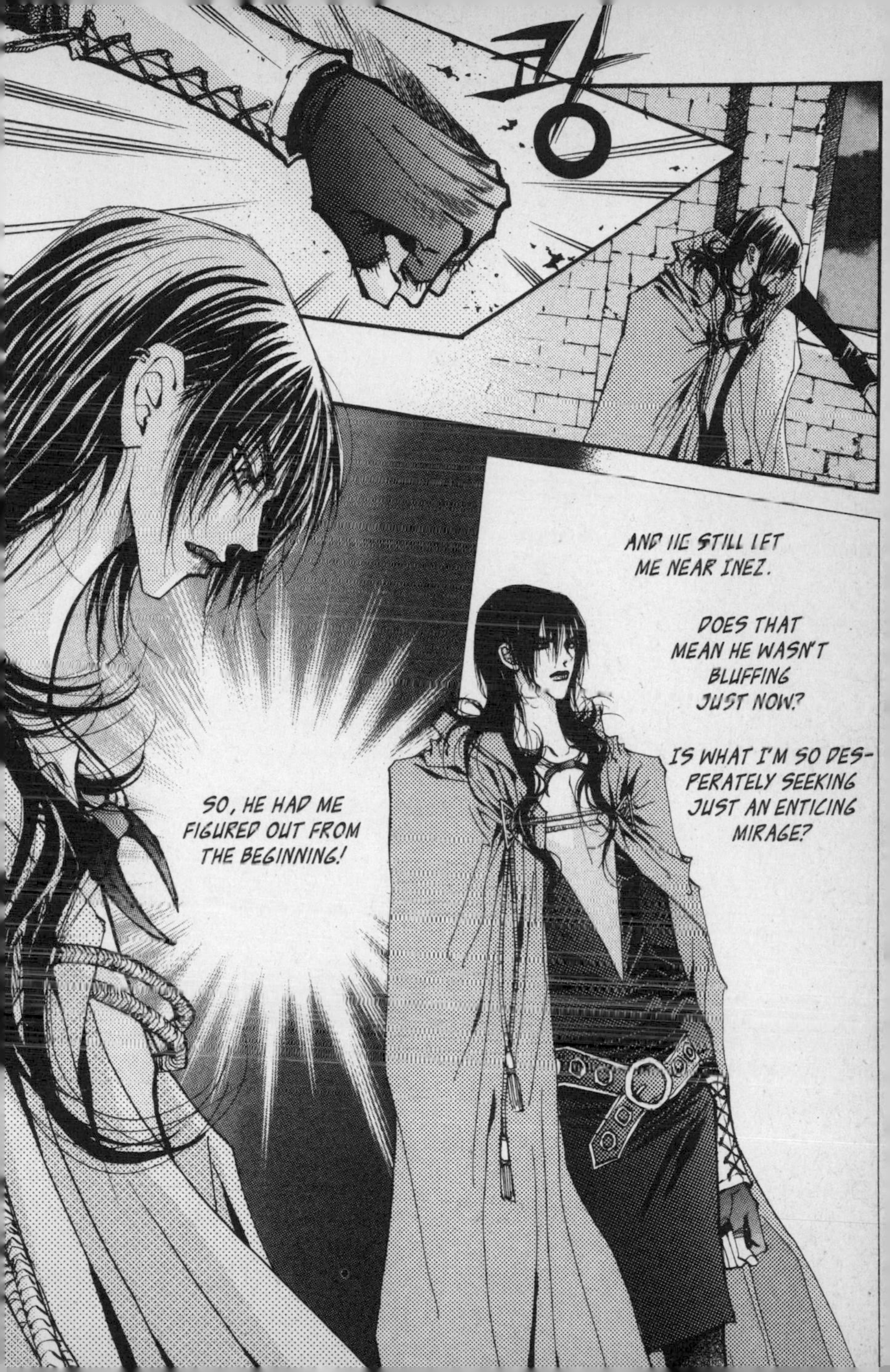
쾅
SO, HE HAD ME FIGURED OUT FROM THE BEGINNING!
AND HE STILL LEFT ME NEAR INEZ.
DOES THAT MEAN HE WASN'T BLUFFING JUST NOW?
IS WHAT I'M SO DESPERATELY SEEKING JUST AN ENTICING MIRAGE?

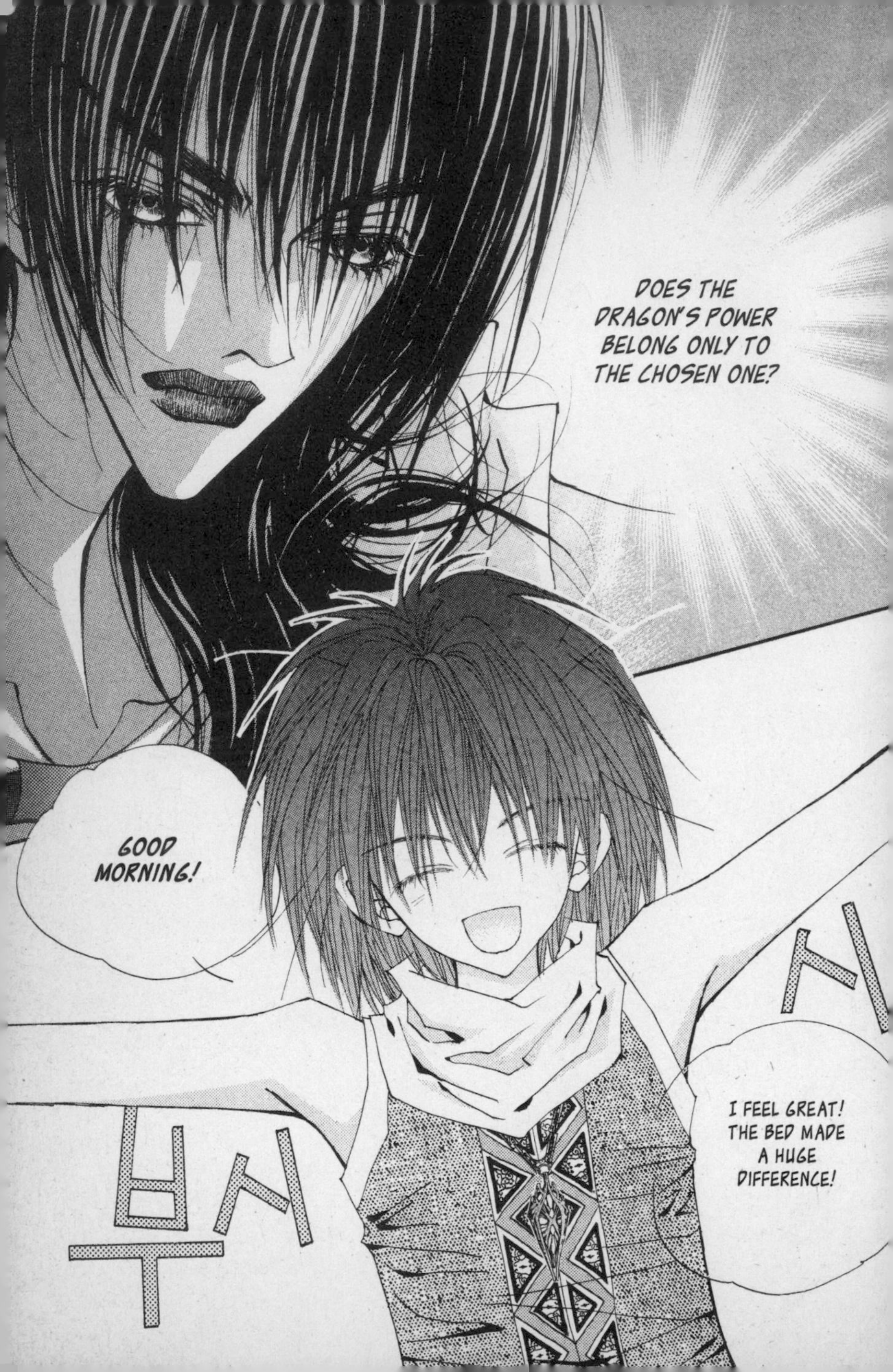
DOES THE DRAGON'S POWER BELONG ONLY TO THE CHOSEN ONE?
GOOD MORNING!
I FEEL GREAT! THE BED MADE A HUGE DIFFERENCE!

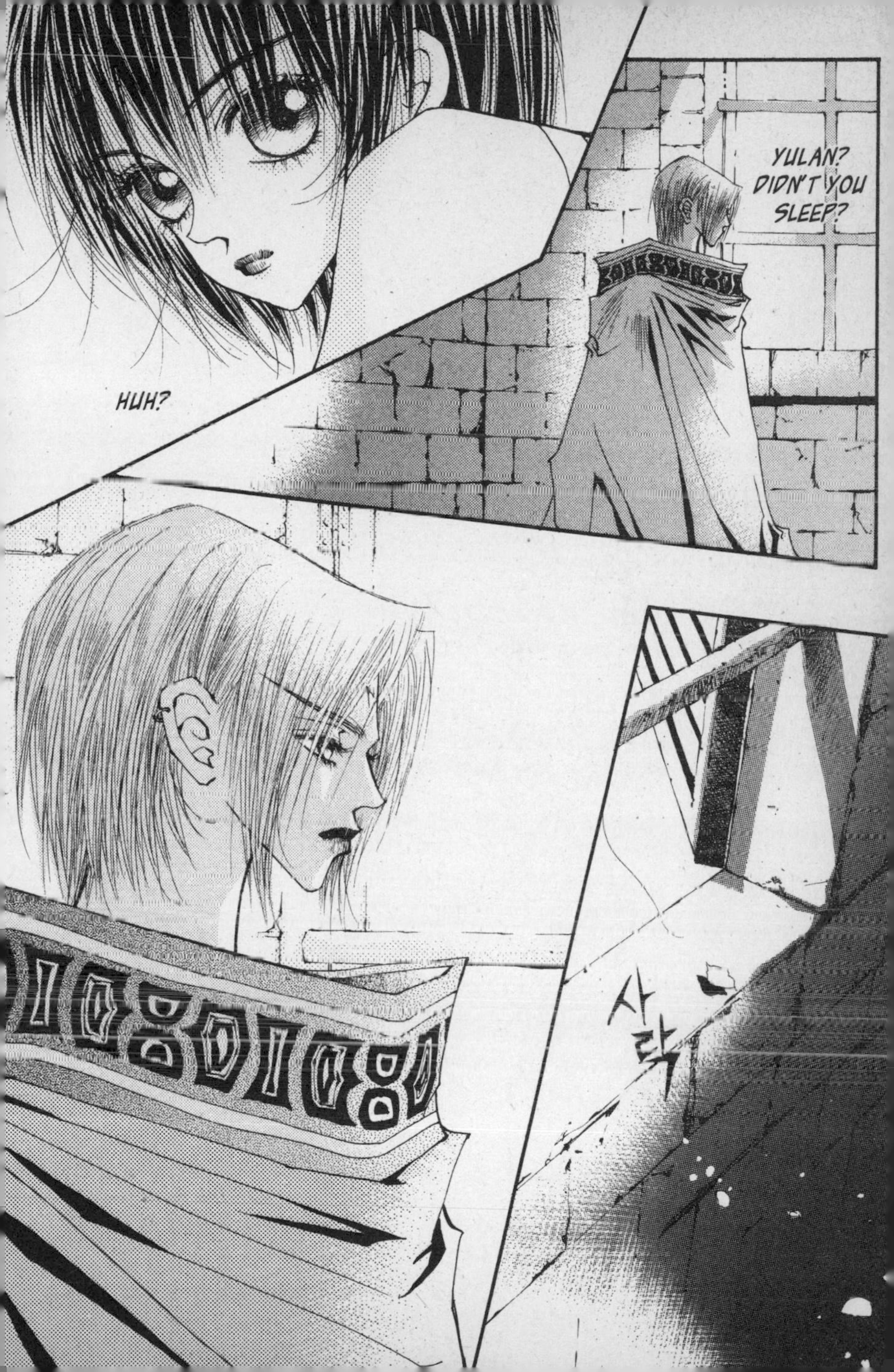
YULAN? DIDN'T YOU SLEEP?
HUH?
사락

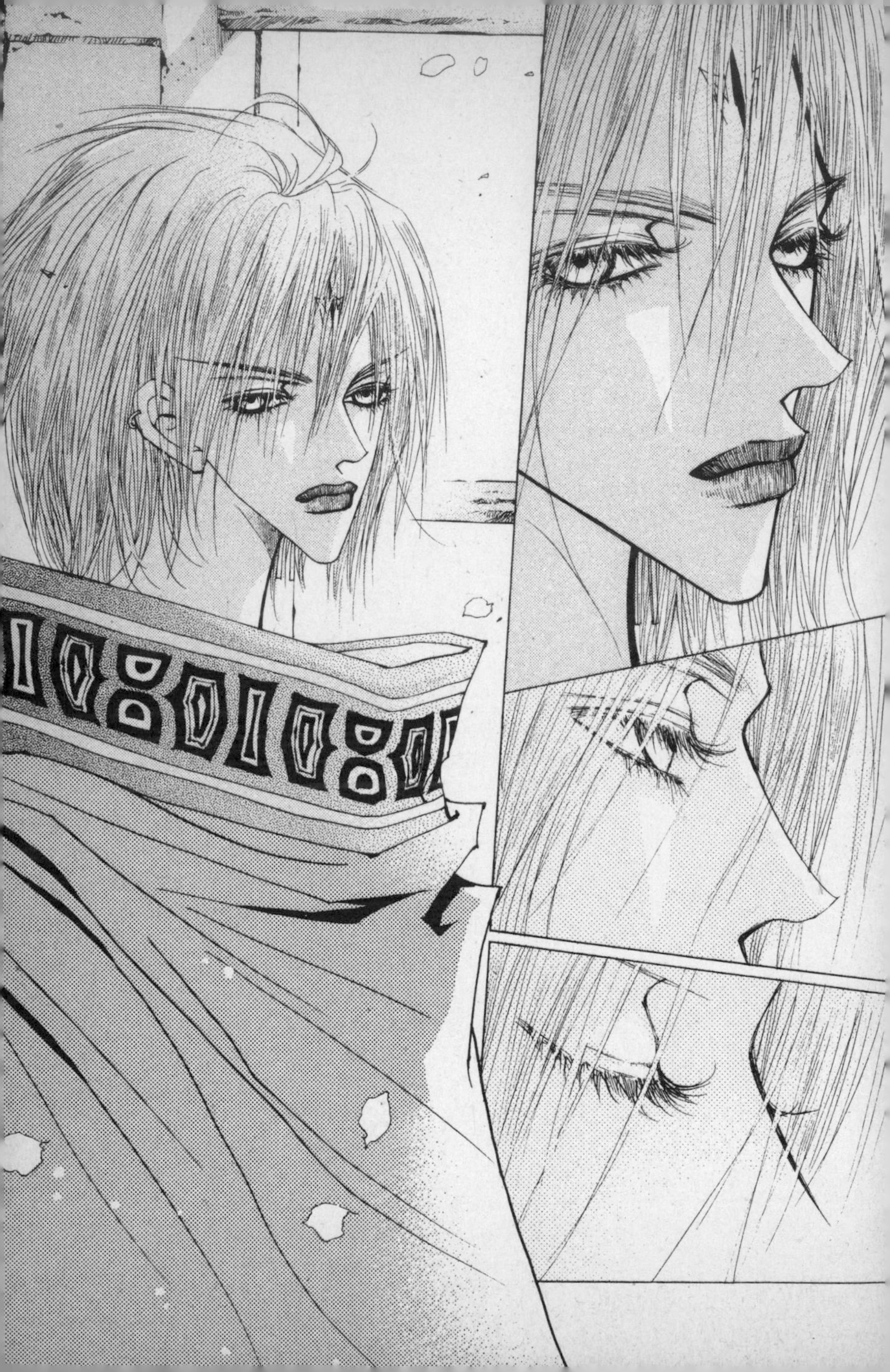

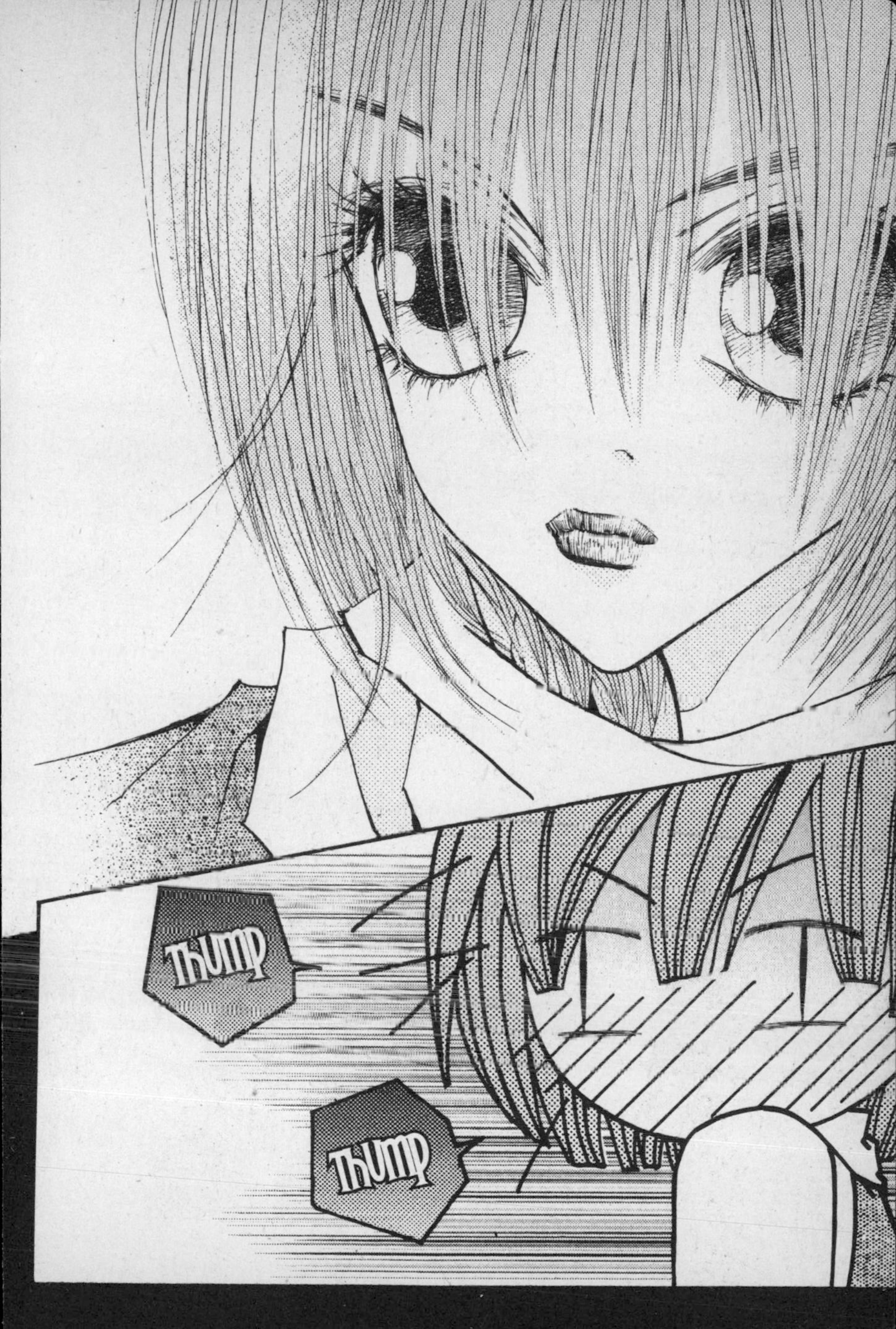
THUMP
THUMP

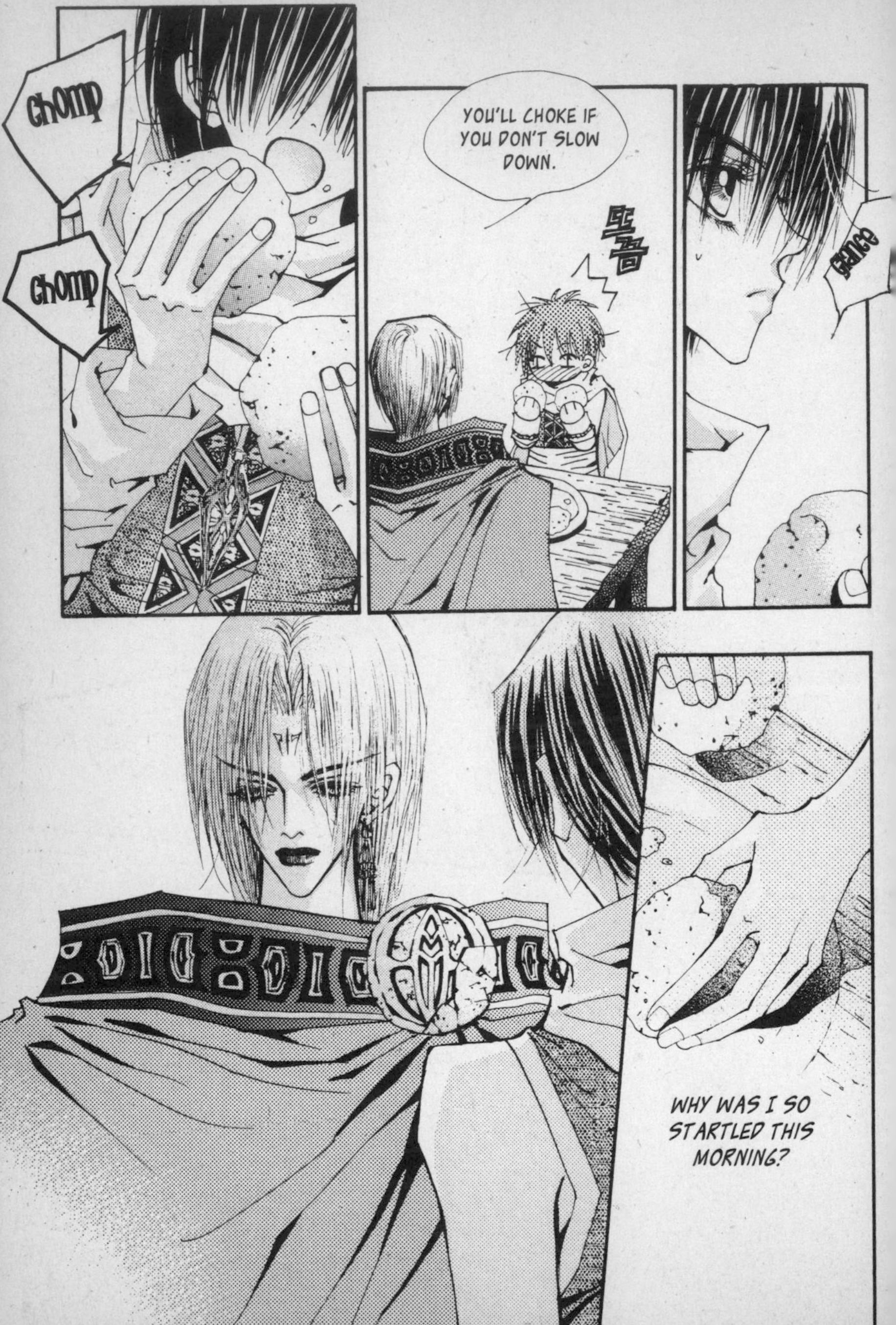
GLANCE
YOU'LL CHOKE IF YOU DON'T SLOW DOWN.
CHOMP
CHOMP
WHY WAS I SO STARTLED THIS MORNING?

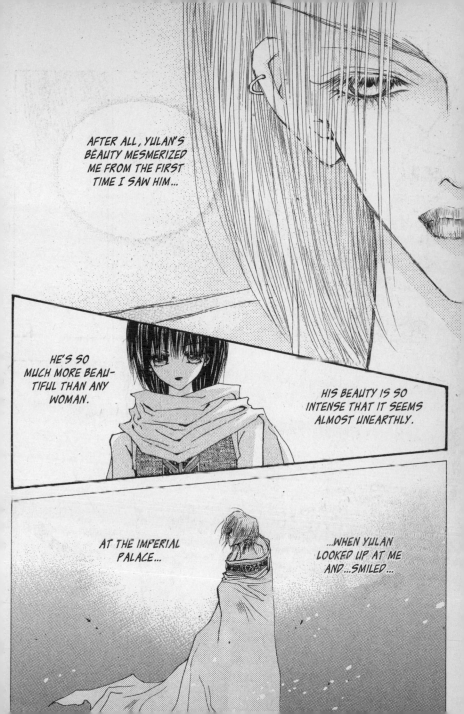

AFTER ALL, YULAN'S BEAUTY MESMERIZED ME FROM THE FIRST TIME I SAW HIM...

HE'S SO MUCH MORE BEAUTIFUL THAN ANY WOMAN.

HIS BEAUTY IS SO INTENSE THAT IT SEEMS ALMOST UNEARTHLY.

AT THE IMPERIAL PALACE...

...WHEN YULAN LOOKED UP AT ME AND...SMILED...

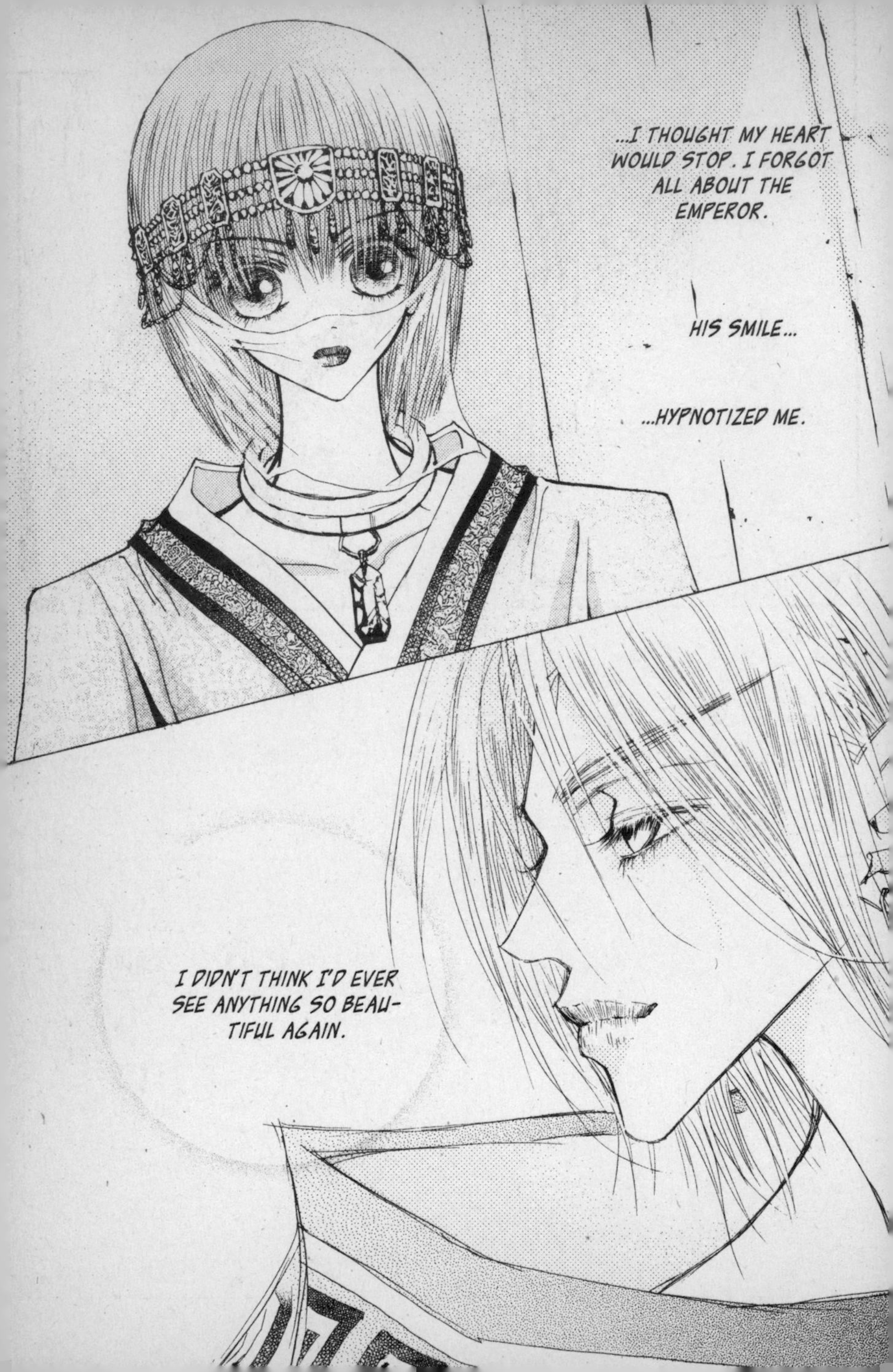
...I THOUGHT MY HEART WOULD STOP. I FORGOT ALL ABOUT THE EMPEROR.
HIS SMILE...
...HYPNOTIZED ME.
I DIDN'T THINK I'D EVER SEE ANYTHING SO BEAU-TIFUL AGAIN.

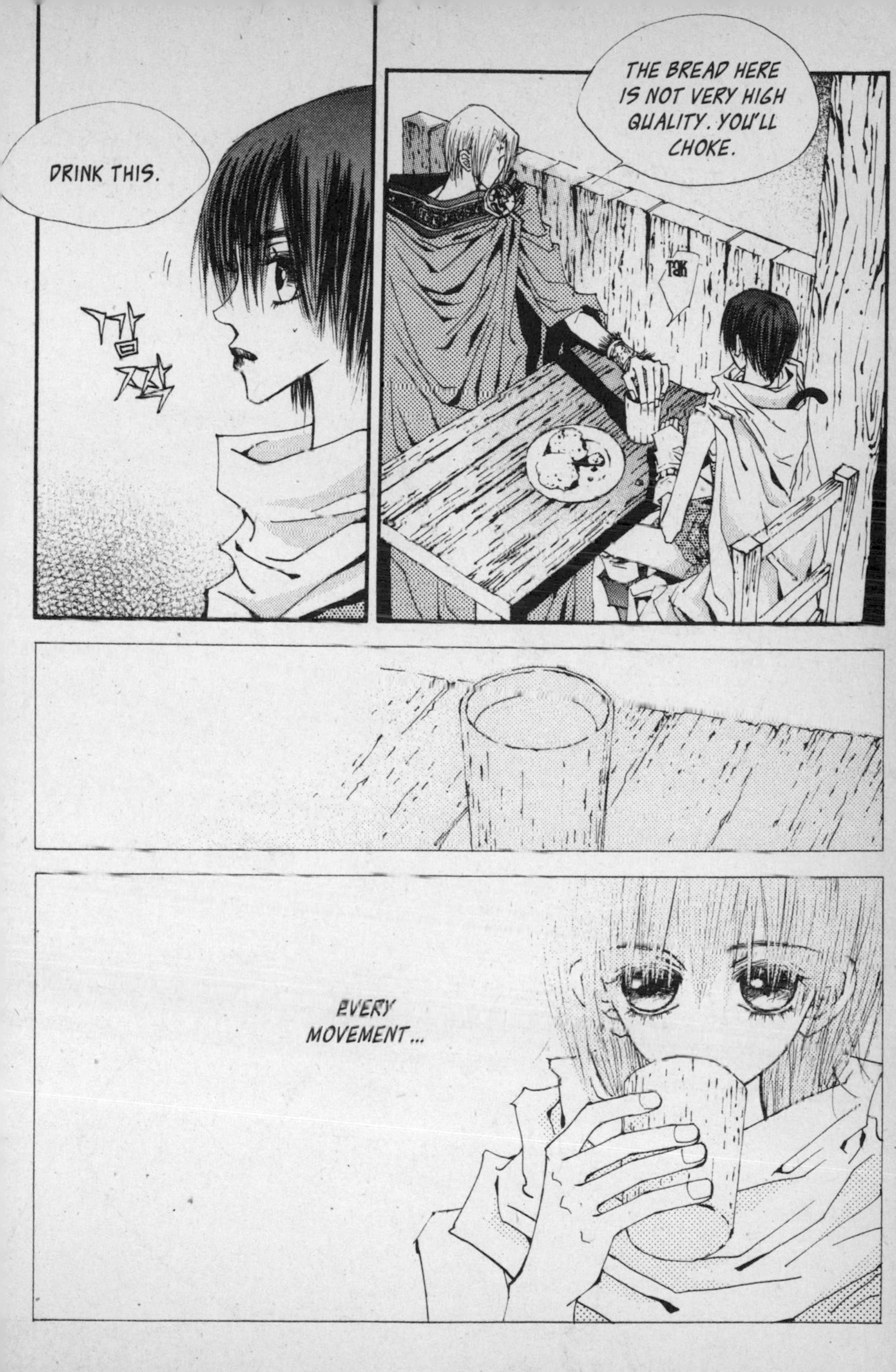
DRINK THIS.
깜짝
THE BREAD HERE IS NOT VERY HIGH QUALITY. YOU'LL CHOKE.
TAK
EVERY MOVEMENT...

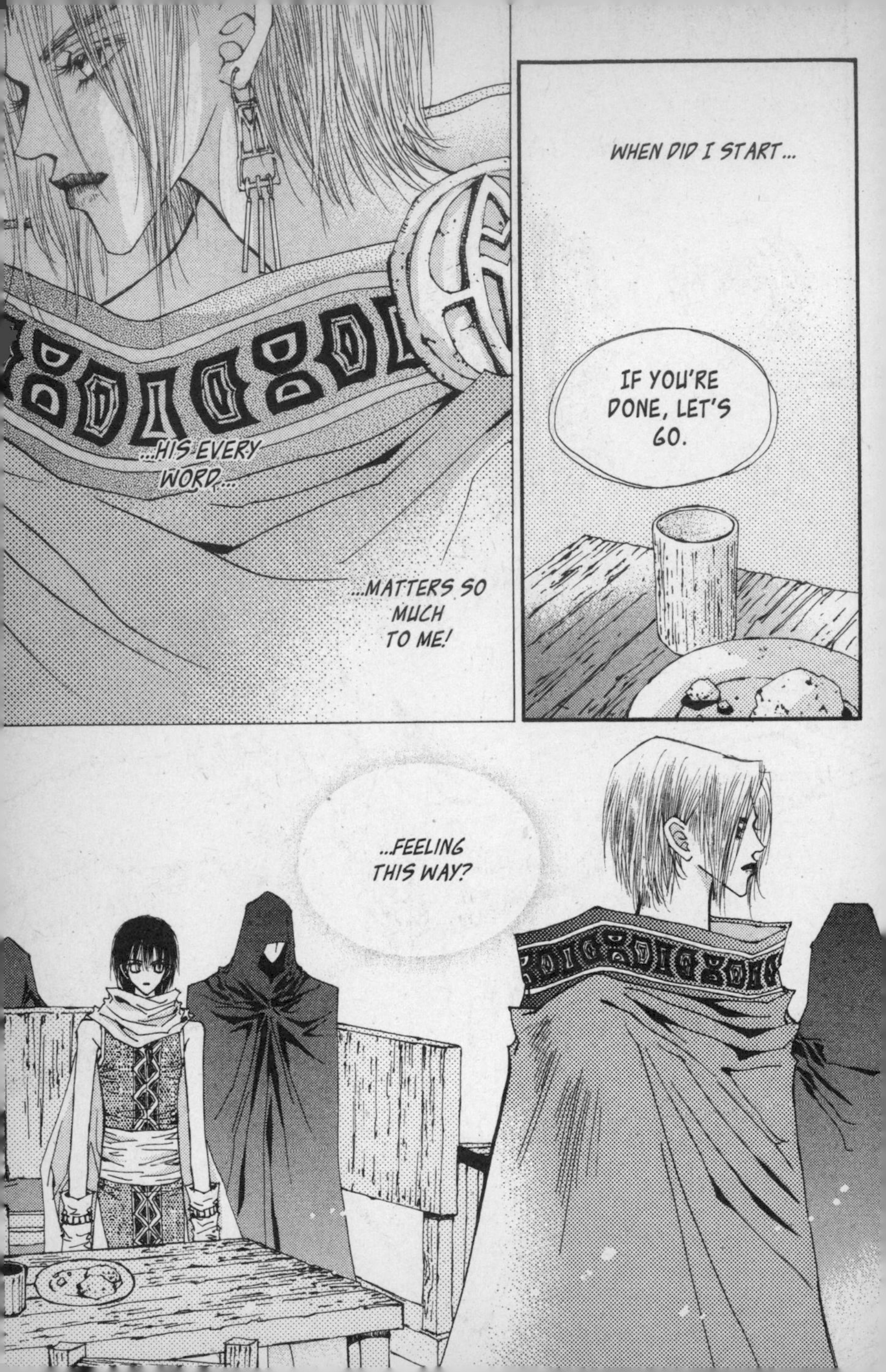
WHEN DID I START...
IF YOU'RE DONE, LET'S GO.
...HIS EVERY WORD...
...MATTERS SO MUCH TO ME!
...FEELING THIS WAY?

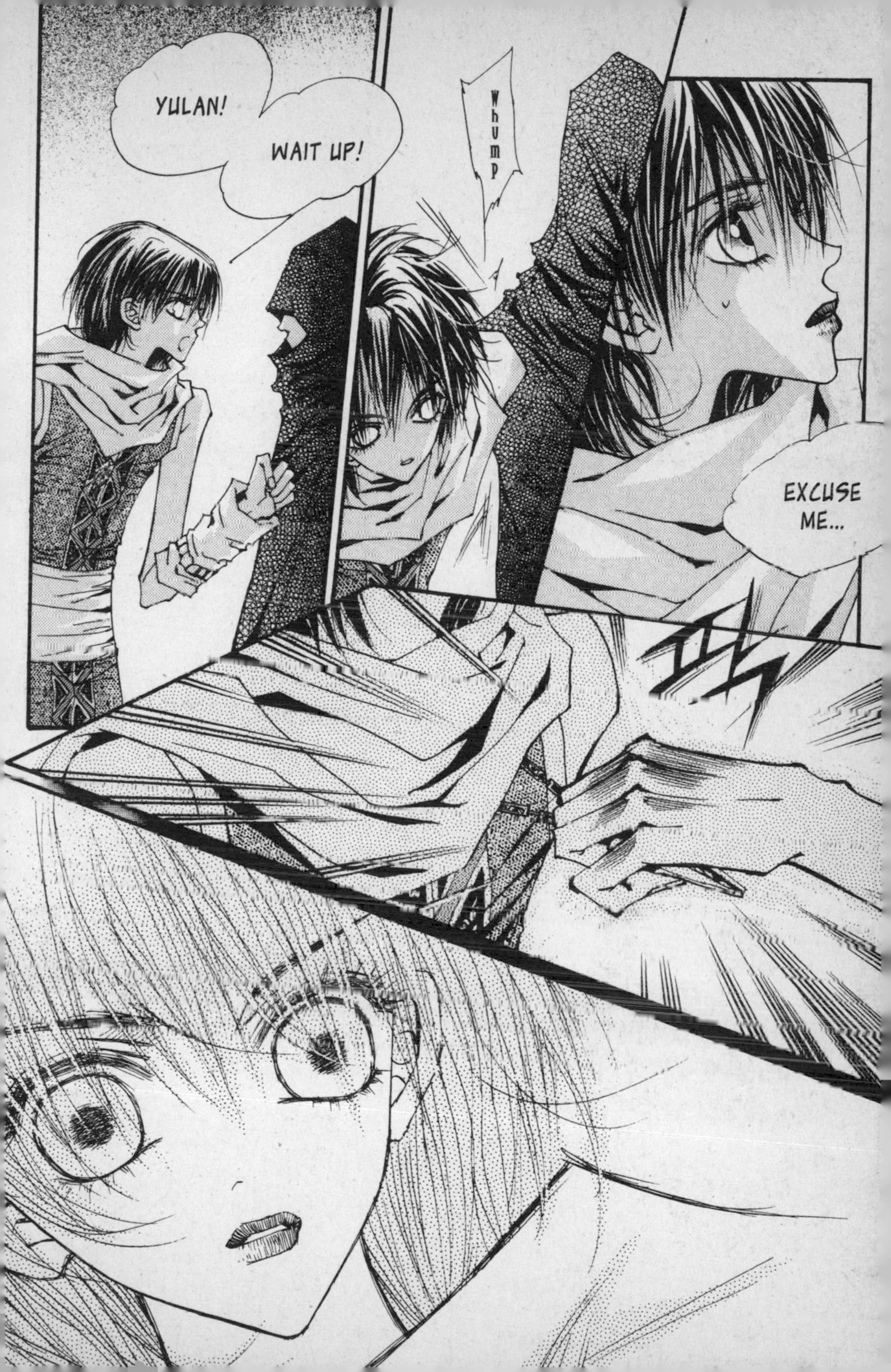
EXCUSE ME...
WHUMP
YULAN!
WAIT UP!

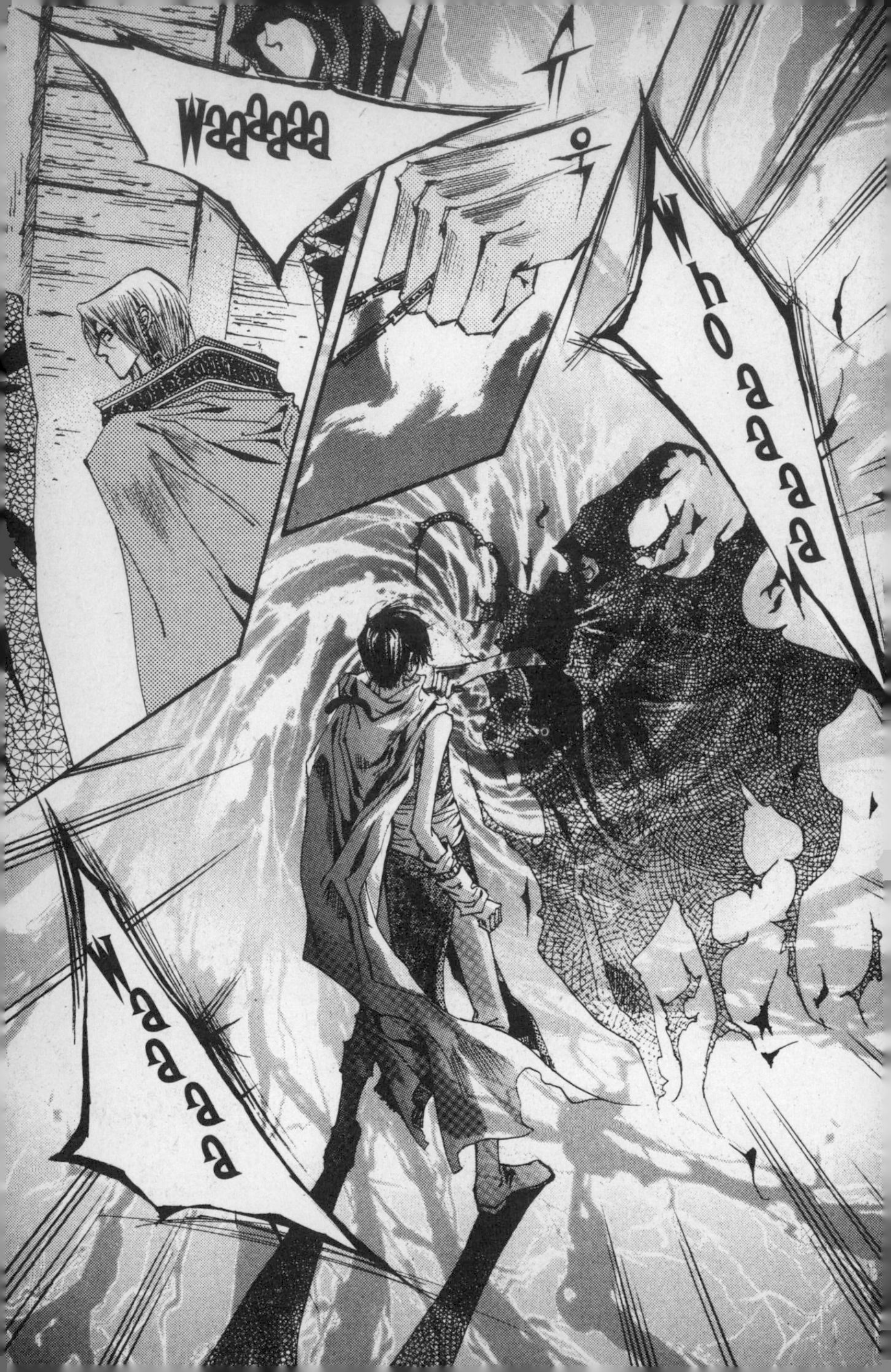
Waaaaaa
Whoaaaaa
Waaaaa

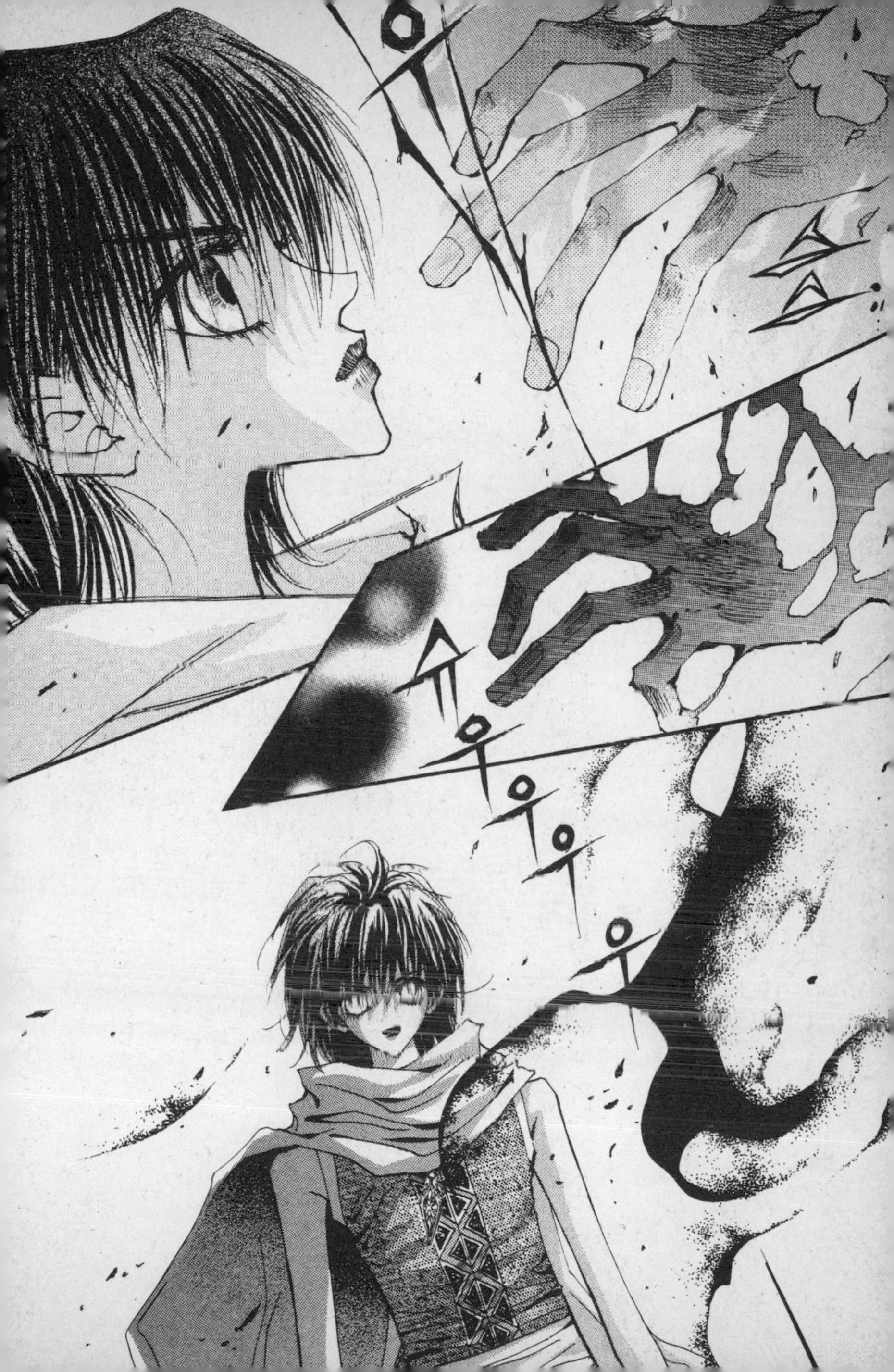
슈우우우우

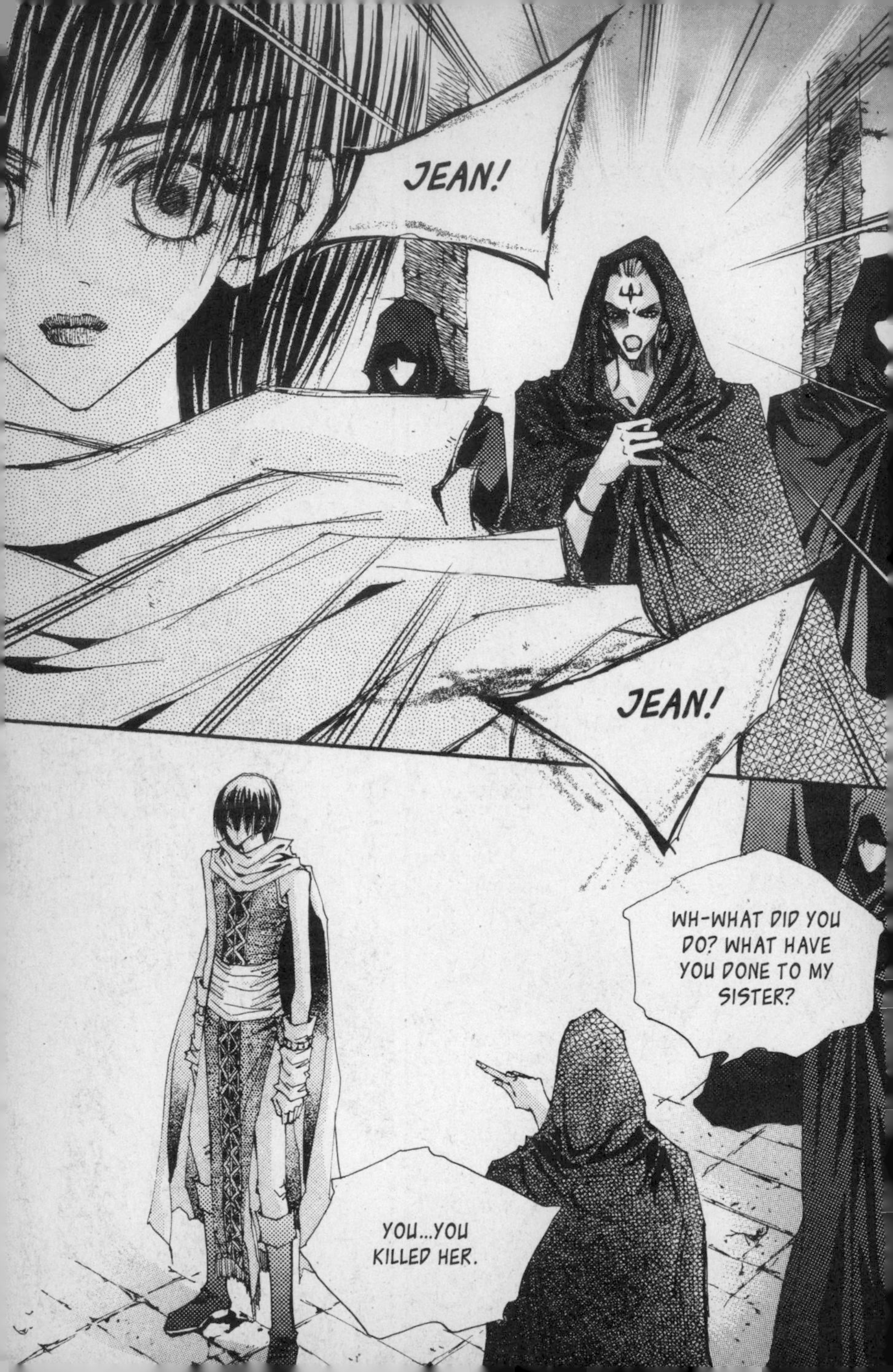
JEAN!
JEAN!
WH-WHAT DID YOU DO? WHAT HAVE YOU DONE TO MY SISTER?
YOU...YOU KILLED HER.

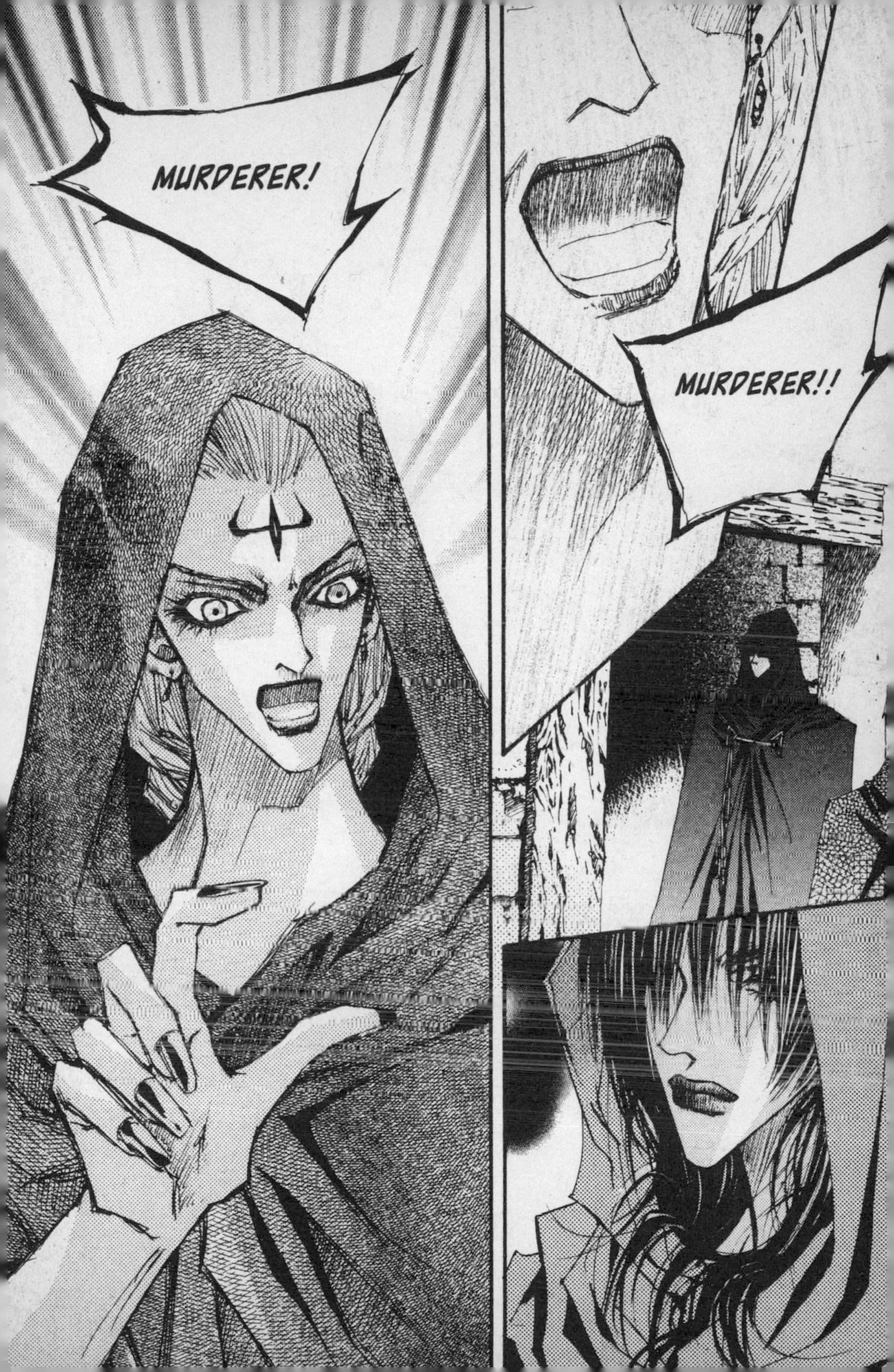
MURDERER!!
MURDERER!

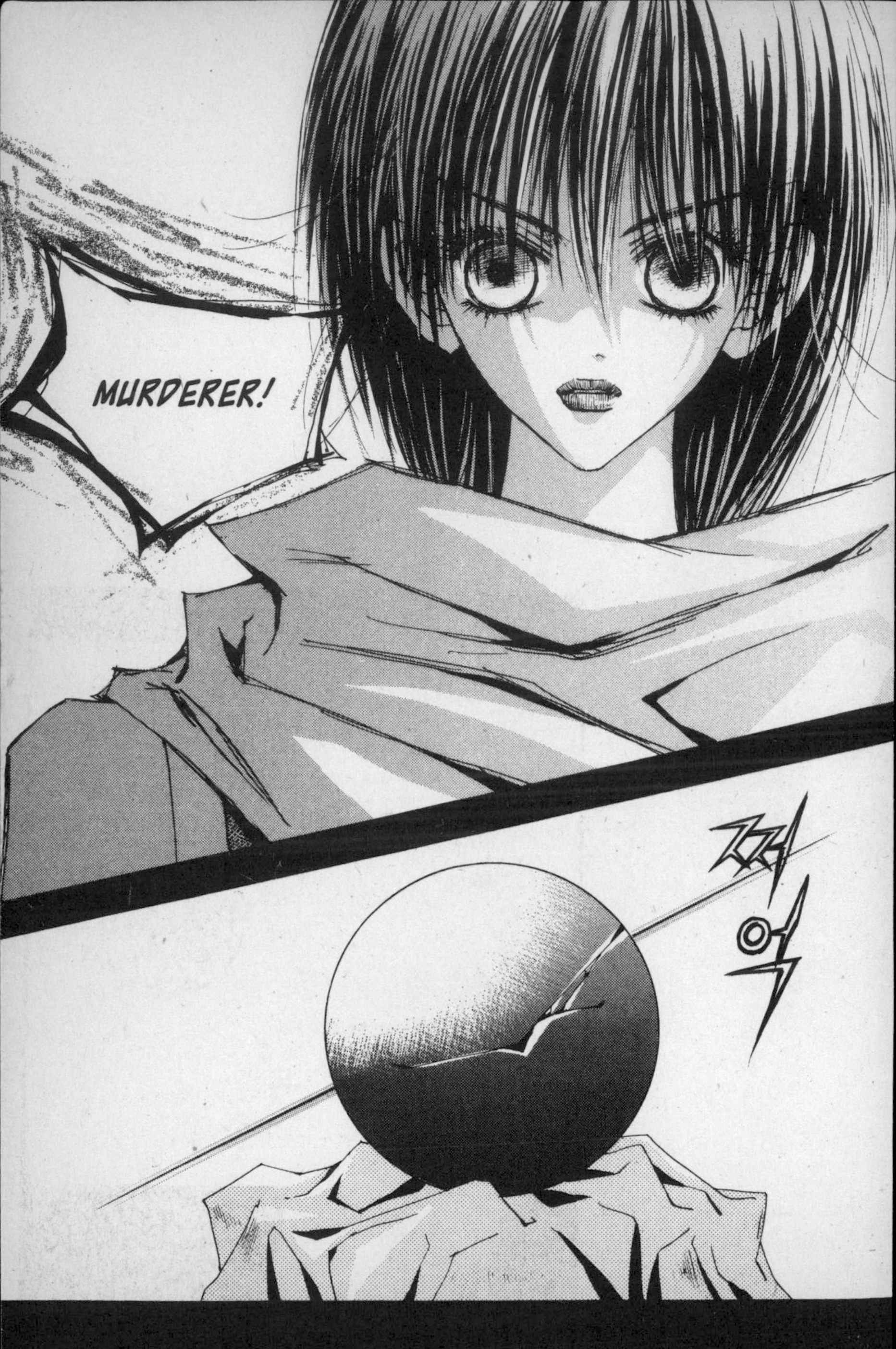
MURDERER!

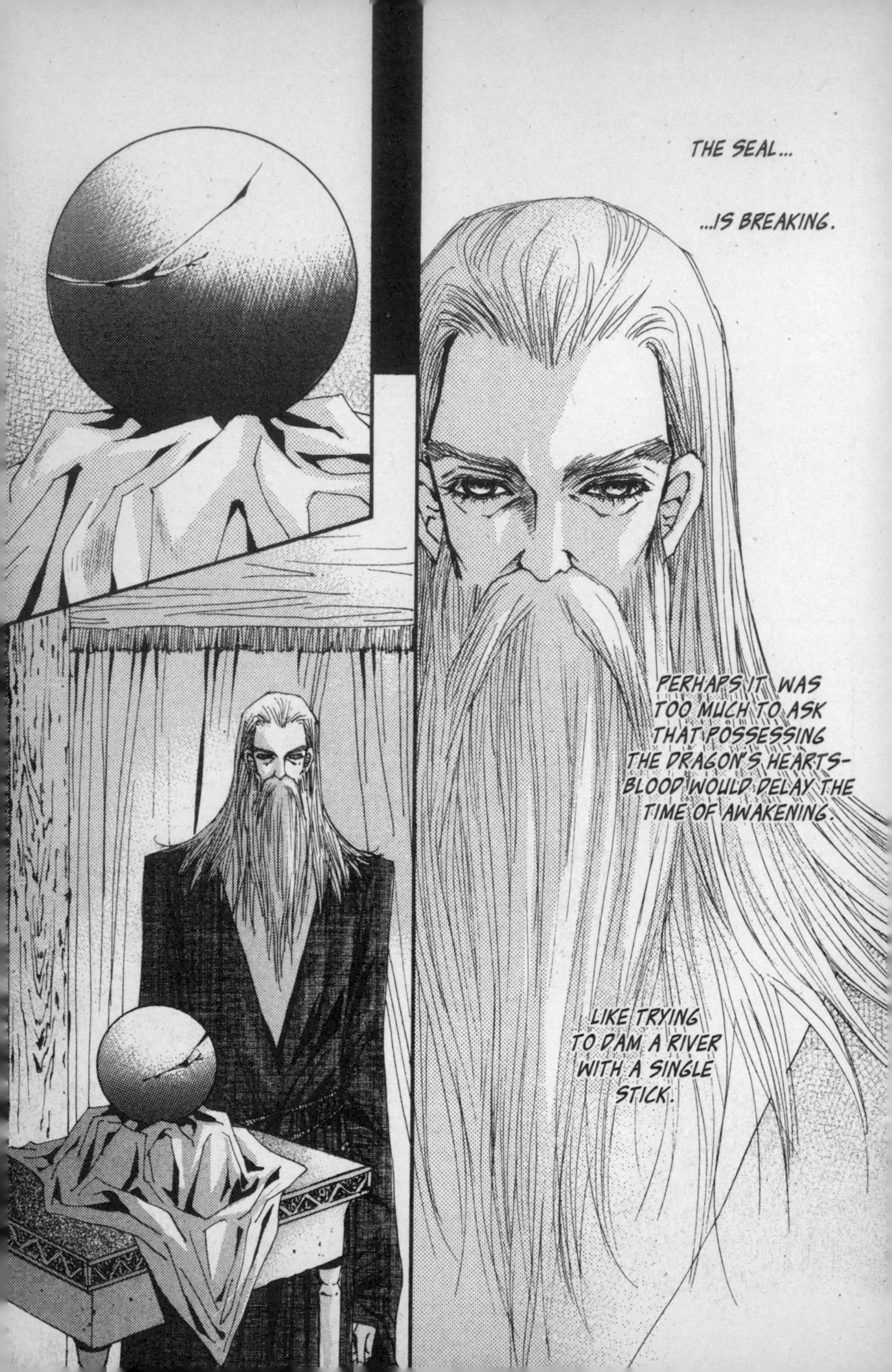
THE SEAL...
...IS BREAKING.
PERHAPS IT WAS TOO MUCH TO ASK THAT POSSESSING THE DRAGON'S HEARTS-BLOOD WOULD DELAY THE TIME OF AWAKENING.
LIKE TRYING TO DAM A RIVER WITH A SINGLE STICK.

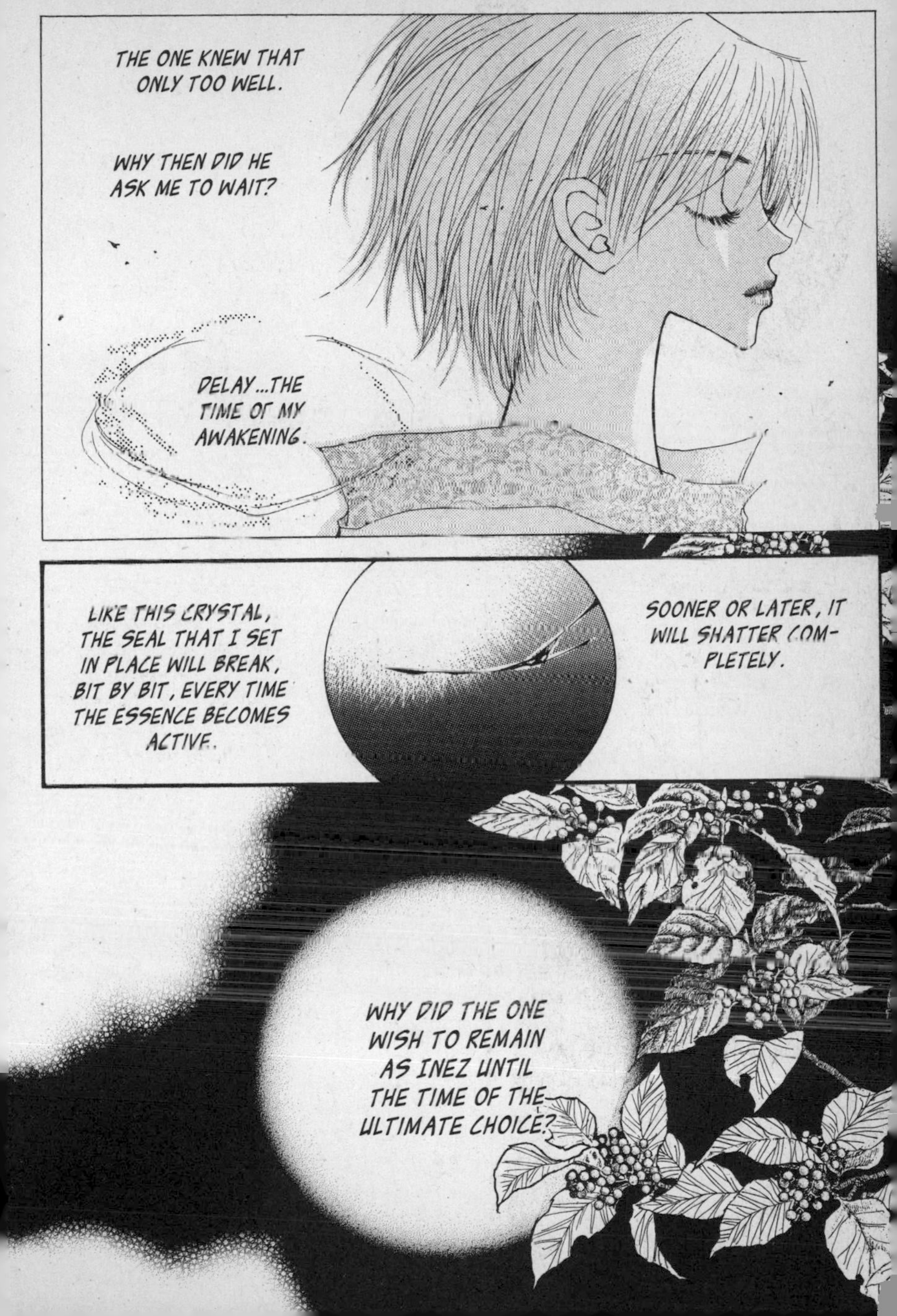
THE ONE KNEW THAT ONLY TOO WELL.
WHY THEN DID HE ASK ME TO WAIT?
DELAY...THE TIME OF MY AWAKENING.
SOONER OR LATER, IT WILL SHATTER COM-PLETELY.
LIKE THIS CRYSTAL, THE SEAL THAT I SET IN PLACE WILL BREAK, BIT BY BIT, EVERY TIME THE ESSENCE BECOMES ACTIVE.
WHY DID THE ONE WISH TO REMAIN AS INEZ UNTIL THE TIME OF THE ULTIMATE CHOICE?

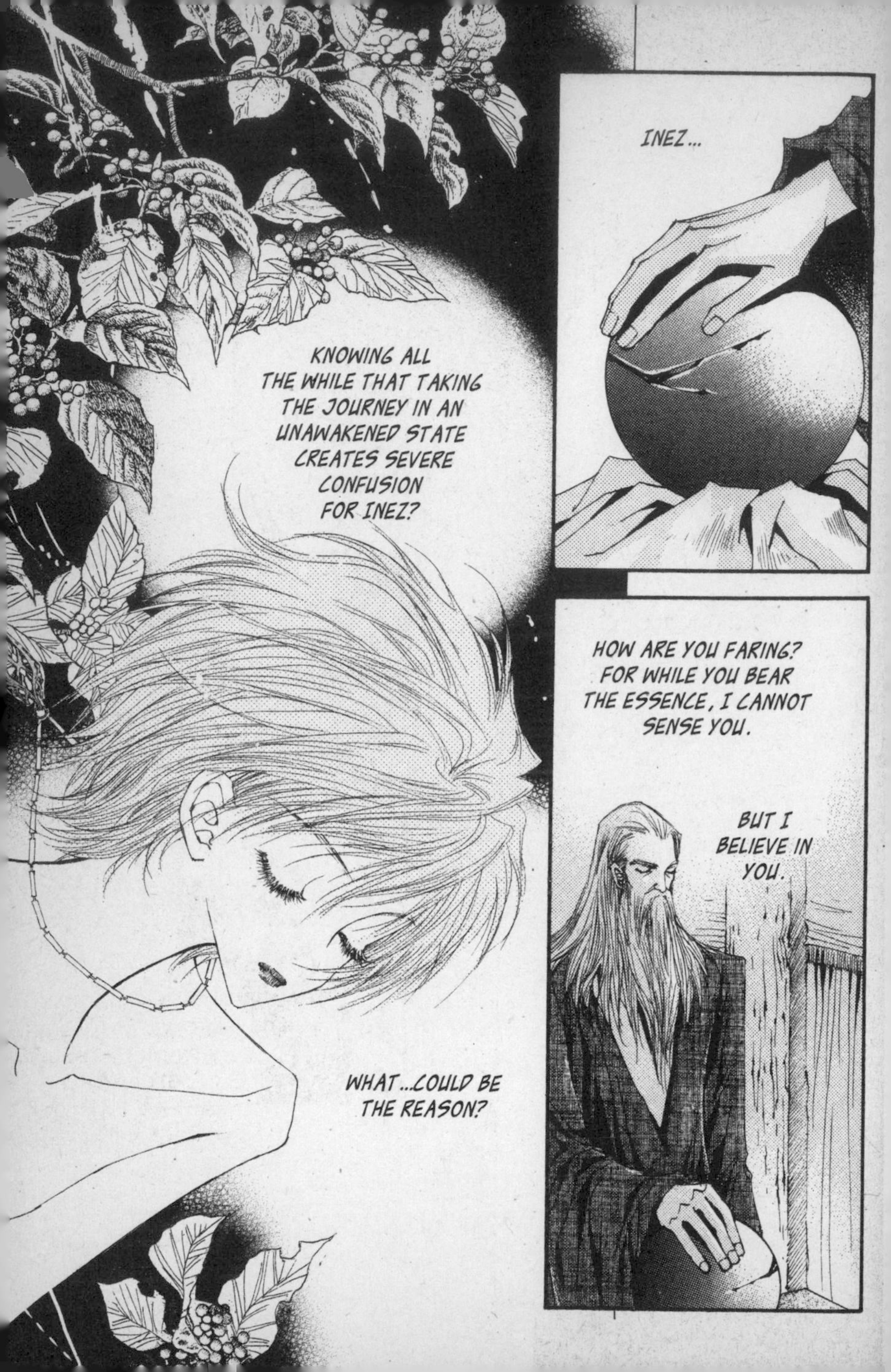
INEZ...
HOW ARE YOU FARING? FOR WHILE YOU BEAR THE ESSENCE, I CANNOT SENSE YOU.
BUT I BELIEVE IN YOU.
KNOWING ALL THE WHILE THAT TAKING THE JOURNEY IN AN UNAWAKENED STATE CREATES SEVERE CONFUSION FOR INEZ?
WHAT...COULD BE THE REASON?

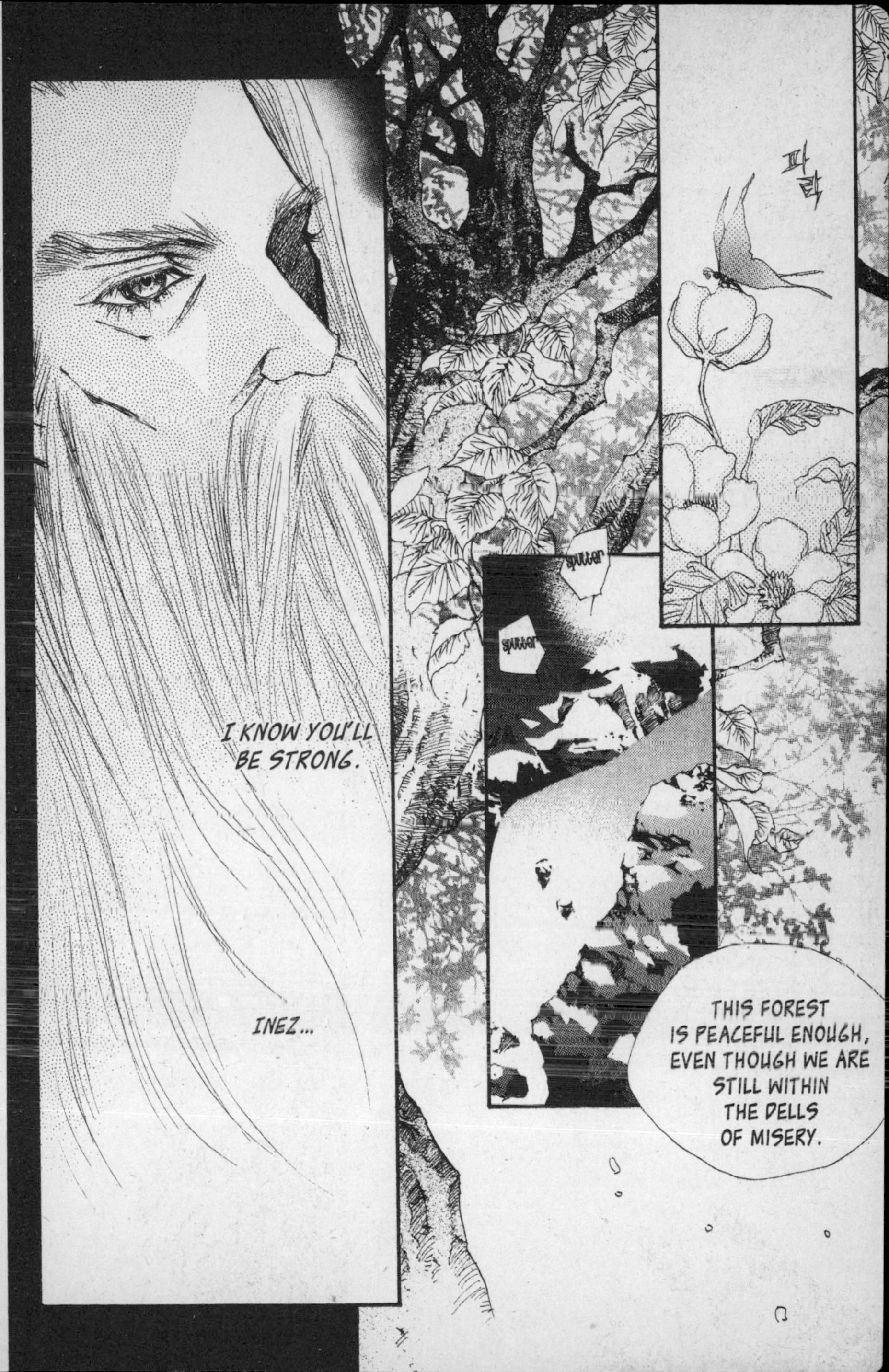
I KNOW YOU'LL BE STRONG.
INEZ...
파락
sputter
sputter
THIS FOREST IS PEACEFUL ENOUGH, EVEN THOUGH WE ARE STILL WITHIN THE DELLS OF MISERY.

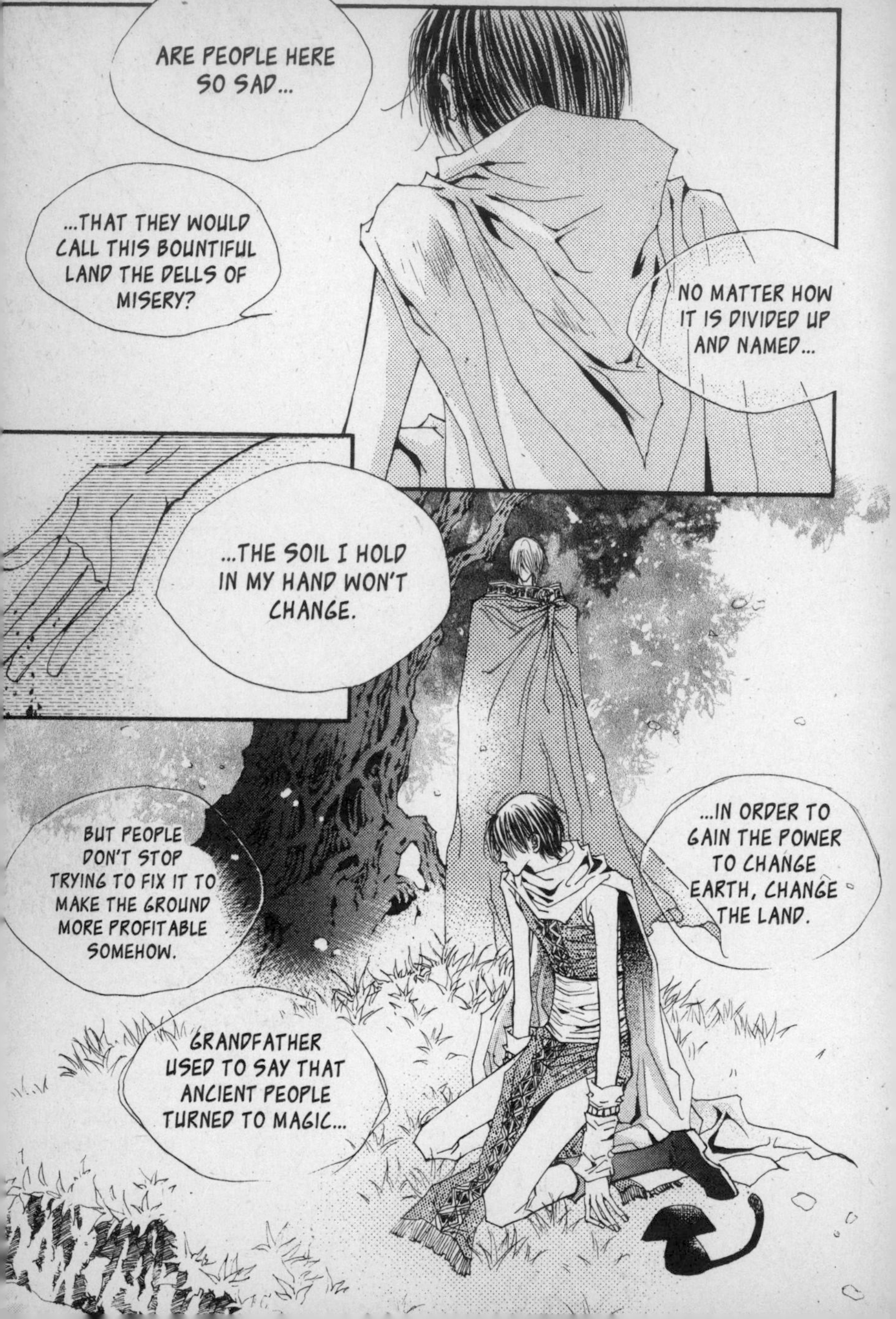
ARE PEOPLE HERE SO SAD...
...THAT THEY WOULD CALL THIS BOUNTIFUL LAND THE DELLS OF MISERY?
NO MATTER HOW IT IS DIVIDED UP AND NAMED...
...THE SOIL I HOLD IN MY HAND WON'T CHANGE.
BUT PEOPLE DON'T STOP TRYING TO FIX IT TO MAKE THE GROUND MORE PROFITABLE SOMEHOW.
GRANDFATHER USED TO SAY THAT ANCIENT PEOPLE TURNED TO MAGIC...
...IN ORDER TO GAIN THE POWER TO CHANGE EARTH, CHANGE THE LAND.

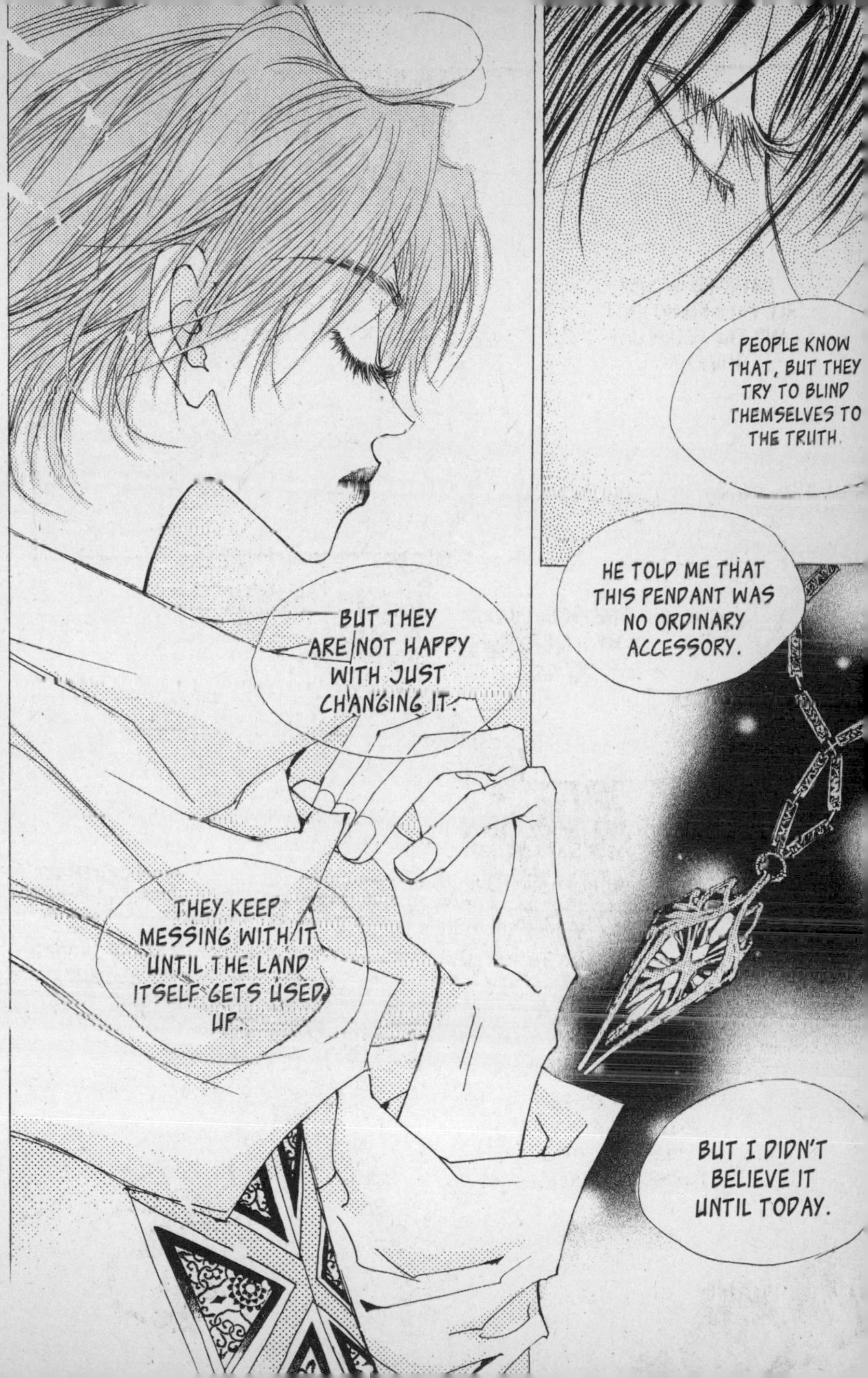
BUT THEY ARE NOT HAPPY WITH JUST CHANGING IT.
THEY KEEP MESSING WITH IT UNTIL THE LAND ITSELF GETS USED UP.
PEOPLE KNOW THAT, BUT THEY TRY TO BLIND THEMSELVES TO THE TRUTH.
HE TOLD ME THAT THIS PENDANT WAS NO ORDINARY ACCESSORY.
BUT I DIDN'T BELIEVE IT UNTIL TODAY.

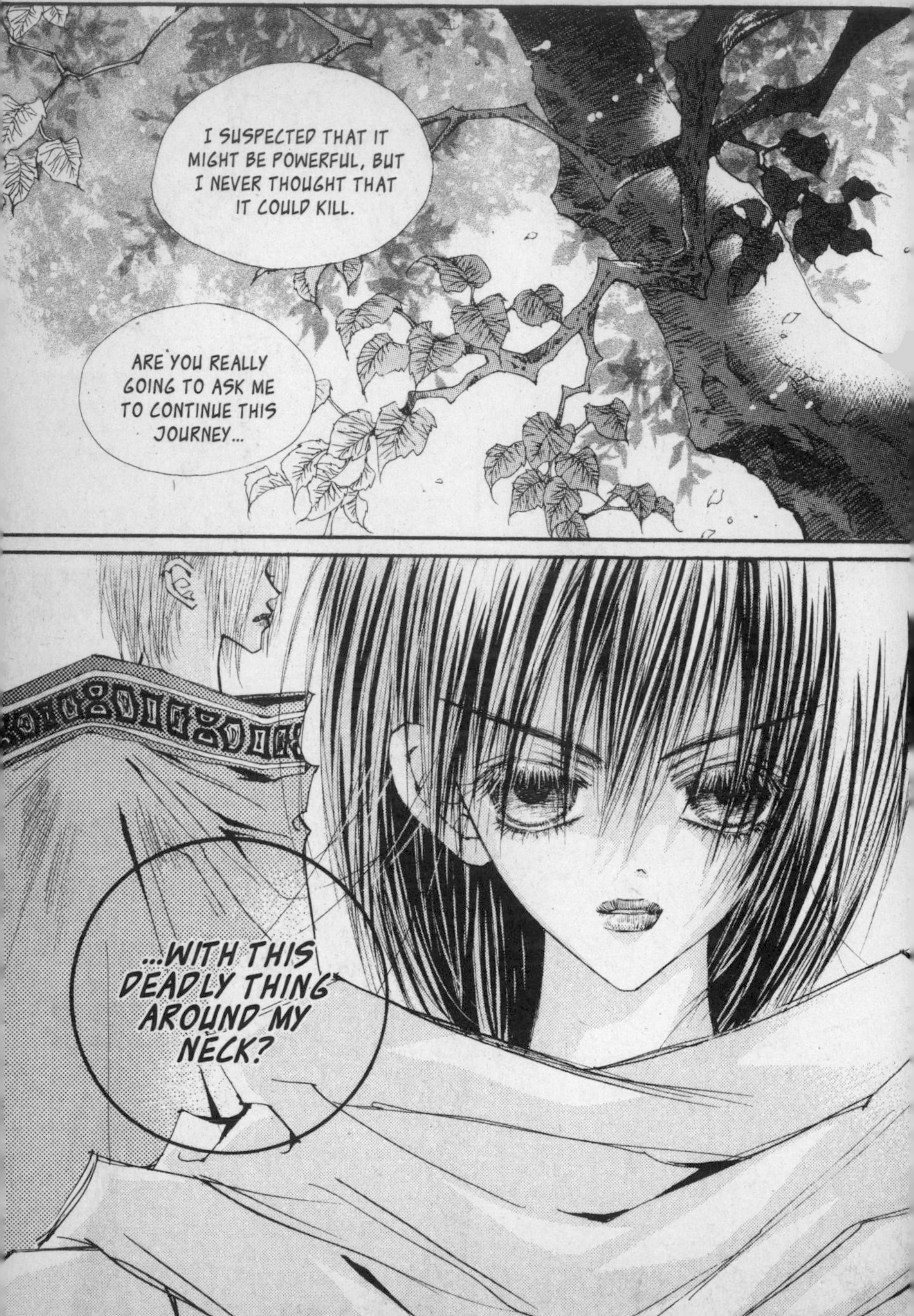
I SUSPECTED THAT IT MIGHT BE POWERFUL, BUT I NEVER THOUGHT THAT IT COULD KILL.
ARE YOU REALLY GOING TO ASK ME TO CONTINUE THIS JOURNEY...
...WITH THIS DEADLY THING AROUND MY NECK?

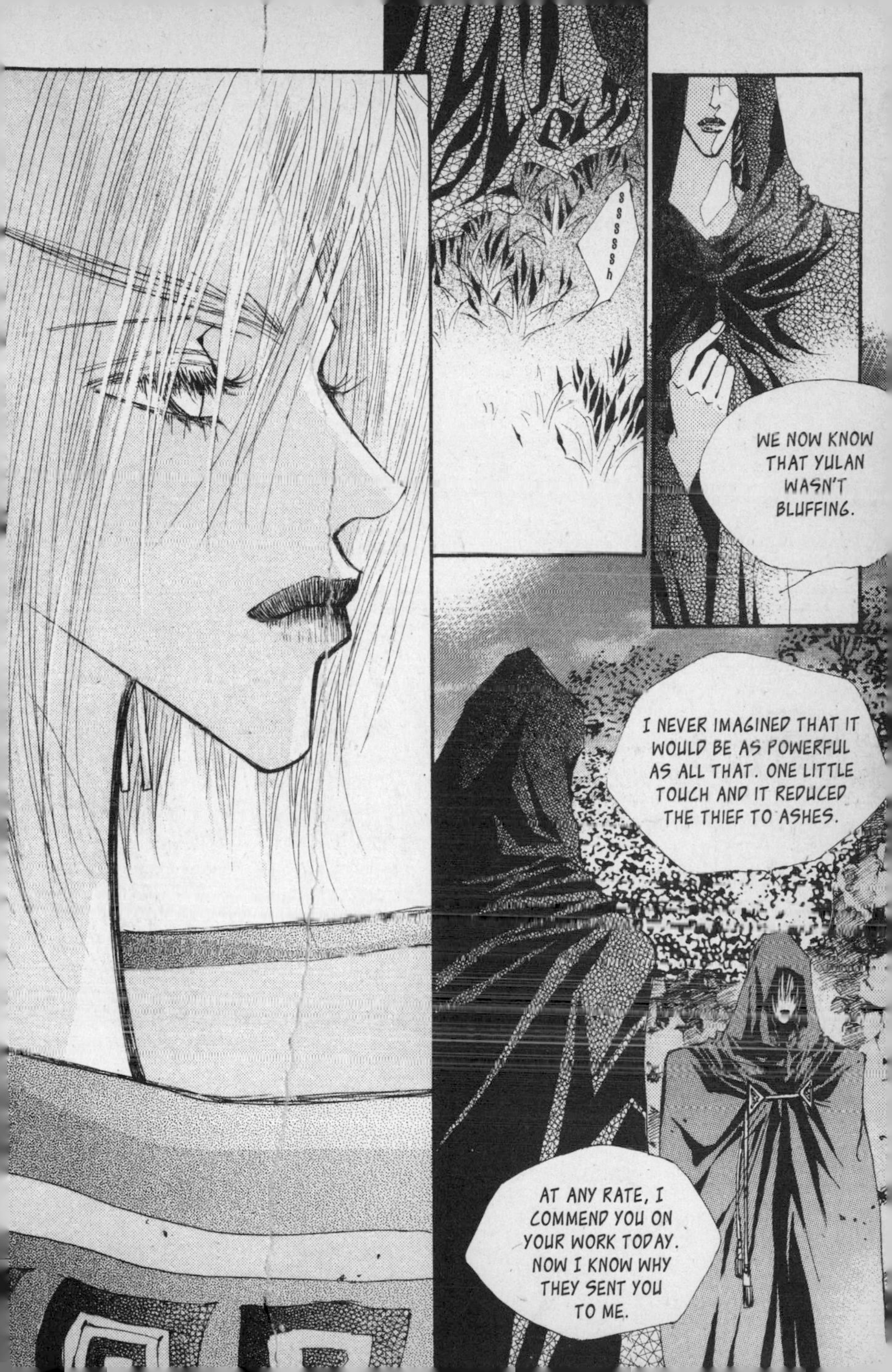

ssssssh
WE NOW KNOW THAT YULAN WASN'T BLUFFING.
I NEVER IMAGINED THAT IT WOULD BE AS POWERFUL AS ALL THAT. ONE LITTLE TOUCH AND IT REDUCED THE THIEF TO ASHES.
AT ANY RATE, I COMMEND YOU ON YOUR WORK TODAY. NOW I KNOW WHY THEY SENT YOU TO ME.

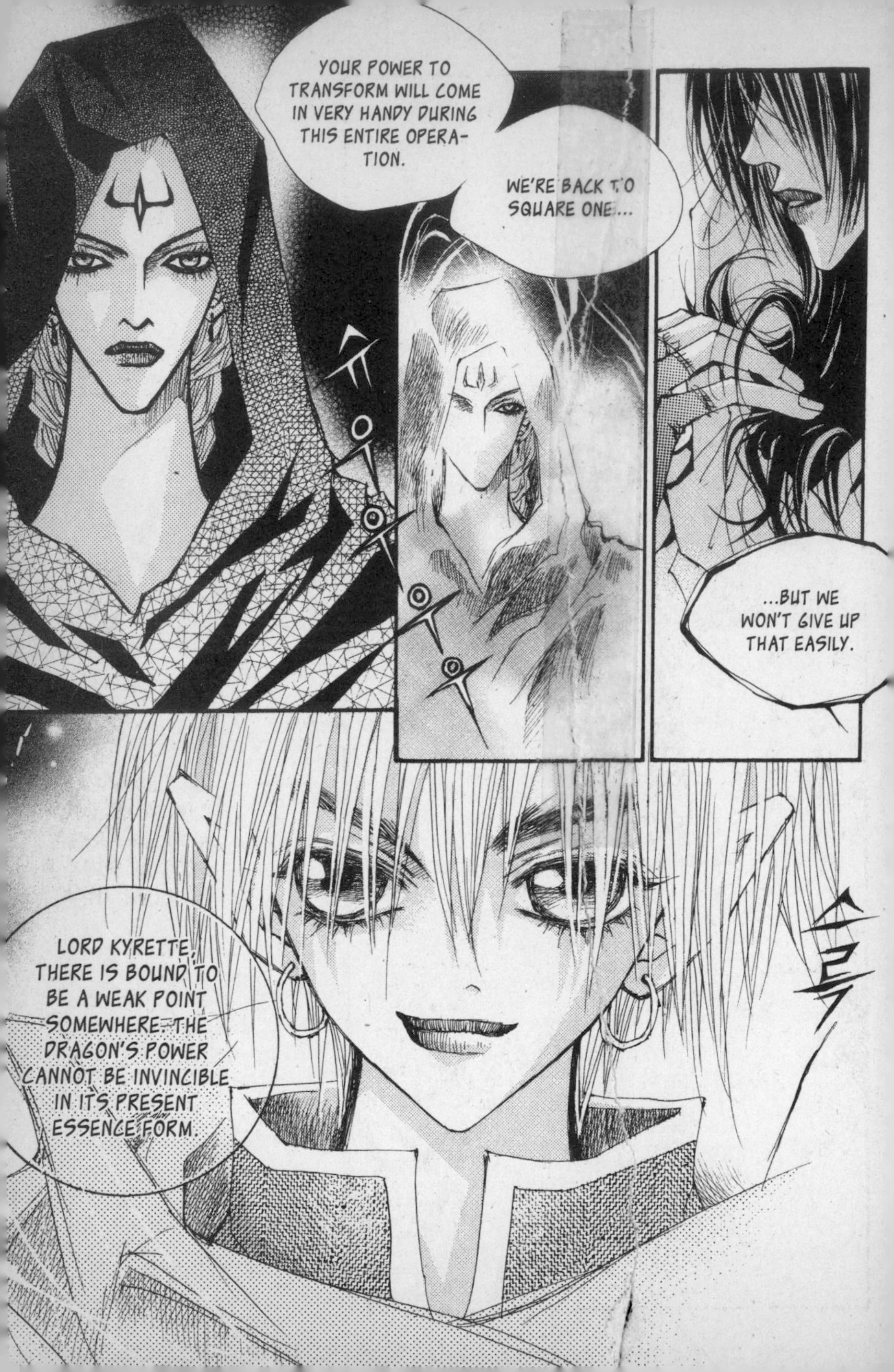
YOUR POWER TO TRANSFORM WILL COME IN VERY HANDY DURING THIS ENTIRE OPERATION.
WE'RE BACK TO SQUARE ONE...
...BUT WE WON'T GIVE UP THAT EASILY.
LORD KYRETTE, THERE IS BOUND TO BE A WEAK POINT SOMEWHERE. THE DRAGON'S POWER CANNOT BE INVINCIBLE IN ITS PRESENT ESSENCE FORM.

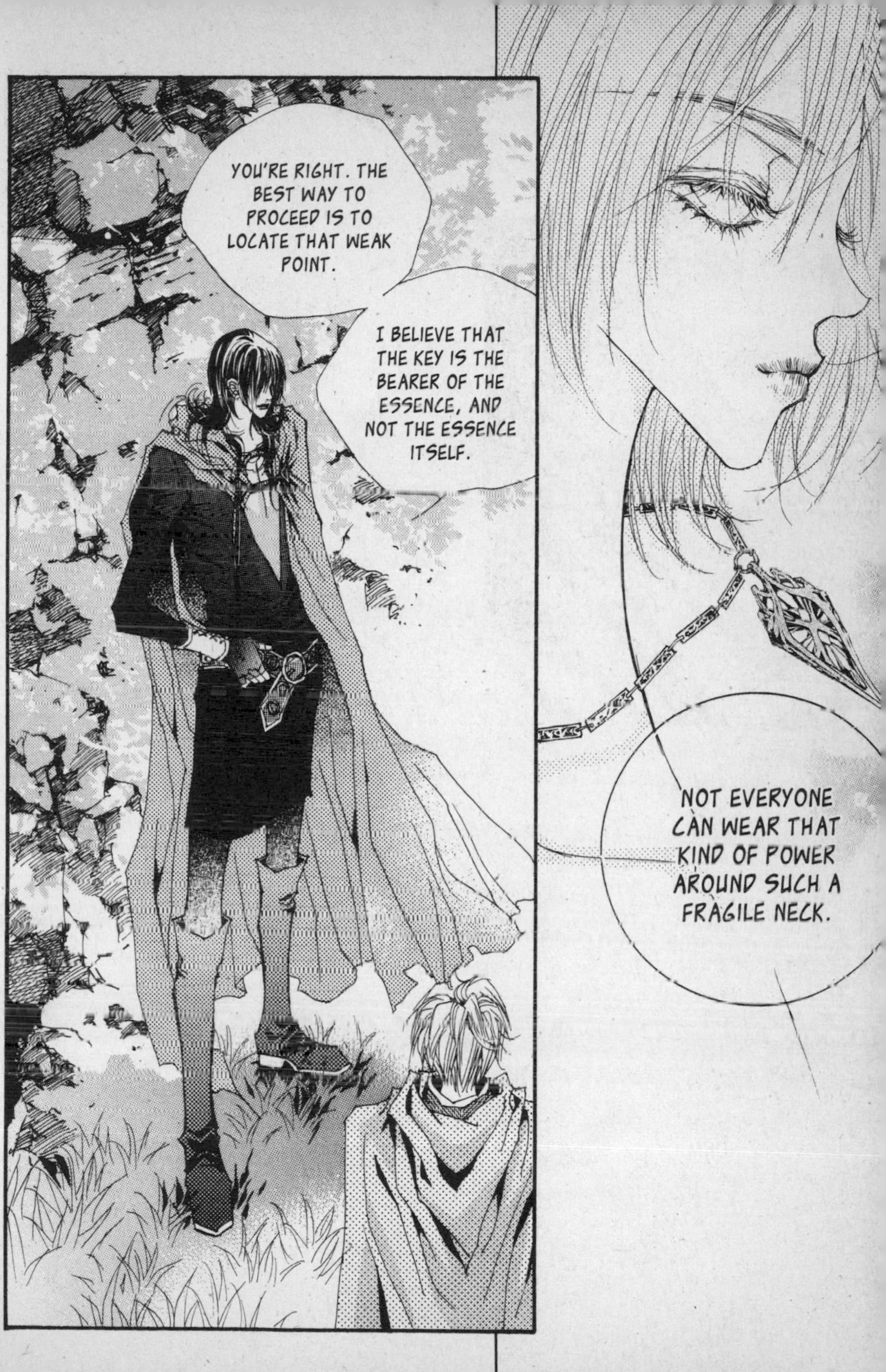
NOT EVERYONE CAN WEAR THAT KIND OF POWER AROUND SUCH A FRAGILE NECK.
YOU'RE RIGHT. THE BEST WAY TO PROCEED IS TO LOCATE THAT WEAK POINT.
I BELIEVE THAT THE KEY IS THE BEARER OF THE ESSENCE, AND NOT THE ESSENCE ITSELF.

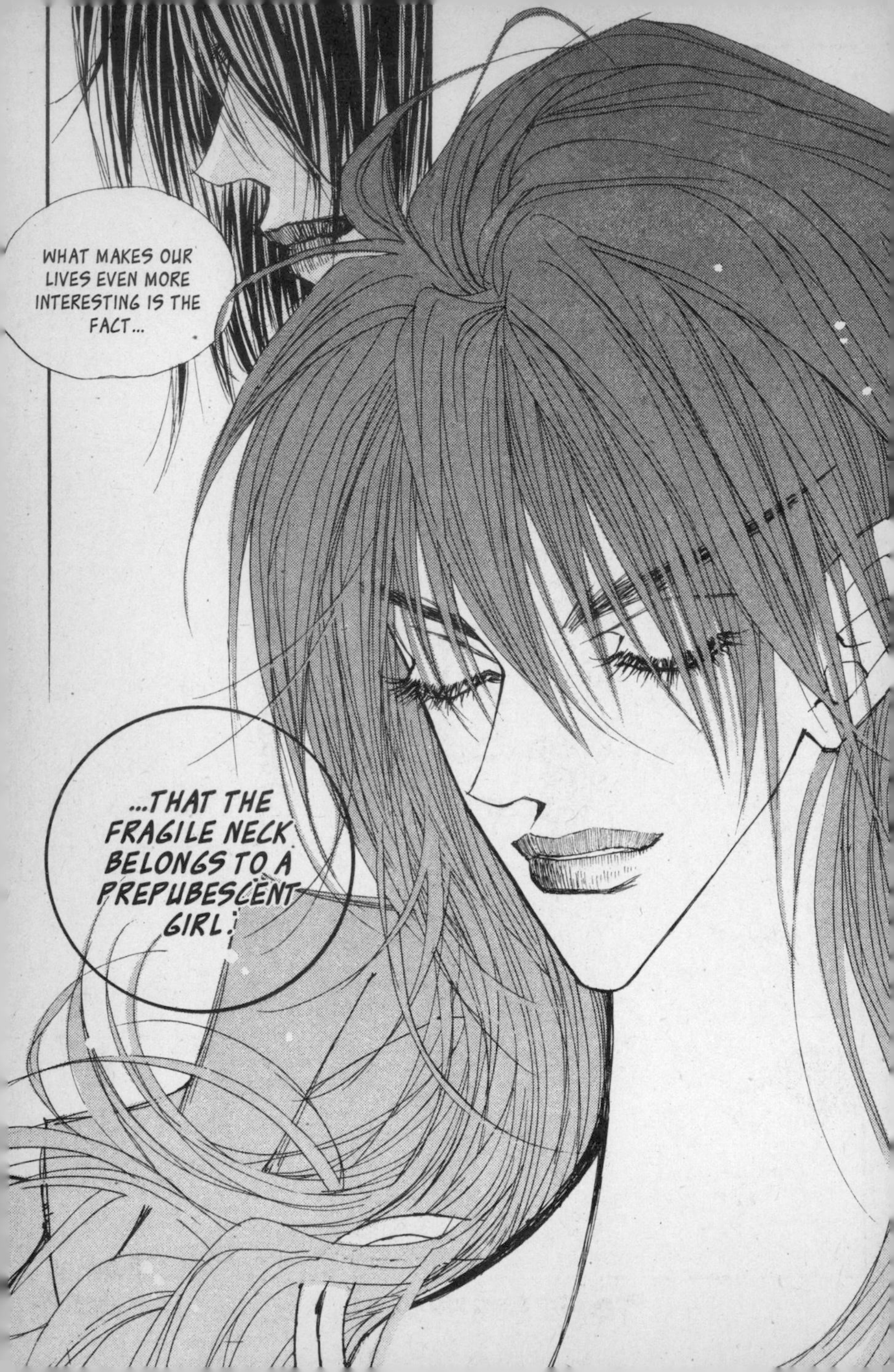
WHAT MAKES OUR LIVES EVEN MORE INTERESTING IS THE FACT...
...THAT THE FRAGILE NECK BELONGS TO A PREPUBESCENT GIRL.

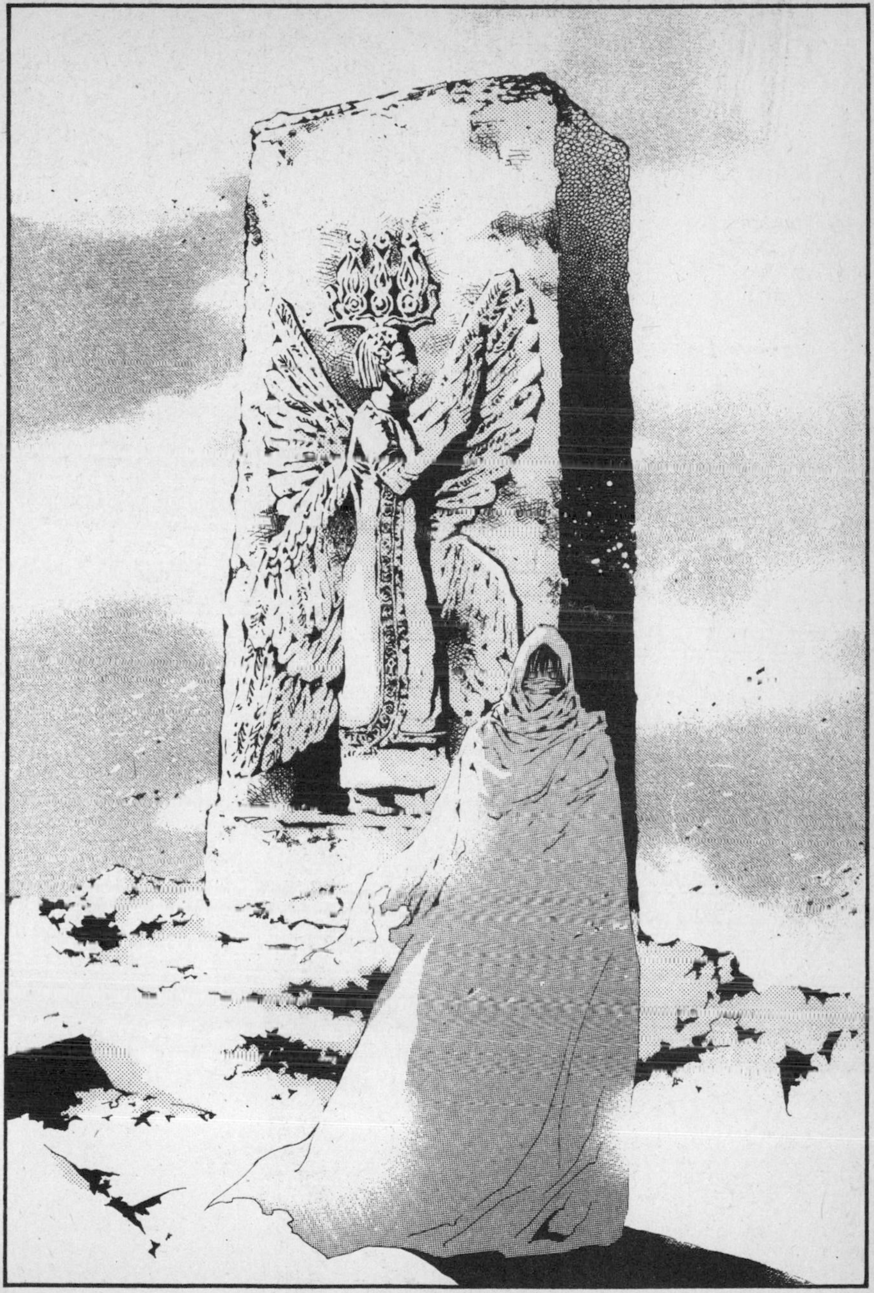

TO BE CONTINUED IN ARCANA VOLUME 5!

THE QUEST CONTINUES IN

ARCANA

VOLUME 5

AS THE SNOW CONTINUES TO FALL UPON THE
KINGDOM OF YOUNG INEZ'S HOMELAND, THE
SITUATION BECOMES INCREASINGLY DIRE BY
THE DAY. THE BEING WHO CAN BRING PEACE
AND STABILITY TO THE LAND IS "THE ONE" WHO
RESIDES WITHIN THE CORPOREAL FORM OF
INEZ. BUT NOW WISE KAAGER STRUGGLES WITH
THE WEIGHT OF THE DECISION HE MUST MAKE,
AND THE CONSEQUENCES THAT MAY RESULT
ONCE THE SAVIOR IS RETURNED TO THE LAND...

THERE'S INTRIGUE AND ADVENTURE IN EVERY
PAGE OF THE NEXT VOLUME OF
ARCANA!

TOKYOPOP SHOP

WWW.TOKYOPOP.COM/SHOP

HOT NEWS!

Check out the **TOKYOPOP SHOP!** The world's best collection of manga in English is now available online in one place!

BIZENGHAST POSTER

PRINCESS AI POSTCARDS

WWW.TOKYOPOP.COM/SHOP

Check out all the sizzling hot merchandise and your favorite manga at the shop!

I Luv Halloween Glow-In-the-Dark STICKERS!

I LUV HALLOWEEN BUTTONS & STICKERS

- LOOK FOR SPECIAL OFFERS
- PRE-ORDER UPCOMING RELEASES
- COMPLETE YOUR COLLECTIONS

I LUV HALLOWEEN © Keith Giffen and Benjamin Roman. Princess Ai © & ™ TOKYOPOP Inc. Bizenghast © M. Alice LeGrow and TOKYOPOP Inc.

LIFE
BY KEIKO SUENOBU

Ordinary high school teenagers...
Except that they're not.

LIFE ™

© Keiko Suenobu

OT
OLDER TEEN
AGE 16+

READ THE ENTIRE FIRST CHAPTER ONLINE FOR FREE:

Ayumu struggles with her studies, and the all-important high school entrance exams are approaching. Fortunately, she has help from her best bud Shii-chan, who is at the top of the class. But when the test results come back, the friends are surprised: Ayumu surpasses Shii-chan's scores and gets into the school of her choice—without Shii-chan! Losing her friend is so painful for Ayumu that she starts cutting herself to ease her sorrow. Finally, Ayumu seeks comfort in a new friend, Manami. But will Manami prove to be the friend that Ayumu truly needs? Or will Ayumu continue down a dark path?

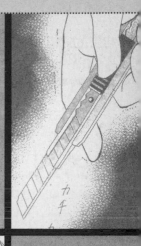

Volume 1
LIFE
Keiko Suenobu

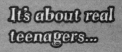

It's about real teenagers...

It's about real high school...

It's about real life.

BIZENGHAST

Dear Diary,
I'm starting to feel

T
TEEN
AGE 13+

Preview the manga at:
www.TOKYOPOP.com/bizenghast

When a young girl moves to the forgotten town of
Bizenghast, she uncovers a terrifying collection of lost
souls that leads her to the brink of insanity. One thing
becomes painfully clear: The residents of Bizenghast are
just dying to come home. ART SUBJECT TO CHANGE © Mary Alice LeGrow and TOKYOPOP Inc.

that I'm not like other people...

Bizenghast ™

The gothic fantasy masterpiece
continues in June...

SPOTLIGHT
TOKYOPOP MANGA SUPPLEMENT

FRUITS BASKET
BY NATSUKI TAKAYA

Fruits Basket ™

Tohru Honda was an orphan with no place to go...until the mysterious Sohma family offers her a place to call home. Tohru's ordinary high school life is turned upside down when she's introduced to the Sohmas' world of magical curses and family intrigue. Discover for yourself the Secret of the Zodiac, and find out why *Fruits Basket* has won the hearts of readers the world over!

THE BESTSELLING MANGA IN THE U.S.!

T TEEN AGE 13+

© Natsuki Takaya

FOR MORE INFORMATION VISIT WWW.TOKYOPOP.COM